Rigid school curricula emphasizing and assessing low-level skills perpetuate the wildly damaging assumption that elementary learners are incapable of engaging in substantive intellectual work. *Sensemaking in Elementary Science* offers an aspirational, yet achievable vision for science teaching and teacher education to guide bold changes in the landscape of elementary science. This book will become a well-worn, go-to resource for those working to make high-quality elementary science a reality.

Heidi Carlone, Ph.D., *Hooks Distinguished Professor of STEM Education, The University of North Carolina at Greensboro, USA*

Sensemaking in Elementary Science

Grounded in empirical research, this book offers concrete pathways to direct attention towards elementary science teaching that privileges sensemaking, rather than isolated activities and vocabulary. Outlining a clear vision for this shift using research-backed tools, pedagogies, and practices to support teacher learning and development, this edited volume reveals how teachers can best engage in teaching that supports meaningful learning and understanding in elementary science classrooms.

Divided into three sections, this book demonstrates the skills, knowledge bases, and research-driven practices necessary to make a fundamental shift towards a focus on students' ideas and reasoning, and covers topics such as:

- An introduction to sensemaking in elementary science;
- Positioning students at the center of sensemaking;
- Planning and enacting investigation-based science discussions;
- Designing a practice-based elementary teacher education program;
- Reflections on science teacher education and professional development for reform-based elementary science.

In line with current reform efforts, including the Next Generation Science Standards (NGSS), *Sensemaking in Elementary Science* is the perfect resource for graduate students and researchers in science education, elementary education, teacher education, and STEM education looking to explore effective practice, approaches, and development within the elementary science classroom.

Elizabeth A. Davis is Professor of Science Education at University of Michigan, USA.

Carla Zembal-Saul is the Kahn Professor of STEM Education at The Pennsylvania State University, USA.

Sylvie M. Kademian is Lecturer of Science Education at University of Michigan, USA.

Teaching and Learning in Science Series

Series Editor: Norman G. Lederman

Reconceptualizing STEM Education
The Central Role of Practices
Edited by Richard A. Duschl, Amber S. Bismack

Supporting K-12 English Language Learners in Science
Putting Research into Teaching Practice
Edited by Cory Buxton, Martha Allexsaht-Snider

Reframing Science Teaching and Learning
Students and Educators Co-developing Science Practices
In and Out of School
Edited by David Stroupe

Representations of Nature of Science in School Science Textbooks
A Global Perspective
Edited by Christine V. McDonald, Fouad Abd-El-Khalick

Teaching Biology in Schools
Global Research, Issues, and Trends
Edited by Kostas Kampourakis, Michael Reiss

Theory and Methods for Sociocultural Research in Science and Engineering Education
Edited by Gregory J. Kelly and Judith Green

Supporting Self-Directed Learning in Science and Technology
Beyond the School Years
Edited by Léonie Rennie, Susan M. Stocklmayer, and John K. Gilbert

Sensemaking in Elementary Science
Supporting Teacher Learning
Edited by Elizabeth A. Davis, Carla Zembal-Saul and Sylvie M. Kademian

For more information about this series, please visit: www.routledge.com/ Teaching-and-Learning-in-Science-Series/book-series/LEATLSS

Sensemaking in Elementary Science

Supporting Teacher Learning

Edited by
Elizabeth A. Davis,
Carla Zembal-Saul, and
Sylvie M. Kademian

NEW YORK AND LONDON

First published
by Routledge
52 Vanderbilt Avenue, New York, NY 10017

and by Routledge
2 Park Square, Milton Park, Abingdon, Oxon OX14 4RN

Routledge is an imprint of the Taylor & Francis Group, an informa business

© 2020 Taylor & Francis

The right of Elizabeth A. Davis, Carla Zembal-Saul, and Sylvie M. Kademian to be identified as the authors of the editorial material, and of the authors for their individual chapters, has been asserted in accordance with sections 77 and 78 of the Copyright, Designs and Patents Act 1988.

All rights reserved. No part of this book may be reprinted or reproduced or utilized in any form or by any electronic, mechanical, or other means, now known or hereafter invented, including photocopying and recording, or in any information storage or retrieval system, without permission in writing from the publishers.

Trademark notice: Product or corporate names may be trademarks or registered trademarks, and are used only for identification and explanation without intent to infringe.

Library of Congress Cataloging-in-Publication Data
A catalog record for this title has been requested

ISBN: 978-1-138-38694-5 (hbk)
ISBN: 978-1-138-38695-2 (pbk)
ISBN: 978-0-429-42651-3 (ebk)

Typeset in Bembo
by Taylor & Francis Books

To the next generation of science learners, including Lucy, Zach, and Lottie.

Contents

List of Figures	xii
List of Tables	xiv
About the Editors	xv
About the Contributors	xvi
Acknowledgments	xx

Working Toward a Vision of Sensemaking in Elementary Science:
An Introduction to *Sensemaking in Elementary Science: Supporting
Teacher Learning*   1
ELIZABETH A. DAVIS, CARLA ZEMBAL-SAUL, AND SYLVIE M. KADEMIAN

SECTION I
Images of the Possible   13

1 Positioning Students at the Center of Sensemaking: Productive
   Grappling with Data   15
   CARLA ZEMBAL-SAUL AND KIMBER HERSHBERGER

2 Portrait of a First-Grade Teacher: Using Science Practices to
   Leverage Young Children's Sensemaking in Science   31
   AMBER S. BISMACK AND LEIGH ANN HAEFNER

3 Science, Engineering, Literacy, and Place-Based Education:
   Powerful Practices for Integration   46
   JENNIFER L. CODY AND MANDY BIGGERS

4 Literacy Practices for Sensemaking in Science that Promote
   Epistemic Alignment   64
   LEEANNA HOOPER AND CARLA ZEMBAL-SAUL

x *Contents*

5 *Response*: Making Sense of Sensemaking in Elementary
   Education—Perspectives from Identity and Implications for
   Equity   78
   LUCY AVRAAMIDOU

6 *Response:* Integrating and Supporting Science Practices in
   Elementary Classrooms   87
   KATHERINE L. MCNEILL

SECTION II
Promising Practices, Tools, and Frameworks   95

7 Approximations of Practice: Scaffolding for Preservice Teachers   97
   ELIZABETH A. DAVIS

8 Planning and Enacting Investigation-based Science Discussions:
   Designing Tools to Support Teacher Knowledge for Science
   Teaching   113
   SYLVIE M. KADEMIAN AND ELIZABETH A. DAVIS

9 Scaffolding Beginning Teaching Practices: An Analysis of the
   Roles Played by Tools Provided to Preservice Elementary
   Science Teachers   129
   SARAH J. FICK AND ANNA MARIA ARIAS

10 Using Tools to Notice Student Ideas and Support Student
   Sensemaking in Rehearsal and Classroom Lesson Reflections   145
   AMANDA BENEDICT-CHAMBERS

11 A Framework for the Teaching Practice of Supporting Students
   to Construct Evidence-Based Claims Through Data Analysis: A
   Lens for Considering Teacher Learning Opportunities   161
   ANNA MARIA ARIAS

12 *Response:* Scaffolds, Tools, and Transitions Toward Disciplined
   Improvisation   178
   MATTHEW KLOSER AND MARK WINDSCHITL

Contents   xi

SECTION III
Supportive Contexts for Professional Learning   187

13 Designing a Practice-Based Elementary Teacher Education
Program and Supporting Professional Learning in Science
Teaching   189
ELIZABETH A. DAVIS, ANNEMARIE S. PALINCSAR, AND
SYLVIE M. KADEMIAN

14 Learning to Teach Science in an Elementary Professional
Development School Partnership   204
CARLA ZEMBAL-SAUL, BERNARD BADIALI, BRITTANY MUELLER, AND
ALICIA M. MCDYRE

15 Starting Small: Creating a Supportive Context for Professional
Learning that Fosters Emergent Bilingual Children's
Sensemaking in Elementary Science   218
MEGAN HOPKINS, CARLA ZEMBAL-SAUL, MAY H. LEE, AND
JENNIFER L. CODY

16 *Response:* Supporting Elementary Teacher Learning to Teach
Science   233
JAN H. VAN DRIEL

17 *Response:* Two Lenses for Looking at Supportive Contexts for
Science Teacher Learning   241
KATHLEEN ROTH

Conclusion: Reflections on Science Teacher Education and
Professional Development for Reform-Based Elementary Science   251
CORY T. FORBES

Index   266

Figures

1.1	Data Collection for the Distances Marbles Rolled at Different Ramp Heights	20
3.1	Our Integration Framework	50
3.2	Student Writing Sample of a Claim-Evidence-Reasoning Framework	55
3.3	MAP Reading Scores Across Three Iterations of the Unit	56
3.4	Mark-Ups of a Student's Work with a Newspaper Article	57
3.5	Claims and Evidence Board for Geology Unit	59
4.1	Ms. Meryl's Pattern of Instruction	68
8.1	Conceptual Framework for Knowledge Needed for Science Teaching Knowledge	115
9.1	Lesson Planning Tool	133
9.2	Theory of Action for the Support Provided by Tools	134
9.3	Scientific Modeling Tool	135
9.4	Sensemaking Planning Tool	136
9.5	Explore Observation Tool	137
9.6	Approximation Reflection Tool	138
11.1	Goals for Elementary Students Described in NGSS	163
11.2	The Students Constructing Evidence-Based Claims Framework: Science Practice of Constructing Evidence-Based Claims in Elementary Classroom	164
11.3	The Supporting Evidence-Based Claims Framework to Describe the Teaching Practice of Supporting Students to Construct Evidence-Based Claims Through Data Analysis	166
11.4	The Decomposed Practice of Supporting Students to Analyze the Data from the EEE Framework	172
11.5	The Decomposed Practice of Supporting Students to Make Claims Justified by Evidence and Reasoning from the EEE Framework	172
11.6	Learning Opportunities Across the Teacher Education Program	175
13.1	Timeline of the Four-Semester Elementary Teacher Education Program	193

16.1	The Interconnected Model of Teacher Professional Growth	235
18.1	Conceptual Model of Instructional Practice	255

Tables

3.1	Five-Paragraph Essay Organizer Scaffold	53
4.1	Pedagogical Shifts in Implementing Literacy for Sensemaking in Science	74
6.1	Themes for Integrating and Supporting Science Practices	88
7.1	Examples of Structuring and Problematizing Intentions	100
7.2	Continuum of Authenticity and Complexity	101
7.3	Peer-Teaching Rehearsal Experiences in a Science Methods Course	102
7.4	Design Questions for *Structuring* Novices' Learning	108
7.5	Design Questions for *Problematizing* Novices' Work	109
8.1	Suite of Tools Designed to Support Teacher Knowledge for Science Teaching	116
9.1	Coding Schemes, Example Codes, and Example Tools	133
10.1	Supporting Student Sensemaking in Rehearsal and Classroom Lesson Reflections	151
13.1	Teacher Education Pedagogies	192
17.1	Three Types of Assistance for Supporting Teachers	245
17.2	Multiple Fronts for Supporting Teacher Learning	246

About the Editors

Elizabeth A. Davis is a science educator, teacher educator, and learning scientist at the University of Michigan. She is especially interested in beginning elementary teachers, teachers learning to engage in rigorous and consequential science teaching, and the roles of curriculum materials and practice-based teacher education in promoting teacher learning.

Carla Zembal-Saul is a teacher educator and scholar of science education at Penn State. Her research and practice explore how elementary teachers learn to engage children in scientific discourse and practices. She is interested in the ways in which science affords opportunities for English learners to participate productively in meaningful, equitable, and caring academic and language learning.

Sylvie M. Kademian is a science teacher educator. She is specifically interested in supporting the development of beginning teachers and the use of tools designed to support beginning teachers to enact investigation-based science discussions in a way that prioritizes students' ideas and sensemaking.

About the Contributors

Anna Maria Arias is a science teacher educator and researcher at Kennesaw State University. Her research centers on supporting elementary teacher learning to create meaningful, rigorous learning opportunities where students integrate science practice and content. She is especially interested in the role of curriculum materials, practice-based teacher education, and the development of practice.

Lucy Avraamidou is a former elementary school teacher and a science educator at the University of Groningen in the Netherlands. Her research is associated with theoretical and empirical explorations of what it means to widen and diversify STEM participation in school and out-of-school settings through the lens of science identity.

Bernard Badiali is an associate professor of education in the Department of Curriculum and Instruction at The Pennsylvania State University. Dr. Badiali's main teaching and research activities have been in the areas of school/university relationships, professional development, school renewal, supervision, and curriculum. He has consulted with numerous colleges and universities throughout the United States as well as more than 100 school districts in the US and abroad and has published articles in numerous educational journals.

Amanda (Mandy) Benedict-Chambers is a science educator and teacher educator at Missouri State University. A former elementary and middle school teacher, her work focuses on supporting preservice elementary teacher learning, helping teachers engage in rigorous, ambitious teaching in science, and using tools and practice-based teacher education to promote teacher noticing and practice.

Mandy Biggers is a science educator and science teacher educator in the department of Biology at Texas Woman's University where she works with preservice elementary and secondary science teachers. A former middle and high school teacher, her research interests center around

About the Contributors   xvii

science and engineering practices, and the interactions of teachers and their science and engineering curricula.

Amber S. Bismack is a graduate student in science education at the University of Michigan. Her interests include supporting elementary teachers' development of their knowledge and teaching practices for engaging students in equitable science learning, particularly through the use of the science practices.

Jennifer L. Cody is a fifth-grade teacher and researches student voice and issues of participatory democracy in her classroom. As a graduate student in science education at Penn State, her research interests lie in the realms of science education, language acquisition, and place-based learning.

Sarah J. Fick is a science educator, teacher educator, and learning scientist at the University of Virginia. She is interested in the tools that students and teachers need in order to develop the ability to answer questions and solve problems using science and engineering processes, with a particular focus on the crosscutting concepts, the lenses we use to make sense of science.

Cory T. Forbes is a science educator and science teacher educator whose teaching and research efforts focus on K–16 science teaching and learning. He works with preservice and in-service elementary teachers, supporting their efforts to cultivate student-centered elementary science learning environments.

Leigh Ann Haefner is a science educator and teacher educator at Penn State Altoona. Her work with preservice teachers focuses on learning to develop meaningful science and integrated STEM learning experiences that supports student talk and sensemaking in science.

Kimber Hershberger is a retired third-grade teacher and SCIED instructor for Penn State. She is currently working as an elementary STEM coach for an urban school district. She is passionate about guiding teachers to include NGSS science and engineering practices in their science lessons. In addition, her work includes helping teacher teams and school districts create content storylines using CER as a guide for helping students to collect evidence and look for patterns in their data.

LeeAnna Hooper is a former elementary school teacher and a current elementary science teacher educator at The Pennsylvania State University. LeeAnna's primary research interest centers around the integration of discipline specific literacy practices as a means to support student sensemaking in elementary science. In particular, she explores the ways in which teacher's design and enact literacy events that serve to shape epistemic practices that are shared and used within a learning community.

Megan Hopkins is a scholar of teacher education and education policy at the University of California, San Diego. A former bilingual teacher, her

xviii *About the Contributors*

work focuses on developing systems of support for teachers of immigrant students and students designated as English learners, and on fostering equitable STEM learning environments that privilege students' linguistic and cultural assets and ways of knowing.

Matthew Kloser is the Director of the Notre Dame Center for STEM Education. He is a former high school science teacher and a current science teacher educator. He investigates how teachers take up core science instructional practices and has a special focus on teaching and learning in biology classrooms.

May H. Lee is a former elementary school teacher and project coordinator at The Pennsylvania State University. She is interested in the language and literacy development of emergent bilinguals in K-6 contexts. She works on a project that examines ways to provides job-embedded professional development that helps educators support and challenge their emergent bilinguals.

Alicia M. McDyre is a former middle school science teacher and science teacher educator. Currently, she directs the Curriculum and Instruction field experiences office at The Pennsylvania State University while helping provide professional development for elementary educators tackling adoption of NGSS.

Katherine L. McNeill is a former middle school teacher and a science educator at Boston College. She is interested in how to support students with diverse backgrounds in the science practices. She works on projects focused on the design of curriculum, assessments, and professional development materials to support students and teachers in the science practices.

Brittany Mueller is currently a third-grade teacher in the state of New York. She graduated from the Schreyer Honors College at The Pennsylvania State University with a BS in Childhood and Early Adolescent Education. She has a special interest in locating and expanding on cross curricular connections between the NGSS and other subject areas that are taught in the elementary classroom.

Annemarie S. Palincsar is the Jean and Charles Walgreen Jr. Chair of Reading and Literacy, Arthur F. Thurnau Professor, and a teacher educator at the University of Michigan. Annemarie's primary research interest is in sensemaking and knowledge building with multiple media, especially in the context of project-based scientific inquiry.

Kathleen Roth, researcher at California State Polytechnic University-Pomona, is passionate about improving K-6 science teaching and learning. Her research demonstrates the effectiveness for teachers and students of a video-based, analysis-of-practice teacher professional development program and the scalability of this approach in a high-needs district through the development of teacher leaders.

Jan H. van Driel is a professor of science education at the University of Melbourne, Australia. His main interest concerns the professional learning of science teachers during pre-service teacher education and in the context of their work, in particular, related to implementing innovations.

Mark Windschitl is a professor of science education at the University of Washington. He studies how preservice and early career science teachers develop repertoires of practice that are shared with a larger community, and how these communities work on the effectiveness and equity of practice over time.

Acknowledgments

Collectively, the authors and editors of this volume would like to express our appreciation for the elementary students, teachers, preservice teachers, administrators, and teacher educators with whom we have worked over the years. We feel grateful to be able to learn with and from the people in the elementary education systems in which we participate.

Working Toward a Vision of Sensemaking in Elementary Science

An Introduction to *Sensemaking in Elementary Science: Supporting Teacher Learning*

Elizabeth A. Davis
UNIVERSITY OF MICHIGAN

Carla Zembal-Saul
THE PENNSYLVANIA STATE UNIVERSITY

Sylvie M. Kademian
UNIVERSITY OF MICHIGAN

Most elementary teachers are responsible for all academic subjects including language arts, mathematics, social studies, and science. Some teach additional subjects like art, music, and computer literacy. Within science, elementary teachers are responsible for life science, physical science, and earth and space science, and now, engineering. They need to teach these disciplines through authentic science and engineering practices and to thread a set of crosscutting concepts through their lessons across the year (National Research Council, 2012). And, they need to do so in a way that empowers and makes central the ideas and experiences of *each child* in the classroom, including those who have been traditionally marginalized in science (e.g., Calabrese Barton and Tan, 2010; Carlone *et al.*, 2011). This is an exceptionally tall order. Elementary teaching, far from being the job of simply "nurturing children" as it is depicted in popular culture, requires academically rigorous, coherent, and extensive preparation to help novices develop a rich knowledge base across multiple disciplines and learn to engage in skillful, equitable, and just teaching practice.

Current reforms in science education urge educators to take seriously the right of all youth to experience rigorous and consequential science learning (cf. Roth, 2014). We see elementary science as an opportunity to engage children in sensemaking about natural phenomena using scientific claims, evidence, and reasoning. The *Framework for K-12 Science Education* (National Research Council, 2012) and the subsequent *Next Generation Science Standards* (NGSS Lead States, 2013) put forward a vision for what "three-dimensional" science learning can entail, including the integration of disciplinary core ideas, science and engineering practices, and crosscutting concepts, toward the goal of rich sensemaking about scientific phenomena. Children are capable of engaging in this kind of sensemaking (e.g., Metz, 2000)—but it is challenging for teachers to learn to support them in doing so (Davis *et al.*, 2006). In addition, science teachers' opportunities for professional learning are typically scattered, short-term, incoherent, and idiosyncratic (NASEM, 2015). Typical elementary teaching in US schools and globally involves mainly lists of science terms and/or discrete hands-on activities that do not drive toward a coherent understanding of big ideas in science—when science is taught at all (Banilower *et al.*, 2018). With this book, our goal is to support a fundamental shift away from activity-oriented and vocabulary-centered elementary science teaching toward instruction and assessment that is aligned with the vision of current reforms—that is, toward elementary science teaching that privileges sensemaking for all children. We build on work from many elementary science educators who bring important lenses to their work, such as the use of modeling or other science practices in elementary science, a focus on the nature of science, or an emphasis on equity (e.g., Abell, 2006; Akerson and Hanuscin, 2007; Manz, 2015; Mensah, 2011; Roth *et al.*, 2011; Schwarz, 2009), and we hope that the book reflects the many influences on our thinking.

We acknowledge the work of colleagues whose scholarship focuses on elementary school science, and whose work has informed our research and practice (Abell, 2006; Roth *et al.*, 2011). These scholars bring important lenses to the work of teacher and student learning, such as equity and identity (e.g., Calabrese Barton and Tan, 2010; Carlone *et al.*, 2011; Mensah, 2011), scientific practices such as argumentation and modeling (e.g., Manz, 2015; Schwarz, 2009), and the nature of science (e.g., Akerson and Hanuscin, 2007). Their contributions have helped us situate our focus on sensemaking in the larger landscape of elementary science education.

Sensemaking in Elementary Science

Odden and Russ (2018) point out the tension between an increasing interest in sensemaking as a theoretical construct in the science education literature and the lack of agreement that exists about the nature of sensemaking. They propose that sensemaking is a "dynamic process of building or revising an explanation" (p. 191) to determine the mechanism behind a phenomenon. They note the importance of connecting everyday knowledge and formal knowledge, while checking "that those connections and ideas are coherent, both with one another and with other ideas in one's knowledge system" (p. 192).

We find this framing to be useful in that it characterizes what students are doing when they are sensemaking. In our work, we further emphasize the social discursive practices learners employ when they collaboratively work

Introduction: Toward Sensemaking 3

to figure something out—whether it be students negotiating, critiquing, and refining explanations for natural phenomena or teachers making sense of some aspect of learning and teaching. Further, we perceive an urgent need to address equitable access when it comes to opportunities to experience rigorous and consequential sensemaking in science, which we address through our research and practice with future and current teachers.

We define sensemaking in a way that builds on Odden and Russ's (2018) conceptualization and is consistent with the *Framework*; we see sensemaking in science as entailing deeply understanding—"figuring out"—disciplinary core ideas and crosscutting concepts in science *through* authentic engagement in science practices, including the discourse they entail. Children learn through meaningful experiences with natural phenomena that are mediated by and include the opportunity to ask questions, collect data, identify patterns, construct explanations, build arguments, develop and use models, and all sorts of other science practices. These practices offer opportunities to broaden teachers' perceptions of who is successful in science, helping to address age-old biases that have served to marginalize certain groups (cf. NGSS Lead States, 2013, Appendix D). Indeed, prioritizing sensemaking provides a space for teachers to recognize the diverse resources and abilities of their students. Teaching in a way that prioritizes children's ideas and children's voices allows (and expects) even young children to be held to rigorous science standards, while acknowledging that children will bring different ideas and experiences to the table and that the way children will express their understandings will vary. This prioritization of sensemaking helps to inform how equitable and just science teaching is conceptualized at the elementary level.

Theories of Teacher Learning and Practice

The kinds of equitable sensemaking opportunities in science described previously are unlikely to occur, though, without a vision of what it can look like and without coherent learning opportunities and contexts and powerful tools and pedagogies for teacher learning. We address these problems in *Sensemaking in Elementary Science: Supporting Teacher Learning*. Throughout, we foreground issues around supporting children's sensemaking. Readers should bear in mind the overarching orientation that sensemaking is crucial in working toward more equitable and just science teaching, and more rigorous and consequential science learning experiences for all children.

The chapters in this volume build on theories of teacher learning and teaching practice. Situated, sociocultural, and practice-based theories guide our work. Thus, we see teacher learning as social, distributed, and situated in practice (e.g., Putnam and Borko, 2000). New and experienced teachers learn with others; they use tools and other forms of support to guide their thinking; and they learn to engage in the work of teaching through experiences that are more and less proximal to the classroom and that are

4 Davis, Zembal-Saul, and Kademian

situated within educational systems. Teacher education, in turn, can entail seeing "practice" as a profession, as a kind of move that one makes in the classroom, and—as a verb—the work one does to become more skillful with those moves and in that profession (Lampert, 2010). By focusing the second section of the book on promising tools, frameworks, pedagogies, and practices, we highlight the social, distributed, and situated nature of learning to teach. Section II highlights how we support novices in working to develop teaching practices (moves) that draw on both a rich knowledge base and a set of commitments to justice and equity. The third section of the book focuses on supportive contexts; we foreground the situated and the social nature of the work. This third section emphasizes the development of systems of supports that promote rigorous, consequential, and equitable teaching.

We take an inclusive view of who serves as a teacher educator, including not only university-based individuals who teach in teacher education programs, but also school- and community-based individuals who support professional learning in other ways. We treat readers as sensemakers and invite them to make connections between the examples in the book and their own contexts and practice.

Research–Practice Networks in Elementary Science Teacher Education: Our Communities of Practice

Throughout the book, we draw on work that was done or originated at two universities: Pennsylvania State University and the University of Michigan. The teacher education programs at these universities each have unique characteristics. Penn State engages beginning teachers in practitioner inquiry (Badiali *et al.*, 2012; Zembal-Saul, 2009). Preservice teachers learn to systematically examine their own practice in the context of school-university partnerships, working side-by-side with experienced mentor teachers and professional development associates who share a coherent vision of the program and profession. The University of Michigan's practice-based teacher education program emphasizes learning to engage skillfully in a set of high-leverage teaching practices and developing robust content knowledge for teaching, as well as establishing a set of ethical obligations that guide equitable teaching (Davis and Boerst, 2014). Preservice teachers experience a range of pedagogies of practice (Grossman et al., 2009) and use carefully designed tools (Windschitl, *et al.*, 2012) as they learn to do the work of teaching.

The three of us work at these two universities. Zembal-Saul is a faculty member at Penn State. Davis is a faculty member at the University of Michigan. Kademian is a lecturer at Michigan, having completed her doctoral work at Michigan as well. All three of us are active and provide leadership in our elementary teacher education programs and work to support professional learning in our programmatic contexts. The other authors whose work is spotlighted in this book worked with one or more of us in doing the work of teacher education. For example, some of the participating authors were graduate students who apprenticed with us in learning the work of teacher education, who have now gone on to other university settings and are working within their own teacher education programs. Other participating authors are faculty colleagues working in the same programs. Still other participating authors are teachers in professional development schools with which we partner and in which we grow. The responding authors, on the other hand, bring outside perspectives from within the US and other countries. In sum, the authors of this book are connected through a web of professional networks, and share a common vision: a vision that entails supporting elementary teachers in learning to do sophisticated intellectual work with their students.

Overview of the Book

In the pages that follow, we provide an overview of each section of the book. In Section I, we ask, *What does the new vision of science learning espoused in the Framework for K-12 Science Education and the Next Generation Science Standards look like in K-5 classrooms?* In this section, we present a series of cases—we consider these to be images of the possible that can help us envision a new kind of teaching and learning. These cases focus on unique classrooms, teachers, and children. Each case, in fact, is grounded within the professional development school collaboratively developed by faculty, teachers, and other educators connected to Penn State. The first chapter, by Zembal-Saul and Hershberger, highlights how a fourth grade teacher and her class work together to organize data collection and data analysis to support sensemaking. We know this kind of scientific work can be challenging for students and teachers alike, and having an image of how children can engage in sensemaking around data is important for shifting educators' ideas of what is possible. This chapter is followed by a case from a first-grade classroom. Here, Bismack and Haefner explore how the teacher engages children in the kinds of science practices explicated in the *Framework*. They focus on how these practices allow the teacher to support and leverage children's scientific sensemaking. A third case, by Cody and Biggers, explores multiple disciplinary practices—in science and engineering as well as in literacy—and connects these to place-based education. In this case, the teacher draws on literacy strategies, engineering challenges, field trips, guest speakers, and persuasive writing in the context of an interdisciplinary unit on water. The chapter illustrates how the teacher and children's collaborative work help the children to see how science connects to their lives, thus supporting their sensemaking. A final case explores the literacy practices a teacher engages students in and the ways in which they support sensemaking in science. Hooper and Zembal-Saul focus on how literacy practices for science teaching—engaging students with multiple science-specific texts; eliciting and using students' ideas through talking,

6 Davis, Zembal-Saul, and Kademian

writing and drawing; and tying words to meaning—promote an epistemic view of science that entails the social construction of knowledge through science practices. More typical attempts to integrate English Language Arts instruction with science tend to promote an epistemic view of science as a static body of facts.

In their responses to the chapters in Section I, Avraamidou and McNeill take up and highlight issues of identity, equity, and instruction that privileges students' engagement in and with science practices. These complementary response chapters help to highlight some of the important themes in these images of the possible.

In each of these images of the possible in Section I, we attempt to illustrate how elementary teachers can support young children's sense-making in science. Our intent is to help other elementary educators, including elementary science teacher educators, to be able to envision the kinds teaching we can work toward in elementary classrooms. Section II then takes that as a starting place to explore *how* we can support teachers in learning to do that kind of work. Learning to engage in teaching that privileges sensemaking is important in all settings, but particularly so in communities undergoing rapid demographic change. All children deserve to experience rigorous, equitable and consequential science learning opportunities espoused in the *Framework*, and all new teachers deserve to know how to support every child in their class in doing so.

In Section II we ask, *What conceptually and empirically grounded tools, frameworks, pedagogies, and practices hold promise for supporting teacher learning?* In this section, we explore vehicles for supporting teachers' professional learning in initial teacher education. Each of these chapters reports on work that either happened at the University of Michigan or grew out of work there. For two decades, Davis has led a group of elementary science teacher educators—the Elementary Science Methods Planning Group—and each of the authors of the chapters in Section II are or were members of that group.

In the chapter that opens this section, Davis focuses on the design of different teacher education experiences within a science methods course, exploring how each "approximation of practice"—including rehearsals and small-scale science teaching—employed in the course serves as scaffolding to both structure and problematize the preservice teachers' learning. The chapter closes with a set of design guidelines for teacher educators hoping to incorporate a practice-based approach to elementary science teacher education. The second chapter in this section focuses on the design of conceptual tools that can support the development of novice teachers' content knowledge for teaching science. Kademian and Davis describe the intentional design and adaptation of these conceptual tools—which include frameworks, templates, rubrics, and other forms of scaffolding—and map them on to specific elements of teacher knowledge. The third chapter in this section continues this focus on tools. Here, Fick and Arias examine how preservice elementary teachers take up and use the tools they are provided. The authors of this chapter are situated in different teacher education programs but initiated their learning as teacher educators together; some of the tools presented here evolved from the same teacher education program where the authors did their graduate work and some grew in their unique contexts, supporting coherence across the chapters and helping to illustrate the fruitful evolution of such tools across time and space. The fourth chapter in this section looks at how preservice teachers can be supported in understanding their students' sensemaking through analyzing student work artifacts and using other forms of support. Within the context of a practice-based science methods course that involves the pre-service teachers in rehearsing science lessons, Benedict-Chambers explores how rehearsals can support novices in learning to use evidence about student thinking to guide their instruction. In the final chapter in this section, Arias looks at how preservice teachers developed their knowledge and practice to support elementary children in analyzing data and constructing evidence-based claims about natural phenomena—some of the same conceptual space as Zembal-Saul and Hershberger explored in Section I. Taking a longitudinal approach, Arias looks carefully at preservice teachers' knowledge and practice at multiple points across the two-year program.

The response chapter for this section, by Kloser and Windschitl, empha-sizes the importance of tools, frameworks, and other forms of support, and extends the work presented in these chapters by noting the importance of novice teachers engaging in disciplined (or principled) improvisation as they use tools and frameworks in their teaching.

In each of the chapters in Section II, we explore different ways of supporting preservice elementary teachers of science in learning to engage elementary children in the kinds of three-dimensional learning and sensemaking around natural phenomena that we privilege throughout this book and that were highlighted in the cases presented in Section I. The authors demonstrate their respect for the complexity of elementary science teaching, and each chapter captures some of that complexity. Section III builds on the previous two sec-tions by moving our thinking forward to the *contexts* in which teachers' pro-fessional learning can take place. This is important because teachers' opportunities for professional learning are often scattered and incoherent (NASEM, 2015). Conceptualizing coherent and focused contexts in which teachers can learn helps to address that issue.

In Section III, we ask, *How can we create coherent and supportive contexts for powerful teacher learning across the professional continuum?* Here, we address issues related to developing spaces that can support professional learning. The first chapter in this section describes the design of the University of Michigan's elementary teacher education program—a program that was re-envisioned to be grounded in three areas: a set of high-leverage teaching practices, content knowledge for teaching, and a set of ethical obligations. The pro-gram prioritizes teachers working to promote children's sensemaking, and these three dimensions of the program are woven together to help begin-ners learn to promote more equitable learning experiences for children. In

8 Davis, Zembal-Saul, and Kademian

this chapter, Davis, Palincsar, and Kademian focus on an early class on children as scientific sensemakers and a later science teaching methods class. Together with some of the chapters from Section II, this chapter provides insight into the careful design of one practice-based teacher education program and how such a design can support professional learning of well-started beginners. Next, Section III shifts the focus to work at Penn State University and productive partnerships. One chapter explores a long-standing, nationally recognized school–university partnership. Co-authored by researchers, partnership faculty, and a program graduate, Zembal-Saul, Badiali, Mueller, and McDyre describe the historical underpinnings of the partnership, address the design features of the partnership, and highlight the potential of practitioner inquiry as signature pedagogy to support professional learning of novice and experienced teachers alike. The final chapter in this section extends further to describe a new partnership between a university and a school district situated in a nascent immigrant community. Here, Hopkins, Zembal-Saul, Lee, and Cody address how they engage practicing elementary teachers in professional learning opportunities that promote equitable participation of emergent bilingual children in meaningful science learning and language development. The need to start small when building trusting relationships, understanding the organizational context, seeking authentic complementarities in project and district initiatives, and garnering support for this kind of work are identified as critical factors for advancing the project.

In these two last chapters of Section III, a more expansive vision of a teacher education program is taken. The authors in these chapters explore how collaborative partnerships *across constituencies* can support professional learning. The ideas presented throughout Section III build on the recommendations of a report on teachers' opportunities for professional learning (NASEM, 2015) in that they illustrate ways of attending to teachers' individual and collective needs, conceptualizing systems for support, and building on research on teaching and learning. The response chapters in this section, by Van Driel and by Roth, draw on different lenses for looking at the work presented, including a model of teachers' professional growth (used by Van Driel) and the lenses of "multiple meanings" (of support and supportive contexts) and "multiple fronts" we need to attend to in conceptualizing supportive spaces for teacher learning (used by Roth). Together, these response chapters help to highlight themes that cut across the three chapters in the section.

The final chapter of the book, by Forbes, provides a conclusion that synthesizes the themes across the three sections of the book. Specifically, Forbes highlights overarching elements of teacher learning and teaching, identifies key characteristics of effective elementary science teaching and learning, and pulls together key features of elementary science teacher learning experiences—doing so in each case by drawing from and situating within the chapters of the book. In so doing, Forbes helps to synthesize across those chapters, and to push the authors' and the field's thinking about ways we can work toward elementary instruction that supports every child in engaging in rich sensemaking in science.

Advancing Sensemaking in Elementary Science through Teacher Education

This volume, then, is intended to inform a wide range of teacher educators who work with elementary teachers of science to support a fundamental shift toward a new vision of science teaching that supports all children in experiencing rigorous and consequential science learning. We fully recognize that teaching science can be a challenge, especially for beginning elementary teachers (Davis *et al.*, 2006)—and indeed, with the new expectations of the *Framework* and the NGSS, all teachers are novices in some ways (NASEM, 2015; see, e.g., Zembal-Saul and Hershberger, this volume, Chapter 1).

Learning to teach at the elementary level is daunting. Elementary teachers require many areas of mastery. Yet because of the very real constraints on initial teacher preparation and ongoing professional learning in science, it is a challenge to support elementary teachers in developing the knowledge and practices necessary to engage children deeply in sensemaking in science. A central tenet that guides all of the authors contributing to this book is that we must create opportunities for new teachers to develop a beginning repertoire of ideas, strategies, tools, and abilities (Davis and Smithey, 2009)—in other words, to help them be well-started beginners (Hollon *et al.*, 1991). And furthermore, we must help teachers who are no longer at the beginning of their career to *continue* to learn, grow, and develop—to see children as capable and to refine ideas, strategies, tools, and abilities to support their learning. We hope that the book informs a range of elementary science teacher educators in working toward these goals.

References

Abell, S. (2006). Challenges and opportunities for field experiences in elementary science teacher preparation. In K. Appleton (Ed.), *Elementary Science Teacher Education* (pp. 73–89). Mahwah, NJ: Lawrence Erlbaum Associates.

Akerson, V., and Hanuscin, D. (2007). Teaching nature of science through inquiry: Results of a 3-year professional development program. *Journal of Research in Science Teaching*, *44*(5), 653–680.

Badiali, B., Zembal-Saul, C., DeWitt, K. and Stoicovy, D. (2012). Shared inquiry: The professional development school as a laboratory of practice for preparing the next generation of teacher educators. In *Placing Practitioner Knowledge at the Center of Teacher Education: Rethinking the Policy and Practice of the Education Doctorate.* Greenwich, CT: Information Age Publishing.

Banilower, E., Smith, P. S., Malzahn, K., Plumley, C., Gordon, E., and Hayes, M. (2018). *Report of the 2018 NSSME+*. Chapel Hill, NC: Horizon Research, Inc.

Calabrese Barton, A. and Tan, E. (2010). We be burnin'! Agency, identity and science learning. *The Journal of the Learning Sciences, 19*(2), 187–229.

Carlone, H. B., Haun-Frank, J., and Webb, A. (2011). Assessing equity beyond knowledge- and skills-based outcomes: A comparative ethnography of two fourth-grade reform-based science classrooms. *Journal of Research in Science Teaching, 48*(5), 459–485.

Davis, E. A., and Boerst, T. (2014). Designing elementary teacher education to prepare well-started beginners. Retrieved from http://www.teachingworks.org/images/files/TeachingWorks_Davis_Boerst_WorkingPapers_March_2014.pdf

Davis, E. A., and Smithey, J. (2009). Beginning teachers moving toward effective elementary science teaching. *Science Education, 93*(4), 745–770.

Davis, E. A., Petish, D., and Smithey, J. (2006). Challenges new science teachers face. *Review of Educational Research, 76*(4), 607–651.

Grossman, P., Compton, C., Igra, D., Ronfeldt, M., Shahan, E., and Williamson, P. (2009). Teaching practice: A cross-professional perspective. *Teachers College Record, 111*(9), 2055–2100.

Hollon, R., Roth, K., and Anderson, C. (1991). Science teachers' conceptions of teaching and learning. In J. Brophy (Ed.), *Advances in Research on Teaching, Vol. 2: Teachers' Subject Matter Knowledge and Classroom Instruction* (pp. 145–185). Greenwich, CT: JAI Press.

Lampert, M. (2010). Learning teaching in, from, and for practice: What do we mean? *Journal of Teacher Education, 61*(1–2), 21–34.

Manz, E. (2015). Resistance and the development of scientific practice: Designing the mangle into science instruction. *Cognition and Instruction, 33*(2), 89–124.

Mensah, F. (2011). A case for culturally relevant teaching in science education and lessons learned for teacher education. *The Journal of Negro Education, 80*(3), 296–309.

Metz, K. (2000). Young children's inquiry in biology: Building the knowledge bases to empower independent inquiry. In J. Minstrell and E. Van Zee (Eds.), *Inquiring into inquiry learning and teaching in science*. Washington, DC: American Association for the Advancement of Science.

NASEM (National Academies of Sciences Engineering and Medicine). (2015). Science Teachers' Learning: Enhancing Opportunities, Creating Supportive Contexts (Committee on Strengthening Science Education through a Teacher Learning Continuum Board on Science Education and Teacher Advisory Council Division of Behavioral and Social Science and Education Ed.). Washington, DC: National Academies Press.

National Research Council. (2012). A framework for K-12 science education: Practices, crosscutting concepts, and core ideas. Committee on a Conceptual Framework for New K-12 Science Education Standards. Board on Science Education, Division of Behavioral and Social Sciences and Education. Washington, DC: National Academies Press.

NGSS Lead States. (2013). Next Generation Science Standards: For States, By States. Washington, DC: National Academies Press.

Odden, T. O. B. and Russ, R. S. (2018). Defining sensemaking: Bringing clarity to a fragmented theoretical construct. *Science Education.* doi:10.1002/sce.21452.

Putnam, R. and Borko, H. (2000). What do new views of knowledge and thinking have to say about research on teacher learning? *Educational Researcher, 29*(1), 4–15.

Roth, K. (2014). Elementary science teaching. In N. Lederman and S. Abell (Eds.), *Handbook of Research on Science Teaching (Vol. II)*. New York: Routledge.

Roth, K., Garnier, H., Chen, C., Lemmens, M., Schwille, K., and Wickler, N. (2011). Videobased lesson analysis: Effective science PD for teacher and student learning. *Journal of Research in Science Teaching*, *48*(2), 117–148.

Schwarz, C. (2009). Developing preservice elementary teachers' knowledge and practices through modeling-centered scientific inquiry. *Science Education*, *93*(4), 720–744.

Windschitl, M., Thompson, J., Braaten, M., and Stroupe, D. (2012). Proposing a core set of instructional practices and tools for teachers of science. *Science Education*, *96*(5), 878–903.

Zembal-Saul, C. (2009). Learning to teach elementary school science as argument. *Science Education*, *93*(4), 687–719.

Section I
Images of the Possible

1 Positioning Students at the Center of Sensemaking
Productive Grappling with Data

Carla Zembal-Saul
THE PENNSYLVANIA STATE UNIVERSITY

Kimber Hershberger
STATE COLLEGE AREA SCHOOL DISTRICT, PA (RETIRED)

Acknowledgments

Thank you to Ms. Medina and her class for welcoming us to join them in learning science. It was a pleasure to participate in such a vibrant intellectual community. This work was funded in part by the Gilbert and Donna Kahn endowed professorship for STEM education.

Introduction

As part of a unit on energy, Ms. Medina and her fourth-graders (10-year-olds) were investigating phenomena related to energy and energy transfer using roller coasters. The teacher's goal was to support students in making sense of the cause–effect relationships between the height of the track's starting point and the rolling marble. Ms. Medina created the context for investigation by showing a short video of a cart moving along a roller coaster track through loops, inclines, and drops. She invited students to discuss their observations and questions. Together the class framed the question: How does the roller coaster have enough "power" to go all the way? Ms. Medina then introduced an initial semi-structured investigation in which students manipulated long tracks made from pipe insulation, adding dictionaries underneath the ramps to systematically adjust the height of the starting point. Students measured the distances the marbles rolled at each height and used a prepared data table to record their results. Ms. Medina encouraged students to collect the most accurate data possible, but did not impose specific conditions. During the investigation, she moved from group to group attending to students' observations and questions. She noticed that students were talking about both the distances the marbles traveled and their speed. What did Ms. Medina do with these new insights?

The predominant use of hands-on activities in elementary school science is difficult to disrupt, especially given the outward appearance of student engagement. Children clearly enjoy working in small groups, interacting with materials, and playing games. They often participate more actively in hands-on science activities than in instruction associated with other subject areas. As long as there is a science topic, a plethora of activities are readily available that require little modification to implement in the classroom. But what does it really mean for children to be engaged in scientific discourse and practices as part of rigorous, equitable and consequential science learning?

In this chapter we delve deeper into how teachers can engage students with data in productive ways—what counts as evidence, why and how data are collected, how data can be organized and represented in order to recognize patterns and relationships, and how data are transformed through analysis to construct claims. Moreover, we seek to frame generating and making sense of data as an invitation to participate in making sense of the world and how it works as part of school science. We extend and utilize the vignette of 'Ms. Medina and Marbles in Motion' later in this chapter to illustrate sensemaking moments in which she used her understanding of a coherent science content storyline (Reiser, 2013; Roth *et al.*, 2011, Taylor *et al.*, 2017), which she co-designed with teachers and researchers, and students' ways of knowing to create an equitable and productive context for participation in scientific discourse and practices. This "image of the possible" highlights the ways in which data discussions can serve as a lever for shifting away from step-by-step activities toward more epistemically rich science learning opportunities.

Sensemaking in Elementary School Science

If coming to understand the world by engaging in scientific discourse and practices is the centerpiece of next generation science learning, then creating equitable access for students to participate productively in the intellectual work of sensemaking is the hallmark of effective science teaching. Scholars have characterized sensemaking in science as attending not only to what students understand about the world, but also their ways of and processes for knowing (Rosebery and Warren, 2008). Children are capable of asking testable questions about how the world works and engaging in the kinds of scientific reasoning necessary to make sense of phenomena (Duschl *et al.*, 2007; Metz, 2000). The implications for elementary teachers are daunting. Not only must they understand and be pedagogically fluent with core ideas in science and scientific practices, they also need to place children's ideas and thinking at the forefront of their short-term and long-term planning, responsiveness during teaching, and formative assessment practices (Hammer, 1995).

Claims-Evidence-Reasoning and Sensemaking

In the period since *What's Your Evidence? Engaging K-5 Students in Constructing Explanations in Science* (Zembal-Saul *et al.*, 2013) was published, our thinking and pedagogical practices related to crafting, enacting, and analyzing coherent and consequential science learning opportunities for children have continued to evolve. We have persisted in our school-based work with preservice and practicing elementary teachers with the explicit intention of moving beyond a focus on activities toward sensemaking in science, which requires giving priority to evidence (Avraamidou and Zembal-Saul, 2005). However, the challenges associated with this work have been well documented (Davis *et al.*, 2006).

The publication of *What's Your Evidence? (WYE)* was timely in that it coincided with the release of *A Framework for K-12 Science Education: Practices, Crosscutting Concepts, and Core Ideas* (National Research Council, 2012) and the *Next Generation Science Standards: For States, By States* (NGSS Lead States, 2013). *WYE* focuses on pedagogical and assessment practices for use by elementary teachers as they learn to engage their students in arguing from evidence and constructing scientific explanations for phenomena. The approaches featured in *WYE* align with several essential shifts that serve as the foundation for a new vision for students' meaningful science learning and scientific practices. Central to this vision is making sense of the natural and designed world (Duschl *et al.*, 2007; Hammer, 1995; National Research Council, 2012) in ways that interconnect science content and scientific practices and build in sophistication over time.

Not only does *WYE* align with the *Framework,* it provides "images of the possible" of classroom science teaching (e.g., vignettes and videos). The book grew out of research and practice associated with funded projects on scientific argumentation and explanation-building at Boston College (McNeill) and Penn State University (Zembal-Saul). The Claims–Evidence–Reasoning (CER) framework (McNeill and Krajcik, 2008) was employed as a powerful scaffold for working with preservice and practicing teachers when planning, teaching, assessing, and analyzing science learning opportunities. These shifts in understanding and pedagogy are challenging for many educators, especially at the elementary level where teachers are prepared to teach all subject areas and whose teaching responsibilities have targeted priority areas for high stakes assessment (i.e., mathematics and literacy).

While we continue to view CER as a powerful framework for co-constructing evidence-based explanations—one that is both accessible and reasonable to elementary teachers and students—our initial conceptualization for constructing explanations in elementary school science have evolved. For example, we now emphasize the use of the CER framework as a heuristic for evidence-based arguments (Zembal-Saul, 2018b; Zembal-Saul *et al.*, 2013). In practice, multiple iterations of negotiating, interrogating, and refining sequences of evidence-based claims taken together build toward explaining phenomena. Ideally, these sequences have predictive power for more sophisticated questions and explanations, as well as potential for making connections across units of instruction. In addition, CER provides consistency for engaging in scientific discourse and practices when it is used to inform instructional supports for sensemaking, such as talk moves, writing heuristics, explanation mapping tools, and attention to developing classroom norms. Finally, we frame content storylines based on CER sequences as productive tools for teacher decision-making prior to, during, and after instruction.

Our work with content storylines (Zembal-Saul *et al.*, 2013) was inspired by the results of the TIMSS Video Study (Roth *et al.*, 2006) and the overwhelming emphasis of discrete activities in school science in the United States. In their conceptualization of a coherent science content storyline, Roth and colleagues (2006, 2011) make a strong case for learning goals, coherence, and sequencing—an intentional move away from an activity orientation to teaching science. Reiser (2013) further elevated the role of content storylines in providing coherence for phenomena-based, three-dimensional science teaching and learning.

Interestingly, in our early work with CER-based science storylines, we underestimated their potential as a vehicle for turning over responsibility from teachers to students for the intellectual work of constructing explanations. It is this last point that the case of Ms. Medina serves to address.

Beyond Activities and Vocabulary

Scientists, philosophers of science, and science educators agree that the lock-step "scientific method" portrayed in school science does not accurately represent the work of scientists and engineers. A focus on "final form science and textbook-driven instruction" (Duschl *et al.*, 2007, p. 13) is characteristic of "doing school" rather than authentic, productive participation in science (Duschl, 2000; Lemke, 1990). Moreover, it does not acknowledge students as being capable of participating productively in scientific practices and knowledge-building. An activity focus can direct students through discrete experiences with features of scientific processes. However, activities tend to promote emphasis on academic vocabulary through the well-meaning approach of bringing scientific topics to life (Hooper and Zembal-Saul, this volume, Chapter 4). While a "flashy hook" may capture students' attention in the moment, without the robust intellectual work of puzzling with data, this approach accomplishes little in the way of advancing the vision for students' sensemaking in science.

The teachers with whom we collaborate recognize the power of prioritizing the construction of explanations from evidence and the importance of shifting the work of knowledge building from teachers to students, especially during class discussions (Schoerning *et al.*, 2015). As our collaborations and co-design progressed, some teachers experimented with

Positioning Students at the Center 19

handing over other aspects of doing science to their students, such as asking scientific questions, making decisions about what data to collect and how, as well as organizing and representing data in multiple ways to uncover patterns and relationships. Scholars refer to control over knowledge and knowledge building as *epistemic authority* and concur that teachers should position students as being capable of this challenging intellectual work as part of productive sensemaking (Carlone *et al.*, 2011; Stroupe, 2014).

When collaborating teachers invited students to assume greater responsibility for sensemaking, they also began to place less emphasis on vocabulary and more emphasis on informal formative assessments (e.g., classroom discourse, drawings/diagrams and written explanations) in order to better understand students' ideas and the ways in which they were making sense of phenomena. Acceptance of "kid talk" during sensemaking advances the aim of shifting power dynamics to be more inclusive of students' diverse ways of knowing and thinking. Next, we share an example of this kind of work on the part of a teacher to shift epistemic authority for sensemaking from her to students.

From the Classroom

Recall Ms. Medina and her class from the beginning of the chapter. Ms. Medina is an experienced fourth grade teacher who consistently uses CER to frame science teaching and learning. She is active professionally at the local and national levels with science reform, and she has participated in ongoing professional learning focused on science teaching, learning, and assessment. We developed the vignette from video of classroom practice taken from a larger research project and professional development partnership (Zembal-Saul, Badiali, Mueller, and McDyre, this volume, Chapter 14) in which there is a shared commitment to practitioner inquiry (Cochran-Smith and Lytle, 2009; Dana and Yendol-Silva, 2009).

When we left the initial vignette, Ms. Medina's class was investigating the relationship between the height of the ramp and the effect on the rolling marble. She noticed that students were observing and discussing differences in both speed and distance, even though the table she provided for recording data focused on distance. Although there is much about science teaching and learning to consider through this vignette, we highlight how Ms. Medina used phenomena to create equitable access to productive participation in scientific practices; anticipated and leveraged opportunities that invited student input in generating and analyzing data; and addressed core science ideas and associated academic vocabulary when students were ready to pursue causal explanations. We view the teacher's co-design and use of a CER-informed content storyline as being critical to her ability to shift responsibility for sensemaking from herself to students.

20   *Zembal-Saul and Hershberger*

Ms. Medina and Marbles in Motion

The day after students' initial investigation, Ms. Medina gathered the class together for a science talk with the goal of analyzing data and making claims about how the height of the ramp affected the distance the marble rolled. She projected a sample data sheet on the whiteboard (Figure 1.1), and students reviewed the data their groups had recorded in their science journals. The teacher guided them to look for patterns in the data set. Recall that even though Ms. Medina did not impose strict criteria for data collection, she did provide a data table that allowed for systematic attention to the height of the ramp (in dictionaries) and the distance traveled by the marble.

TEACHER: Open up [your science journals] to your data collection sheet. Turn and talk with people around you. What claims can you make from the data to address the question of the impact of the height of the track on the distance the marble rolled?

Students talk in their small groups, discussing their claims and writing them on their data sheets. Ms. Medina circulated around the class listening to students' discussions, sometimes asking them questions and looking at the claims their group made.

TEACHER: Who would like to share the claim your group made? S1?
S1: The marble went further each time.
TEACHER: Does anybody agree with S1? S2 can you read what you wrote for your claim?
S2: It goes faster and further as we added more.
S3: It goes faster and further as we added more dictionaries.
TEACHER: Do you guys agree with her? She says that it went faster and further as the height increased. What are your thoughts on that?

Height: 1 Dictionary	Distance: (inches)		Height: 2 Dictionaries	Distance: (inches)
Trial 1	30		Trial 1	44
Trial 2	36		Trial 2	41
Trial 3	33		Trial 3	45
Average	33		Average	43
Height: 3 Dictionaries	Distance: (inches)		Height: 4 Dictionaries	Distance: (inches)
Trial 1	50		Trial 1	76
Trial 2	55		Trial 2	80
Trial 3	53		Trial 3	82
Average	53		Average	79

Figure 1.1 Data Collection for the Distances Marbles Rolled at Different Ramp Heights

S1: We don't know for sure if it rolled faster, but we just saw that it went further each time.

TEACHER: Why are you saying we don't know for sure?

S4: Because we didn't use a stopwatch or one of those things that can detect the amount of speed it went.

TEACHER: What does your chart show?

S5: It just shows evidence that it went further each time but it never showed evidence that it went faster.

Because she had circulated around the classroom and listened to the students' discussions about the claims they could make from their data, Ms. Medina knew that some groups had included both distance and speed in their claims, while others only used distance. She intentionally invited students to share examples of differing claims during the science talk. When one student read a claim that included both speed and distance, the teacher did not correct it. Rather, she turned it back to the class by restating the claim and asking students to respond. Ms. Medina repeatedly asked students what their data showed. Students were able to agree that the first investigation only showed how the distance the marble traveled increased as the height of the top of the track increased. Ms. Medina accepted students' colloquial use of the term "speed."

Because Ms. Medina knew that students were talking about both distance and speed as they investigated the marble rolling down the ramp, she intentionally planned to use the class discussion for students to negotiate parameters for a subsequent investigation of how fast the marbles rolled down tracks of varying height. As the science talk continued, the class crafted the new wondering: *How does the height of the roller coaster affect how fast the marble goes?* Students were especially interested in whether to time the marble when it stopped rolling or at the end of the ramp. In fact, they were divided on this point. As the students talked through when and how to stop measuring time, several of them asked to use the whiteboard to make their thinking visible through drawings and diagrams—a practice familiar to them from their science journals.

The class was actively engaged in making decisions about how data would be generated, and many members of the class participated in the discussion. After listening carefully to other students' ideas about how to record how fast the marble traveled down the track, they worked together to create a way to stop the marble and established a common distance from the end of the track to take their time measurement. Ms. Medina redirected students to data they had already collected to make informed choices about how to design the investigation. After negotiating these decisions, students addressed how to record their data. They decided to use a data table with multiple trials similar to the one from the initial investigation (Figure 1.1). Students then used their first data set to predict that the marbles would go faster as the ramp height increased. In this way, Ms. Medina's data table served to support both how students designed their investigation and thought about collecting data in a systematic way. Equally as important, the initial investigation also informed students' predictions about the relationship between the height of the ramp and time. It was not until the next day that they actually conducted the investigation and went through another iteration of analyzing data from which they negotiated the evidence-based claim: *As we increased the height of the top of the track, the marble went faster.* At this point, Ms. Medina introduced the scientific terminology that students had derived through their investigation—speed is the distance traveled per unit of time.

At this point in the unit, Ms. Medina's students began asking questions about *why* the height of the track influenced the speed and distance of the marble. Put another way, students' investigation of patterns in data and basic relationships among variables created the need to explain. Ms. Medina recognized the transition in students' questions and timed the introduction of energy (previously called power by students) as necessary for the class to use as reasoning in the co-construction of their CER sequences—connecting the speed of an object to its energy (NGSS, 4-PS3–1). The rest of Ms. Medina's content storyline also capitalized on students' emerging interests in understanding the how and why of energy transfer and transformation.

Discussion: Inviting and Sustaining Sensemaking

Here, we highlight four main features that address the importance of sharing epistemic authority with students to puzzle with data as they learn science concepts, as well as how to participate productively in other scientific practices. These themes focus on what the teacher is intentionally doing during instruction:

1 Preparing a content storyline to guide responsive pedagogy;
2 Using phenomena to create equitable access and productive participation in scientific practices;
3 Anticipating and leveraging opportunities that invite student input in generating and analyzing data;
4 Addressing core science ideas and associated academic vocabulary when students are ready to pursue causal explanations.

The role of the CER framework is addressed as an important feature in each of these themes.

The Role of Content Storyline

Ms. Medina does not operate from an activity-based orientation. Rather, she used the CER framework as a way to organize her planning and teaching, as well as establish norms for talking and doing science with students. She co-designed the content storyline for this unit collaboratively with colleagues who used the NGSS performance expectations (4-PS3–1, 4-PS3–2) to frame what students need to understand and be able to do by the end of the unit of instruction (see Appendix). She intentionally identified an anchor phenomenon (i.e., roller coasters staying on the track and making it to the end) that provided a captivating context for sustained investigation of energy transfer and transformation. With these bookends in place, Ms. Medina and her colleagues were able to consider the kinds of experiences with phenomena and data students would need in order to make sense of core science ideas, as well as the sequence in which the resulting claims would be useful to students as they developed a scientific explanation appropriate to fourth grade.

In working with practicing teachers who are in the early stages of moving away from an activity-based approach to science teaching, we have found that co-designing a content storyline with more experienced others is a powerful process for learning (see Appendix). By thinking through CER sequences based on core ideas and anchored in explaining real world phenomena, teachers' attention shifts to the kinds of evidence students will require for a complete explanation. They also begin to attend to how the explanation will build over time and the extent to which they can move students toward a scientific understanding. Many teachers who do this work carry their storylines with them during instruction as a tool for bringing them back to the core ideas and scientific practices in the midst of the hustle and bustle of interactive, student-centered investigations and data-based discussions. While content storylines are valuable to those involved in their co-design, they are not necessarily readily passed along to those outside the process of creating them.

Phenomena as a Vehicle for Equitable Access

Scholars have documented that teachers have reduced expectations for who they perceive to be "low ability" students (e.g., Zohar, 2007). This trend extends to students who live in poverty or differ culturally and linguistically from dominant groups in science and engineering fields (Duschl *et al.*, 2007; Lee and Buxton, 2010). Lee *et al.* (2013) address the inherent challenges of achieving the vision for students' science learning from the *Framework* given the linguistic demands of the scientific practices. The authors emphasize that science and engineering practices are highly interrelated, and they suggest that successful engagement in one of the practices creates opportunities for effective engagement in others (see also Bismack and Haefner, this volume, Chapter 2).

The vignette of Ms. Medina's class illustrates that productive engagement in scientific practices for every child begins with opportunities to interact with phenomena in ways that create shared experiences from which scientific questions can be collaboratively generated and investigated. Ms.

24   *Zembal-Saul and Hershberger*

Medina was intentional about *how* she introduced students to energy through moving objects. She was aware that defining energy at the beginning of the unit was not likely to be fruitful, so she engaged students in making observations using the roller coaster video that elicited their questions, ideas, and ways of knowing about objects in motion. The teacher then prepared a semi-structured investigation that invited every child in her class to experience marbles in motion on tracks of varying heights. This can be viewed as *leveling the playing field* from an equity standpoint (Zembal-Saul, 2018a). "Playing" with the homemade roller coasters provided a shared experience and gave every student access to emergent patterns associated with increasing the height of the top of the track. By doing this, Ms. Medina increased the likelihood of greater student participation and ownership in discussions of data.

Placing Students at the Center of Sensemaking in Science

Sharing more responsibility for the intellectual work of doing science, both what to investigate and how, as well as accepting students' ways of knowing, are fundamental to the sensemaking process (Rosebery and Warren, 2008). It is not that Ms. Medina relinquished all responsibility for learning to students; rather, she created inclusive opportunities for sensemaking before and during instruction, and she proactively invited students to take greater responsibility for making sense of phenomena during the lessons. The practice of noticing and responding to sensemaking moments during the act of teaching is a high-leverage practice (Ball and Forzani, 2009) that novice and experienced teachers alike find challenging (NASEM, 2015; Levin *et al.*, 2009).

Ms. Medina is a responsive teacher. She intentionally balanced her understanding of the terrain of unit content with students' contributions, questions, and struggles. Whenever possible, she used her knowledge of students to plan opportunities for them to notice and ask questions about aspects of the phenomenon that would be productive in building a scientific explanation over time (Arias, this volume, Chapter 11). While teaching, Ms. Medina didn't just walk from group to group to see if students were on task and/or provide procedural feedback; rather, she actively watched and listened to their ideas to inform subsequent instruction and explanation construction. In this vignette, more specifically, she listened for ideas that could spur debate, as well as negotiation, about what new data were needed and how to generate them. Put another way, she embraced uncertainty, improvised, and gave students opportunities to make decisions about how to make sense of marbles in motion (Manz, 2016; Schoerning *et al.*, 2015).

Ms. Medina also sought out opportunities for disagreement and argumentation as invitations for sensemaking—about science ideas and scientific practices—as opposed to signals for her to explain the normative answers or scientific methods. Importantly, she accepted "kid talk" and a variety of ways of representing knowledge, such as drawings and diagrams, during sensemaking discussions. Her goal was the productive participation of as many students as possible, with an emphasis on what they were understanding as opposed to whether they were using appropriate academic vocabulary. This broadens the class's concept of what it means to be scientifically proficient, supporting a more equitable instructional experience. This kind of responsiveness is not possible without a sophisticated sense of the science storyline, as well as a worldview that values individual students' contributions for advancing the sensemaking of the entire class.

Toward Causal Explanations in Elementary Science

Explaining phenomena is central in the work of scientists. The *Framework* states, "A major activity of science is investigating and explaining causal relationships and the mechanisms by which they are mediated. Such mechanisms can then be tested across given contexts and used to predict and explain events in new contexts" (National Research Council, 2012, p. 84). Translating this into practice in school science has proven to be challenging (Braaten and Windschitl, 2011), especially at the elementary level. To this point, we find it compelling that Ms. Medina orchestrated opportunities for questions that require *how* and *why* accounts to emerge from students' experiences with the homemade roller coasters and the investigation of simple relationships. The class became dissatisfied with relationships between the height of the track and the speed at which the marble moves. Ms. Medina recognized this moment as one in which students are ready for the introduction of energy as a core science idea to help advance their understanding of the phenomenon. Until that time, she accepted "kid talk" (e.g., power for energy) in framing the questions and in sensemaking discussions of how to generate and analyze data.

While CER is useful as a heuristic in the development of causal explanations, Ms. Medina's use of this approach was completely non-algorithmic. She moved fluidly between questions, evidence, claims, and reasoning in response to her students' ideas, questions, and interests. She did this with a deep understanding of the content and practices, as well as the storyline. Moreover, Ms. Medina was intentional about not only engaging students in collecting data, but also representing those data in ways that allow patterns to become visible and usable in the sensemaking process. The complexity of this work on the part of Ms. Medina should not be underestimated (Arias, this volume, Chapter 11).

Conclusion

From the beginning, the focus of our work has been to disrupt traditional, activity-centric approaches to teaching science in elementary grades. The question, *What's your evidence?*, emerged from classroom-based research with

26 *Zembal-Saul and Hershberger*

preservice and practicing teachers, and represents the importance of pressing for evidence in the construction of scientific explanations (Zembal-Saul, 2009). This chapter began with the goal of addressing the rest of the story—what comes *before* negotiating claims from evidence as fundamental to the sensemaking process. Ms. Medina's vignette highlights the potential of engaging students with phenomena and puzzling through what data to collect and how to record and analyze them as an invitation to equitable and productive participation in science practices and as a means of shifting epistemic authority from teachers to students (Stroupe, 2014).

Throughout the chapter, we have foregrounded the importance of teachers having a strong grasp of both the phenomenon students will be working to understand, as well as the scientific explanation they intend for students to construct. Engaging teachers in the co-design of content storylines is a powerful mechanism for professional learning and the development of "near horizon vision" (e.g., unit level; adapted from Ball *et al.*, 2008). Such vision requires moving away from day-to-day, hands-on activities toward organizing learning opportunities that build coherently throughout a unit, are sequenced to explain phenomena in increasingly complex ways, and are epistemically sound. Additionally, near horizon vision is essential in becoming a more responsive teacher—one who anticipates, attends to, and leverages students' ways of knowing, even when they disagree with one another and/or deviate from canonical science in the moment. Recall how Ms. Medina created the space for students' thinking about speed and distance to persist while guiding them to recognize the need for additional investigation.

It is an exciting time to be engaged in research and practice with elementary teachers as they embark on the challenging journey of shifting from traditional science instruction to positioning students to assume more authority in the process of sensemaking. The scientific practices are deeply interconnected, and making progress with one practice creates opportunities to make progress with others (Lee *et al.*, 2013; see also Bismack and Haefner, this volume, Chapter 2; Cody and Biggers, this volume, Chapter 3). We hope that Ms. Medina's story inspires you to consider how to invite students to grapple with data as part of the sensemaking process in science.

Appendix: Science Content Storyline Planning Guide

NGSS Performance Expectation

The process of building the science content storyline is non-linear and iterative. Begin by considering what students will understand and be able to explain about the phenomenon by the end of instruction. *Unpack and review DCIs, SEPs, and CCCs.*

What is the phenomenon that students will investigate?

Describe the phenomenon and how students will engage with it? Why do you think it will be interesting to students? What is the complete explanation you intend for students to construct?

What prior knowledge, local knowledge, lived experiences, and interests are students likely to have? How will you uncover this information and create opportunities to build upon it?

Claims are based on the big science ideas necessary to explain the phenomena. *What are these ideas and is there a way to sequence them coherently (B)? What might an age-appropriate version of the claim/statement sound like (B)?*

Claims should be grounded in evidence and respond to a question that students are investigating about the phenomenon. *What questions will you use to drive instruction (A)? How might you elicit students' questions for this purpose (E)? Which questions require descriptive answers and which require causal explanations (A, E)?*

Whenever possible, young students should engage directly with phenomena and collect and analyze data necessary to explain it. When raw data are transformed through the process of analysis and sensemaking, they become useful as evidence. Claims emerge from evidence and in response to questions, not the other way around.

Once the science ideas needed for the explanation are identified and sequenced, consider how students will collect data for each CER sequence (C). If an activity does not serve the purpose of generating data that will help students understand and explain the phenomena, drop it! Data collection opportunities should be intentionally designed for the storyline. Whenever possible, consider how students can be included in making decisions about how to collect, organize, and analyze data (C, E).

Reasoning is used to further make connections between evidence and claim (D). Sensemaking discussions play an important role in making students' reasoning visible. *What might it sound like for students to elaborate on how data support a claim they are negotiating? What science terms might be useful for this purpose and when/how will you introduce them? What questions will you ask to facilitate reasoning, support negotiation of claims, and prompt arguing from evidence (E)?*

Question (A)	Claim (B)	Evidence (C)	Reasoning (D)	Notes (E)

References

Avraamidou, L., and Zembal-Saul, C. (2005). Giving priority to evidence in science teaching: A first-year elementary teacher's specialized knowledge and practice. *Journal of Research in Science Teaching, 42*(9), 965–986.

Ball, D. L., and Forzani, F. M. (2009). The work of teaching and the challenge for teacher education. *Journal of Teacher Education, 60*(5), 497–511.

Ball, D. L., Thames, M. H., and Phelps, G. (2008). Content knowledge for teaching, what makes it special? *Journal of Teacher Education, 59*(5), 389–407.

Berland, L. K., and Reiser, B. J. (2009). Making sense of argumentation and explanation. *Science Education, 93*(1), 26–55.

Braaten, M., and Windschitl, M. (2011). Working toward a stronger conceptualization of scientific explanation for science education. *Science Education, 95*(4), 639–669.

Carlone, H. B., Haun-Frank, J., and Webb, A. (2011). Assessing equity beyond knowledge- and skills-based outcomes: A comparative ethnography of two fourth-grade reform based science classrooms. *Journal of Research in Science Teaching, 48*(5), 459–485.

Cochran-Smith, M. and Lytle, S. (2009). *Inquiry as stance: Practitioner research for the next generation.* Teachers College Press.

Dana, N. and Yendol-Silva, D. (2009). *The reflective educator's guide to classroom research: Learning to teach and teaching to learn through practitioner inquiry* (2nd edn.). Thousand Oaks, CA: Corwin Press.

Davis, E. A., Petish, D., and Smithey, J. (2006). Challenges new science teachers face. *Review of Educational Research, 76*(4), 607–651.

Duschl, R. A. (2000). Making the nature of science explicit. In R. Miller, J. Leech, and J. Osborne (Eds.), *Improving Science Education: The Contribution of Research* (pp. 187–206). Philadelphia, PA: Open University Press.

Duschl, R. A., Schweingruber, H., and Shouse, A. W. (Eds.). (2007). *Taking Science to School: Learning and Teaching Science in Grades K-8.* Washington, DC: National Academies Press.

Engle, R. A., and Conant, F. R. (2002). Guiding principles for fostering productive disciplinary engagement: Explaining an emergent argument in a community of learners classroom. *Cognition and Instruction, 20*(4), 399–483.

Hammer, D. (1995). Student inquiry in a physics class discussion. *Cognition and Instruction, 13*(3), 401–430.

Lee, O. and Buxton, C. (2010). *Diversity and Equity in Science Education: Research, Policy and Practice.* Multicultural Series. New York: Teachers College Press.

Lee, O., Quinn, H., and Valdés, G. (2013). Science and Language for English Language Learners in Relation to Next Generation Science Standards and with Implications for Common Core State Standards for English Language Arts and Mathematics. *Educational Researcher, 42*(4), 223–233.

Lemke, J. L. (1990). *Talking Science: Language, Learning, And Values.* Norwood, NJ: Ablex Pub. Corp.

Levin, D. M., Hammer, D., and Coffey, J. E. (2009). Novice teachers' attention to student thinking. *Journal of Teacher Education, 60*(2), 142–154.

Manz, E. (2016). Examining evidence construction as the transformation of the material world into community knowledge. *Journal of Research in Science Teaching, 53*(7), 1113–1140.

McNeill, K. L., and Krajcik, J. (2008). Scientific explanations: Characterizing and evaluating the effects of teachers' instructional practices on student learning. *Journal of Research in Science Teaching*, *45*(1), 53–78.

Metz, K. (2000). Young children's inquiry in biology: Building the knowledge bases to empower independent inquiry. In J. Minstrell and E. Van Zee (Eds.), *Inquiring into Inquiry Learning and Teaching in Science*. Washington, DC: American Association for the Advancement of Science.

NASEM (National Academies of Sciences Engineering and Medicine). (2015). *Science Teachers' Learning: Enhancing Opportunities, Creating Supportive Contexts* (Committee on Strengthening Science Education through a Teacher Learning Continuum Board on Science Education and Teacher Advisory Council Division of Behavioral and Social Science and Education Ed.). Washington, DC: National Academies Press.

National Research Council. (2012). *A Framework for K-12 Science Education: Practices, Crosscutting Concepts, and Core Ideas*. Washington, DC: National Academies Press.

NGSS Lead States. (2013). *Next Generation Science Standards: For States, By States*. Washington, DC: National Academies Press.

Reiser, B. (2013, September). What professional development strategies are needed for successful implementation of the Next Generation Science Standards?Invitational Symposium on Science Assessment. ETS K-12 Center.

Rosebery, A. S., and Warren, B. (2008). *Teaching Science to English Language Learners: Building on Students' Strengths*. Arlington, VA: NSTA Press.

Roth, K.J., Druker, S.D., Garnier, H.E., Lemmens, M., Chen, C., Kawanaka, T., Rasmussen, D., Trubacova, S., Warvi, D., Okamoto, Y., Gonzales, P., Stigler, J., and Gallimore, R. (2006). *Teaching Science in Five Countries: Results from the TIMSS 1999 Video Study (NCES 2006–2011)*. US Department of Education, National Center for Education Statistics. Washington, DC: US Government Printing Office.

Roth, K. J., Garnier, H., Chen, C., Lemmens, M., Schwille, K., and Wickler, N. I. Z. (2011). Videobased lesson analysis: Effective science PD for teacher and student learning. *Journal of Research in Science Teaching*, *48*(2), 117–148.

Schoerning, E., Hand, B., Shelley, M., and Therrien, W. (2015). Language, access, and power in the elementary science classroom. *Science Education*, *99*(2), 238–259.

Stroupe, D. (2014). Examining classroom science practice communities: How teachers and students negotiate epistemic agency and learn science-as-practice. *Science Education*, *98*(3), 487–516.

Taylor, J., Roth, K.Wilson, C., Stuhlsatz, M. and Tipton, E. (2017). The effect of an analysis-of-practice, videocase-based, teacher professional development program on elementary students' science achievement. *Journal of Research on Educational Effectiveness*, *10*(2), 241–271.

Zembal-Saul, C. (2009). Learning to teach elementary school science as argument. *Science Education*, *93*(4), 687–719.

Zembal-Saul, C. (2018a). *KLEWS to Formative Assessment for 3D Science*. Lansing, MI: Michigan Formative Assessment Academy.

Zembal-Saul, C. (2018b). Research and practice on science teachers' continuous professional development in argumentation. In S. Erduran (Ed.), *Argumentation in Chemistry Education: Research, Policy and Practice*. Advances in Chemistry Series. London: Royal Society of Chemistry.

Zembal-Saul, C., McNeill, K. L., and Hershberger, K. (2013). *What's Your Evidence?: Engaging K-5 Children in Constructing Explanations in Science*. Boston, MA: Pearson Higher Education.

Zohar, A. (2007). Science teacher education and professional development in argumentation. In S. Erduran and M. P. Jiménez-Alexandre (Eds.), *Argumentation in Science Education* (pp. 245–268). New York: Springer.

2 Portrait of a First-Grade Teacher

Using Science Practices to Leverage Young Children's Sensemaking in Science

Amber S. Bismack
UNIVERSITY OF MICHIGAN

Leigh Ann Haefner
THE PENNSYLVANIA STATE UNIVERSITY [1]

In the primary grades it is important to not only help students "like" science (Furtak and Alonzo, 2010), but to use students' interests to leverage their learning. This can be challenging for elementary teachers when they are expected to teach all subjects while also integrating the disciplinary core ideas, science practices, and crosscutting concepts in their science instruction (Marx and Harris, 2006; NGSS Lead States, 2013). Though this is challenging, it is not impossible. In this chapter, we characterize how one experienced early elementary teacher met these expectations by using the science practices during a sensemaking discussion to help her students connect their prior experiences with new concepts.

Teaching for Scientific Sensemaking

Scientific sensemaking involves constructing, articulating, and defending one's ideas of the phenomena being studied based on evidence (Berland and Reiser, 2009). The science practices—the ways science professionals engage in their work—can be used to support scientific sensemaking. For example, developing explanations of phenomena is one way to engage in scientific "knowledge building" (Scardamalia and Bereiter, 2006). Common science practices in elementary classrooms—and those we focus on in this chapter—include asking questions, conducting investigations, analyzing and interpreting data, engaging in arguments from evidence, and constructing explanations. Each practice supports students' scientific sensemaking in different ways.

Asking scientific questions involves constructing questions that are investigable (National Research Council, 2012). Though potentially engaging for students, the questions in elementary classrooms are often teacher- or curriculum-created, thereby not providing students opportunities to learn how to construct investigable questions that build from their own experiences and curiosities (Biggers, 2017).

32 Bismack and Haefner

Conducting investigations involves systematically collecting data about phenomena to answer a scientific question or revise an existing theory or explanation (National Research Council, 2012). If possible, having students conduct investigations where they gather their own data can support their understanding of what data is needed to make sense of the phenomena.

Analyzing and interpreting data is central for scientific sensemaking because it requires students to identify patterns and relationships in first- or second-hand data. The patterns and relationships are used to answer the scientific question or to support or refute a theory or explanation (National Research Council, 2012). This social practice emphasizes the importance of consensus-building (Rivet and Ingber, 2017).

In elementary classrooms, two synergistic science practices are scientific argumentation and explanations. Engaging in scientific argumentation involves using evidence to persuade someone of one's ideas or to evaluate different ideas (Berland and Reiser, 2009; National Research Council, 2012; Zembal-Saul, 2009). When students engage in scientific argumentation, it can appear as the back-and-forth interaction between students as they discuss and debate their ideas about science using evidence (e.g., Osborne *et al.*, 2004). Often, in elementary classrooms, this type of interaction occurs in the service of constructing explanatory accounts of phenomena. In both argumentation and explanation-construction, evidence identified from the data is used to support claims (Berland and McNeill, 2011).

Though all science practices are critical for engaging students in scientific sensemaking, these are some science practices that provide foundations for all students, including young students, to make sense of and think critically about the world around them (Metz, 2011).

Students' Engagement in Scientific Sensemaking

When given adequate support all students can engage in the science practices. For example, fading scaffolds have been found to support middle school students in constructing scientific explanations (McNeill and Krajcik, 2008). Also, upper elementary students' articulation of their own scientific questions and construction and analyses of models of data support their scientific sensemaking (Lehrer and Schauble, 2002). Even young elementary students can make sense of scientific phenomena when designing and conducting their own scientific investigations (Metz, 2011). These represent examples of students constructing explanations, asking questions, analyzing and interpreting data, and planning and conducting investigations. Like science professionals, the students constructed their own scientific knowledge when engaging in the science practices.

Prioritizing Students and Inquiry when Teaching for Scientific Sensemaking

Engaging students in scientific sensemaking means focusing on students and what they bring to the classroom. One way is to provide opportunities to investigate phenomena that are interesting and challenge students' prior ideas (National Research Council, 2005). Teachers can use open-ended questioning strategies to elicit students' ideas (Harris *et al.*, 2012) and engage students in discussions that prioritize their ideas, which not only supports their sensemaking but also represents science as a social, collaborative enterprise (National Research Council, 2005). Prioritizing students' ideas in sensemaking discussions means introducing scientific language after students have had the opportunity to discuss the phenomena using their everyday language (Brown and Ryoo, 2008; see also Zembal-Saul and Hershberger, this volume, Chapter 1; Hooper and Zembal-Saul, this volume, Chapter 4).

The Claim-Evidence-Reasoning instructional scaffold is one way teachers have supported students in scientific sensemaking. This scaffold supports students in developing claims that answer scientific questions about phenomena that are based on evidence collected from investigations or other learning activities. The reasoning enables students to articulate the ways in which the evidence supports the claim, often using scientific principles (e.g., McNeill *et al.*, 2006). The scaffold also serves as a formative assessment of students' emerging understandings (Zembal-Saul *et al.*, 2013). For a further explanation of the instructional scaffold and how teachers go about engaging in this complex work, see Zembal-Saul and Hershberger (this volume, Chapter 1).

Overview of Methods

This qualitative case study (Stake, 2000) investigated the science teaching practices of one in-service teacher, Ms. Kerry. We used open coding of the video recordings of Ms. Kerry's science teaching to investigate how she structured the sensemaking discussions, as well as how she elicited, responded to, and moved student thinking forward. Sample codes included sharing data, developing a claim, re-evaluating data to see what was missed, and adding consensus evidence. We also conducted three semi-structured interviews with Ms. Kerry highlighting her views of science teaching and learning, her professional context and experience, and her planning and instruction.

We used this coding to develop three vignettes that represent how Ms. Kerry (a) drew on children's own language to guide a science discussion, (b) leveraged students' initial ideas to inform current and further investigations, and (c) guided students' analyses of their data. After presenting these vignettes in the following sections, we discuss how the science practices supported students' sensemaking and ways teachers can engage in this work.

Scientific Sensemaking in First Grade

First-Grade Teacher: Ms. Kerry

Ms. Kerry[2] taught first-grade to 17 students during the final year of her 35-year teaching career. As a science teacher, she believed her role was to teach the curriculum content objectives, align content with students' capabilities, and use sensemaking discussions to support student learning. She explained that, "you need to provide experiences…to [see] what the students know and what their misconceptions are" (Interview 2).

This study analyzed portions of Ms. Kerry's teaching of two units about States of Matter and Magnets. Each large, multi-week unit covered a breadth of concepts within the theme. We chose to focus on the magnets and states of matter lessons due to Ms. Kerry's use of content-rich, science sensemaking discussions. Each lesson was structured around an investigation question and began with Ms. Kerry eliciting students' initial ideas and wonderings. Then, students collected and recorded data during small group investigations with adult guidance. Lastly, Ms. Kerry led a whole class discussion where the children identified patterns in their observations/data to construct a scientific explanation that answered the investigation question. Though time-consuming—the science lessons were about 60 minutes or more in length—Ms. Kerry emphasized the importance of science by structuring her day to accommodate the time.

Vignette 1: Using Children's Talk to Develop Science Explanations

In this lesson from the States of Matter unit early in the school year, the children investigated a *mystery matter* (melted crayon) to answer the question, *How can you change a liquid into a solid?*

TEACHER: Let's talk about what we noticed.

STUDENT 1: First it was a liquid and then it turned into a solid.

TEACHER: [referencing their investigation question] So we were able to turn a liquid into a solid? Can someone add on to that?

STUDENT 2: First it was liquid, and then the way it turned into a solid is that you had to let it sit.

TEACHER: You had to let it sit? If I take a liquid and I just let it sit, it will just turn into a solid? If I poured a liquid into a dish and let it sit, it would just turn into a solid?

STUDENT 3: No, because water needs to be cold to turn into ice.

TEACHER: Is that what happened today? Did the liquid we saw today turn cold? How do you know it turned colder?

STUDENT 3: Yes, because we could feel the heat on our hands and that meant the heat was leaving.

TEACHER: So the heat was leaving the liquid? Can someone else add on to that?

STUDENT 4: When the warmth was leaving and it made the liquid into a solid.

STUDENT 5: The warmth ... you could feel it coming out into the air and it just turned into a solid.

Ms. Kerry repeated this idea and asked the class whether they agreed, disagreed, or wanted to add on. Thinking the class had reached consensus, Ms. Kerry shifted the conversation to developing a claim from the evidence.

TEACHER: Our question was *How can you change a liquid into a solid?* What claim would answer that question? [writing on the board *You can change a liquid into a solid by_____.*]

STUDENTS: By letting it sit.

Rather than correcting them or redirecting them back to the previous discussion, Ms. Kerry starts the conversation over.

TEACHER: Is that what you think did it? Just letting it sit for a little bit?

STUDENT 6: Yes.

STUDENT 7: No.

TEACHER: Wait, I hear a yes and I hear a no. If I take a liquid and pour it in a container and let it sit, it would turn into a solid?

STUDENT 8: You need it hot because when all the steam comes out it turns into a solid.

TEACHER: Then what was it that was turning it into a solid?

STUDENT 8: The heat was going away.

After several more minutes, Ms. Kerry identified two primary and opposing ideas where students struggled with the distinction: 1) Letting a liquid sit for a while will turn it into a solid, and 2) Heat needs to leave before it will turn into a solid.

TEACHER: I want you to think about what we saw happening. Was the mystery matter just sitting there or was it the heat leaving that turned it into a solid? I want you to think about this for a minute. If I set a pan of water on the table and just let it sit, would it turn to a solid?

STUDENTS: No.

TEACHER: No? Then do you think the warmth leaving is different than something just sitting there?

STUDENTS: Yes.

Ms. Kerry scaffolded the claim development further by writing the following on chart paper:

1   We started with a liquid
2   _____
3   We ended with a solid

TEACHER: [pointing to the blank line] What happened in here and how do we know?

36 *Bismack and Haefner*

STUDENT 9: The heat leaves.
TEACHER: How do we know the heat left?
STUDENT 9: Because we could feel the heat.
TEACHER: Oh, we could feel it.

Ms. Kerry writes on the middle line: *We felt the heat leave.*

TEACHER: Okay, let's see. [reading the three lines] We started with a liquid, we felt the heat leave, and we ended with a solid. Is that what we saw with the mystery matter?

The students finally agree that the warmth leaving the liquid caused it to turn into a solid. After developing a whole-class evidence-based claim, students returned to their seats and wrote the claim with evidence in their science notebooks. Lastly, the students conducted a similar investigation by collecting temperature data before and after the phase changes and used this to support and confirm the evidence-based claim.

This vignette illustrates how prioritizing children's talk, using investigation-based data, and allowing children time to identify patterns in data can support their sensemaking. Throughout the discussion, students used their own words and ideas to support, clarify, compare, and refute each other's ideas until there was a consensus. Ms. Kerry continuously referred back to the observations and expected students to use data to support their own ideas or refute another's idea. Facilitating children's talk and reasoning about data was a repetitive, reiteration of the discussion that was time-consuming yet crucial for all students' sensemaking.

Vignette 2: Eliciting Students' Prior Knowledge to Leverage Science Learning

Ms. Kerry's spring Magnets unit began with students sharing experiences with magnets, which included, "stick them together" and "if you don't do it right, they won't stick, they won't touch each other." With each experience, Ms. Kerry responded with surprise and amazement. "You are telling me that two magnets can stick together?" Toward the end of this discussion, she introduced science vocabulary. "I am going to teach you the science word for *stick*. When they go together, we call that *attract*. Wow, the magnet *attracted* through the table?" From this point on, she used the scientific terminology with the students. After this initial discussion, the students worked in small groups (without magnets) to sort a bag of objects into three piles, predicting which objects *would* attract a magnet, objects that *would not* be attracted, and objects they were uncertain about. When finished, they returned to the carpet to discuss this.

TEACHER: [laying objects out on the carpet] Were there any objects that you definitely thought would be attracted to a magnet?
STUDENT 1: The paperclip.

Portrait of a First-Grade Teacher   37

TEACHER: What was it about the paperclip that made your team pretty sure it would be attracted to a magnet?

STUDENT 1: It's metal.

TEACHER: Are you thinking if something is metal you are pretty sure it would be attracted to a magnet?

STUDENT 1: Yes.

> As more students affirmed that a magnet would be attracted to metal, Ms. Kerry asked if they could write down that metal objects are attracted to magnets. Most students agreed.

STUDENT 2: No, not all. There is some that attract and some that don't attract. Like copper!

TEACHER: Does anyone want to respond to what he just said? He doesn't think all metals are attracted.

STUDENT 3: I think he is right because [holding up an object] this has metal, but it won't really stick because it has softer things around it.

TEACHER: It sounds to me like you are thinking that if the metal is covered with something it won't be attracted to the magnet?

STUDENT 3: Yes

STUDENT 4: [pointing to the covering] I disagree. That is actually very, very thin but this [picking up another object] is very, very thick. So, if it tried to go through this it couldn't go through, but it can go through that [pointing to the original object].

TEACHER: She is saying no—a magnet can't go through anything, but you think a magnet can be attracted through thin things but not thick things? It sounds like we have a difference of opinion and something we are wondering about. One: Will magnets actually attract through things? And two: Does it matter how thick it is? Will a magnet attract through something thick?

> Ms. Kerry redirects students back to the original idea of whether all metal is attracted to a magnet. Some students agree and others disagree.

TEACHER: This seems like something else we are wondering about. Are magnets attracted to all metals or just some metals?

> Both wonderings were recorded on chart paper and the conversation continued around other objects, with wonderings recorded when disagreements arose about weight, shape, size, hardness, and material.

About a third of the lesson was spent in this initial discussion, which was followed by students working in groups to test objects in their piles and a subsequent discussion of the results.

This vignette illustrated how Ms. Kerry used her previous experiences teaching magnets to anticipate students' prior ideas and provide opportunities for them to share and discuss those ideas. The discussions were used to generate testable questions, which informed current and future lessons. Ms. Kerry also purposefully

38   Bismack and Haefner

provided a diverse array of materials for the students to examine and sort prior to testing the materials with magnets. As a result, students made detailed observations of the objects and Ms. Kerry used those to raise questions about the materials. This illustrates how rich and meaningful discussions of children's observations and predictions and their justification for those predictions can support more thoughtful testing and eventual understanding of properties of materials.

Vignette 3: Helping Children Find Patterns in Data

To begin the third magnets lesson Ms. Kerry introduced students to different magnets (bar, disk, rod, ring, and horseshoe magnets) and posed a new question: *Are certain parts of a magnet stronger than other parts of a magnet?* They tested the magnets by determining how many paperclips each could hold. Ms. Kerry showed that two paperclips are not attracted to each other if there is no magnet and compared it to a magnet with two paperclips in a chain. The class discussed how more magnets in a chain means the magnet is stronger than magnets with fewer paperclips in a chain. When the testing was complete, the class discussed their results.

STUDENT 3: The first time we tested the ring we got two paperclips, but then when we tested the end, we got three paperclips. When we tried the rings, at first, we got two and three but then we tried it again and we got three and three. We wanted to test it again because all the magnets always had two sides.

TEACHER: What do you mean by two sides?

STUDENT 3: Like, if you are using the horseshoe it is two and two, if you are using the big magnet, it is four and four.

TEACHER: I am having trouble understanding what you saw. Can someone help me understand this?

STUDENT 3: Because we all had the same magnets that we used, all the magnets have two strongest parts.

TEACHER: [holding up a bar magnet] Were there certain parts on this magnet that were stronger than others?

STUDENT 4: The black part.

TEACHER: [pointing to the middle of the magnet] This part in the middle here?

STUDENT 4: It wasn't that strong.

TEACHER: Did anyone else see that same thing?

Students nod in agreement.

TEACHER: What about this horseshoe magnet? What were the strong parts in this one?

STUDENT 5: [touching the two ends of the magnet] These two.

TEACHER: [pointing to the middle] Was this part as strong as those parts?

STUDENT 5: No

Portrait of a First-Grade Teacher   39

STUDENT 6: It didn't hold one there.

TEACHER: [holding a small rectangular magnet] What about this magnet? Were all four sides just as strong?

STUDENT 7: No, one side wasn't that strong.

To illustrate the pattern, Ms. Kerry drew a picture of each magnet on chart paper.

TEACHER: I hear you saying that you noticed the bar magnet had two sides that were stronger than the other sides?

STUDENTS: Yes.

Ms. Kerry circled the ends (poles) on her drawing of the bar magnet. Then she pointed at the horseshoe magnet.

TEACHER: And the horseshoe had two sides stronger than the rest of the horseshoe?

STUDENTS: Yes.

Ms. Kerry circled the ends (poles) of the horseshoe magnet. Ms. Kerry continued circling and labeling the remaining drawings, illustrating the pattern in the data.

TEACHER: It seems like no matter what group you worked in, everybody saw that each magnet had two parts that were stronger than other parts of the magnet?

Students nod in agreement.

TEACHER: I want you to think about how you would answer the question: *Are some parts of the magnet stronger than others?* What would you say?

STUDENT 8: Yes, they have two strong parts on the magnets.

STUDENT 3: Yes, they have only two strong parts on the magnet and the others are not strong enough to hold the clips.

Ms. Kerry wrote the claim: Yes, each magnet has two parts that are strong.

TEACHER: [turning back to the class] How do you *know* that some sides are stronger?

STUDENT 9: Some can hold more paperclips.

TEACHER: Oh, so these sides held more paperclips!

Ms. Kerry asked students to share some numbers that each side held and recorded them on the drawings.

TEACHER: Let's go back to our claim. Each magnet has two parts that are strong. Would you say that is a pretty accurate claim?

Students nod in agreement.

TEACHER: [pointing to the drawings] This is evidence that supports this claim. Now I am going to give you some scientific reasoning. You discovered something that scientists discovered! Every magnet, no matter where you find it, has two parts that are stronger and they have a special scientific name. They are called *poles*.

Ms. Kerry asked if students had heard the word "pole" before and after some discussion, students say the North Pole.

TEACHER: Yes, the poles have names! One pole is the north pole and one is the south pole. All magnets have a north and a south pole.

STUDENT 10: On the big magnet there was an S and N.

TEACHER: You saw that? The reason they got their names is if you hold a magnet from a string and let it spin, when it stops spinning, the north pole of the magnet will point toward the real North Pole. The south pole will point toward the real South Pole.

In this lesson, the children identified and made sense of patterns in the data. The students recognized that every magnet had "two strong parts," which represented the core science concept of magnetic poles. Ms. Kerry drew on multiple sets of data to help her students reach a consensus and develop their claim. Ms. Kerry also used the sensemaking discussion to introduce science terminology after the students had an appropriate and contextualized understanding of the science concept. This was a typical practice in her science lessons.

Leveraging the Science Practices to Support Learning Science Concepts

Engaging students in the science practices supports students in making sense of science concepts, which was Ms. Kerry's focus for her science teaching. She used the science practices to help her students confront their own preconceived notions of the world. To do this, different science practices were foregrounded and backgrounded, as demonstrated by the vignettes, depending on students' needs. Four science practices—asking scientific questions, conducting scientific investigations, analyzing and interpreting data, and constructing scientific explanations—were featured in these vignettes, though these were not the only science practices students engaged in throughout the year (e.g., elementary scientific argumentation frequently appeared in sensemaking discussions).

Asking Scientific Questions

Asking scientific questions can be a powerful way to connect with students' own interests and curiosities (National Research Council, 2012), yet this is not typical in elementary classrooms (Biggers, 2017). Ms. Kerry pushed beyond the "typical" classroom to develop the investigation questions based on her students' own curiosities. For example, she used the initial exploration of materials magnets do and do not attract in order to elicit students' wonderings (questions) and reframe those wonderings into investigable questions. Though the students were not focused on what makes questions investigable, Ms. Kerry did demonstrate how science is guided by questions that are typically based on our own curiosities and wonderings (Reiser *et al.*, 2017).

Conducting Scientific Investigations

To give meaning to students' scientific questions, students need opportunities to investigate them (Crawford, 2000), which helps students learn how data is collected and used to answer scientific questions (Zembal-Saul *et al.*, 2013). Ms. Kerry purposefully gave her students opportunities to collect data about phenomena (magnets and materials) that could be used to answer the student- and teacher-driven questions. She demonstrated how, with careful planning and scaffolding, even young children can engage in this critical science practice (Metz, 2011).

Analyzing and Interpreting Data Using Sensemaking Discussions

Analyzing and interpreting data typically occurs during the sensemaking discussion after students have collected the data (Arias, this volume, Chapter 11; Rivet and Ingber, 2017), though this portion of a science lesson is often eliminated or shortened due to time constraints (Bismack *et al.*, 2014). Ms. Kerry made time for all students to analyze the data and used open-ended questioning and probing of students' language (Arias, this volume, Chapter 11; Harris *et al.*, 2012) to push students to draw on the data to make sense of the phenomena. She also re-tested materials during these discussions in response to alternative claims and to remind students to attend to the data. This science practice is the core of scientific sensemaking in that it allows students to confront their preconceived notions of the phenomena (Zembal-Saul *et al.*, 2013).

While analyzing the data, Ms. Kerry called attention to contrasting student ideas or pushed back on an idea (e.g., "Did anyone see anything different?"). This is an elementary form of scientific argumentation (Berland and McNeill, 2011; Zembal-Saul, 2009). Students were encouraged to discuss and evaluate alternative claims based on the evidence—often without even knowing they were doing so. Engaging in this practice emphasized the importance of consensus building when interpreting data and that the consensus is what guides understanding (and validation) of the claims.

Constructing Scientific Explanations

To help students formalize their understandings, Ms. Kerry had students construct a claim supported by evidence—a heuristic designed to support students' construction of explanations that was modified to fit the needs of young children (McNeill *et al.*, 2006; Zembal-Saul *et al.*, 2013). To do this, Ms. Kerry used her students' everyday language that was often not scientific in nature to discuss what was happening in the phenomena. When she introduced scientific terminology, she did so toward the end of the discussion—after her students already recognized and discussed what was happening. For example, in vignette three, Ms. Kerry introduced the word "pole" only after the students identified the poles on the magnets—and she used the terminology to introduce the concept of the Earth having two poles. Similar to work with older elementary students, introducing scientific terminology after students have made sense of the concepts instead of before supports deeper science learning (Brown and Ryoo, 2008).

In summary, each science practice was a tool that Ms. Kerry used to leverage students' ideas in ways that supported their scientific sensemaking. Her use of the science practices was intentional, fluid, iterative, and time-consuming, but served to support students' understanding of the science concepts.

Productive Science Teaching Takes Time and Requires Intentional Planning

Engaging in the type of science teaching demonstrated by Ms. Kerry and advocated in current science reform takes time (National Research Council, 2012; NGSS Lead States, 2013). For example, a majority of Ms. Kerry's science lessons involved taking time to discuss the ideas the students held about the phenomena (Carroll, 1989; Michaels and O'Connor, 2017). Her teaching differed from typical elementary classrooms where sensemaking discussions get shortened or eliminated due to time constraints, which limits students' opportunities to engage in scientific sensemaking (Bismack *et al.*, 2014). Scientific sensemaking is particularly important for students with minimal science experiences, as well as for English Language Learners who are working to make sense of the norms of science, science concepts, and language used (Buxton and Lee, 2014).

Teachers need to engage in year-long planning to create opportunities in which every child can engage in all of the science practices, because no single lesson or even a single unit could effectively engage students in all of the practices. Teachers must foreground and background different science practices at different times based on the unit goals and students' needs. For example, early in the year Ms. Kerry foregrounded conducting investigations and analyzing and interpreting data. In contrast, later in the year Ms. Kerry foregrounded asking questions and constructing student-created explanations once her students gained more science experience. Prioritizing the necessary time and opportunities for students to make sense of phenomena and foregrounding and backgrounding science practices targets the needs of all students, particularly those with minimal science experiences and English Language Learners (Buxton and Lee, 2014; Schwarz *et al.*, 2017).

Can Teachers Really Engage in this Type of Complex Science Teaching?

This case illustrated how one experienced elementary teacher productively engaged her students in scientific sensemaking, but it begs the question: *Can any teacher teach science that engages students in this type of scientific sensemaking?* We argue that all teachers can do this, but it may involve shifts in how they plan and view science teaching and learning. The shifts include centralizing students and their ideas, leveraging the science practices to support science learning, and prioritizing the learning of science concepts over scientific language.

- *Centralizing students and their ideas.* Teachers need to recognize that all students' capabilities and interests in science and beyond can be used as tools to support their learning. For example, Ms. Kerry elicited students' ideas that she knew they held and used those ideas and questions to guide further investigations. She also consistently used students' own language to discuss ideas.
- *Leveraging the science practices to support science learning.* The science practices can serve as tools to engage students in investigating and sensemaking that confronts their alternative ideas. For example, comparing data about crayons hardening with an alternative material (e.g., water) pushed back against the idea that "letting something sit" would cause a material to change state. The focus on analyzing data, as well as the other science practices, helped students make sense of the phenomena. Though time consuming, this was critical for supporting the learning needs of all students (Buxton and Lee, 2014; Carroll, 1989).
- *Prioritizing the learning of science concepts over scientific terminology.* Often elementary science is taught with a focus on scientific terminology (Banilower *et al.*, 2013). In contrast, Ms. Kerry and others (e.g., Brown and Ryoo, 2008) demonstrated that students' science learning is enhanced when learning the concepts is prioritized over learning scientific terms. After students have developed an understanding of the phenomena, scientific terminology can be woven into discussions to give students accurate language to describe the phenomena (e.g., "poles" on magnets to replace "parts" of magnets). Doing so allows teachers to draw on all students' language and experiences to guide discussions and help them make connections to science concepts, which is particularly supportive of English Language Learners among others (Buxton and Lee, 2014).

These are only a few shifts that teachers may need to make to support *all* students in learning science. Helping teachers learn how to engage in this type of work will be challenging, yet necessary. Teacher education programs, professional development opportunities, and curriculum materials will need to foreground the teaching of the science practices as tools for facilitating the learning of science concepts (National Academies of Sciences Engineering and Medicine, 2015). Leveraging science practices to learn science concepts can support all students' engagement in science—and is possible for all teachers.

Notes

1 Authors contributed equally to the work in this paper and share first authorship.
2 A pseudonym is used to reserve the participant's anonymity.

References

Banilower, E. R., Smith, P. S., Weiss, I. R., Malzahn, K. M., Campbell, K. M., and Weis, A. M. (2013). *2012 NSSME Report of the 2012 National Survey of Science and Mathematics Education*. Chapel Hill, NC: Horizon Research, Inc.

Berland, L. K., and McNeill, K. L. (2011). For whom is argument and explanation a necessary distinction? A response to Osborne and Patterson. *Science Education*, *96*(5), 808–813.

Berland, L. K., and Reiser, B. J. (2009). Making sense of argumentation and explanation. *Science Education*, *93*(1), 26–55.

Biggers, M. (2017). Questioning questions: Elementary teachers' adaptations of investigation questions across the inquiry continuum. *Research in Science Education*, *48*(1), 1–28.

Bismack, A. S., Arias, A. M., Davis, E. A., and Palincsar, A. S. (2014). Connecting curriculum materials and teachers: Elementary science teachers' enactment of a reform-based curricular unit. *Journal of Science Teacher Education*, *25*(4), 489–512.

Brown, B. A., and Ryoo, K. (2008). Teaching science as a language: A "content-first" approach to science teaching. *Journal of Research in Science Teaching*, *45*(5), 529–553.

Buxton, C. and Lee, O. (2014). English learners in science education. In N. G. Lederman and S. K. Abell (Eds.), *Handbook of Research on Science Education* (Vol. II). New York:Routledge, Taylor & Francis.

Carroll, J. B. (1989). The Carroll model: A 25-year retrospective and prospective view. *Educational Researcher*, *18*(1), 26–31.

Crawford, B. A. (2000). Embracing the essence of inquiry: New roles for science teachers. *Journal of Research in Science Teaching*, *37*(9), 916–937.

Furtak, E. M., and Alonzo, A. C. (2010). The role of content in inquiry-based elementary science lessons: An analysis of teacher beliefs and enactment. *Research in Science Education*, *40*(3), 425–449.

Harris, C. J., Phillips, R. S., and Penuel, W. (2012). Examining teachers' instructional moves aimed at developing students' ideas and questions in learner-centered science classrooms. *Journal of Science Teacher Education*, *23*(7), 769–788.

Lehrer, R., and Schauble, L. (2002). *Investigating Real Data in the Classroom: Expanding Children's Understanding of Math and Science*. New York: Teachers College Press.

Marx, R. W., and Harris, C. J. (2006). No child left behind and science education: Opportunities, challenges, and risks. *Elementary School Journal*, *106*(5), 467–477.

McNeill, K. L., and Krajcik, J. S. (2008). Scientific explanations: Characterizing and evaluating the effects of teachers' instructional practices on student learning. *Journal of Research in Science Teaching*, *45*(1), 53–78.

McNeill, K. L., Lizotte, D. J., Krajcik, J. S., and Marx, R. W. (2006). Supporting students' construction of scientific explanations by fading scaffolds in instructional materials. *Journal of the Learning Sciences*, *15*(2), 153–191.

Metz, K. E. (2011). Disentangling robust developmental constraints from the instructionally mutable: Young children's epistemic reasoning about a study of their own design. *The Journal of the Learning Sciences*, *20*(1), 50–110.

Michaels, S., and O'Connor, C. (2017). From recitation to reasoning: Supporting scientific and engineering practices through talk. In C. V. Schwarz, C. Passmore and B. J. Reiser (Eds.), *Helping Students Make Sense of the World Using Next Generation Science and Engineering Practices*. Arlington, VA: NSTA Press.

National Academies of Sciences Engineering and Medicine. (2015). *Science Teachers' Learning: Enhancing Opportunities, Creating Supportive Contexts*. Washington, DC: National Academies Press.

National Research Council. (2005). *How Students Learn: History, Mathematics, and Science in the Classroom*. Washington, DC: National Academies Press.

National Research Council. (2012). *A Framework for K-12 Science Education: Practices, Crosscutting Concepts, and Core Ideas*. Washington, DC: National Academies Press.

NGSS Lead States. (2013). *Next Generation Science Standards: For States, By States*. Washington, DC: Achieve, Inc.

Osborne, J., Erduran, S., and Simon, S. (2004). Enhancing the quality of argumentation in school science. *Journal of Research in Science Teaching*, *41*(10), 994–1020.

Reiser, B. J., Brody, L., Novak, M., Tipton, K., and Adams, L. (2017). Asking questions. In C. V. Schwarz, C. Passmore and B. J. Reiser (Eds.), *Helping Students Make Sense of the World Using Next Generation Science and Engineering Practices*. Arlington, VA: NSTA Press.

Rivet, A., and Ingber, J. (2017). Analyzing and interpreting data. In C. V. Schwarz, C. Passmore and B. J. Reiser (Eds.), *Helping Students Make Sense of the World Using Next Generation Science and Engineering Practices*. Arlington, VA: NSTA Press.

Scardamalia, M., and Bereiter, C. (2006). An architecture for collaborative knowledge building. In E. De Corte, M. C. Linn, H. Mandl and L. Verschaffel (Eds.), *Computer-Based Learning Environments and Problem Solving*. New York: Springer, Inc.

Schwarz, C. V., Passmore, C., Reiser, B. J. (2017). Moving beyond "knowing about" science to making sense of the world. In C. V. Schwarz, C. Passmore and B. J. Reiser (Eds.), *Helping Students Make Sense of the World Using Next Generation Science and Engineering Practices*. Arlington, VA: NSTA Press.

Stake, R. E. (2000). Case studies. *Handbook of Qualitative Research*. Thousand Oaks, CA: Sage Publications, Inc.

Zembal-Saul, C. (2009). Learning to teach elementary school science as argument. *Science Education*, *93*(4), 687–719.

Zembal-Saul, C., Hershberger, K., and McNeill, K. L. (2013). *What's Your Evidence? Engaging K-5 Students in Constructing Explanations in Science*. Upper Saddle River, NJ: Pearson Education.

3 Science, Engineering, Literacy, and Place-Based Education
Powerful Practices for Integration

Jennifer L. Cody
THE PENNSYLVANIA STATE UNIVERSITY

Mandy Biggers
TEXAS WOMAN'S UNIVERSITY

Science, Engineering, Literacy, and Place-Based Education: Powerful Approaches for Curriculum Integration

Each year, fifth-grade students take a trip to the local wastewater treatment plant to supplement our environmental science unit. Generally, they walk around the facility on a tour led by one of the technicians. The students sometimes ask questions centered on what the technician is explaining. Never did the students initiate questions or ask questions tied to what they were learning in the curriculum. This year was different. The students were engaged in a unit that intentionally integrated engineering tasks into the science curriculum. Specifically, an engineering unit culminating with the construction of water filters. The field trip occurred after the students participated in the engineering tasks and after they were able to conduct some water quality tests. Additionally, the students considered a question during the field trip: "How does the wastewater treatment facility turn 'dirty' water (influent) into 'clean' water (effluent)?" In years past, students thought the field trip was interesting and appreciated learning what happens to the water after they flush the toilet or take a shower. However, this time, the technical details of the water treatment did not escape them. They were interested in the ways in which the filters were constructed and with which materials. Also, they understood the terms "influent" and "effluent." When they returned to school after the field trip, the students were motivated to write about their experience and were also able to compose written informational pieces centered on the wastewater treatment, which allowed them to use what they learned to inform their own water filter designs. How did we reach this level of authentic engagement with the fifth-grade students?

In a series of popular books, "A Series of Unfortunate Events," the Baudelaire children experience multiple unfortunate events in an attempt to learn about their parents' deaths and keep their fortune out of the hands of a mysterious villain (Snicket, 1999). In the fall of 2015, we had our own series of events, but ours turned out to be serendipitous rather than unfortunate. In this chapter, we describe how we planned and enacted a new water quality unit that incorporated not only science and engineering, but also literacy practices and argumentation, all set in the context of a local place-based issue. We argue that integration of this format is complex, but approachable as we encourage readers to consider our multiple iterations of the original unit, as well as the impact on students' interest and learning. Moreover, we recommend beginning with one point of integration into science lessons, rather than attempting to integrate all of the pieces we put together ... in what *could* have very well become our own unfortunate series of events.

Given the inclusion of engineering practices in the Next Generation Science Standards (NGSS Lead States, 2013), we incorporated elements of engineering design from the Engineering is Elementary (EiE, 2011) curriculum resource and a science curriculum resource centered on water quality from Project-Based Inquiry Science (Kolodner, 2015). Our goal was to strengthen the connection between engineering and science in ways that are meaningful to students. Aligning the separate curriculum materials was not enough, however. We originally chose these resources because they dealt with the same environmental science topic (water quality), but the work was far from over once we selected the particular curricular resources. Even though the topics were aligned, the curricula were not integrated. The work of integrating these into a cohesive storyline is what we describe in this chapter. We wanted to ensure the engineering unit was not an "add-on" at the end of the science unit or simply a way to "kick off" the science unit. These considerations were at the forefront of our thinking as we sought to find more engaging ways to incorporate engineering, local issues, and literacy practices into science teaching. We wanted to push past students describing *what* happened and aim for students to reason about *why* a phenomenon occurred (Osborne and Patterson, 2011). This is the essence of argumentation and sensemaking in science classrooms (Zembal-Saul and Hershberger, this volume, Chapter 1).

In the district in which this study took place, there are no student textbooks, and the fifth-grade science curriculum resource was authored by the district in 1999. As a result, we began to investigate ways to create coherent science content storylines (Reiser, 2013) to effectively and efficiently bring science, engineering, and literacy units together in meaningful ways for students. We recognize that readers will not have the same set of circumstances on which we capitalized, particularly the relevant local issue and its connection to the curriculum. It is our hope, however, that there are ways to incorporate aspects of our approach into other contexts. Our story is meant to inspire, not prescribe or overwhelm.

How the Unit Came About

We are a partnership between a fifth-grade teacher (first author) and a university faculty member (second author). When we realized our shared interest in the integration of engineering practices, we began to contemplate ways to work together to bring more engineering into the elementary classroom. During our early days working together, a local event erupted with the potential to affect the drinking water source of our students. Spotlighting the issue of equitable access to water as it was happening in the backyard of the students was a big undertaking; we knew this from the beginning, but decided that the trade-off of embedding the local water issue into the unit would be worthwhile for our students, and it would bring a sense of meaning and purpose to their learning. Our town was in the middle of a heated deliberation about whether a luxury university student housing development should be built near the aquifer that supplies the community with water. The housing proposal was met with strong community resistance (e.g., Hartley, 2015). This issue had the potential to impact students in the classroom directly because it was their drinking water supply that was at stake.

The unit described in this chapter was not designed overnight, but was built after several iterations. During the 2013–2014 school year, the first author implemented a new teacher-created, environmental science unit with a content storyline centered on water quality. The following year, she integrated the PBIS resource "Living Together" (Kolodner, 2015) into the water quality storyline. Throughout the lessons, it was evident that students were reading and writing more informational texts in science in addition to the usual reading and writing curriculum. The two of us began collaborating during the 2015–2016 school year, and we incorporated engineering into the existing version of the water quality unit. This collaboration resulted in the third iteration of the unit, which included a fully integrated version of the previous teacher-created content storyline, science inquiry practices from the PBIS (Kolodner, 2015) curriculum, and (new) the Engineering is Elementary (EiE, 2011) curriculum.

It is this third iteration that provides the centerpiece for this chapter. Why the need for all the work of aligning and integrating these curriculum materials? The short answer is that no curriculum exists that seamlessly integrates science and engineering practices, literacy practices, and local issues.

The Changing Landscape of Elementary Science

As elementary teachers feel the pressure of recent education reform and compartmentalized standards, there is often a resulting lack of priority on science for a more intense focus on literacy and math (Marx and Harris, 2006; Roseman and Koppal, 2008). On average, elementary-age students in grades K-3 only spend 19 minutes a day on science. On the other hand, students of the same age receive about 54 minutes per day of mathematics instruction and 89 minutes per day of English-language arts instruction (National Academies of Science, Engineering and Medicine, 2015).

Dewey (1929) argued that science learning cannot come from isolated ideas but rather must derive from a "relatively coherent system" of ideas that "reciprocally confirm and illuminate one another" (p. 22). Science should not be a compartmentalized, occasional part of a student's day. Teachers and districts are beginning to recognize the need for integrating science and literacy (NRC, 2014). Instructional time was not the only factor influencing our desire to integrate curricula. Science and literacy go hand in hand, and in order to provide students with opportunities to engage in science practices, students need literacy instruction that is epistemically aligned (Hooper and Zembal-Saul, this volume, Chapter 4).

Moreover, students often struggle to learn science content when they are unable to see a connection between lessons or the ways in which the lessons connect directly to their lives. Engaging students in scientific practices as part of learning science content "…can provide a meaningful context for literacy activities in that it creates a motivating purpose for students to use language to negotiate meaning and figure out something new about the way the world works" (Zembal-Saul et al., 2013, p. 11). A significant aspect of developing and implementing science and engineering practices in elementary classrooms (especially teaching students how to develop scientific argumentation skills) is the need for increased emphasis on English language arts.

Because of the diminished time allotted for elementary school science, and limited preparation of elementary teachers in science (Eshach, 2003), elementary educators tend to rely heavily on curriculum materials (Biggers, 2018). Often, science curriculum resources are outdated and contain lessons with few, if any, authentic connections with other subjects, such as engineering, math, or English language arts (Moscovici and Nelson, 1998). As mentioned above, one way to meet standards while engaging students in meaningful science and engineering practices is to center teaching and learning on local and interdisciplinary units of study. Science offers multiple entry-points for meeting the demanding expectations of current curriculum reform in other subjects, such as math, engineering, and literacy. Also, when students are able to make connections between their lives and school, they are more engaged in what is being taught (Sobel, 2005).

Students who experience a participatory model of learning identify as community stakeholders, think critically, and are engaged in learning the science behind an issue in order to gather evidence to support their thinking (Molnar-Main, 2017). This model of learning includes valuing student voice and questions that drive academic investigations. Because this type of application of science is meaningful, it impacts a student's ability to become scientifically literate and to demonstrate their understanding through authentic assessment experiences. According to *Taking Science to School*, "Accomplished learners know when to ask a question, how to challenge claims, where to go to learn more, and they are aware of their own ideas and how these change over time" (National Research Council, 2007, p. 19).

The Integration Framework

Building on these ideas, in planning for this unit, we configured a framework of contemporary features of science and engineering practices, literacy practices, and place-based instruction that increased the amount of meaningful reading, writing, speaking, and listening done in the classroom (see Figure 3.1). Next, we describe each piece of the integration framework highlighting in particular the science practices and the place-based context. We describe how we harnessed this framework to increase students' sensemaking skills.

Science and Engineering Practices

To promote alignment with scientific practices and core science ideas, we selected a Project-Based Inquiry Science (PBIS) curriculum from *It's About Time* called "Living Together" (Kolodner, 2015). PBIS lessons emphasize a problem solving approach that helps students make sense of science. The lessons pose the umbrella question "*How does water quality affect the ecology of a community?*" and provide students with many opportunities to circle back to revisit the overarching question. In the scenario of the lessons, students learn that a company plans to build a factory in the fictitious town, Wamego. Students use this fictitious context to test water quality, study macroinvertebrates, consider pollution possibilities, and make a recommendation to the Wamego town governing board as to whether or not the town should allow the company to build their factory near the river.

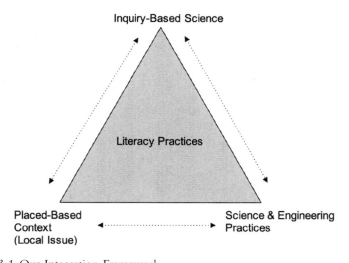

Figure 3.1 Our Integration Framework

Within the PBIS curriculum, we emphasized a claim-evidence-reasoning framework to support students' generation of claims that emerged from evidence for the questions. Generating claims from evidence is one of the eight science and engineering practices in the NGSS (NGSS Lead States, 2013). It is a practice that should be integral at all grade levels, and one in which even very early learners can be successful (Metz, 2008).

An increased emphasis on engineering practices in the NGSS (NGSS Lead States, 2013) was an additional concern because we recognized that the published PBIS lessons did not emphasize engineering practices. Because the NGSS are relatively new, few elementary science curricula include engineering practices. This leaves teachers who intend to incorporate engineering with options of (1) creating their own engineering activities, (2) finding engineering activities online, or (3) using a curriculum that emphasizes engineering for elementary students.

We decided on a curriculum resource called Engineering is Elementary (EiE, 2011). In particular, we chose the EiE (2011) resource "Water, Water Everywhere: Designing Water Filters," as it seemed to most closely align with the PBIS water quality lessons. EiE provided opportunities for students to develop an understanding of the technical aspects of water filters through the engineering design process.

Place-Based Education

Place-based education is a common-sense way to encourage civic engagement in science. It is

> a vibrant approach to education that takes students out into the communities, to learn, to do and to grow as human beings. Students are given the opportunity to learn subject matter in deep and lasting ways, understand the places they live in and participate in community renewal.
> (Demarest, 2016)

Since we decided to center the unit on the local issue, it was necessary to replace some of the PBIS texts with informational texts relevant to our local issue. As a result, we pulled a number of newspaper articles (e.g., Hartley, 2015) that helped provide sufficient contextual information. We kept the basic structure of the PBIS lessons, but replaced the town of Wamego with our local township, and the factory with the proposed luxury university student housing development.

Literacy Practices

One inherent problem with pulling current newspaper articles is that newspapers are often written above a fifth-grade reading level (Johns and Wheat, 1984). Our fifth-graders needed some scaffolding in order to

52 *Cody and Biggers*

successfully access the content of these relevant texts. We were able to employ specific literacy strategies, such as marking up the text, talking to the text, and partner reading so that the students could more easily decipher the higher-level text. We also developed and supported literacy practices that tied to science practices, including argumentation and communication.

How the Unit was Enacted

Here, we describe the details of the enactment of our final water quality unit. The unit lasted over 40 days, so we describe a broad overview of the unit and detail a few of the significant points of integration. Overall, we taught the EiE lessons first followed by the PBIS lessons, with the entire unit embedded within local context and supported by literacy strategies.

We began the unit with the engineering lessons. In the "Water, Water Everywhere" (EiE, 2011) series of lessons, students begin by reading a story about a young girl in India who tries to save a turtle from the polluted Ganges river. This poses the purpose for a design challenge later in the lessons, and introduces students to the engineering design process. Next, students look at a mural of a fictitious community and point out places where natural and human-made contamination could possibly occur. This introduces them to the career of environmental engineers. Students then test several different filter materials (i.e., sand, gravel, coffee filters) with different types of contaminated water. They take what they learned during these tests into the engineering design challenge where they design a filter to clean a mystery sample of contaminated water.

We followed up the engineering lessons with a field trip to our local water treatment facility. As mentioned in the opening vignette, students attend a field trip to a local wastewater treatment facility. This field trip had been in place for decades as it ties to the original environmental science unit. However, the new science unit provided entrée for students to experience the field trip in a more purposeful and important way. Since students learned about engineering water filters and different filter materials before attending the field trip, their questions during the trip were more focused and intentional. They learned that it no easy task to clean contaminated water. Many walked away from the trip with big questions and important observations. One student said, "This is only one treatment facility on the planet. I wonder how many there are in the world. Can you imagine what would happen if we weren't cleaning the water we use? Would we run out of water?"

Once students had experience with engineering water filters and local environmental engineering, we introduced them to the local issue of the proposed housing development. We posed the same questions from the engineering lessons about how the building project could possibly contribute to increased contamination in land, air, and water in the local area. They quickly realized the possible pollution and its consequences, and the rest of the unit was centered on this local issue.

Reading local newspaper articles coupled with the science investigations about water quality provided students with information and observations, which allowed them to communicate effectively with local officials, scientists, and community members. An invited speaker on the township board of supervisors spoke to the class in favor of development. In addition, a supervisor-elect, who was adamantly opposed to the development, addressed the students. Both speakers were able to present scientific data to bolster their respective stances, and it was interesting to see the students change their position multiple times as each speaker presented data. This use of data helped students experience a real-life example that emphasizes the science practice of argumentation from evidence.

By examining this local water issue, students learned the structures of local government, and they researched the natural and human history of our local area. We conducted a number of water quality tests (including pond water, farm water, drinking water, etc.) using indicators such as pH, dissolved oxygen, temperature, and turbidity. Students used the evidence gained from these tests to generate claims backed by evidence to answer the overarching question "*How does water quality affect the ecology of a community?*" They used scientific reasoning to communicate their findings, oral and written, to local officials and the general public.

The students used multiple sources of information and data to make claims about whether their local township should allow the luxury student housing to be built. In order to formatively assess students and visibly represent their claims, we created an evidence board, similar to those in the published PBIS lessons, to post evidence that each group of students used to justify their position about the development. Evidence collected included such things as water quality test results, data gathered from interviews with experts, and photos taken while running model simulations.

The culminating activity for our unit was for our students to author evidence-based recommendations for the consideration of the local board of supervisors as they began to deliberate about the housing development. We provided each student with scaffolding in the form of a five-paragraph organizer (see Table 3.1). Students were encouraged to use their evidence as the pillars for their "supporting ideas" in the body paragraphs of the essay to back up their claims. This unit was not the students' first experience with the practices of creating evidence-based claims; they were familiar with and proficient at these skills. Our students were excited to begin this authentic

Table 3.1 Five-Paragraph Essay Organizer Scaffold

	1st ¶ Introduction (Main Idea + Overview)	
2nd ¶ Supporting Evidence #1	3rd ¶ Supporting Evidence #2	4th ¶ Supporting Evidence #3
	5th ¶ Conclusion (Summary + Recommendations)	

54 Cody and Biggers

writing project, and dove into the assignment because they recognized the opportunity to make a difference in the community. This writing prompt reinforced the sensemaking practices the students had been building throughout the unit.

Every lesson in the place-based, interdisciplinary unit served a purpose and was integral to our content storyline. In addition, each lesson helped the students put more pieces of the puzzle together in answering the over-arching question of the unit (*How does water quality affect the ecology of a community?*). As we worked through the unit, students were continuously reminded that they would ultimately be making written, evidenced-based recommendations to the township board of directors. This served as an authentic way to assess student understanding of the unit because it required them to draw on all of the evidence amassed over the course of the unit in order to make their final proposals.

What We Learned

As readers might imagine, we learned much through this experience. The students were highly motivated during this unit and engaged in all aspects of the school day. Parents reported that their children could not wait to get to school to share new information because they were so interested in reading the newspaper and watching the local news in the evenings. One notable product of this work had to do with discussions with parents during parent–teacher conferences during which parents explained that their children shared vast amounts of information with them about water filters, the importance of water quality, and technical information about wastewater treatment. Here we describe some of the affordances of the integrated unit including: (1) student learning; (2) depth of discussions; (3) allocation of skills to other content areas; (4) connection to the subsequent science unit; and (5) student excitement surrounding engineering tasks.

Student Learning Across Content Areas

We observed student growth across content areas. For example, students were able to articulate water quality test results to their families. In addition, they were able to argue using the evidence gathered during the science investigations when discussing pros and cons of the housing development. We saw an increase in writing assessment stamina and the processing of content when we used non-fiction writing rubrics. Students were able to systematically draw on their critical thinking skills and develop a logical argument. Figure 3.2 shows a student writing sample of their question (*How does the University Area Joint Authority turn dirty water [influent] into clean water [effluent]?*), claim (*UAJA turns influent water into effluent water by using a multiple step filtering process*), evidence, and reasoning about the water treatment

Science, Engineering, Literacy, and Place   55

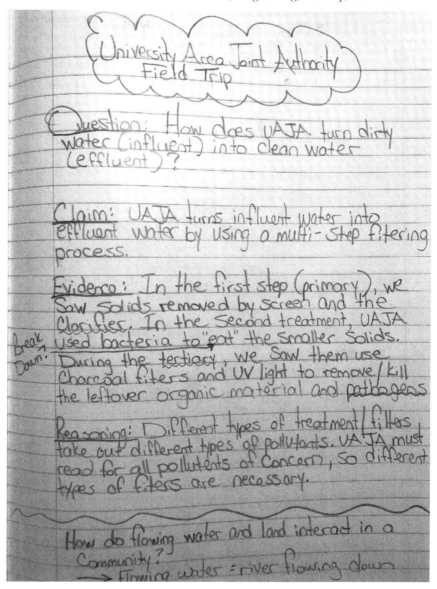

Figure 3.2 Student Writing Sample of a Claim-Evidence-Reasoning Framework

facility. This particular example (representative of an average fifth-grade student response) represents how the students were able to take the content knowledge from the engineering and science units to the field trip in order to ask in-depth, meaningful questions that added to their evidence-based claims about water filter materials.

Data gathered during the 2013–2014 school year (content storyline iteration of the unit) served as a baseline for the comparison of district-level reading assessment data using the Measurement of Academic Progress (MAP) testing developed by Northwest Evaluation Association (NWEA). On average, scores increased 2.47 points from the fall (September 2013) to the winter (January 2014) benchmark assessment (see Figure 3.3). Specifically, students seemed more adept at considering bias and understanding point-of-view in texts. While a number of factors could account for these score changes, no new curricular resources were enacted in the areas of math, reading, or writing. The greatest curriculum changes occurred around science as outlined by this chapter and therefore are likely factors in the increased student academic achievement.

During 2014–2015 (content storyline + PBIS iteration of the unit) student scores on the reading MAP assessment improved an average of 5.31 points from the fall (September 2014) to the winter (January 2015) benchmark assessment (see Figure 3.3). While many factors may have contributed to this improvement, we suspect that one key factor was the integrated unit.

During the 2015–2016 school year (the school year of the unit described in this chapter: content storyline + PBIS + EiE iteration), student performance of reading and writing increased again, with an average improvement of 6.55 from the fall (September 2015) to the winter (January 2016) benchmark assessment (see Figure 3.3).

Deeper Discussions

Throughout the unit, students engaged in numerous science talks during which evidence was the centerpiece (and civil discourse was a must). During

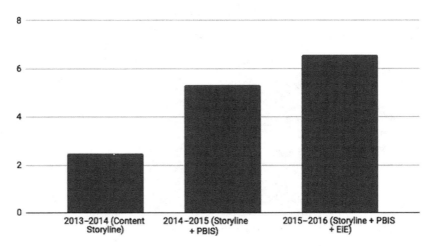

Figure 3.3 MAP Reading Scores Across Three Iterations of the Unit

these discussions, students learned to weigh multiple sides of an argument. They became skilled at determining stakeholders and understanding that there are many benefits and trade-offs in most situations. The ability of students to converse with adults regarding the issues at hand was notable and due in part to the confidence they developed as a result of the integrated unit. This increased their opportunities for sensemaking about the phenomena. In addition, students learned how to approach and analyze newspaper articles and read for comprehension (see Figure 3.4). Students worked with a partner to mark items in the article they felt were important

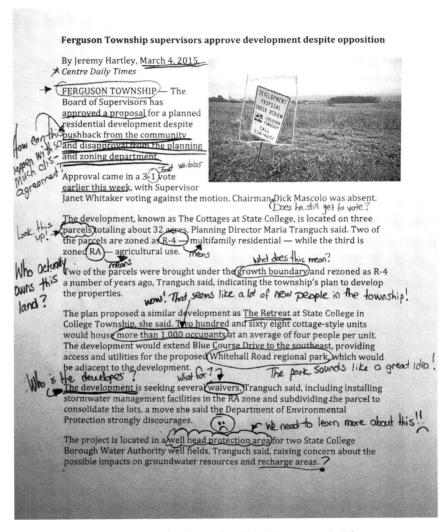

Figure 3.4 Mark-Ups of a Student's Work with a Newspaper Article

by underlining (i.e., "pushback from the community"), things they were unsure about by circling (i.e., "agricultural use, multi-family use"), and also circling benefits and trade-offs (i.e., "Whitehall Road Regional Park").

We were particularly impressed with the level of sophistication of the students' discussions when guest speakers came to talk with them about different aspects of the development. The students were able to draw upon the technical aspects of the various water quality tests, their firsthand experience with wastewater treatment, and the engineering of the water filters to ask informed questions. One of the guest speakers was a township supervisor who was a proponent of the development. The students expressed their concerns about the number of cars that would be traveling in an area that has seen little traffic compared to what was being proposed. The supervisor explained to the students that new bus routes on along the road would help alleviate some of the traffic. A student spoke up and shared that, although buses may seem like a good idea, they bring their share of pollution and problems to the area. "What about the fact that buses will have to stop along the road to pick up and drop off riders? This will cause traffic to slow down or stop and will possibly cause traffic jams. Also, buses pollute, too." This student went on to explain that they learned that there are benefits and trade-offs in every situation and the supervisors should make sure they consider all of the scenarios.

This discussion was not prompted or prepared in advance. The students in the class took on stakeholder identities because they were invested in keeping their drinking water safe. However, it extended beyond drinking water. Throughout the unit, they began to think about all of the different stakeholders and also other environmental impacts.

Allocation of Skills to Other Content

Not only were students able to successfully deliberate about the science concepts addressed by the unit, we also observed that students were using similar skills during reading class. A small group of students was working on an in-depth book study and were asked to demonstrate their understanding of the author's purpose in writing in their journals. We overheard the students in the group discussing if they could use the words "claim and evidence" to write the paragraph. The first student wrote the following paragraph:

> The author's purpose in Chapter 4 is to create a funny and light-hearted moment in order to help everyone stop crying. The evidence for this is on page 87 when the author wrote, "The noise that came out of that boy was like … ." The author did this because if he hadn't caused the children to laugh, the resolution of the plot would not have matched the rest of the story.

Connection to Next Science Unit: Geological Process

Next in the sequence of fifth-grade science units was Geological Processes. It was fascinating to see students make connections between the environmental science (water quality) unit and Earth's processes. Using a structure similar to that laid out in this chapter, students learned about the process of hydraulic fracturing (fracking), which is an issue affecting Pennsylvania and other states. They read newspaper articles about well contamination as a result of fracking, watched videos of interviews with people whose lives were changed for the better because of fracking, and hosted visitors from South Africa and from the United States Geological Survey. Students considered the stakeholders, benefits, and trade-offs. In addition, they referred back to their knowledge of water quality testing to make an informed recommendation to the group from South Africa working to decide whether or not their community should introduce fracking as a way to generate income. In addition, the fifth-graders prepared an informational video, which they shared with the group from South Africa. Within this work, the integration of science, engineering, and a shared environmental issue drove the students' motivation and interest. Just as in the Water Quality unit, the students visualized their working claims on a project board in the classroom (see Figure 3.5).

Excitement about the Engineering Process

Students engaged in the engineering process in substantive ways. Building water filters was the first time fifth-grade students were formally introduced

Figure 3.5 Claims and Evidence Board for Geology Unit

60   *Cody and Biggers*

to the engineering design process and the first time they participated in such an in-depth and purposeful engineering experience. We were struck by their enthusiasm during the engineering work. We felt it was important to capitalize on this level of enthusiasm and purposefully integrated an engineering task into the fracking unit to help students understand the importance of engineers in finding and extracting natural gas, describing the layers under the Earth's surface, and understanding how fossil fuels are formed and where they come from.

Conclusion

Teaching and learning are complex activities, as evidenced by the multiple points of integration we attempted in this unit. Recall that our goal of this chapter was to inspire rather than direct a certain method of teaching and/or learning. In our case, this "image of the possible," as highlighted in this section of the book, is meant to illustrate a glimpse of how one integrated curricular unit played out in a fifth-grade classroom. We hope that there is a piece of what we attempted that struck a chord with readers, revealing possibilities for integration in order to increase opportunities for sensemaking. We recognize that this was a large undertaking—attempting to integrate science, engineering, and a local issue all while emphasizing literacy strategies to support students' learning.

Student engagement made instruction appear effortless; however that is misleading. Substantial time and effort was invested in planning and implementing this integrated and place-based unit. The challenge of integrating so many moving parts—two sets of curricula, finding resources for the local housing issue that would be beneficial to the unit, lining up speakers and field trips—it took a lot of advance organizing and planning.

This type of teaching and learning requires that teachers consider a multitude of factors in order to effectively engage students in productive struggles. The intent of this facilitating productive struggles is to push students out of their comfort zones because this is where the most learning occurs. Much of this work cannot be accomplished without first developing an inclusive and engaging learning environment where students will flourish on the road to becoming lifelong learners. As a result, students are able develop collaborative relationships in order to productively participate in scientific practices and reflection in order to formulate questions about phenomena, investigate those questions, and build explanations based on evidence.

Choosing curriculum aligned to the same topic is only a first step. The real integration took intentional planning, and developed over the three iterations of the unit. Our goal of integration was not to add more for the sake of adding more. We aimed to help students make sense of a local issue by integrating scientific and engineering practices. By integrating these strands, our students saw science as a meaningful way of investigating the world around them. They embedded themselves in the local issue with strong claims supported with evidence collected over the course of the unit.

Recall that one of our original goals was to not tack engineering on as an "add-on" at the end of the science lessons. We believe that by introducing the engineering challenge first followed by a closely related field trip, the students' level of engagement in the topic brought their interest into the science lessons. This and the incorporation of the local issue helped take this integrated unit to levels we had never achieved before in both student interest and also academic achievement.

We hope that there is a glimmer of inspiration within these pages that will push other educators out of their comfort zones to try a new form of integration. Integration of literacy into science (or science into literacy) helps tackle the challenge of lack of time to teach everything. We also highlight the fact that we approached this unit from two different backgrounds: one of a classroom teacher and one of a university faculty member. Our different expertise brought aspects to the unit that we would not have considered alone. Integration brings experts together in new and exciting ways to transform teaching and learning.

Our series of events could have very easily turned more toward the "unfortunate" nature as in the Lemony Snicket books! While we chose to integrate all four areas (science, engineering, local issue, literacy), starting with one single point of integration is a first step, as we did in the initial pilot versions of this unit. Here we leave the reader with a few suggestions to inspire an integrated unit.

- Science and Engineering. Find engineering lessons that complement existing science lessons and try them out. Purposefully incorporating an engineering challenge is one way to add student engagement to any science topic. It does not have to include an entirely new set of curriculum materials.
- Science and Literacy. Bring literacy strategies into existing science lessons. Give students opportunities to speak, listen, read and write in authentic ways, be it journals, prompts, listing evidence and making claims, or writing letters about what they are learning that build on evidence.
- Science and Local Issues. Science happens all around us, every single day. Our local communities are filled with current events that beg to be brought into the classroom. Issues such as pollution, landfills, recycling, public transportation, and water quality are a few that come to mind that would make for great lessons on argumentation when appropriately integrated into the science curriculum.

References

Biggers, M. (2018). Questioning questions: Elementary teachers' adaptations of investigation questions across the inquiry continuum. *Research in Science Education*, *48*(1), 1–28.

Boston Museum of Science. (2019). Engineering is Elementary. Retrieved from: http://www.mos.org/eie/

62 *Cody and Biggers*

Demarest, A. (2016). Our curriculum matters. Retrieved February 17, 2016, from: http://www.ourcurriculummatters.com/What-is-place-based-education.php.

Dewey, J. (1929). The sources of a science of education. New York: H. Liveright. Retrieved from: https://archive.org/details/sourcesofascienc009452mbp

EiE (Engineering is Elementary). (2011, February). Water, water everywhere: designing water filters. Retrieved from: http://www.eie.org/eie-curriculum/cur riculum-units/water-water-everywhere-designing-water-filters

Eshach, H. (2003). Inquiry-events as a tool for changing science teaching efficacy belief of kindergarten and elementary school teachers. *Journal of Science Education and Technology*, *12*(4), 495–501.

Hartley, J. (2015, March 4). Ferguson Township supervisors approve development despite opposition. *Centre Daily Times*. Retrieved July 8, 2018, from: https://www.centredaily.com/news/local/community/state-college/article42909045.html

Johns, J. L., and Wheat, T. E. (1984). Newspaper readability: Two crucial factors. *International Literacy Association and Wiley*, *27*(5), 432–434. Retrieved July 8, 2018, from: http://www.jstor.org/stable/40032569

Kolodner, J. L. (2015). *Project-Based Inquiry Science: Living Together* (15th edn.). Armonk, NY: It's About Time.

Marx, R. W., and Harris, C. J. (2006). No child left behind and science education: Opportunities, challenges, and risks. *Elementary School Journal*, *106*(5), 467–477.

Metz, K. E. (2004). Children's understanding of scientific inquiry: Their conceptualization of uncertainty in investigations of their own design. *Cognition*, *22*(2), 219–290.

Metz, K. E. (2008). Narrowing the gulf between the practices of science and the elementary school classroom. *The Elementary School Journal*, *109*(2), 138–161.

Molnar-Main, S. (2017). *Deliberation in the Classroom: Fostering Critical Thinking, Community, and Citizenship in Schools*. Dayton, OH: Kettering Foundation.

Moscovici, H., and Nelson, T. H. (1998). Shifting from activitymania to inquiry. *Science and Children*, *35*(4), 14.

National Academies of Sciences, Engineering, Medicine. (2015). *Science Teachers' Learning: Enhancing Opportunities, Creating Supportive Contexts*. Committee on Strengthening Science Education through a Teacher Learning Continuum. S. Wilson, H. Schweingruber, N. Nielsen (Eds.). Washington, DC: National Academies Press.

National Research Council. (2007). *Taking Science to School: Learning and Teaching Science in Grades K-8*. Washington, DC: National Academies Press.

National Research Council. (2014). *Literacy for Science: Exploring the Intersection of the Next Generation Science Standards and Common Core for ELA Standards: A Workshop Summary*. Steering Committee on Exploring the Overlap between "Literacy in Science: and the Practice of Obtaining, Evaluating, and Communicating Information."H. Rhodes, M. Feder (Rapporteurs). Washington, DC: National Academies Press.

NGSS Lead States (2013). *Next Generation Science Standards: For States, By States*. Washington, DC: National Academies Press.

Osborne, J., and Patterson, A., (2011). Scientific argument and explanation: A necessary distinction? *Science Education*, *95*(4), 627–638.

Reiser, B.J. (2013, September). What Professional Development Strategies Are Needed for Successful Implementation of the Next Generation Science Standards?Symposium conducted at the meeting of the Invitational Research Symposium on Science Assessment, Washington, DC.

Roseman, J. E., and Koppal, M. (2008). Standards to improve K-8 science curriculum materials. *Elementary School Journal, 109*(2), 104–122.

Schoenbach, R. (2012). *Reading for Understanding: How Reading Apprenticeship Improves Disciplinary Learning in Secondary and College Classrooms.* San Francisco, CA: Jossey-Bass.

Snicket, Lemony. (1999) *A Series of Unfortunate Events: The Bad Beginning.* London: HarperCollins.

Sobel, D. (2005). *Place-Based Education: Connecting Classrooms and Communities.* Great Barrington, MA: Orion Society.

Zembal-Saul, Carla, McNeill, Katherine L. and Hershberger, Kimber. (2013). *What's Your Evidence?: Engaging K-5 Students in Constructing Explanations in Science.* London: Pearson.

4 Literacy Practices for Sensemaking in Science that Promote Epistemic Alignment

LeeAnna Hooper and Carla Zembal-Saul
THE PENNSYLVANIA STATE UNIVERSITY

Introduction

"How can we lift a load into our treehouse?" Ms. Meryl barely has time to say those nine words before her group of third-graders who are settled in a circle on the carpet at the front of the room begin to whisper their ideas to each other enthusiastically. Ms. Meryl's question serves as an anchor for a third-grade unit on simple machines. Before students begin to develop a plan for lifting a basket of books into a two-story treehouse structure in the corner of their classroom, they must develop a conceptual understanding of how simple machines work. To do that, Ms. Meryl has planned a lesson that introduces a lever as a simple machine. Ms. Meryl, an experienced teacher, has posed a challenge to her class, "I want you to think of a way for a simple machine to lift your teacher."

In this chapter, we take a look into Ms. Meryl's third-grade classroom to examine the teaching practices that she employs to connect literacy and science instruction in support of her students' sensemaking of important disciplinary core ideas and participation in epistemic practices. It is a case of how an experienced elementary teacher, whose approach to science teaching focused on engaging students in constructing scientific explanations and arguing from evidence, incorporates literacy practices for sensemaking in science.

Elementary School Science and Literacy

Students' early experiences in science are essential to their ongoing science learning and development. Beginning in elementary school, students should be given opportunities to ask questions and inquire about natural phenomena, engage in scientific practices and discourse, and begin to develop an understanding of what it means to reason with scientific ideas. These early experiences serve as a foundation for continued engagement in scientific practices and discourse throughout middle and high school. As described in the introductory chapter (see Davis, Zembal-Saul, and Kademian, this volume, Introduction), shifts in science teaching practices that are highlighted in science education reform emphasize the need for students to have sustained opportunities to investigate phenomena through participation in scientific practices and discourse, and by developing increasingly sophisticated understandings of disciplinary core ideas.

Literacy plays a critical role in learning science. In light of decades of research on student learning in science, researchers advocate for students' engagement in scientific practices as a way to make sense of core science ideas. Scientific practices require a language-rich, sensemaking process that includes, "using cognitive, social, and language skills" (National Research Council, 2014, p. 11). Historically, science education researchers agree that reading, writing, and talk are core practices of science (Cervetti *et al.*, 2012), but yet there are inconsistencies in defining literacy as it pertains to science. In reform documents that predate the *Next Generation Science Standards* (NGSS) (NGSS Lead States, 2013), literacy in the discipline focused on the goal of citizens becoming scientifically literate to inform participation in a democratic society. We take the stance that literacy serves an essential role in what it means to participate productively in learning science. Currently, however, literacy practices in science teaching typically result in teaching vocabulary and learning science through non-fiction texts (Hand, 2007). This approach to stands in stark contrast to the idea of providing students with opportunities to learn the language and practices of science through active engagement in investigations and rich discourse (see also Bismack and Haefner, this volume, Chapter 2).

In response to competing perspectives on literacy and science, presenters at a workshop hosted by the Board on Science Education highlighted the importance of capitalizing on science as a vehicle for engaging learners in literacy development (National Research Council, 2014). The members of the workshop addressed having students go beyond reading and writing *about* science, asserting instead that literacy practices should be utilized to support student engagement in the scientific practices necessary for sensemaking in science. Drawing heavily on this report, we advocate literacy *for* science, in which teachers support students in making sense of phenomena using scientific ideas and participating in epistemic practices (Kelly, 2008) of science.

We build upon this critical work and refer to our approach as *Literacy Practices for Sensemaking in Science* to emphasize the fundamental intersections of literacy practices that engage students in co-constructing deep understanding about how the world works in ways that epistemically align with the spheres of activity of scientists and engineers (National Research Council, 2012).

Literacy Practices for Engaging Students in a Science Learning Community

To examine these proposed literacy practices for sensemaking in science, we use a situative perspective of learning in which communities of practice, cognitive apprenticeship, and discourse are all central components to

66 *Hooper and Zembal-Saul*

describe how children learn to engage in science practices. We acknowledge that various communities of practice shape learners, and over time participation in these communities influence cultural practices, discourse patterns, and belief systems (Lave *et al.*, 1991). Thus, the tools and language patterns of an elementary science learning community become essential components to examine when identifying how teachers use literacy practices for sensemaking in science. Students' understanding of the epistemic practices of science, that is the specific ways in which "members of a community propose, justify, evaluate, and legitimize claims within a disciplinary framework" (Kelly, 2008, p. 99), should be prioritized by teachers as they are equally important as learning the content of science. Children must engage in doing science, and understand how individuals reason with science ideas.

Learners enter into new learning communities with experiences and understandings of the world (Lave *et al.*, 1991). Moreover, discourse plays a central role in helping teachers to uncover a student's prior knowledge to leverage her/his prior experiences and ideas to support sensemaking (Bransford *et al.*, 1999). Therefore, teachers must be fluent in listening for and uncovering these experiences (Levin *et al.*, 2009; Coffey *et al.*, 2011) in the service of moving the entire learning community forward as students co-construct explanations of a scientific phenomenon (Davis, Palincsar, and Kademian, this volume, Chapter 13).

A Case of Literacy *for* Science Teaching and Learning

In this section, we share the case of an experienced elementary teacher, Ms. Meryl, to illustrate the sophisticated knowledge for science teaching and promising pedagogical practices needed to engage students productively in literacy practices for sensemaking in science. We were intentional in identifying a teacher who had participated in extensive and ongoing research-based professional development for more than a decade. In doing so, we were able to focus on the literacy practices that emerged from Ms. Meryl's approach to science teaching and learning. Ms. Meryl maintained a heightened focus on how to support her students in making sense of core science ideas and the processes by which scientific ideas are negotiated and shared.

About Ms. Meryl

Ms. Meryl would be the first to tell you that her passion and comfort for teaching science were not present at the start of her career. Instead, she would explain that her enthusiasm and what seems like an effortless approach to teaching science grew as the result of her drive to confront her discomfort with teaching science. To strengthen her science teaching practices, Ms. Meryl joined a school-university partnership (see Zembal-Saul, Badiali, Mueller and McDyre, this volume, Chapter 14) midway through her career. As a result of this partnership, she worked with researchers on argumentation and explanation in elementary school science for more than fifteen years. Ms. Meryl co-authored multiple manuscripts for publication, presented at numerous conferences, and participated in facilitating science education professional development for teachers across the country. Ms. Meryl also co-taught elementary science methods courses for preservice teachers and served as a classroom mentor for 12 years. She was familiar with the NGSS and used the standards regularly as a tool for planning the science content storylines that framed her instruction.

Ms. Meryl's Approach to Sensemaking

Ms. Meryl's approach to sensemaking in science was remarkably consistent and yet responsive to students' ideas and interests. She employed an instructional pattern that incorporated a variety of opportunities for students to engage in talk, investigation, and reasoning. Her approach to planning and enacting instruction relied on a coherent sequence of concepts that developed over time as students moved through investigating phenomena related to negotiating the meaning of science ideas. In the vignette that follows, we highlight a lesson that focused on investigating and negotiating meaning for the force–distance relationship that explains how levers make work easier. In planning for the unit, Ms. Meryl identified the lever as the initial simple machine to be investigated given the easily observable and compelling illustration of the force–distance relationship. She dedicated multiple days of instruction to provide students with experiences that taken together support them in uncovering the evidence necessary to develop the force–distance relationship that underlies how other simple machines work.

Over the course of the lesson, Ms. Meryl's pattern of instruction capitalized on the interplay between whole group and small group discourse. Ms. Meryl's intentional use of a variety of discourse formats for science talk provided additional pathways for all students to make sense of core science ideas. Ms. Meryl consistently began lessons by engaging students in whole group discussion to have them interact socially and over time with a science concept (McDonald and Kelly, 2012; Mortimer and Scott, 2003). It is through these discourse-rich opportunities for sensemaking that students had a chance to participate in intellectual work with peers, access the reasoning of others, experience how a community deals with uncertainty, and begin to observe changes in thinking over time (Mortimer and Scott, 2003). Ms. Meryl utilized small group discussion for conferring with students during investigations and writing, and she embedded strategies, such as "turn and talk," in whole group discussions known as science conferences. Through this interplay of whole group and small group discourse, learners were invited to pull together their existing ideas and points of view with new ideas that were presented through talk. This resulted in a form of reasoning that required students to act on their ideas (Colley and Windschitl, 2016). Ms. Meryl's movement between whole group and small group discussion, investigation, and writing explanations (Figure 4.1) allowed for students to elaborate on ideas, question the coherence of an idea, assess the credibility of an idea, and represent ideas in various forms (Michaels *et al.*, 2008). The kinds of interactions found in Ms. Meryl's lessons allowed students to articulate and negotiate their ideas through talk and thus engage in sensemaking (Mortimer and Scott, 2003).

This approach to sensemaking can be observed in a vignette in which we illustrate features of Ms. Meryl's science teaching and highlight examples of *Literacy Practices for Sensemaking in Science* in the context of science instruction.

Vignette of Ms. Meryl's Teaching

The science lesson featured here focused on the introduction of levers to investigate balanced and unbalanced forces (NGSS 3-PS2–1; NGSS Lead States, 2013). Ms. Meryl posed a challenge to her third-grade class: *"I want you to think of a way for a simple machine to lift your teacher."* She invited one of the smallest students in the class, Julie, to the front of the room and asked the class again if there was a way for her to lift the teacher. Over the next 13 minutes, Ms. Meryl facilitated a discussion in which the students talked through various proposals. Ms. Meryl asked them to use the whiteboard to draw plans for the class to see. After one student explained her idea of a ramp, another student, Amy, excitedly decided that a lever would work and drew her idea on the board. She explained that a plank could work as a lever with a block that she called a *"velcrum"* (meaning fulcrum) placed under it. Utilizing Amy's idea without correcting her vocabulary, Ms. Meryl brought in a plank of wood and brick. Setting the materials in the center of the circle of students, she asked them, *"How could we set this up so that Julie could lift me?"* Ms. Meryl invited students to manipulate the materials as they shared their thinking about how to set up a lever. Questions arose about where the brick/fulcrum should be placed, where Julie (applied force) should step onto the plank, and where the teacher (load) should stand. The discussion culminated with students identifying and labeling the essential

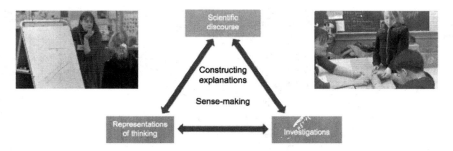

Figure 4.1 Ms. Meryl's Pattern of Instruction

parts of a lever, but the question remained about where the fulcrum should be placed so that Julie could lift the teacher.

In the next part of the lesson, Ms. Meryl provided an opportunity for the students to investigate the placement of the fulcrum using Lego^{TM}. In small groups, students tested various configurations and made observations about the placement of the fulcrum. Ms. Meryl visited each group to confer with them, asking them to explain their thinking using evidence from the investigation. Ms. Meryl encouraged language that focused students on observations that were important to developing an understanding of how levers work, such as "farther away from the load" and "closer to the load." After making and testing levers with Lego^{TM}, students began to use the language modeled by the teacher in subsequent whole group science conferences. Students communicated their interpretations of the Lego^{TM} investigation and applied their developing understanding of how levers work to revise their proposals about how to use a lever to lift the teacher. Drawing upon their investigation of Lego^{TM} levers, students set up the board and brick with the fulcrum closest to the load, and Julie was easily able to lift Ms. Meryl. Ms. Meryl guided students through the process of negotiating a claim from evidence that answered the question, *"How can we lift the teacher?"* Utilizing the claim-evidence-reasoning (CER) framework (McNeill and Krajcik, 2008; McNeill and Krajcik, 2011) discussed by Zembal-Saul and Hershberger (this volume, Chapter 1), Ms. Meryl then asked the students to write an evidence-based explanation in their science notebooks along with a diagram of the lever scenario.

The next day, Ms. Meryl began her science lesson with students co-constructing a shared definition for the term *fulcrum*. She gave students time to talk with their peers and share ideas, before engaging in whole group discussion. The class collaboratively defined fulcrum as, *"the point on which the lever sits or moves."* At that point, Ms. Meryl introduced a non-fiction text that she had at the ready and asked her students to compare their definition to the one found in a text.

Literacy Practices for Sensemaking in Elementary Science

In the case of Ms. Meryl's lever lesson, we can identify three *Literacy Practices for Sensemaking in Science* that were consistently evident in her science teaching across analysis of the entire unit of instruction: (1) engaging students with multiple science-specific texts; (2) eliciting and using students' ideas through talking, writing and drawing; and (3) tying words to meaning. Ms. Meryl's pattern of instruction moved back and forth fluidly from engaging students in scientific discourse to investigating phenomena to constructing and using of a variety of science texts (e.g., drawings, written and oral explanations, vocabulary in context). Of particular interest, we saw her intentionally model scientific discourse and reasoning with students in small and whole group formats to have them make sense of levers and the

70   *Hooper and Zembal-Saul*

underlying force–distance relationship. In the following section, we unpack each *Literacy Practice for Sensemaking in Science* from Ms. Meryl's instruction. We assert that unlike traditional approaches to integrating literacy and science, Ms. Meryl's science teaching demonstrates careful alignment of literacy practices and the epistemic practices of science.

Engaging Students with Multiple, Science-Specific Texts

While texts are essential to the framing of literacy, we entered into the process of analyzing Ms. Meryl's teaching practices with the perspective that merely reading about science (informational books and websites) is insufficient for meaningful science learning (National Research Council, 2014). This prompted us to examine Ms. Meryl's teaching for how she approached texts, with emphasis on those that are important to scientists and learning science. We found strong support for models, evidence-based explanations, and representations of data (e.g., data tables, graphs, charts, argument maps) that were produced and used by students during scientific investigations as powerful texts for sensemaking. The intellectual work of authoring, interpreting, communicating, and critiquing science texts across the domains of literacy (talking, listening, writing, and reading) is a prime example of reconsidering traditional informational texts to include those essential for productive participation in the epistemic practices of science and sensemaking. This perspective on science-specific texts, in which explicit connection are made among the language of science in various text forms (Pearson *et al.*, 2010), remains uncommon in elementary school science.

Evidence of Ms. Meryl's use of science-specific texts is prominent in the vignette. Ms. Meryl's science instruction involved students in communicating and analyzing ideas using evidence, which served as both a sensemaking practice and literacy practice. In the vignette, Ms. Meryl consistently facilitated discourse-rich interactions and modeled the norms of using evidence to support and critique ideas. For instance, she prompted small groups to explain their Lego^{TM} levers using data from their investigation. Also, she orchestrated co-construction of a claim from evidence in whole group discussion before asking students to write and draw the scientific explanation independently.

Finally, the vignette illustrates that Ms. Meryl understood that science texts take a variety of forms and that students must have multiple opportunities to engage with science texts to make sense of the core ideas embedded in the lesson. Ms. Meryl leveraged students' authoring, reading, interpreting, and critique of diagrams as ways of supporting sensemaking. As students negotiated an understanding of levers, they not only developed a shared language for talking about the features of levers, but they also produced shared norms for drawing and communicating their lever systems to make sense of the diagrams produced by their peers. These practices took place in the broader

Literacy Practices for Sensemaking   71

context of developing norms for participating in scientific practices. The teacher recognized that engaging students in constructing and critiquing science texts served as opportunities for them to learn the science, as well as how science is done.

Eliciting and Using Students' Ideas Through Talking, Writing, and Drawing

While our initial examination of Ms. Meryl's teaching practices focused on how she elicited students' ideas, we were equally attentive to how she used students' ideas as resources to advance sensemaking in science for the entire learning community. To better understand this literacy practice for sensemaking in science we first revisit Ms. Meryl's approach to making students' ideas visible. In the vignette, we see Ms. Meryl provide her students with an opportunity to share their initial ideas about the investigation through drawing diagrams. Ms. Meryl knew that drawings lend themselves to making students' thinking public. She also was aware that in doing this work, students often propose a seesaw as a way to lift the teacher. By having students draw their ideas on whiteboards and explain them to one another, Ms. Meryl elicited the seesaw idea for the whole group. This initial idea can be utilized by Ms. Meryl to move the group towards investigating the lever as a simple machine and more specifically, foreground the force–distance relationship through the placement of the fulcrum on a lever. Finally, Ms. Meryl knew in advance the direction in which she intended to move the class through the simple machines content storyline. Her overarching goal remained the idea that simple machines can be used to make work easier. Thus, she listened for those ideas throughout the whole group discussion to capitalize on central ideas as they arose.

Eliciting students' ideas, while important, is insufficient for sensemaking in science. Once students' ideas are public, the teacher must have a sense of what to do with them in the moment to support learning (Levin *et al.*, 2009; Coffey *et al.*, 2011; see Davis, Zembal-Saul, and Kademian, this volume, Introduction). Ms. Meryl anticipated that having students draw and discuss their ideas about how to lift a teacher would result in a lever being proposed. She was prepared with materials that she could then use for students to identify and construct shared meaning for the associated vocabulary. Ms. Meryl also demonstrated her ability to listen for, be responsive to, and leverage particular ideas required to construct an explanation for why levers make work easier. Ms. Meryl's use of the Lego[TM] systems, in addition to a life-sized lever, provided multiple opportunities for the students to propose, test, and revise their thinking. This sequence of investigating the force–distance relationship allowed students to collect, analyze, and discuss data iteratively. Moreover, students discussed and negotiated their models and applied their emerging thinking to new problems (from Lego[TM] to lifting the teacher). This required students to communicate their ideas in shared language, listen to the ideas of others, and agree/disagree with their peers using evidence.

72 Hooper and Zembal-Saul

Ms. Meryl was thoughtful in her approach to this complex work, and it was evident that her teaching was informed by an understanding of the scientific explanation she intended for students to construct from evidence across multiple investigations. This greater vision (Ball, 1993) of where she was headed with her class allowed her to make effective in the moment decisions about how to address students' ideas (Zembal-Saul and Hershberger, this volume, Chapter 1).

Tying Words to Meaning

Students engaged in learning science are also learning the unique disciplinary language of science. Yore *et al.* (2003) highlight the integral role that language plays in science, as a means to "doing" science, as well as constructing an understanding of scientific ideas. Over the course of several decades, as the result of a climate of high stakes assessment, vocabulary instruction has maintained a prominent place in elementary school science (Marx and Harris, 2006). Teachers recognize a need for students to know academic vocabulary to succeed on standardized tests, which contributes to instruction that focuses on pre-teaching or front-loading science terms. It is common for elementary teachers to address science vocabulary through direct instruction and memorization, followed by a quick hands-on activity. Teaching science in this way falls short of aligning with the epistemic practices of science and presents significant barriers to students developing a conceptual understanding of scientific ideas.

In examining Ms. Meryl's approach to vocabulary instruction, and the use of language in science learning, we observe her utilizing a repertoire of strategies to support the students in making sense of the language of science in the context of doing science. Her approaches to assisting students in learning the language of science positions all of them as capable learners. This work began in the planning process when Ms. Meryl determined the core science ideas essential to the study of simple machines. Specific to the lever lessons, Ms. Meryl identified *lever, fulcrum, effort,* and *force* as necessary for helping students make sense of and articulate their learning about levers as a simple machine. As students engaged in drawing their ideas of a simple machine that could be used to lift the teacher, Ms. Meryl invited them to put into words what they were proposing. As students articulated their ideas, she listened to their words and their ideas, waiting for moments when she could build from their words to introduce key vocabulary terms that would be used throughout the lesson. In the vignette, Amy proposed the idea of a lever and suggested that a *velcrum,* placed under the plank of wood, could help make the lever move. Hearing the word *velcrum* prompted Ms. Meryl to introduce the term *fulcrum* to the class. She reinforced the use of this word by labeling the fulcrum on the life-size model of the lever, as well as holding students accountable for the use of the term *fulcrum* when discussing their investigation findings in both small group and whole group discussion. In this way, Ms. Meryl capitalized on multiple opportunities to tie words to meaning.

Although Ms. Meryl elicited and used students' ideas to introduce the term fulcrum, she did not explicitly define fulcrum for the students. Instead, she engaged the students in an investigation of levers using Lego™ and provided ample time for them to discuss their findings and use their evidence to co-construct an explanation. The definition of fulcrum came *after* students had experienced investigating and explaining levers (see Bismack and Haefner, this volume, Chapter 2). On day two of the lesson, Ms. Meryl invited students to think about how they would define the term "fulcrum." In a whole group discussion, she asked the students to recall the role of the lever in their diagrams to determine how they would define this term. After several minutes of whole group and small group discussion, the students co-constructed the definition of fulcrum, stating that the fulcrum is the "point on which the lever sits or moves."

Students' abilities to engage in the intellectual work of co-constructing a definition for fulcrum is grounded in the work that Ms. Meryl did with her class from day one. Ms. Meryl's success in tying words to meaning was contingent on several important strategies. To present science vocabulary in the context of doing science, Ms. Meryl paid close attention to the timing and the way in which children introduced words with ideas. Also, Ms. Meryl understood that students make sense of academic vocabulary when a learning community uses a new term over time and attached to students' experiences with investigating and discussing the force–distance relationship. Lastly, Ms. Meryl held the students accountable for using the term in their science talk and writing. As a whole class, the students were doing the work to make sense of the term fulcrum, and Ms. Meryl orchestrated classroom talk for students to negotiate a meaningful and contextualized definition for the term.

Putting it all Together

In this case study, we set out to highlight literacy *for* science by describing the range of ways in which one educator used literacy practices to support sensemaking in science. Ms. Meryl's focus on giving priority to evidence and explanation revealed notable alignment between literacy practices and epistemic practices of science. These literacy practices for science teaching include: (1) engaging students with multiple science-specific texts (e.g., models, evidence-based explanations, representations of data, and student-created science texts); (2) eliciting and using students' ideas through talking, writing and drawing; and (3) tying words to meaning. We hope that sharing Ms. Meryl's practices may support other educators in making pedagogical shifts in their science teaching to meet the literacy demands for supporting students' sensemaking in science.

74 *Hooper and Zembal-Saul*

Our work assumes capitalizing on science instruction for literacy and language development in early grades is a potential inroad for more meaningful science teaching and learning. Taking up these practices requires that teachers transform how they conceptualize the use of literacy practices in science instruction. As mentioned previously, teachers often have students read non-fiction texts *about* science, pre-teach vocabulary *about* science, and engage students in talking *about* scientific ideas. These ways of utilizing literacy practices in science become more about how to do the lesson, rather than a focus on how science is done (Jiménez-Aleixandre *et al.*, 2000).

Literacy practices for sensemaking in science seek to shift away from an "*about*" model to one that privileges literacy *for* science in the context of epistemic practices (see Table 4.1). A literacy *for* science approach positions students not merely as recipients of knowledge through texts, but also as producers and critics of scientific texts. Instead of reading about science we advocate for *co-constructing, critiquing, and using* a variety of scientific texts to support students sensemaking in science. Finally, there remains a dire need to transition away from memorizing science vocabulary to a sensemaking perspective in which students *negotiate shared meaning* of scientific vocabulary in the context of doing science.

Implementation of literacy practices for sensemaking in science requires a commitment to responsive teaching (Levin *et al.*, 2009; Coffey *et al.*, 2011), a nuanced understanding of core science ideas and how they build and connect, and fluency in scientific discourse and practices. Ms. Meryl's case advances the notion that teachers must have a coherent and well-developed plan for students' participation in iterative cycles of data collection and explanation construction for productive sensemaking. Ms. Meryl's science teaching also illustrates the complexity of reconceptualizing literacy practices in ways that are aligned with the epistemic practices of science and the role they play in sensemaking. As shown in the vignette, literacy practices for sensemaking in science are interconnected, complex and work synergistically with science practices to support sensemaking in elementary science.

Table 4.1 Pedagogical Shifts in Implementing Literacy for Sensemaking in Science

Literacy in Elementary School Science	*Literacy for Sensemaking in Science*
Frontloading and memorizing science vocabulary	Negotiating shared meaning of scientific vocabulary in the context of doing science
Reading and writing informational texts about science	Co-constructing, critiquing, and using a variety of science texts including models, representations of data, etc.
Speaking and listening about science; IRE discourse	Public discourse and reasoning using scientific norms and conventions

In the current context of science education, classroom teachers are tasked with the challenging work of navigating how to leverage literacy practices for sensemaking in science, and they must be given appropriate supports to do this (Kademian and Davis, this volume, Chapter 8). In our work with preservice and in-service elementary teachers, we see the promise of framing science teaching as a sensemaking process that necessarily requires literacy practices for science. Examples of these practices across a variety of age levels and school contexts can be used by science teacher educators and researchers as images of the possible when re-considering the intersections of literacy and science teaching. Ms. Meryl's approach to science teaching focused on capitalizing on literacy to engage students in constructing evidence-based explanations serves as an image of what is possible.

If we return to the beginning of Ms. Meryl's lesson in which she poses the question, *How can we lift the teacher?*, we can see that Ms. Meryl did more than engage her students in a scientific question that motivates them to investigate. She has posed a question that invites her students to investigate a core idea, and she skillfully has planned for instruction that begins to support her students in developing the literacy tools needed to make sense of scientific concepts. Her ability to engage her students in literacy-rich instruction that promotes scientific discourse and reasoning demonstrates what can be possible when teachers are intentional in bringing science and literacy and together.

Contribution to Sensemaking and Images of the Possible

The case of Ms. Meryl's literacy practices for sensemaking in science provides insights into what the shift from "doing school" to "doing science" can look like in elementary school. In taking a close look at Ms. Meryl's approach to sensemaking and her ability to use literacy practices to support students in talking, listening, reading, and writing *for* science, we have a better sense of the kinds of instruction needed to disrupt traditional approaches to and purposes for integrating literacy and science. Examining the practices of experienced teachers becomes critical for engaging in continued discussion around the shared problem space of barriers to teaching science in elementary school. This chapter serves as another entry point for looking at the problems of practice in elementary science teaching and presenting possible approaches that teachers can take for promoting sensemaking in science teaching and learning. As other authors in this section have addressed (e.g., Bismack and Haefner, this volume, Chapter 2; Cody and Biggers, this volume, Chapter 3), how teachers facilitate and position students engaged in scientific discourse and practices is critical to their learning. Patterns of instruction used by master teachers should be leveraged for developing strategies and practices for supporting students in making sense of the practice of science and uncovering science ideas. A teacher's ability to plan for instruction that centers on science as a social practice,

76 Hooper and Zembal-Saul

engages students in the epistemic aims of science, as well as elicit and use students' science ideas in instruction helps us better understand what remains possible in making sense of science with young children.

A very warm thank you to Ms. Meryl and her students for allowing us to be a constant presence in their classroom and to learn from them.

References

Ball, D. L. (1993). With an eye on the mathematical horizon: Dilemmas of teaching elementary school mathematics. *The Elementary School Journal, 93*(4), 373–397.

Bransford, J. D., Brown, A. L., and Cocking, R. R. (Eds.). (1999). *How People Learn: Brain, Mind, Experience, and School.* Washington, DC: National Academies Press.

Cervetti, G. N., Barber, J., Dorph, R., Pearson, P. D., and Goldschmidt, P. G. (2012). The impact of an integrated approach to science and literacy in elementary school classrooms. *Journal of Research in Science Teaching, 49*(5), 631–658.

Coffey, J. E., Hammer, D., Levin, D. M., and Grant, T. (2011). The missing disciplinary substance of formative assessment. *Journal of Research in Science Teaching, 48*(10), 1109–1136.

Colley, C. and Windschitl, M. (2016). Rigor in elementary science students' discourse: The role of responsiveness and supportive conditions for talk. *Science Education, 100*(6), 1009–1038.

Hand, B. M. (2007). *Science Inquiry, Argument and Language: A Case for the Science Writing Heuristic.* Rotterdam, The Netherlands: Sense Publishers.

Jiménez-Aleixandre, M. P., Rodriguez, A. B., and Duschl, R. A. (2000). "Doing the lesson" or "doing science": Argument in high school genetics. *Science Education, 84*(6), 757–792.

Kelly, G. J. (2008). Inquiry, activity, and epistemic practice. In R. Duschl, and R. Grandy (Eds.), *Teaching Scientific Inquiry: Recommendations for Research and Implementation* (pp. 99–117). Rotterdam, The Netherlands: Sense Publishers.

Lave, J., Wenger, E., and Wenger, E. (1991). *Situated Learning: Legitimate Peripheral Participation.* Cambridge: Cambridge University Press.

Levin, D. M., Hammer, D., and Coffey, J. E. (2009). Novice teachers' attention to student thinking. *Journal of Teacher Education, 60*(2), 142–154.

McDonald, S. P., and Kelly, G. J. (2012). Beyond argumentation: Sense-making discourse in the science classroom. In M. Khine (Ed.), *Perspectives on Scientific Argumentation* (pp. 265–281). Dordrecht, The Netherlands: Springer.

McNeill, K. L., and Krajcik, J. (2008). Scientific explanations: Characterizing and evaluating the effects of teachers' instructional practices on student learning. *Journal of Research in Science Teaching, 45*(1), 53–78.

McNeill, K. L., and Krajcik, J. S. (2011). *Supporting Grade 5–8 Students in Constructing Explanations in Science: The Claim, Evidence, and Reasoning Framework for Talk and Writing.* Boston, MA: Pearson.

Marx, R., and Harris, C. (2006). No Child Left Behind and science education: Opportunities, challenges, and risks. *Elementary School Journal, 106*(5), 467–477.

Michaels, S., O'Connor, C., and Resnick, L. B. (2008). Deliberative discourse idealized and realized: Accountable talk in the classroom and in civic life. *Studies in Philosophy and Education, 27*(4), 283–297.

Mortimer, E., and Scott, P. (2003). *Meaning Making in Secondary Science Classrooms*. New York: McGraw-Hill Education.

National Research Council. (2012). *A Framework for K-12 Science Education: Practices, Crosscutting Concepts, and Core Ideas*. Washington, DC: National Academies Press.

National Research Council. (2014). *Literacy for Science: Exploring the Intersection of the Next Generation Science Standards and Common Core for ELA Standards: A Workshop Summary*. Washington, DC: National Academies Press. Retrieved from: https://doi.org/10.17226/18803.

NGSS Lead States. (2013). *Next Generation Science Standards: For States, By States*. Washington, DC: National Academies Press.

Pearson, P. D., Moje, E., and Greenleaf, C. (2010). Literacy and science: Each in the service of the other. *Science, 328*(5977), 459–463.

Yore, L., Bisanz, G. L., and Hand, B. M. (2003). Examining the literacy component of science literacy: 25 years of language arts and science research. *International Journal of Science Education, 25*(6), 689–725.

5 *Response*: Making Sense of Sensemaking in Elementary Education

Perspectives from Identity and Implications for Equity

Lucy Avraamidou
UNIVERSITY OF GRONINGEN, THE NETHERLANDS

Introduction: From *Inquiry* to *Sensemaking*

The four chapters of Section I are rooted within reform recommendations that marked the last decade in North America emphasizing scientific practices in science teaching and learning. Even though the chapters are situated in the context of North America, they also have implications for science education in contexts outside of North America. The authors draw upon recommendations of the *Framework for K-12 Science Education* which provided the blueprint for developing the *Next Generation Science Standards* (National Research Council, 2012). Unlike previously published reform documents, the framework uses the term "scientific practices" instead of "science process" or "inquiry skills" in order to emphasize not only skills but also knowledge that is specific to each practice. These practices have been used by different researchers in various contexts in different places of the world, to design and implement teacher preparation programs, curriculum materials, and classroom interventions that emphasize the engagement of students in planning and carrying out investigations and constructing evidence-based explanations. As Zembal-Saul *et al.* (2013) argued,

> not only should students understand and be able to apply scientific ideas to explain natural phenomena but they should also be able to generate and evaluate scientific evidence, construct and debate evidence-based explanations, and participate productively in a community of science learners.
>
> (p. 17)

Indeed, the current science education standards movement has renewed expectations for children on what to do, how to think, and how to engage in scientific practices. However, this amalgam of expectations brings challenges to contextualizing science instruction because the recommendations continue to require fundamental shifts in best practices for teaching and learning science. As a matter of fact, the recommendations create ambitious expectations for beginning elementary school teachers, especially when not all elementary school teachers have the ideal training, support or resources to enact science education reform. Hence, a question emerges: *How can teachers translate these reform recommendations and the urgency for attention to the epistemic aspects of science into practice?*

This is precisely what the authors of the four chapters have done: they have provided concrete images from the elementary school classroom of how these reform recommendations look in practice. In reviewing the four chapters, the emphasis on the epistemic aspects of science becomes clear across all of them. Essentially, these four chapters constitute an attempt to provide a set of diverse and concrete images of how teaching with an emphasis on the epistemic aspects of science, and specifically during sensemaking, looks in practice in the context of elementary education. This is important in light of literature pointing to the challenges that elementary teachers, who are trained as generalists, face in enacting reform recommendations (Davis et al., 2006). Collectively, the four chapters provide evidence that generalists are capable of engaging in reform-oriented science practices and offer examples of how these reform practices look within various science units in different classrooms and school districts, and with students of different ages (6–11 years old). The unique contribution of the chapters to conceptualizing sensemaking, in my view, is found in the form of responses to the following two crucial questions: *When students are sensemaking, what are they doing? When teachers are supporting sensemaking, what are they doing?* In this commentary chapter, I discuss the enactment of sensemaking through the lenses of "equity" and "identity," under the following two headings: (a) perspectives from identity; and (b) implications for equity. But, before doing so, I offer a brief overview of the content of the four chapters as a means for providing a common ground for understanding what follows.

An Overview of the Chapters

In their chapter, Zembal-Saul and Hershberger (Chapter 1) put forward an argument about positioning students at the center of sensemaking as a means for disrupting traditional approaches to science teaching in elementary grades, which emphasize hands-on activities. With an emphasis on how teachers engage students in generating, recording, and analyzing data, the authors offer a vignette, part of a unit on energy, of an elementary teacher that illustrates sensemaking moments. The vignette highlights the ways in which the teacher engages her fourth-grade students (9–10 years old) in investigating phenomena related to energy and energy transfer using roller coasters. In doing so, the vignette focuses on the ways in which a teacher:

80 *Avraamidou*

(a) used phenomena to create equitable access and engagement with science; and (b) prioritized the construction of explanations from evidence. Throughout sensemaking the teacher paid special attention to "kid talk" during sensemaking. This emphasis on "talking science" served as a means for engaging students in reasoning about data as well as a means for including and embracing students' diverse ways of reasoning and appropriating scientific vocabulary.

With an emphasis on teachers' practices, Bismack and Haefner (Chapter 2) provide research evidence of how an experienced teacher leveraged the science practices and children's talk as a way to help first-graders (6 years old) make sense of concepts related to magnets and magnetism. Following an analysis of videos of the teacher's science teaching, as well as three interviews, the authors developed three vignettes that provide a detailed account of the ways in which this teacher engaged her students in scientific practices. Central in these vignettes was the nature of classroom discourse or the sensemaking discussions in which the construction of evidence-based claims was central. Each of these vignettes highlights different aspects of teacher practices that support sensemaking: (a) drawing on children's own language; (b) leveraging students' initial ideas; and (c) students' analyses of their data.

Cody and Biggers present an "image of the possible," which illustrates the benefits of integrating science and engineering practices, literacy and place-based instruction, in a way intended to increase fifth-grade students' (10–11 years old) opportunities to make sense of scientific phenomena. In enacting this unit, the authors engaged students in different kinds of activities: reading of a story, a field trip to the local wastewater treatment facility, carrying out water quality tests, researching the natural and human history of the local area, reading local newspapers, communicating with local officials, scientists, and community members, and writing to local officials and the general public. In discussing the affordances of this integrated unit through an example of student writing in the form of claim-evidence-reasoning, the authors referred to the following: (a) student learning across content areas; (b) depth of discussions; (c) transfer of skills to other content areas; (d) connection to the subsequent science unit; and (e) student excitement surrounding engineering tasks.

Hooper and Zembal-Saul (Chapter 3) situate their chapter in a third-grade classroom (8–9 years old). The case highlights an experienced teacher's practices for integrating literacy and science instruction. The vignette presented in this chapter focuses on the teacher's consistent approach to sensemaking which employs an instructional pattern that moves across varied opportunities for students to engage in talk, investigation, and reasoning. Following an analysis of the vignette, the authors identified three literacy practices that emerged: (a) engaging students with multiple science-specific texts; (b) eliciting and using students' ideas through talking, writing and drawing; and (c) tying words to meaning.

Perspectives from Identity

In reading the chapters through an identity lens, it becomes apparent that the teachers featured in the vignettes were able to enact reform-based practices, which reflects an aspect of the nature of their science identities. But why might the construct of identity be useful in our understanding of and efforts to examine how sensemaking is conceptualized and enacted in the elementary school classroom? Because as Gee (1999) argued, identity refers to "the kind of person one is seeking to be and enact in the here and now" (p. 13) and "being recognized as a certain kind of person in a given context" (p. 99). Hence, in the context of the school classroom, the kind of teacher someone is and is recognized to be by their students, especially in relation to reform recommendations, could be better understood through the construct of identity. As Luehmann (2007) has argued,

> Becoming a science teacher who values and engages in reform-based practices involves much more than acquiring a new set of knowledge and skills, and that this process could be better understood and supported once we think of it as developing a new professional identity as a reform-minded science teacher.
>
> (p. 823)

In attempting to examine teacher identity, Gee's (2000) conceptualization of identity provides a useful analytical framework, consisting of the following types of identity: (a) *nature-identity*, which refers to a state developed from forces in nature; (b) *institution-identity*, which refers to a position authorized by authorities within institutions; (c) *discourse-identity*, which refers to an individual trait recognized in the discourse and dialogue with "rational" individuals; and (d) *affinity-identity*, which refers to the experiences shared in the practice of "affinity groups" (p. 100). In this chapter, I argue that discourse identity might offer a valuable lens in examining the ways in which teachers provide opportunities for students to engage in sensemaking. From a sociocultural point of view, a person's speech is a marker of identity (Lemke, 2008). In analyzing the vignettes offered in the chapters, different episodes can be identified that illustrate the teachers' discourse identities and how these might have implications for addressing goals related to equity.

For example, Bismack and Haefner, in their chapter (Chapter 2), offer three vignettes that represent how the teacher-participant in their study leveraged science practices to support her students' sensemaking. The following extracts from the third vignette provide evidence of this teacher's reform-based discourse identity, as she engaged students in making meaning of their data through a classroom discussion. Following a discussion about the outcomes of the students' experiments with magnets, the teacher stated: *It seems like no matter what group you worked in, everybody saw that each magnet*

82   *Avraamidou*

had two parts that were stronger than other parts of the magnet? Following on from this, the teacher posed a question that prompts students in making a claim: *Ok, I want you to think about how would you answer the question: are some parts of the magnet stronger than others? What would you say?* The students offered various answers, and following on these, the teacher prompted them to think about their evidence: *How do you know that some sides are stronger?* What's evident in this classroom discourse is how the teacher guided students through the processes of sensemaking and specifically, for the purpose of developing evidence-based claims, while also using the terms "evidence" and "claim." Based on this, I would argue that this extract provides evidence of the reform-based nature of this teacher's discourse identity.

Another example that points to how a reform-based teacher identity looks in practice is found within Zembal-Saul and Hershberger's chapter (Chapter 1). Different episodes found in the opening vignette of the chapter provide evidence of how the teacher was able to enact her reform-based identity in the context of a unit on energy, by engaging students in forming questions and designing investigations in order to collect data that would help them respond to the question: *How does a roller coaster have enough "power" to go all the way?* An example of the emphasis placed on evidence-based claims is found in the following direction that the teacher gave to the class: *What claims can you make from the data to address the question of the impact of the height of the track on the distance of the marble rolled?* A fundamental dimension of the nature of (student) science identity that is exemplified in this chapter is what the authors refer to as "social sensemaking," which emphasizes how, as members of a community, students make meaning through social interactions. This was evident in different episodes presented in the chapter as for example, in the opening of the lesson when the teacher said: *"Turn and talk with people around you ... ."* As becomes clear in this chapter, work in small groups and opportunities for exchanging and negotiating ideas was at the heart of this teacher's practices. Such "social" opportunities to negotiate understandings and develop shared meanings are essential to identity-based research.

The nature of the discourse identity of the teacher who features in Hooper and Zembal-Saul's chapter is exemplified through different episodes that are shared in the vignette. The vignette from this classroom begins with a challenge posed to the students: *"I want you to think of a way for a simple machine to lift your teacher,"* which focused on the introduction of levers to investigate balanced and unbalanced forces. Following on this, the teacher facilitated a classroom-discussion in which the students talked through various ideas, and explained them in different forms of literacies, as a means for eliciting students' ideas. The students then engaged in carrying out investigations with Lego^{TM} for the purpose of developing a claim from evidence. Similar to all other chapters, in this one, the teacher's discourse identity is reform-based and emphasizes students' co-constructing explanations of natural phenomena based on evidence and through social interactions as members of a community.

Implications for Equity

Sensemaking, or how students make sense of science, has been receiving increased attention by researchers in various parts of the world. Despite its widespread use in science education research, sensemaking remains a fragmented theoretical construct which lacks a universally agreed definition (Odden and Russ, 2018). In the four chapters reviewed, however, a unity exists across conceptualizations of sensemaking, which places emphasis on students' construction and articulation of evidence-based ideas of phenomena. As such, the four chapters highlight the roles, practices, and discourses of both students and teachers during sensemaking. A deeper examination of these roles, practices, and discourses illuminates the nature of the identities of these teachers and how their enactment promotes goals related to equity. In what follows, I offer a discussion of the content of the chapters by applying perspectives from equity-based research:

> Equity in science education requires that all students are provided with equitable opportunities to learn science and become engaged in science and engineering practices; with access to quality space, equipment, and teachers to support and motivate that learning and engagement; and adequate time spent on science. In addition, the issue of connecting to students' interests and experiences is particularly important for broadening participation in science.
>
> (National Research Council, 2012, p. 28)

In analyzing the vignettes offered in the chapters, different episodes or moments can be identified that illustrate practices that promote equity.

An interesting example is found in Cody and Bigger's chapter (Chapter 3) where they describe a field trip to the local water treatment facility. The fact that the *local* context defines the context of the unit points to the importance of place, defined as a space with meaning created by experiences, and which has been addressed in identity-based research in light of goals related to equity (Avraamidou, 2018). The locality of the context supported the enactment of culturally relevant practices such as engaging students in reading local newspaper articles as well as providing them with opportunities to communicate effectively with local officials, scientists, and community members. This approach placed all students in the center and as insiders within their community, their local context. As such, the unit not only takes into consideration the students' interests, cultural repertoires, and their own experiences with the context, but it also engages students in creating culturally relevant meaning. Such an emphasis on how students locate themselves in the context includes and embraces students' personal cultural repertoires which relates directly to equity goals.

In light of goals related to equity, Hooper and Zembal-Saul's chapter (Chapter 4) has a unique contribution to make because of its emphasis on

84 *Avraamidou*

the role of language in supporting scientific literacy development. This chapter presents a teacher who focuses her attention on the language of science and uses different strategies to support students in making sense of the language of science, or as the authors state, "tying words to meaning." From an equity perspective, what is important to take away from this chapter is how the teacher used a variety of means and forms to engage students in the language of science, namely: drawings, talk, representations of data, and explanations as science texts. As such, these practices provided a diverse set of literacies that offered inclusive opportunities for all students to engage with the language of science.

Practices that serve as examples of inclusive learning opportunities were also evident in Zembal-Saul and Hershberger's chapter (Chapter 1), in which they shared vignettes from a classroom where the teacher constantly navigated between small-group and whole-group discussions. What this points to is a shift of the power or authority of knowledge from the teacher to the students given that throughout the lesson students are placed in the center of sensemaking as constructors of knowledge. Additional practices that pay attention to equity goals are also found in two forms: (a) acceptance of "kid talk" and a variety of ways of representing knowledge and communicating during sensemaking; and (b) providing opportunities for all students to create shared experiences and common points of departure. This was especially evident in the introduction of the lesson, when the teacher began with a roller coaster video but also throughout the lesson, as the teacher constantly invited *all* students to engage in sensemaking.

Contributions and Implications

The four chapters offer a range of important insights into scientific practices in the context of elementary education and contribute in novel ways to sensemaking research at both a theoretical and methodological level. Collectively, these chapters might assist teachers, researchers, and teacher educators in realizing the goals of the reform, emphasizing scientific practices and sensemaking while improving learning opportunities for all students. Through concrete examples from the classroom, the chapters offer a unique contribution to conceptualizing sensemaking because they offer responses to the following two crucial questions: *When students are sensemaking, what are they doing? When teachers are supporting sensemaking, what are they doing?* When students are sensemaking, they engage in scientific practices and evidence-based discussions about science concepts, or more specifically, they engage in reasoning and problem-solving strategies used in scientific practice. But, how is sensemaking mediated by teachers? With evidence gathered from the chapters reviewed here, teachers might support sensemaking by providing students with opportunities and tools to make sense of the world they live in, to engage in scientific practices and to reason about data and ideas for the purpose of developing explanations. Such opportunities and tools might include eliciting existing knowledge through questioning, engaging students in authentic experimentation, collecting and interpreting evidence, argumentation, and explanation development. During students' engagement in evidence-based investigations, teachers support them to participate productively in classroom talk and to use of scientific language through collaborative and dialogic interactions and by constantly reflecting, while ensuring that all students' ideas and cultural repertoires are considered.

Despite their differences on scope and learning contexts, all four chapters exemplify the value of sensemaking in the elementary school classroom, serving at the heart of the account of scientific practices. One limitation of the findings of these studies is that they cannot be generalized beyond the context in which they took place—a context that is largely homogeneous and monocultural. Given the rapidly increasing ethnic, cultural, and linguistic diversity in the world, I would urge the authors to consider goals related to supporting non-dominant students in engaging in sensemaking and identity development. This is important given research evidence pointing to the fact that students from non-dominant linguistic backgrounds (e.g., bilingual) may experience identity conflict when appropriating scientific language (Brown, 2006).

The purpose of this commentary chapter was to discuss these chapters through perspectives on identity and equity. Based on the brief analysis of the chapters through identity and equity, I would argue that identity can offer a valuable lens to examine both teachers' and students' science identities when engaging in sensemaking. At the same time, an equity perspective might point to the desired outcome of improving learning opportunities for all students through sensemaking. Adopting such perspectives in sensemaking holds certain implications for research. Hence, I would recommend that researchers turn their attention to an examination of what it would mean to conceptualize sensemaking through the lens of identity for the purpose of promoting goals related to equity. While a wealth of research studies exist that examine teacher/student identity development and students' engagement in sensemaking, these two research areas remain detached from each other. With evidence drawn from the chapters reviewed, I would argue that the constructs of identity and sensemaking interrelate given that engaging students in scientific practices models the nature of science and the work of scientists, which might impact students' science identities, or, put simply, students grappling with the question: *Is science Me or is science Other?* This is especially relevant when teaching in diverse contexts and aiming at addressing goals related to equity. Below are research questions that might be worth further exploration: In what ways might sensemaking support non-dominant students' sense of belonging in science? In what ways does engaging with sensemaking support non-dominant students in identifying with science? What is the interplay between teachers' discourse-identities and students' development of strong science identities in the context of sensemaking? What is the role of students' social positioning and personal cultures in sensemaking and how can equitable sensemaking be promoted both in and out-of-classroom contexts? In what ways can sensemaking support students with diverse ethno-linguistic backgrounds to engage in scientific discourse as means for cultural border crossing and science identity formation? I end my response by posing a research question that draws directly from perspectives on identity and equity, and which holds promise for broadening and diversifying participation in science: *In what ways might sensemaking support students, especially those who have traditionally been excluded and marginalized from science, in developing disruptive science identities that allow them to position themselves as insiders in scientific practices?*

References

Avraamidou, L. (2018). Stories we live, identities we build. *Cultural Studies of Science Education*. DOI: 10.1007/s11422–11017–9855–9858.

Brown, B. A. (2006). "It isn't no slang that can be said about this stuff": Language, identity, and appropriating science discourse. *Journal of Research in Science Teaching*, *43*(1), 96–126.

Davis, E. A., Petish, D., and Smithey, J. (2006). Challenges new science teachers face. *Review of Educational Research*, *76*(4), 607–651.

Gee, J. P. (1999). *An Introduction to Discourse Analysis: Theory and Method*. New York: Routledge.

Gee, J. P. (2000). Identity as an analytic lens for research in education. *Review of Research in Education*, *25*, 99–125.

Lemke, J. L. (2008). Identity, development and desire: Critical questions. In C. R. Caldas-Coulthard and R. Iedema (Eds.), *Identity Trouble* (pp. 17–42). London: Palgrave Macmillan.

Luehmann, A. L. (2007). Identity development as a lens to science teacher preparation. *Science Education*, *91*(5), 822–839.

National Research Council. (2012). *A Framework for K-12 Science Education: Practices, Crosscutting Concepts, and Core Ideas*. Washington, DC: National Academies Press.

Odden, T. O. B. and Russ, R. S. (2018). Defining sensemaking: Bringing clarity to a fragmented theoretical construct. *Science Education*. DOI:10.1002/sce.21452.

Zembal-Saul, C., McNeil, K. L., and Hershberger, K. (2013). *What's Your Evidence? Engaging K-5 Children in Constructing Explanations in Science*. Boston, MA: Pearson Higher Education.

6 *Response:* Integrating and Supporting Science Practices in Elementary Classrooms

Katherine L. McNeill
BOSTON COLLEGE

As described throughout the first section of this book, with recent reform efforts (National Research Council, 2015) and standards such as the NGSS (NGSS Lead States, 2013) the vision of elementary science has shifted. Elementary science should not focus solely on defining terms or memorizing science facts (such as a force is a push or a pull). It also should not focus on science process skills, the scientific method or other "contentless" activities (such as writing a procedure for making a peanut butter and jelly sandwich). Instead, the current vision of elementary science advocates for students making sense of real-world phenomena as they use evidence to construct and critique multiple explanations or models. Yet this shift towards science-as-practice is often not prevalent in elementary classrooms. Furthermore, if science practices are included in elementary school science, instruction often focuses on a subset of the science practices, such as planning and carrying out investigations, with limited opportunities for students to engage in sensemaking around constructing explanations, developing models or engaging in argument from evidence (McNeill *et al.*, 2018).

Themes from Images of the Possible

The four chapters in Section I, *Images of the Possible*, provide invaluable examples and strategies for integrating the science practices into elementary classrooms. Across these chapters, some common themes are highlighted related to the science practices. Table 6.1 includes a summary of the themes, which cut across the different chapters, and are critical for integrating and supporting science practices in elementary classrooms. These themes offer concrete strategies for developing rich science instruction for every student. In this section, each theme is described in more detail using examples from across the different chapters.

Phenomena

Each of the classroom cases includes a shared phenomenon to ground and elicit student questions to support science instruction. Using a phenomenon

88 *McNeill*

Table 6.1 Themes for Integrating and Supporting Science Practices

Theme	Examples from Chapters
Phenomena: Start science instruction with a **phenomenon to** integrate science practices into instruction.	Ms. Cody's fifth-grade water unit (Cody and Biggers, this volume, Chapter 3) was motivated by a local phenomenon—the town was debating whether to build a luxury university student housing development near the aquifer that supplies the community with water. This phenomenon was used to introduce the question, *How does water quality affect the ecology of a community?*
Evidence: **Evidence** plays a key role in all of the science practices.	Ms. Medina and Marbles in Motion (Zembal-Saul and Hershberger, this volume, Chapter 1) illustrates how students can collect data and use that evidence to making claims about their investigation. In addition, this focus on evidence raised important questions and ideas about future data the class needed to make claims about speed.
Student-driven discourse: Students' participation in and doing the **heavy lifting** in scientific **discourse** is essential for the science practices.	Ms. Kerry's case (Bismack and Haefner, this volume, Chapter 2) of exploring a melted crayon illustrates first-graders engaging in rich student-driven discourse. Instead of Ms. Kerry correcting the claim that a liquid turns into a solid "By letting it sit," she redirected the question to the class: "Is that what you think did it? Just letting it sit for a bit?" which encouraged multiple students to share ideas and questions in collaborative sensemaking.
Experience before scientific vocabulary: Students should engage in rich investigations and discourse focused on science ideas before the teacher introduces scientific vocabulary.	Ms. Meryl's third-grade unit (Hooper and Zembal-Saul, this volume, Chapter 4) illustrates how students can engage in social sensemaking using the science practices before being introduced to scientific vocabulary. For example, Ms. Meryl's students engaged in two days of investigations about levers before she co-constructed with her class the definition for the term "fulcrum." She used the students experiences to define as a class a fulcrum as "the point on which the lever sits or moves."

to begin a unit can look very different from previous models of science instruction which often started by providing students with the name of a topic using academic language (e.g., *We are now going to start a unit on simple machines. Who can tell me what a simple machine is?*). Instead, starting science units with an anchoring phenomenon provide a common experience for every student that leads to questions that can motivate the unit storyline as students engage in science practices to make sense of the phenomenon (Reiser *et al.*, 2017). This anchoring phenomenon can engage students and empower them to help drive the instruction with their own questions.

To select and use phenomena in science instruction, it can be helpful to consider two key elements of a phenomenon: 1) It needs to be observable in a classroom; 2) It can either be from a natural or designed system (Lowell and McNeill, in press). In terms of observable, this can take on many forms such as an in-class investigation, a video, or a written case. Students need to somehow observe the phenomena in order to have a shared experience that offers greater equity and access for all students. Since all students have this common experience, regardless of their background outside of school, this provides each student with an entry point to notice, wonder and develop their own questions. There are many different types of phenomena that students can observe. Natural phenomena are ones that occur in the world around us (e.g., *Why does the glass break when a singer hits a specific pitch?*), while designed phenomena involve engineered solutions to questions or problems by humans (e.g., *How can I design a boat that will stay afloat holding the most weight?*). Across all of these different types of phenomena, they serve a common purpose to ground students in a shared experience that drives student wonderings and questions to motivate their engagement and sense-making using science practices.

All four teacher cases in this section are grounded in phenomena. In the case of Ms. Medina, students observed a video of a cart moving along a roller coaster track through loops, inclines and drops before launching into their own investigations. For Ms. Kerry's first-grade classroom students investigated the phenomenon of a melted crayon to explore the question, *How can you change a liquid into a solid?* In Ms. Cody's case of her fifth-grade students the science unit was motivated by a local phenomenon—the town was deliberating over whether to build a luxury university student housing development near the aquifer that supplied the community with water. This phenomenon was used to motivate the driving question, *How does water quality affect the ecology of a community?* Ms. Meryl's third-grade unit began with a phenomenon in their classroom. In the corner of her room was a two-story treehouse structure and students were challenged to develop a plan to bring a basket of books into the treehouse. The unit centered around this phenomenon with the overarching question of, *How can we lift a load into our treehouse?* In order to answer this question, students not only needed to engage in science practices but also develop a conceptual understanding of simple machines.

In all four of these examples, using a phenomenon as an initial driver not only engaged students in the science practices, but also supported students' development of disciplinary core ideas as they made sense of the phenomenon. The four examples also illustrate the range of phenomena that can be used to motivate and support student learning. Phenomena can be introduced to students through a video (e.g., roller coaster), science investigation (e.g., melted crayon), a local issue (e.g., housing development near an aquifer) or an example (e.g., treehouse with books in classroom). These four cases illustrate that there are many ways to design and use phenomena, but

90   *McNeill*

that across these diverse ways phenomena play a key role in the shift to elementary science-as-practice. This shift provides greater student access and engagement in making sense of the world around them.

Evidence

Evidence is an essential component of science classroom instruction that actively engages students in science practices for the purpose of sensemaking (McNeill and Berland, 2017). In science, evidence is data, such as observations or measurements, about the natural or designed world. Evidence is linked to all eight of the science practices whether it is thinking about what evidence to collect (e.g., asking scientific questions), collecting the evidence (e.g., conducting investigations), making sense of the evidence (e.g., analyzing and interpreting data, constructing explanations) or critiquing competing ideas using evidence (e.g., engaging in argument from evidence). Evidence use is threaded throughout a unit as the science story unfolds. Purposefully integrating evidence use in science classrooms can help move instruction away from final form science in which students are memorizing ideas that are being given to them by the teacher or a text (McNeill and Berland, 2017). Instead, students figure out their questions and wonderings by collecting, using, and making sense of evidence.

Across all four cases, students worked with evidence during different science practices. In the case of Ms. Medina, students grappled with the evidence they had collected in their first investigation as well as what evidence they needed to collect in the future. While engaging in sensemaking about the data they collected about the distance traveled by the marble in relation to the height of the ramp, students generated questions about the speed of the marble. In order to answer this question about speed, students considered what data they needed and how to generate that evidence. The focus on evidence both pushed their understanding of the current investigation, but also encouraged them to think about next steps in the science storyline of their unit. In Ms. Kerry's first-grade classroom, she continuously referred students back to their observations and data as they debated two potential claims related to the melted crayon changing from a liquid to a solid—just let it sit versus heat needs to leave. She encouraged the students to use the evidence as they engaged in sensemaking about the competing claims. In Ms. Cody's fifth-grade water unit about their local community, students collected and made sense of evidence from multiple sources including science investigations, local newspaper articles and speakers who came to their class to discuss the potential impact of the housing development project on local water quality. For example, when the speakers came to class they presented scientific data for their particular stance, which students had to make sense of in relation to a real-life example. Finally, Ms. Meryl's third-grade class also relied on evidence as they engaged in sensemaking to develop a richer understanding of simple machines. For example, they began by exploring levers using both Lego™ and a plank of wood and a brick to collect data. They used this evidence to construct a claim that answers the question, *How can we lift the teacher?* Across all of these cases, students used evidence to make sense of the phenomena and develop richer conceptual understandings as the story of the unit unfolded.

Student-Driven Discourse

The authors of this section also clearly highlight and illustrate the importance of student-driven discourse in these science practice rich classrooms. Students engage in productive discourse with their peers as they investigate phenomena and make sense of their evidence. This can look very different from traditional science instruction in which the talk predominately comes from the teacher as s/he explains science ideas to the class. The ownership and culture shifts from teacher-directed to student-driven discourse in these elementary classrooms.

Making students' ideas public through talk encourages the development of a community in which the whole class works together to build understandings of phenomena. By using "talk moves" such as "What's your evidence?," "Does it always work that way?," and "Do you agree/disagree? (and why?)," teachers can support a shift in their classroom discourse in which students do more of the heavy lifting such as the reasoning and figuring out about evidence and science ideas (Michaels and O'Connor, 2017). This requires a shift in the role of the teacher from doing things "for" students to doing things "with" students. By using talk moves and other strategies, teachers can encourage students to reason and collaboratively engage in sensemaking.

For example, in the case of Ms. Medina after completing an investigation in which students collected data about *distance,* she did not correct a student who read a claim with both speed and distance. Instead, she restated the claim and turned it back to the class encouraging greater student sensemaking and ownership of these ideas. This talk move resulted in the class developing a new question—*How does the height of the roller coaster affect how fast the marble goes?* In Ms. Kerry's case, her first-grade students engaged in rich discourse as they debated different claims for how to change a liquid into a solid. Some students thought "you had to let it sit" while other students thought "the warmth was leaving it made the liquid into a solid." Instead of simply providing students with the scientifically accurate answer, Ms. Kerry used talk moves to support the students in helping each other develop a richer understanding of these science ideas. During Ms. Cody's fifth-grade unit on water quality, students engaged in discussions in which they weighed different sides of arguments and considered the perspectives of multiple stakeholders in relation to their local water quality issue. Ms. Meryl's instruction with her third-grade students relied heaving on student discourse in both whole group and small group discussions. She encouraged her students to engage in rich social sensemaking through science talk.

92 *McNeill*

Together these examples illustrate the importance of science talk within elementary classrooms as students engage in science practices. The role of the teacher is not to dominate the discourse or to give the students the correct answer. Instead, the teacher is a facilitator who works "with" students to support the class in thinking together as they ask questions and use evidence to make sense of phenomena and science ideas.

Experience before Scientific Vocabulary

In addition to discourse, language is essential in science instruction in elementary classrooms. The science practices are language intensive as they require students to read, write, view, speak and listen as they engage in the processes of constructing and critiquing explanations and models (Lee *et al.*, 2013). Although the science practices are language intensive, this does not advocate for the preteaching of scientific vocabulary. Instead, research suggests the importance of every student, including English learners, using their everyday languages and experiences to *first* make sense of phenomena rather than beginning instruction by introducing and defining science terminology (González-Howard and McNeill, 2016). This can look different from previous science units that may have started with providing students with academic language and defining the terms for them (e.g., *We are starting a unit on solids. A solid is a type of matter that has a definite shape, volume and mass*). Instead, students should develop scientific language through their active participation in science practices and rich discourse as they engage in sensemaking with their peers.

The cases in this chapter highlight the importance of experiencing science using the practices before defining key science vocabulary. Furthermore, they highlight the importance of focusing on a few key science terms rather than a long list of new scientific vocabulary. For example, in the case of Ms. Medina, students discussed and developed investigations on how to measure speed during their investigations of roller coasters before she introduced the scientific definition that speed is the distance traveled per unit time. In Ms. Kerry's unit on magnets, she first encouraged her first-graders to share their experiences with magnets using their everyday language. After discussing their ideas about how magnets "stick them together" she then introduced the science vocabulary of "attract" as a science word for "stick." In Ms. Meryl's class focused on *How can we lift a load into our treehouse?*, they spent two days investigating levers before defining the "fulcrum" as a class. She leveraged the students' experiments with both Lego™ and a wooden plank and brick to experience the science ideas before co-constructing the definition of a fulcrum as "the point on which the lever sits or moves."

As illustrated throughout these chapters (and discussed in detail in Hooper and Zembal-Saul, this volume, Chapter 4) beginning teaching with direct instruction of scientific terms and definitions can serve as a barrier for student learning. Instead, students need to experience the science ideas as they use science practices to wrestle with phenomena. After experiencing the key disciplinary ideas, scientific vocabulary should then be introduced and tied to those experiences to promote deeper meaning and equitable instruction for all students. It is important to consider both the timing and the way we introduce scientific vocabulary to elementary students as we support them in engaging in science.

Summary

All four chapters provide rich images of teachers and students engaged in science-as-practice in elementary classrooms. These *Images of the Possible* allow us to envision elementary science instruction that meets the call in recent reform efforts and science standards for science practices. Threaded throughout these images are four themes related to:

1 phenomena;
2 evidence;
3 student-driven discourse; and
4 experience before scientific vocabulary.

All four of these elements provide important guidelines and strategies to consider as we support and integrate science practices into elementary classroom instruction. Utilizing these strategies can help us shift away from traditional science instruction in which students are memorizing science facts or engaged in "contentless" activities to three-dimensional science instruction that supports all students in access and opportunities for meaningful science instruction. These strategies can help create a classroom culture in which the teacher works *with* the students as they make sense of the natural and designed worlds around them.

References

González-Howard, M. and McNeill, K. L. (2016). Learning in a community of practice: Factors impacting English-learning students' engagement in scientific argumentation. *Journal of Research in Science Teaching, 53*(4), 527–553.

Lee, O., Quinn, H. and Valdés, G. (2013). Science and language for English language learners in relation to Next Generation Science Standards and with implications for common core state standards for English language arts and mathematics. *Educational Researcher, 42*(4), 223–233.

Lowell, B. R. and McNeill, K. L. (in press). Keeping critical thinking afloat: Shifting from activity-based to phenomenon-based planning. *Science Scope.*

McNeill, K. L. and Berland, L. (2017). What is (or should be) scientific evidence use in K-12 classrooms? *Journal of Research in Science Teaching, 54*(5), 672–689.

McNeill, K.L., Lowenhaupt, R., and Katsh-Singer, R. (2018). Instructional leadership and the implementation of the NGSS: Principals' understandings of science practices. *Science Education, 102*(3), 452–473.

Michaels, S. and O'Connor, C. (2017). From recitation to reasoning: Supporting scientific and engineering practices through talk. In C. V. Schwarz, C. M. Passmore, and B. J. Reiser (Eds.), *Helping Students Make Sense of the World Through Next Generation Science and Engineering Practices* (pp. 311–336). Arlington, VA: NSTA Press.

National Research Council. (2015). *Guide to Implementing the Next Generation Science Standards*. Washington, DC: National Academies Press.

NGSS Lead States. (2013). *Next Generation Science Standards: For States, By States*. Washington, DC: National Academies Press.

Reiser, B. J., Novak, M., and McGill, T. A. W. (2017). *Coherence from the Students' Perspective: Why the Vision of the Framework for K-12 Science Requires More Than Simply "Combining" Three Dimensions of Science Learning*. Washington, DC: National Academies of Sciences, Engineering, and Medicine, Board on Science Education.

Section II

Promising Practices, Tools, and Frameworks

7 Approximations of Practice
Scaffolding for Preservice Teachers

Elizabeth A. Davis
UNIVERSITY OF MICHIGAN

Acknowledgments

I appreciate the opportunity to work with my colleagues in the Elementary Science Methods Planning Group and the many preservice teachers who have helped me learn and grow as an elementary science teacher educator over my years at the University of Michigan.

Approximations of Practice: Scaffolding for Preservice Teachers

Teacher educators have traditionally relied on pedagogies of reflection and investigation (Grossman *et al.*, 2009b), and supported beginning teachers in developing an important knowledge base and analytic skills for teaching (Ball and Forzani, 2009). But teaching is interactive, contingent, and intricate (Ball and Forzani, 2009; Grossman *et al.*, 2009a), with students contributing ideas in real time and with teachers needing to support the learning of students with different needs, backgrounds, interests, and experiences. How can they learn to engage in elementary science teaching of the sort described in this volume (e.g., Bismack and Haefner, this volume, Chapter 2; Zembal-Saul and Hershberger, this volume, Chapter 1)?

Pedagogies of practice (Grossman *et al.*, 2009a; or pedagogies of enactment, Grossman *et al.*, 2009b) are teacher education pedagogies (including representations, decompositions, and approximations of practice) that support learning to do the actual work of teaching, centered on developing a set of high-leverage or core teaching practices (e.g., Ball and Forzani, 2009; Windschitl *et al.*, 2012). Practice-based teacher education does not simply increase the time preservice teachers spend in the field. Instead, it is "professional training that attempts to focus novices' learning more directly on the work of teaching rather than on traditional academic or theoretical topics," with focus on a set of high-leverage practices drawing on a rich knowledge base (Forzani, 2014, p. 357; Grossman *et al.*, 2009b; Zeichner, 2012). I explore the role *approximations of practice* can play in scaffolding preservice teachers in learning to teach, with the goal of helping teacher educators design more effective and efficient learning experiences. I use the

98   *Davis*

work of one preservice teacher to illustrate these approximations and how they serve to scaffold.

Theoretical Framework

Teacher learning is situated, social, and distributed; preservice teachers construct knowledge and appropriate practice together with others and through using tools (Putnam and Borko, 2000; Vygotsky, 1978). Preservice teacher learning entails learning to do the practices of teaching that will be used in classrooms; the learning is *situated* within the profession. Because of the complex nature of those practices, initial work may be more simple and less authentic (e.g., eliciting one child's ideas before attempting to do so with a whole class of children; cf. Davis, Palincsar, and Kademian, this volume, Chapter 13). Preservice teachers learn with others more knowledgeable than themselves (such as their mentor teachers, field instructors, and other teacher educators) as well as other preservice teachers, so their learning is *social*. Because learning entails gaining access to and skill in the authentic knowledge and practices of a profession, preservice teachers move toward increasingly authentic teaching experiences, and more knowledgeable others help them learn within those experiences. Preservice teacher learning is *distributed* across these communities of practice or social systems and across tools that support their performance. Through supporting situated, social, and distributed learning of teaching practice, approximations of practice can help preservice teachers learn to teach.

Approximations of practice are "opportunities for novices to engage in practices that are more or less proximal to the practices of a profession" (Grossman *et al.*, 2009a, p. 2058)—for example, teaching a small group of students (see, e.g., Lampert *et al.*, 2013). High-leverage teaching practices that might be worked on through approximations of practice could include eliciting students' science ideas, leading a whole class discussion, or meeting with a parent (Davis and Boerst, 2014; Kazemi *et al.*, 2009; Grossman *et al.*, 2009b).

Approximations of practice are intended to support preservice teachers in engaging in deliberate practice (Lampert *et al.*, 2013). Deliberate practice refers to the purposeful, effortful activities in which individuals engage with the intent of optimizing their improvement in their performance of an endeavor (Ericsson *et al*, 1993). Approximations allow learners to experience "instructive failure" (Grossman *et al.*, 2009a, p. 2077)—they allow room for error in a safe, low-stakes environment. The goal is careful attention to and reflection on the particulars of instructional moves in relationship to learners and content.

Based on this description, I argue that approximations of practice serve as scaffolded learning experiences for preservice teachers. *Scaffolding*—associated with Vygotsky's (1978) notion of a zone of proximal development and consistent with a view of learning as situated, social, and distributed—implies that given appropriate assistance, a learner can attain a goal or engage in a practice otherwise out of reach (Wood, Bruner, and Ross, 1976). Van de Pol *et al.* (2010), analyzing the literature on scaffolding, identified categories of *scaffolding intentions*: support of learners' (a) metacognitive activity, (b) (socio)cognitive activity,[1] and (c) affect. While these categories—like most such frameworks—are imperfect in that some forms of scaffolding work toward multiple goals, the framework serves as an analytic tool to identify similarities across scaffolding.

Metacognitive scaffolding can include promoting monitoring and helping the learner maintain direction—essentially, helping the learner to continue to focus on and move toward the goal, as well as to articulate their ideas. *Sociocognitive* scaffolding can involve both conceptual and procedural scaffolding and can include, for example, support that narrows options (in the scaffolding literature, this is referred to as reducing the degrees of freedom, restricting the problem space, and narrowing choices). It also can include helping the learner identify what is important (marking critical features of the task and highlighting the task's salient features) and providing help (in the form of expert guidance and by highlighting gaps or problems with the understanding or performance). *Affective* scaffolding can include managing the learner's frustration (e.g., by calibrating the provision of expert guidance) and creating interest, curiosity, and engagement.

Scaffolding in any of these categories can *structure* a task—that is, "address the challenges learners face ... to make [a task] more tractable" or manageable for learners (Reiser, 2004, p. 274). Reiser continues, "The core idea [of structuring] is that by providing structure or constraints, perhaps in the form of explicit direction or by narrowing choices, the complexity facing the learner is reduced and the problem solving is more tractable" (p. 283). Table 7.1 gives examples of how scaffolding can structure a task for learners (drawing on, e.g., Reiser, 2004; Van de Pol *et al.*, 2010; Wood *et al.*, 1976, and organized using Van de Pol *et al.*'s framework).

Approximations of practice, ideally, structure the task. In learning to teach, the "task" that is being worked on is some aspect of the work of teaching (Ball and Forzani, 2009)—perhaps, a teaching practice or set of practices. Approximations of practice provide structure for this work—for example, through decomposing a practice and highlighting its salient features. Approximations reduce the complexity of the practice or compilation of practices, by foregrounding some aspects of teaching while backgrounding others, while helping the novice to maintain attention on the goal and controlling frustration with teaching's complexities.

Scaffolding in any of the three categories can also serve to *problematize* tasks—"to shape tasks for learners in ways that make their problem solving more productive" (Reiser, 2004, p. 274). The goal of this scaffolding mechanism of problematizing is to "guide the learner into facing complexity in the domain that will be productive for learning" (p. 288). In doing so, the support makes the task more complex, more interesting, and non-trivial. Table 7.1 also gives examples of how scaffolding can problematize a task. Not surprisingly, some scaffolding both structures *and* problematizes.

100   *Davis*

Table 7.1 Examples of Structuring and Problematizing Intentions

	Examples of structuring intentions	*Examples of problematizing intentions*
Primarily *metacognitive* scaffolding	Maintaining direction Promoting monitoring	Maintaining direction "Rocking the boat" (Reiser, 2004, p. 288) when students are not being mindful enough Eliciting articulation Eliciting decisions
Primarily *(socio)cognitive* scaffolding (conceptual and procedural)	Reducing the degrees of freedom Restricting the problem space Narrowing choices Decomposing a complex task Highlighting the salient features of a task Focusing effort Providing expert guidance	Marking critical features of a task Highlighting the salient features of a task Highlighting discrepancies (problems with the "production" or performance) Surfacing gaps and disagreements Focusing attention on issues that need resolution
Primarily *affective* scaffolding	Controlling frustration	Creating interest Recruiting learners to the task Engaging via dissonance or curiosity

Approximations of practice can problematize tasks for preservice teachers. They force attention to the important particulars of a teaching practice; highlight ways that the practice, as enacted, is inadequate (e.g., how a closed-ended question shuts down discussion); and support reflection on the enactment.

Structuring and problematizing allow the task—in this case, the new teaching practice—to be worked on in a meaningful and deliberate way. Reiser (2004) describes the need for careful balance between providing assistance, on the one hand, and ensuring that the work on a task is productive for learning, on the other. Eventually, the learner takes more autonomy and the scaffolding fades, and the practice is developed in more authentic contexts.

I outline three examples from the University of Michigan's elementary science methods class next, to illustrate how teacher educators can design experiences to structure and problematize learning to teach and to increase the effectiveness and the efficiency of our designs.

Practice-Based Experiences: Scaffolding through Structuring and Problematizing

We[2] have organized a series of practice-based elementary science teaching experiences into three types. These approximations of practice include *peer-*

teaching rehearsal experiences, small-scale field-based teaching experiences, and *full teaching experiences*. These fall along a rough continuum (see Table 7.2), increasing in both authenticity and complexity (see, e.g., Grossman *et al.*, 2009b; Lampert *et al.*, 2013). By "authentic" I mean close to the genuine work of classroom teaching. By "complexity" I refer to the number and difficulty of teaching moves being managed at once. The peer-teaching rehearsal experiences are least authentic and complex, as well as the most highly scaffolded, whereas the full lessons are most authentic and complex, and the least scaffolded, demonstrating a gradual release of responsibility. Teacher educators likely see aspects of their own instructional approaches reflected here, though the attention may be at a larger grain size, rather than on developing specific high-leverage teaching practices (Zeichner, 2012).

Some empirical work has explored these approximations of practice in the same university context and elsewhere (e.g., Arias, this volume, Chapter 11; Benedict-Chambers, this volume, Chapter 10), and demonstrate how they support situated, social, and distributed learning. This work, complementing the broader literature base, suggests that each approximation has affordances for preservice teachers' learning. Nelson (2011), for example, found that peer-teaching rehearsals served as existence proofs for preservice teachers, helping them recognize the kinds of science teaching in which they might be able to engage. Benedict-Chambers (2014) noted the importance of roles in peer-teaching rehearsals, describing how acting as a student helped the preservice teachers learn to attend to student thinking. Nelson (2011) found that small-scale teaching experiences, which break a lesson into lesson elements[3], helped preservice teachers to see the value of each part of a science lesson. Teaching full science lessons as described here provides opportunities to practice important aspects of science teaching such as adapting lesson plans to be more inquiry oriented (Forbes and Davis, 2010). Looking across the suite of approximations, Arias (2015; see also Arias, this volume, Chapter 11) found that preservice teachers experienced success in engaging in a sophisticated science teaching practice during the highly scaffolded peer-teaching rehearsals. Their success diminished as they moved into the more complex and less scaffolded full science teaching experiences (see also Kademian, 2017).

Next I illustrate how these approximations of practice both structure (i.e., make practices more tractable or manageable for learners) and problematize (i.e., make practices more complex). I draw on samples of work (written

Table 7.2 Continuum of Authenticity and Complexity

	Peer teaching	*Small-scale field-based teaching*	*Full teaching experiences*
Level of authenticity	Lowest	Middle	Highest
Level of complexity	Lowest	Middle	Highest

102   *Davis*

plans, videorecorded enactments, written reflections) from a purposefully selected preservice teacher, pseudonym "Eliza." I don't intend to provide empirical evidence of these approximations' efficacy for Eliza specifically or her colleagues in general. Rather, I use Eliza's case to illustrate what the approximations are like and how their designs serve to structure and problematize. Eliza was demographically typical of her colleagues (i.e., she was white, female, and approximately 21 years old). Eliza's engagement with the integration of science content and scientific practices was atypical, however, in that she focused her attention on this integration to a greater extent than many of her peers and experienced more success. She thus provides an interesting case to highlight.

Approximation of Practice #1: Peer-Teaching Rehearsal Experiences

The *peer-teaching rehearsal experiences* engage interns (the term for prospective teachers in our program) in the interactional work around science instruction. (See Table 7.3.) Rehearsals provide opportunities for novices to learn to do the work of teaching in low-stakes contexts (e.g., Kazemi *et al.*, 2009; Lampert *et al.*, 2013). Because our science methods class occurs late in our program (see Davis, Palincsar, and Kademian, this volume, Chapter 13, for a description of the course), the peer-teaching experiences are designed to entail multiple science teaching practices (such as eliciting students' ideas about natural phenomena and supporting students in data collection). They are not full science lessons. Each peer-teaching rehearsal experience involves co-planning using an existing lesson plan, enactment in small groups, and co-reflection. For each enactment, a few interns experience the "teacher" role in parallel, working separately with a small group of colleagues as "students" as well as a teacher educator. In the enactment, the teacher educator facilitates in-the-moment feedback and, at times, recommends "stop-actions" and "rewinds." Feedback might provide the "teacher" constructive criticism or publicly highlight an effective instructional move. A

Table 7.3 Peer-Teaching Rehearsal Experiences in a Science Methods Course

Peer teaching experience	Description
Engage	Establish an investigation question and elicit students' initial ideas about a scientific phenomenon (e.g., ideas about force and motion)
Experience	Establish data collection with students and support students in carrying out investigation (e.g., collecting distance data related to balls rolling down a ramp)
Explain+Argue with Evidence	Support students in identifying patterns in data (e.g., mass, distance), generating claims about scientific phenomenon supported by evidence, and applying knowledge to new problems

stop-action allows the intern to pause and regroup before continuing. In a rewind, the intern is given the opportunity to stop the action, and to try an instructional move again, in a different way (cf. Davis *et al.*, 2017; Lampert *et al.*, 2013). For example, after stumbling over how to word a question intended to elicit students' ideas, an intern might be stopped by a teacher educator and asked to develop, and then ask, a better-formulated question. Alternatively, if an intern makes a particularly nice move that serves to broaden the students' sense of who is scientifically proficient, the teacher educator might comment publicly, to highlight ways in which the intern is moving toward more equitable and just science teaching.

I use the case of Eliza to illustrate this approximation.[4] Eliza planned and enacted three peer-teaching lesson portions—segments of a lesson about force and motion (see Table 7.3). For the final element, she was expected to support her "students" in identifying patterns in the data (related to balls of different masses rolling down a ramp) and making a claim supported by evidence. Eliza planned (Eliza Motion lesson plan, 10/28/12) a systematic way of organizing her students' data on the board that would help them see patterns in it. Her plan also included a sentence stem for supporting the claim with evidence. During her enactment, her teacher educator might have signaled these strengths to Eliza and her colleagues as something to notice and replicate; these elements would support engaging each student in rigorous and consequential learning. Her plan did not, however, include a way of having students consider how their own explanation was similar to or different from the other students'. The teacher educator, therefore, might have chosen to pause Eliza's enactment and ask her to use a discourse move to ask students to consider one another's explanations. After her enactment, her colleagues might have discussed the different approaches to data organization and representation possible in this lesson.

The peer-teaching rehearsal experiences are, by design, the most highly structured of the three approximations of practice. Several of the scaffolding intentions support interns *sociocognitively*. These experiences reduce the degrees of freedom for the novices by decreasing the number of students, changing who the students are (to adult colleagues), and limiting the amount of instruction, thus making the performance more accessible for novices (Grossman *et al.*, 2009a). For example, we provide interns with lesson plans to use as well as tools that support their planning (cf. Kademian and Davis, this volume, Chapter 8). Eliza worked from a commercial lesson plan we had provided her, and used tools from the methods class to adapt that lesson for peer teaching. By providing plans and tools, the teacher educator narrows choices, focuses the interns' efforts, and restricts the problem space (cf. Lampert *et al.*, 2013). The plans and accompanying tools also decompose the practice further (e.g., by breaking down a science lesson into sub-components that align with scientific practices such as data collection and data analysis). This decomposition serves to highlight salient features of certain science teaching practices (cf. Arias, this volume, Chapter 11). For example, Eliza focused a portion of her plan and enactment on data analysis and another portion on making a claim supported by evidence—both science practices highlighted by the decomposition tools. Furthermore, the teacher educator, informed by a feedback guide aligned with a class framework, provides real-time feedback and expert guidance during the enactment, making suggestions that may limit the degrees of freedom further. The intern's colleagues can highlight salient features of the practice as well. The peer-teaching experiences further structure the learning through "stop actions" and "rewinds," giving the intern an opportunity to pause to collect her thoughts or, if something has gone awry, to try it again (Lampert *et al.*, 2013; see also Davis *et al.*, 2017). Eliza, for example, could have tried in real time having students respond to one another's explanations.

The structured design of the peer-teaching rehearsal experiences also demonstrates *metacognitive* scaffolding. Through the teacher educator's feedback based on interns' strengths and struggles, the tight parameters around the lesson-portions taught, and the use of rubrics, interns can maintain direction and monitor progress. The teacher educator also facilitates reflection, through written prompts and oral discourse in the class. *Affectively*, the teacher educator helps interns control their frustration by making concrete suggestions for improvements and framing peer-teaching rehearsal as a low-stakes opportunity to learn. Eliza and her colleagues could work together to improve their science teaching practice. In these ways, this approximation of practice serves as scaffolding to make the work of learning to engage in science teaching more tractable for novices—that is, to structure the work.

At the same time, the design of the peer-teaching rehearsal experiences problematizes the work for novices. Interns are expected to teach parts of lessons that entail not just science content, but also scientific practices; this complexifies the work of science teaching beyond what interns may have observed in elementary classrooms. For example, Eliza wasn't teaching about data analysis in the abstract; she was integrating science practices with core ideas related to force and motion. The teacher educator observing the peer teaching enactment is likely to complexify the teaching practice. Eliza's planned public representation for analyzing the data would allow fairly systematic analysis. Many interns, however, fail to plan for how to publicly compile and represent groups' data, leading to stumbling during this portion of the peer teaching rehearsal. If one of Eliza's colleagues exhibited such a struggle, the teacher educator helps to surface gaps and discrepancies between the intern's performance and the goal performance and focus her attention on an issue that needs resolution—namely, the development and use of a representation that will help students see patterns in the data (cf. Arias, this volume, Chapter 11; Kademian and Davis, this volume, Chapter 8; Zembal-Saul and Hershberger, this volume, Chapter 1).

Metacognitively, an interruption like this serves to elicit decisions, as well; Eliza's hypothetical colleague would, in the case described above, need to develop an appropriate representation to use, on the spot. The peer-teaching rehearsal design requires and supports reflection; interns engaged in the peer-teaching experiences reflect on dimensions of the teaching practice. The teacher educator's input also acts *affectively*. The teacher educator works to recruit the interns by helping them see the connection to their own classroom practice. Similarly, the intern's colleagues can spur curiosity about the practice by bringing up experiences from their own work with children. A teacher educator might also spur dissonance (and through it, engagement) by noting a mismatch between an intern's practice (e.g., telling "students" the answer) and their espoused beliefs (e.g., wanting students to construct understandings; see Arias, 2015). All of these characteristics serve to make the practice more complex—to problematize it (Reiser, 2004)—and thus offer the opportunity for more productive learning.

Approximation of Practice #2: Small-Scale Teaching Experiences

The second practice-based experience, the *small-scale field-based teaching experiences,* takes place in elementary classrooms with children. Interns teach portions of lessons to a small group of students or the whole class. This move from rehearsal to practicum classroom is typical in practice-based teacher education.

For example, Eliza taught the central investigation portion of a lesson on the role of decomposers (in this case, earthworms) in her fourth-grade classroom. Eliza's plan (Eliza Worm lesson plan, 10/4/12) and enactment showed her careful work with children on the scientific practice of *observation*, an aspect of science teaching practice not typical in Eliza's placement classroom or in US classrooms in general (Banilower *et al.*, 2013). Eliza asked her students, for example, "What are you noticing about this?" and "You noticed there was a lot of worm poop. What does that tell you?" (Eliza Worm lesson video, October 2012). Thus, due to the intentional design of this approximation, in this lesson-portion, Eliza had the opportunity to support data collection and interpretation—high-leverage science teaching practices—and she drew on her knowledge and skill as a teacher to do so. She was able to practice providing the kind of hands-on investigative experience that helps to bring rigorous and consequential learning to the elementary classroom. She did not bear the burden, however, of launching or closing the lesson.

How do these experiences structure the work? The design of the small-scale, field-based teaching experiences provides numerous examples of *sociocognitive* scaffolding. These reduce the degrees of freedom by limiting the amount of instruction (to one portion of a science lesson—in Eliza's case, the investigation of decomposition cups with and without earthworms) that entails certain teaching practices, and in some cases, the degrees of freedom are further reduced by decreasing the number of students from a whole class to a small group. Here, however, the students are actual elementary children (with their range of backgrounds and experiences), and the length of the instruction may be longer than 15 minutes. These experiences structure the work of teaching by specifying the type of lesson portion to be taught, highlighting salient features of science teaching (i.e., typical lesson segments) while reducing choices and restricting the problem space (e.g., by focusing on investigation-based lessons). Because the experience was designed so that the intern only needed to teach the data collection and data analysis portions of the lesson, Eliza was able to focus on how to support the children's observations of the decomposition cups. The mentor teacher and the intern's field instructor are often both present, and can provide expert guidance and assistance (and potentially *affective* support) if needed. The design also *metacognitively* structures, by maintaining interns' direction through focusing their attention on specific elements of science lessons. Eliza, for example, could focus on supporting students' observations, not (in this teaching experience) on developing arguments. The design also does *affective* work, helping to control frustration by reducing the number of demands on the intern's attention in their early science teaching experiences.

These small-scale, field-based teaching experiences also intentionally problematize the work. The intern is expected to select the lesson to be taught so it aligns with the instructional work in the classroom (thus creating interest in the intern, who is highly invested in the placement classroom—*affective* scaffolding). Furthermore, these lessons are expected to entail both science content and scientific practices; this expectation helps to maintain direction (*metacognitive* scaffolding) and mark critical features (*sociocognitive* scaffolding) of science teaching. Eliza, for example, integrated the science practice of making careful observations with the core ideas related to decomposition (the cycling of matter). Finally, the design of the approximation of practice requires that the intern reflect on the enactment using videorecords (*metacognitive* scaffolding). Eliza's reflection—supported by the design of the assignment, which asked, "A specific place in the video in need of revision is _____ (*insert time stamp*). Why is this move in need of revision? How would you revise it?"—also focused her attention on issues that needed resolution (*sociocognitive* scaffolding): she noted that her students' observations were vague and lacked detail, and she went on to suggest an improvement. In these ways, the small-scale, field-based teaching experiences could problematize the practice and support Eliza and her colleagues in obtaining productive opportunities to learn.

Approximation of Practice #3: Full Teaching Experiences

Finally, the *full teaching experiences*—detailed less fully here because they are more typical in teacher education—provide the opportunity to teach full investigation-based science lessons to a whole class of children. Asking the interns to enact a full science lesson requires them to demonstrate a nontrivial engagement in the task of authentic science teaching. (Eliza taught a

Approximations of Practice 107

lesson exploring the states of matter.) Here, again, the mentor teacher and field instructor provide expert guidance and assistance if needed, providing *sociocognitive* scaffolding associated with structuring the work (as well as potentially *affective* support). Per the assignment design, the intern engages in reflection on the enactment (*metacognitive* scaffolding), identifying video records from the enactment that demonstrate key elements of the teaching practice(s) on which the intern focused. This forces articulation and may focus attention on issues in the enactment itself that need resolution—*metacognitive* and *sociocognitive* supports that problematize. The full teaching experience assignment creates interest (*affective* scaffolding) through connection to the field placement classroom. Thus, the full teaching experience provides some structure, and some problematizing, but is less highly scaffolded and more authentic and complex than either of the other two types of teaching experiences.

Discussion, Implications, and Conclusions

What can we learn about designing teacher education experiences from interpreting approximations of practice through the lens of structuring and problematizing?

First, teacher educators can consider how approximations of practice can structure the work of teaching and thus support learning to teach for novices. Approximations of practice "quiet the background noise" (Grossman *et al.*, 2009a, p. 2083). Table 7.4 provides questions to guide teacher educators' design of approximations of practice that structure.

While making the work of teaching more tractable for novices is important, at the same time, teacher educators must attend to ways in which approximations of practice problematize the work of teaching for interns, fostering deliberate practice. Quieting the background noise does not suffice for promoting teacher learning. Table 7.5 provides design questions that can guide teacher educators in developing approximations of practice that problematize.

Thus, structuring and problematizing help make the practice of teaching both more tractable and more complex. Metacognitively, structuring helps interns stay on track and problematizing helps them recognize that they can improve their practice. Sociocognitively, structuring helps interns see what they should do; problematizing helps them see *how* they can improve. Affectively, structuring keeps interns from getting overwhelmed while problematizing helps them want to improve. The structuring and problematizing roles are each necessary to promote learning (Reiser, 2004).

The design solutions identified in Tables 7.4 and 7.5 take three forms. First, some solutions take the form of *tools* that can be put in place in the teacher education classroom or program and used in approximations of practice (cf. Benedict-Chambers, this volume, Chapter 10; Fick and Arias, this volume, Chapter 9; Kademian and Davis, this volume, Chapter 8). For

108 *Davis*

Table 7.4 Design Questions for *Structuring* Novices' Learning

Design questions for structuring How can the approximation of practice … ?	Examples of design solutions By …
Metacognitive	
… help the novice maintain direction?	… specifying the characteristics of the practice that must be in place … purposeful feedback about the practice
… help the novice monitor their performance?	… providing a rubric keyed to salient features of the practice
Sociocognitive	
… reduce the degrees of freedom, restrict the problem space, and narrow the choices for the novice?	… providing a script or a lesson plan … limiting the time, number of students, or segment of a lesson … changing the "students" to colleagues … providing a task or representation to use
… decompose a complex task for the novice, highlight the salient features, and focus the novice's effort on a key element of the practice?	… focusing on a single practice or element … naming and unpacking a decomposition of a practice or element of instruction … providing a rubric keyed to salient features of the practice
… allow for the provision of expert guidance?	… providing foci for teacher educators' feedback keyed to salient features of the practice … promoting "stop actions" and "rewinds"
Affective	
… help the novice control their frustration?	… setting expectations and clarifying stakes … reducing the number of demands on attention

example, tools can include frameworks that decompose a practice to high-light salient features. Second, design solutions are built into *consistent pedagogies* themselves. For example, the peer-teaching experiences give the possibilities of stop actions and rewinds. *Tools* and *pedagogies* contribute to the effectiveness and efficiency of a teacher education classroom. Interns come to internalize the tools and know what to expect of the pedagogies, particularly when they are used throughout a program (Kademian and Davis, this volume, Chapter 8). Together, these help interns begin to move toward more skillful, equitable, and just science teaching.

Approximations of Practice 109

Table 7.5 Design Questions for *Problematizing* Novices' Work

Design questions for problematizing How can the approximation of practice … ?	Examples of design solutions By …
Metacognitive	
… help the novice maintain direction as they engage in the practice?	… providing expert guidance aimed at improving language or other instructional choices
… disrupt the novice's engagement, when the novice is not being sufficiently mindful?	… focusing attention on the goal to improve one's overall teaching practice
… elicit the novice's articulation?	… prompting reflection … expecting analysis of video records
… elicit decisions by the novice?	… "pausing" the performance to "rewind" the performance of the practice
Sociocognitive	
… mark critical features of the practice and highlight its salient features?	… expecting a more sophisticated or ambitious performance than may be typical in schools (e.g., integrating science content and practice) … using a rubric keyed to salient features of the practice
… highlight problems with the performance, surface gaps in the novice's understanding and disagreements among novices, and focus the novice's attention on issues that need resolution?	… using a rubric keyed to salient features of the practice … providing explicit feedback on instructional choices keyed to salient features … purposeful infusion of typical problems of practice … promoting "stop actions" and "rewinds"
Affective	
… create interest and recruit the novice to the task?	… mapping the approximation to authentic classroom practice … demonstrating connection to improved teaching
… engage the novice in the practice, through generating dissonance or curiosity?	… demonstrating the challenge of a seemingly straightforward practice

The third form of design solution entails purposeful *person-to-person interactions*. A teacher educator must filter the many possible interactions to have with the novice and zoom in on the most important—perhaps guided by a tool. This requires simultaneously taking on multiple roles (e.g., elementary student, teacher, and teacher educator) and responsibilities (e.g., naming the elements of the practice, giving focused feedback; Kazemi *et al.*, 2009). It also requires that the teacher educator draw upon knowledge of preservice

110   *Davis*

teachers in general and of the specific intern who is approximating the practice (cf. Davis *et al.*, 2017). Through the increased efficiency supported by the tools and pedagogies—and the resulting reduction in the teacher educator's cognitive load—the teacher educator can further support the effectiveness of the teacher education experiences.

Too much structure with insufficient problematizing may trivialize the practice and diminish the opportunity to learn. Too little structure with too much problematizing may overwhelm the novice and leave her unable to take up opportunities to learn (Reiser, 2004). Thus, in designing approximations of practice for preservice teachers, teacher educators should attend to how the approximations (a) structure and problematize the work, through attention to (b) sociocognitive, metacognitive, and affective scaffolding intentions and using (c) tools, pedagogies, and social interactions. Doing so can improve the effectiveness, efficiency, and equity of instructional approaches.

Notes

1 Because scaffolding as a construct grew from the tutoring literature, it originally was used in working with a single learner. In recent decades, the construct has been applied in classroom contexts. In keeping with my theoretical perspective, I use "sociocognitive" or "(socio)cognitive" in lieu of "cognitive."
2 I use first-person plural in describing the instructional design for the science methods course due to my long-term collaboration with members of the Elementary Science Methods Planning Group at the University of Michigan; my work with these teacher educators has shaped my knowledge and practice immeasurably. I use first-person singular when referring to my analyses here in this chapter.
3 We use the "EEE+A Framework", an instructional framework for investigative science lessons, to organize our instruction in the science methods class (Benedict-Chambers, 2014; Kademian and Davis, this volume, Chapter 8). Its lesson elements include Engage, Experience (a phenomenon), and Explain+Argue with Evidence. This is a simplification of other instructional frameworks such as the 5E model (Bybee *et al.*, 2006).
4 When I am drawing on written sources or video recordings, I cite them. I do not have video records associated with Eliza's peer-teaching rehearsals, so my comments about the teacher educator's feedback are hypothetical in that case.

References

Arias, A. (2015). Learning to teach elementary students to construct evidence-based claims. (Unpublished doctoral dissertation), University of Michigan, Ann Arbor.
Ball, D., and Forzani, F. (2009). The work of teaching and the challenge for teacher education. *Journal of Teacher Education*, *60*(5), 497–511.
Banilower, E., Smith, P. S., Weiss, I., Malzahn, K., Campbell, K., and Weis, A. (2013, February). *Report of the 2012 National Survey of Science and Mathematics Education*. Retrieved from Chapel Hill, NC: http://www.horizon-research.com/2012nssme/research-products/reports/technical-report/

Benedict-Chambers, A. (2014). Developing professional vision for practice: Preservice teachers using students' scientific ideas in simulations of practice. (Unpublished doctoral dissertation), University of Michigan, Ann Arbor.

Bybee, R., Taylor, J., Gardner, A., Van Scotter, P., Powell, J. C., Westbrook, A., and Landes, N. (2006). *The BSCS 5E Instructional Model: Origins and Effectiveness.* Colorado Springs: BSCS.

Davis, E. A., and Boerst, T. (2014). Designing elementary teacher education to prepare well-started beginners. Retrieved from: http://www.teachingworks.org/images/files/TeachingWorks_Davis_Boerst_WorkingPapers_March_2014.pdf

Davis, E. A., Kloser, M., Wells, A., Windschitl, M., Carlson, J., and Marino, J.-C. (2017). Teaching the practice of leading sensemaking discussions in science: Science teacher educators using rehearsals. *Journal of Science Teacher Education, 28*(3), 275–293.

Ericsson, K., Krampe, R., and Tesch-Römer, C. (1993). The role of deliberate practice in the acquisition of expert performance. *Psychological Review, 100*(3), 363–406.

Forbes, C., and Davis, E. A. (2010). Curriculum design for inquiry: Preservice elementary teachers' mobilization and adaptation of science curriculum materials. *Journal of Research in Science Teaching, 47*(7), 820–839.

Forzani, F. (2014). Understanding "core practices" and "practice-based" teacher education: Learning from the past. *Journal of Teacher Education, 65*(4), 357–368.

Grossman, P., Compton, C., Igra, D., Ronfeldt, M., Shahan, E., and Williamson, P. (2009a). Teaching practice: A cross-professional perspective. *Teachers College Record, 111*(9), 2055–2100.

Grossman, P., Hammerness, K., and McDonald, M. (2009b). Redefining teaching, re-imagining teacher education. *Teachers and Teaching: Theory and Practice, 15*(2), 273–289.

Kademian, S.M. (2017). Supporting beginning teacher planning and enactment of investigation-based science discussions: The design and use of tools within practice-based teacher education. (Unpublished doctoral dissertation), University of Michigan, Ann Arbor.

Kazemi, E., Franke, M., and Lampert, M. (2009). Developing pedagogies in teacher education to support novice teachers' ability to enact ambitious instruction. In R. Hunter, B. Bicknell, and T. Burgess (Eds.), *Crossing Divides: Proceedings of the 32nd Annual Conference of the Mathematics Education Research Group of Australasia* (Vol. 1).

Lampert, M., Franke, M., Kazemi, E., Ghousseini, H., Turrou, A., Beasley, H., and Crowe, K. (2013). Keeping it complex: Using rehearsals to support novice teacher learning of ambitious teaching. *Journal of Teacher Education, 64*(3), 226–243.

Nelson, M. (2011). Approximations of practice in the preparation of prospective elementary science teachers. (Unpublished doctoral dissertation), University of Michigan, Ann Arbor.

Putnam, R., and Borko, H. (2000). What do new views of knowledge and thinking have to say about research on teacher learning? *Educational Researcher, 29*(1), 4–15.

Reiser, B. (2004). Scaffolding complex learning: The mechanisms of structuring and problematizing student work. *The Journal of the Learning Sciences, 13*(3), 273–304.

van de Pol, J., Volman, M., and Beishuizen, J. (2010). Scaffolding in teacher–student interaction: A decade of research. *Educational Psychology Review, 22*, 271–296.

Vygotsky, L. S. (1978). *Mind in Society: The Development of Higher Psychological Processes.* Cambridge, MA: Harvard University Press.

Windschitl, M., Thompson, J., Braaten, M., and Stroupe, D. (2012). Proposing a core set of instructional practices and tools for teachers of science. *Science Education, 96*(5), 878–903.

Wood, D., Bruner, J., and Ross, G. (1976). The role of tutoring in problem solving. *Journal of Child Psychology, 17*, 89–100.

Zeichner, K. (2012). The turn once again toward practice-based teacher education. *Journal of Teacher Education, 63*(5), 376–382.

8 Planning and Enacting Investigation-based Science Discussions

Designing Tools to Support Teacher Knowledge for Science Teaching

Sylvie M. Kademian and Elizabeth A. Davis
UNIVERSITY OF MICHIGAN

Acknowledgments

Parts of this research were funded by a grant from the Gates Foundation to TeachingWorks (see https://library.teachingworks.org). Any opinions, findings, conclusions, or recommendations expressed in this material are those of the authors. The authors thank the elementary interns at the University of Michigan for their participation and the Elementary Science Methods Planning Group for supporting the authors' growth as teacher educators.

Introduction

Using tools designed to support beginning teacher learning is a dimension of teacher educator practice that has been gaining attention in the literature (e.g., Cartier *et al.*, 2013; Ross, 2014; Windschitl *et al.*, 2012). Using teacher educator-provided tools has the potential to support beginning teacher understanding of how to facilitate investigation-based discussions that capitalize on student contributions and foster student sensemaking; this privileging of student ideas supports more equitable and just science teaching. Studies have described the types of tools teacher educators could design and provide to preservice teachers. However, fewer studies have described the design and use of teacher educator-provided tools detailing types of teacher knowledge the tools are intended to support. We describe designing and using a cohesive suite of tools within an elementary science methods course with a focus on supporting beginning teachers' learning to facilitate investigation-based discussions that promote every child's sensemaking.

Context of Tool Use

We designed the tools for use in a science methods course embedded in a master of the arts program with certification in elementary education at the

University of Michigan. The program is 12 months in length, and all participants (called interns) entered the program having previously obtained a bachelor degree; they ranged from 22 to 45 years of age. Interns complete the month-long science methods course—a total of about 36 hours—while completing part of a year-long classroom internship with a mentor teacher in a local elementary school. This classroom internship provides interns the opportunity to enact science lessons with K-5 children. The science methods course is the only course in the program during which science is the content area of focus.[1]

The teacher education program takes a practice-based approach, focusing on the knowledge needed for science teaching while providing opportunities for interns to engage in and discuss the practice of teaching. Practice-based teacher education (Ball and Cohen, 1999; Grossman *et al.*, 2009b; see also Davis, Palincsar, and Kademian, this volume, Chapter 13) has the potential for supporting science teaching that integrates science content and science practices. Current research advocates for using a set of high-leverage practices (Ball *et al.*, 2009) that "build on one another instructionally and play recognizable roles together in a coherent system of teaching" (Windschitl *et al.*, 2012, p. 883). Repeated emphasis on a set of high-leverage practices across a program may support teachers to develop a more appropriate vision of elementary science teaching (cf. Zembal-Saul *et al.*, 2000). By engaging in the high-leverage practices with varying amounts of support, including teacher-educator created tools, beginning teachers develop the ability to use teaching practices productively with children (Ball and Forzani, 2009; Davis and Boerst, 2014; Windschitl *et al.*, 2012). During the science methods course interns have several opportunities to engage in approximations of teaching practice (Grossman *et al.*, 2009a) including *peer-teaching rehearsal experiences* (which take place within the methods classroom) and *field-based teaching experiences* (see Davis, this volume, Chapter 7).

Supporting Specific Types of Teacher Knowledge

Science teaching that integrates scientific content and science practices to empower all learners and engage them in rigorous and consequential science learning requires knowledge for teaching as well as the ability to enact that knowledge in one's teaching practice. Knowledge for teaching science includes subject matter knowledge, such as knowledge of the scientific theory of evolution, and pedagogical content knowledge, such as knowledge of how to present that theory at a level appropriate for elementary-age children (Ball *et al.*, 2008; Magnusson, Krajcik, and Borko, 1999; Shulman, 1986). To design and refine the suite of tools for the science methods course, we utilized Ball and colleagues' (2009) model of essential knowledge of mathematics teaching, adapting this model for use in science education (see Figure 8.1).

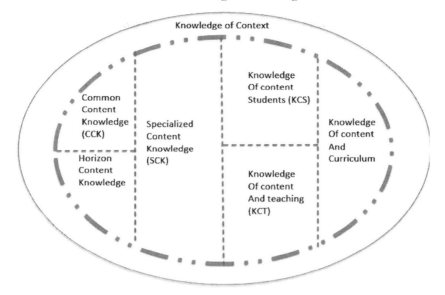

Figure 8.1 Conceptual Framework for Knowledge Needed for Science Teaching Knowledge
Source: Adapted from Ball *et al.*, 2008

For example, common content knowledge includes knowledge of scientific facts, concepts, and nature of science (i.e., substantive and syntactic knowledge; Schwab, 1962). When asking children to construct explanations, a teacher may draw on this knowledge to press children for multiple pieces of evidence to support their claims (cf. Kademian and Davis, 2018).

Design and Modification of a Suite of Tools

We designed and/or modified tools intended to foster development of specific domains of interns' knowledge intended to support interns to engage in productive teaching practices that capitalize on student contributions and student sensemaking (Cartier *et al.*, 2013; Ross, 2014; Windschitl *et al.*, 2012). Several of the tools built on collaborative work within the Elementary Science Methods Planning Group led by Davis at the University of Michigan. We adapted other tools (e.g., the Monitoring Tool described by Cartier and colleagues, 2013) for use in our context. Finally, we developed some of the tools based on observed areas of intern struggle at the time of this study.

A tool operates in the space between an individual and a complex task that might be out of reach for the intern without some form of support or assistance (Cole and Wertsch, 1996). Table 8.1 summarizes the tools and the domains of knowledge they target (see TeachingWorks Resource Library

Table 8.1 Suite of Tools Designed to Support Teacher Knowledge for Science Teaching

Tool Name	Description
Designed to Foster both Subject Matter Knowledge and Pedagogical Content Knowledge	
Instructional Planning Template	A lesson-planning template designed to support teachers' planning of investigation-based science lessons. Prompts teachers to think about and plan for important elements of the lesson including anticipating children's ideas about scientific phenomena, considering how the lesson fits in with the big ideas in science, management considerations for small group work and investigation materials, etc.
Designed to Foster Subject Matter Knowledge	
Card sorting activity	Designed to help support teachers develop and consider the subject matter knowledge important for the focal lessons. Teachers can use their completed card sorting activity to help plan lessons and larger units.
Designed to Foster Pedagogical Content Knowledge	
Engage-Experience-Explain+Argue Framework Reference	Science lesson framework designed to support teachers to engage children in the practices of scientists while learning about scientific content. Outlines what teachers and children do during each element of the framework. Tool provides connections to the NGSS science practices and the high-leverage practices that are cornerstones of the teacher education program.
Talk Moves Tool	Provides specific language that can be used to support productive teacher-to-student and student-to-student dialogue during each element of the EEE+A framework. Tool outlines possible talk moves that can be used to elicit children's ideas, monitor data collection, help children understand the nature of the investigation, press children to provide explanations with justifications, and connect children's ideas.
Alternative Ideas Tool	Provides interns a set of research-based common alternative ideas that children are likely to have about a scientific phenomenon. Tool can be used to anticipate student thinking.
Monitoring Tool	Supports teachers to monitor children while they engage in planning and carrying out investigations. When using this tool, teachers are asked to consider likely student ideas (both scientifically accurate as well as common alternative ideas) and student struggles that are common when engaging in scientific practices.
CER Scaffolding Tool	Provides elementary children a sentence starter and framework for writing evidence-based claims. Helps to remind children of the investigation questions, and the three parts of an evidence-based claim (including using multiple pieces of evidence). Particularly useful for groups of children who are new to the Claim-Evidence-Reasoning framework.

https://library.teachingworks.org/curriculum-resources/ for versions of each tool, including how each serves to advance the goals of more just and equitable science teaching[2]). Like Fick and Arias (this volume, Chapter 9), we emphasize the collaborative, evolving design process for these tools. Besides describing each tool, we address how the tools scaffolded novices' learning to teach science, discuss how we used the tools within the methods course, and identify which domain(s) of knowledge each tool supports.

Instructional Planning Template

The elementary science methods course uses an *Instructional Planning Template* that is aligned with the *Engage, Experience, and Explain+Argue Framework*. Interns are asked to use the *Instructional Planning Template* to prepare all of their lessons associated with assignments in the science methods course. Interns use a similar template throughout their teacher education program (cf. Davis and Boerst, 2014); however, we modified the template for the science methods course specifically to foster planning of investigation-based science lessons. For example, the template prompts the interns to consider common alternative ideas children may have about a particular science topic, requires interns to describe how the individual lesson aligns with the goals of the larger science unit, and provides space for interns to develop a claim based on evidence and reasoning that children should be able to construct after the lesson is complete. Additionally, the *Instructional Planning Template* prompts interns to think about and plan for classroom management associated with handling small group work and investigation materials so children are able to engage in the practices of scientists (e.g., carrying out investigations). The template was developed iteratively over time, providing additional support for interns in areas where our previous research determined areas of teacher struggle (e.g., missed opportunities to press children to provide multiple pieces of evidence) (Arias, 2015; Beyer and Davis, 2009; Fick and Arias, this volume, Chapter 9).

The *Instructional Planning Template* serves as a tool for planning in a similar way to the lesson planning considerations presented by Zembal-Saul *et al.* (2000)—guiding interns' thinking about subject matter knowledge and pedagogical content knowledge. For example, by prompting interns to consider multiple pieces of evidence that could be used to support the scientifically accurate claim for the lesson, interns have the opportunity to develop common content knowledge of the scientific phenomena of focus. With use of the *Instructional Planning Template* interns also have opportunities to build knowledge of content and teaching by determining which pieces of data from the investigation children can use as evidence to support their claims. In so doing, the tool supports interns in designing rigorous, consequential, and coherent science learning experiences for all of the children in their classroom.

The *Instructional Planning Template* pushes interns to think through how the diversity of their students might shape how a lesson unfolds. For example, when planning a lesson a novice teacher may attend to how students will be grouped for small group work, how they plan to interact and gain ideas for each student, how non-normative ideas will be elicited and included, and how learning tasks and assessments will be differentiated based on each student's understanding.

Also, the template is coherent with the overall vision of the teacher education program (Davis and Boerst, 2014). The *Instructional Planning Template* not only provides interns with cohesiveness and a clear trajectory within each lesson they plan (Leinhardt and Greeno, 1986), it also is consistent across their experiences in the program.

Card Sorting Activity

Interns complete the *Card Sorting Activity* in association with the two lessons they plan during the science methods course. These lessons are focused either on the function of plant stems or thermal equilibrium (the peer teaching rehearsal lesson—see Davis, this volume, Chapter 7) and a content area being covered in the intern's field placement classroom (the Lesson in Field Experience lesson or "LiFE" lesson). Rather than using the *Card Sorting Activity* to begin to design their own curriculum like the teachers in Windschitl and colleagues' (2012) study, interns complete the *Card Sorting Activity* to familiarize themselves with the lessons and corresponding preexisting curriculum units used within the methods course.

For the first *Card Sorting Activity*, associated with the peer teaching lesson, interns are given a set of big ideas from the unit curriculum materials and the *Atlas for Science Literacy* (AAAS, 2001). For example, one big idea is "energy has many forms." Then, individually, each intern organizes the big ideas in a two-dimensional space. Interns describe how the ideas relate to one another on lines connecting the big ideas, provide a short summary of how the peer teaching lesson fits into the "bigger picture" being addressed by the unit, and list three questions that arose for them about the science content by completing this activity.

Interns complete the second *Card Sorting Activity* in a similar way. However, interns develop their own set of "big ideas" using the unit curriculum materials associated with the lesson they plan to teach for the Lesson in Field Experience (LiFE) lesson. Again, each intern organizes the big ideas in a two-dimensional space, representing how the ideas are related to one another. Interns can choose to do this assignment individually or collaboratively with others teaching lessons within the same unit.

Informed by Windschitl *et al.* (2015), we adapted the *Card Sorting Activity* to support interns to develop and consider the subject matter knowledge that is important for the focal lessons. Because prior research has found teacher identification of the big ideas as a critical precursor to enacting ambitious science teaching that supports all children's learning (Windschitl *et al.*, 2012), it is important to provide interns with an opportunity to grapple with or refresh their own ideas about the science content.

Completing the *Card Sorting Activity* provides interns an opportunity to develop common content knowledge including details about the mechanistic explanation of the phenomenon children will be investigating. It also provides an opportunity for interns to develop horizon content knowledge (Ball *et al.*, 2008). By considering how the big ideas within the science unit are connected, interns may develop an understanding of the comprehensive science ideas required to help children make sense of the multiple investigations in which they will participate during the larger unit (Windschitl *et al.*, 2012). Having this stronger subject matter understanding themselves can help interns be positioned to support the content learning of all of the children in their classrooms.

Engage-Experience-Explain+Argue Framework

The elementary education science methods course utilizes the *Engage-Experience-Explain+Argue (EEE+A) Framework Reference* for investigation-based elementary science lessons. This tool decomposes science teaching into three elements: *Engage, Experience*, and *Explain and Argue with Evidence*, similar to the 5E model (Bybee *et al.*, 2006; see also Benedict-Chambers, 2016). With this decomposition, we break down teaching into smaller pieces (Grossman *et al.*, 2009a).

During the *Engage Element*, interns support children in identifying an investigation question or problem and elicit ideas about that question. In the *Experience Element*, interns support children in establishing data collection and carrying out the investigation. The *Explain and Argue with Evidence Element* asks interns to support children to analyze data gathered in the *Experience Element* and find patterns within that data. Interns are prompted to help children construct evidence-based claims and apply their knowledge to new situations. Whole-class investigation-based discussions typically occur during the *Explain+Argue Element*; however, the teaching moves made by the intern during the *Engage* and *Experience Elements* shape the enactment of the *Explain+Argue Element*.

We designed the *EEE+A Framework Reference* to support teachers in engaging children in the practices of scientists while learning about scientific content. It outlines what teachers might do during each element, providing decompositions of the larger teaching practices involved in enacting an investigation-based discussion, as well as what children do during each element. Additionally, the tool articulates connections to the *Next Generation Science Standards* science practices, as well as the high-leverage teaching practices that are cornerstones of our teacher education program. Much like the 5E model, the *EEE+A Framework Reference* provides interns with information needed to make decisions about how an investigation-based science

120 *Kademian and Davis*

lesson could be sequenced and provides suggestions for instructional strategies and techniques that are likely to be effective (Bybee *et al.*, 2006).

By providing these suggestions, the *EEE+A Framework Reference* works to foster development of interns' pedagogical content knowledge, specifically their knowledge of content and teaching. For example, by using the *EEE+A Framework Reference* to plan their lessons, interns are prompted to use instructional strategies that support engagement in rigorous and consequential science learning, and allow children to develop scientific claims based on data from the in-class investigation.

Talk Moves Tool

We provide the *Talk Moves Tool* to interns at the beginning of the science methods course. The tool is aligned with the *EEE+A Framework* and outlines specific language in the form of "talk moves" that can be used to elicit ideas, monitor data collection, press children to provide explanations with evidence and justification, and connect to other children's ideas. The talk moves can take the form of questions or statements that are used regularly in a teacher's classroom to support meaningful discourse that leads to sensemaking among the students and teacher.

Using talk moves allows teachers to shift between authoritative and dialogic discourses, both of which are needed to support sensemaking (National Research Council, 2007). Current research states that teachers benefit more from learning specific talk moves (Michaels *et al.*, 2008; National Research Council, 2007) to help children navigate through the practices of explanation construction and argumentation. The *Talk Moves Tool* was designed to suggest talk moves that can be used to support productive teacher-student and student-student dialog during each element of the *EEE+A Framework*. Some of the talk moves are subject-neutral, for example, using the phrase "tell me more about that." Others are science-teaching specific, for example, using the phrase "Given your thinking so far, what do you predict will happen during our investigation and why?" The talk moves specific to science teaching are informed by talk moves for facilitating science discussions in the literature, as well as practitioner resources (e.g., Schweingruber, Shouse, and Michaels, 2007; Zembal-Saul *et al.*, 2013). The *Talk Moves Tool* is also designed to support interns to engage children in the science practices of explanation construction and engagement in argumentation with evidence.

The science-teaching specific talk moves aligned with the *EEE+A Framework* were designed to foster development of pedagogical content knowledge, particularly knowledge of content and teaching. By prioritizing the use of talk moves throughout the teacher education program, we support interns understanding that it is normal for students to have beliefs and understandings about the world based on their personal experiences and/or religious and cultural funds of knowledge. By using talk moves included in the *Talk Moves Tool* in their instruction, interns provide opportunities for *all* students to learn from the questions being asked by the teacher. General talk moves were introduced in other methods courses in the teacher education program; however, this was the first time the interns were exposed to science-teaching specific talk moves. By making the talk moves subject-specific, features of investigation-based science teaching become more salient for beginning teachers, helping them to engage all of their students in the kinds of discourse needed for sensemaking.

Alternative Ideas Tool

The *Alternative Ideas Tool*[3] provides interns with a set of research-based, alternative ideas children are likely to have about scientific phenomena (diSessa and Minstrell, 1998), including those that may arise in the peer teaching lessons. However, the set does not include common alternative ideas for all of the concepts interns might teach for the lessons in the field assignment (LiFE). Within the *Instructional Planning Template*, interns are prompted to consider possible alternative ideas children may have.

Children have a wealth of ideas about natural phenomena based on the world in which they live (diSessa and Minstrell, 1998). While experienced teachers may be able to anticipate these ideas, novice teachers are unlikely to be in a position to do so (e.g., Abell, 2007; Furtak, Thompson, Braaten, and Windschitl, 2012). Thus, providing interns with a list of research-based common alternative ideas provides an opportunity for development of pedagogical content knowledge, particularly knowledge of content and students (Davis and Smithey, 2009). For example, if an intern knows children are likely to think that condensation forms on the outside of a glass of ice water because the water "leaks" through the glass, the intern might plan in advance how to address the idea if it were to arise during an investigation-based discussion. Rather than simply labeling the student's idea as incorrect, the intern may develop a series of questions to ask the student to probe his or her thinking, or point the student toward evidence that might redirect that line of thinking (e.g., observing condensation on a cold mirror) while valuing the idea itself.

Monitoring Tool

We provide interns with an exemplar *Monitoring Tool* (Cartier *et al.*, 2013) at the beginning of the methods course. We created the exemplar *Monitoring Tool* for a lesson focused on supporting children to follow the flow of electric current in a simple circuit. All interns experience this lesson from the "children's perspective" on the first day of the methods course. The instructor uses the monitoring tool as part of her instruction. Following the investigation, the teacher educator and interns reflect on their experiences during the lesson discussing using the tool to monitor interns' ideas. The exemplar lists common researched-based alternative ideas (those which are included in the *Alternative Ideas Tool*) as well as scientifically accurate understandings. Interns are then encouraged to use the exemplar to develop similar *Monitoring Tools* for both their peer teaching lesson and lesson in the field lesson assignments as a way to keep track of children's ideas over the course of the lesson.

When creating the *Monitoring Tool* for each of their lessons, interns identify the features required for the scientific explanation of focus. One of those features might include listing multiple pieces of evidence for each claim being made. By identifying these features, the intern then might use the *Monitoring Tool* to formatively assess children's understandings during the enactment.

Additionally, when creating the *Monitoring Tool*, interns must anticipate common alternative ideas children may have about the science content and likely struggles children may have when engaging in carrying out investigations. For example, an intern may anticipate that children think a "short circuit" means there must be some sort of "break" in the path of electrical current flow. Additionally, interns may anticipate that children may struggle to make clear, complete, and objective observations. In doing so, the intern recognizes that children will come to the investigation with some understandings about the scientific phenomena, and may be better positioned to develop a plan to support children who are struggling with either the scientific content and/or the science practices "without taking over the thinking for them" (Cartier *et al.*, 2013, p.52).

Finally, creating a *Monitoring Tool* may prompt interns to determine how to respond to the work children produce that may not be accurate or complete (Cartier *et al.*, 2013). Interns tend not to think about children's ideas about science phenomena very carefully (Abell, 2007; Davis *et al.*, 2006) and have limited ideas of what to do with children's ideas after eliciting them (Gotwals and Birmingham, 2015; Zembal-Saul *et al.*, 2000). By anticipating ideas children may have about the scientific phenomenon or practice and having a plan for how to value children's thinking, an intern will be better able to plan what to do to guide children toward a more complete understanding while still allowing children to do the cognitive work (Cartier *et al.*, 2013). For example, if an intern determines children struggle to make clear, complete, and accurate scientific observations, they can use the *Monitoring Tool* in conjunction with the *Talk Moves Tool* to develop questions that prompt children to think about the quality of their scientific observation drawings.

By using the *Monitoring Tool* to keep track of children's ideas during investigations, interns have the opportunity to foster development of teacher knowledge of content and students. Rather than circulating only to focus on whether children are on-task and using materials correctly, using the *Monitoring Tool* prompts interns to carefully attend to what children say while they work together in groups. By having the anticipated student

Planning and Enacting Science Discussions 123

ideas, probing questions, and talk moves in hand as the intern checks in with groups of children, they can focus on asking questions to make children's thinking visible and help to clarify children's thinking for other group members (Cartier *et al.*, 2013), allowing those ideas to serve as resources.

Additionally, through using the *Monitoring Tool*, the intern can begin to plan for an investigation-based discussion. By having a record of the ideas that arose during small-group discussions, the intern can begin to select which child or groups they want to contribute at specific times during the investigation-based discussion. For example, if while monitoring children's ideas, one group was discussing why their data were not matching their predictions due to measurement errors, the intern could then plan to have that group contribute to the discussion of probable causes of anomalous data. By noting which groups of children have particularly useful ideas[4] to contribute for specific aspects of the discussion, the intern is better able to facilitate an investigation-based discussion that provides the class with opportunities to both grapple with data and make sense of the disciplinary core ideas driving the lesson.

Providing opportunities to foster intern knowledge of content and students and knowledge of content and teaching, we designed the *Monitoring Tool* with the intent of helping interns anticipate and monitor student ideas about science content and science practices while they engage in planning and carrying out investigations. When creating and using the tool with children, interns consider a variety of factors—the key features that must be present for a scientifically accurate claim based on evidence, the challenges children are likely to encounter, the alternative ideas that are likely to arise, and potentially how to respond to ideas that are not scientifically accurate (Cartier *et al.*, 2013). This can help them hear a range of student thinking and recognize the strength in how children think about science.

Claim–Evidence–Reasoning Scaffolding Tool

We provide interns with the *Claim-Evidence-Reasoning (CER) Scaffolding Tool* at the start of the methods course (cf. McNeill, 2009). The *CER Scaffolding Tool* is designed to be used directly with children. The course instructor models how this tool can be adapted for a lesson focused on the flow of electric current in a simple circuit. Again, interns experience this lesson from the "children's perspective" on the first day of the methods course. As they do so, they complete a worksheet based on the *CER Scaffolding Tool*, which serves as a template. The template provides an example of a claim-evidence-reasoning handout a teacher might use with children during an investigation-based science lesson. Interns are encouraged to make similar handouts for their peer teaching lesson and lesson in the field assignments. The tool also provides suggestions for each grade level. For example, we encourage interns teaching children in grades K-2 to have children draw their predictions rather than write them.

Given current reform efforts focused on engaging children in the science practice of constructing explanations (National Research Council, 2012; NGSS Lead States, 2013) and the difficulties teachers face with engaging children in explanation construction (e.g., Berland and Reiser, 2009; McNeill, 2009), beginning teachers require additional support in doing so. The *CER Scaffolding Tool* serves as a support for children new to using the claim-evidence-reasoning framework for explanations (e.g., McNeill 2009; Zembal-Saul *et al.*, 2013, Zembal-Saul and Hershberger, this volume, Chapter 1). The handout reminds children of the investigation question for the lesson, and the three parts of an evidence-based argument, including multiple pieces of evidence.

In using the *CER Scaffolding Tool*, interns are also reminded of important components of an explanation, potentially fostering development of knowledge of content and teaching. Additionally, interns may be reminded of several important aspects of investigation-based lessons, including asking a scientific question, making predictions with justification, recording and using data collected during the investigation, and finally crafting evidence-based claims that answer the investigation question (cf. Arias, this volume, Chapter 11).

Through using the *CER Scaffolding Tool* interns are provided an additional opportunity to develop knowledge of content and students. Similar to the *Monitoring Tool*, by using the *CER Scaffolding Tool* the intern can recognize that children will come to the investigation with some understandings about the scientific phenomena, and may encourage children to share those ideas by drawing or writing predictions. Interns can then use the handout to formatively assess children's initial understandings and determine patterns in student thinking. By noticing these patterns, the intern may be able to tailor children's experiences to help them progress toward a more accurate understanding of the science content. Interns can also provide an appropriate way of organizing data within the handout that will help children to begin to recognize important patterns in the data, and press children to provide multiple pieces of evidence for their claims, supporting rigorous and consequential science learning. Finally, the intern can use the *CER Scaffolding Tool* to formatively assess children's understanding of the science content after the investigation is complete, and use this data to modify future instruction.

Using the Tools Together

We designed or modified each tool so interns can use them synergistically during the methods course and associated field experience. For example, by aligning the *Talk Moves Tool* and *Instructional Planning Template* with the *EEE+A Framework*, we hoped that interns will be able to integrate the talk moves and overall goals of each element of the framework into their lesson plans.

Planning and Enacting Science Discussions 125

Using a cohesive suite of tools supports intern development as they learn to engage in sophisticated work like facilitating scientific sensemaking discussions. For example, using the *Talk Moves Tool* helps interns to craft questions that elicit both evidence and reasoning, providing additional opportunities for student-to-student discussion. Planning to use the talk moves from the *Talk Moves Tool* allows interns to have a set of questions to ask children to foster engagement in scientific discourse while engaging in science practices (e.g., data analysis, argumentation, and explanation construction) (Kademian and Davis, 2018; see also Michaels *et al.*, 2008).

Furthermore, using the *Alternative Ideas Tool* supports construction of knowledge of content and students (Ball *et al.*, 2008). Within the methods course, interns included research-based alternative ideas in their lesson plans prompting several interns to consider both accurate and non-normative ideas about scientific phenomena as potential responses to open-ended questions throughout the plans (Kademian and Davis, 2018). By including the alternative ideas in their plans, interns are more aware of the differences and nuances in children's ideas and as a result are more able to plan how they can use those ideas as resources in a sensemaking discussion.

Creating tools that can be used together also allows for emphasis on the most salient features of science teaching (e.g., integrating science content and science practices; cf. Benedict-Chambers, this volume, Chapter 10). For example, by using a common instructional planning template throughout the program and modifying the template to include features of each discipline (i.e. science, mathematics, etc.), the features of each discipline are highlighted and made more explicit because the overall structure of the template remains constant.

The suite of tools used the in the science methods course also are aligned with the overarching goals of the teacher education program (e.g., recognizing student ideas as resources; supporting sensemaking for all students). By consistently pressing interns to be aware of and utilize children's ideas (e.g., though using the *Alternative Ideas Tool, Monitoring Tool*, and *CER Scaffolding Tool*), they are more likely to recognize that children typically have ideas about a scientific phenomenon prior to beginning the investigation-based science lesson, and that those ideas serve as resources in science learning (Davis *et al.*, this volume, Introduction). This, in turn, helps these beginning teachers learn to support rigorous and consequential science learning for all students, by giving them vehicles for planning for and enacting instruction that focuses on sensemaking and privileges students' ideas.

In sum, providing conceptual tools is a promising practice that has the potential for supporting novice elementary teachers in becoming well-started beginning teachers (see also Benedict-Chambers, this volume, Chapter 10; Fick and Arias, this volume, Chapter 9). We see evidence of the importance of using a suite of tools in developing interns' knowledge for teaching science as

126 Kademian and Davis

well as their science teaching practice. Thus, by detailing the design and use of each of these tools within our elementary science methods course, we hope this chapter can provide insight for teacher educators working to develop and/ or modify a cohesive suite of tools for use in their own contexts.

Notes

1 This methods course is similar to the one for undergraduates described elsewhere in this volume (Davis, Palincsar, and Kademian, this volume, Chapter 13) with an additional focus on students' ideas and leading discussions.
2 One tool described here, the card sorting activity, was refined into the Big Ideas Tool in the library (https://library.teachingworks.org), in part, based on the research reported here.
3 This tool serves a different purpose from the similarly named tool described by Benedict-Chambers (this volume, Chapter 10).
4 Useful ideas may not always be the scientifically accurate ideas, but rather might be a common alternative idea many children had prior to the start of the investigation. The intern could then follow that idea by prompting children to consider if there is enough evidence to support that idea.

References

AAAS (American Association for the Advancement of Science). (2001). Atlas of Science Literacy. Washington, DC: American Association for the Advancement of Science.

Abell, S. K. (2007). Research on science teacher knowledge. In S. K. Abell and N. Lederman (Eds.), Handbook of Research on Science Education (pp. 1105–1149). Mahwah, NJ: Lawrence Erlbaum Associates.

Arias, A. (2015). Learning to teach elementary students to construct evidence-based claims of natural phenomena. (Unpublished Doctor of Philosophy: Educational Studies). University of Michigan, Ann Arbor, Michigan.

Ball, D. L., and Cohen, D. K. (1999). Developing practice, developing practitioners: Toward a practice-based theory of professional education. In L. Darling-Hammond and G. Sykes (Eds.), Teaching as the Learning Profession: Handbook of Policy and Practice (pp. 3–31). San Francisco: Jossey-Bass.

Ball, D. L., and Forzani, F. (2009). The work of teaching and the challenge for teacher education. Journal of Teacher Education, 60(5), 497–511.

Ball, D. L., Sleep, L., Boerst, T. A., and Bass, H. (2009). Combining the development of practice and the practice of development in teacher education. The Elementary School Journal, 109(5), 458–474.

Ball, D. L., Thames, M. H., and Phelps, G. (2008). Content knowledge for teaching what makes it special? Journal of Teacher Education, 59(5), 389–407.

Benedict-Chambers, A. (2016). Using tools to promote novice teacher noticing of science teaching practices in post-rehearsal discussions. Teaching and Teacher Education, 49, 28–44.

Berland, L. K., and Reiser, B. J. (2009). Making sense of argumentation and explanation. Science Education, 93(1), 26–55.

Beyer, C.J, and Davis, E. A. (2009). Supporting preservice elementary teachers' critique and adaptation of science lesson plans using educative curriculum materials. Journal of Science Teacher Education, 20(6), 517.

Bybee, R. W., Taylor, J. A., Gardner, A., Van Scotter, P., Powell, J. C., Westbrook, A., and Landes, N. (2006). *The BSCS 5E Instructional Model: Origins and Effectiveness*. Colorado Springs: BSCS.

Cartier, J. L., Smith, M. S., Stein, M. K., and Ross, D. K. (2013). *5 Practices for Orchestrating Productive Task-Based Discussions in Science*. Reston, VA: National Council of Teachers of Mathematics.

Cole, M., and Wertsch, J. V. (1996). Beyond the individual-social antinomy in discussions of Piaget and Vygotsky. *Human Development*, *39*(5), 250–256.

Davis, E. A., and Boerst, T. (2014). Designing elementary education teacher education to prepare well-started beginners. *TeachingWorks Working Papers*, 1–21. TeachingWorks, University of Michigan. Retrieved from: http://www.teaching works.org/research-data/workingpapers

Davis, E. A., Petish, D., and Smithey, J. (2006). Challenges new science teachers face. *Review of Educational Research*, *76*(4), 607–651

Davis, E. A., and Smithey, J. (2009). Beginning teachers moving toward effective elementary science teaching. *Science Education*, *93*(4), 745–770.

diSessa, A. A., and Minstrell, J. (1998). Cultivating conceptual change with benchmark lessons. In J. Greeno and S. Goldman (Eds.), *Thinking Practices in Mathematics and Science Learning* (pp. 155–187). New York: Routledge.

Furtak, E. M., Thompson, J., Braaten, M., and Windschitl, M. (2012). Learning progressions to support ambitious teaching practices. In A. Alonzo and A. Gotwals (Eds.), *Learning Progressions in Science: Current Challenges and Future Directions* (pp. 405–433). Rotterdam, The Netherlands: Sense Publishers.

Gotwals, A. W., and Birmingham, D. (2016). Eliciting, identifying, interpreting, and responding to students' ideas: Teacher candidates' growth in formative assessment practices. *Research in Science Education*, *46*(3), 365–388.

Grossman, P., Compton, C., Igra, D., Ronfeldt, M., Shahan, E., and Williamson, P. (2009a). Teaching practice: A cross-professional perspective. *Teachers College Record*, *111*(9), 2055–2100.

Grossman, P., Hammerness, K., and McDonald, M. (2009b). Redefining teaching, re-imagining teacher education. *Teachers and Teaching: Theory and Practice*, *15*(2), 273–289.

Kademian, S. M., and Davis, E. A. (2018). Supporting beginning teacher planning of investigation-based science discussions. *Journal of Science Teacher Education*, *29*(8), 712–740. Retrieved from: https://doi.org/10.1080/1046560X.2018.1504266

Leinhardt, G., and Greeno, J. G. (1986). The cognitive skill of teaching. *Journal of Educational Psychology*, *78*(2), 75.

Magnusson, S. J., Krajcik, J., and Borko, H. (1999). Nature, sources, and development of pedagogical content knowledge for science teaching. In J. Gess-Newsome and N. Lederman (Eds.), *Examining Pedagogical Content Knowledge: The Construct and Its Implications for Science Education* (pp. 95–132). Dordrecht, The Netherlands: Kluwer Academic Publishers.

McNeill, K. L. (2009). Teachers' use of curriculum to support students in writing scientific arguments to explain phenomena. *Science Education*, *93*(2), 233–268.

Michaels, S., O'Connor, C., and Resnick, L. B. (2008). Deliberative discourse idealized and realized: Accountable talk in the classroom and in civic life. *Studies in Philosophy and Education*, *27*(4), 283–297.

National Research Council (NRC). (2007). *Taking Science to School: Learning and Teaching Science in Grades K-8*. Washington, DC: National Academies Press.

128 *Kademian and Davis*

National Research Council. (2012). *A Framework for K-12 Science Education: Practices, Crosscutting Concepts, and Core Ideas.* Washington, DC: National Academies Press.

NGSS Lead States. (2013). *Next Generation Science Standards: For States, By States.* Washington, DC: National Academies Press.

Ross, D. K. (2014). Examining pre-service science teachers' developing pedagogical design capacity for planning and supporting task-based classroom discussions. (Unpublished Doctor of Philosophy: Science Education). University of Pittsburgh, Pittsburgh, PA.

Schwab, J. J. (1962). The teaching of science as enquiry. In *The Teaching of Science* (pp. 3–103). Cambridge, MA: Harvard University Press.

Schweingruber, H. A., Shouse, A. W., Michaels, S., and National Research Council. (2007). *Ready, Set, Science!: Putting Research to Work in K-8 Science Classrooms.* Washington, DC: National Academies Press.

Shulman, L. S. (1986). Those who understand: Knowledge growth in teaching. *Educational Researcher, 15*(2), 4–14.

Windschitl, M., Thompson, J., Braaten, M., and Stroupe, D. (2012). Proposing a core set of instructional practices and tools for teachers of science. *Science Education, 96*(5), 878–903.

Windschitl, M., Thompson, J., Braaten, M., Stroupe, D., Chew, C. and Wright, B. (2015). Ambitious science teaching. Retrieved from http://ambitiousscienceteaching.org/

Zembal-Saul, C., Blumenfeld, P., and Krajcik, J. (2000). Influence of guided cycles of planning, teaching, and reflection on prospective elementary teachers' science content representations. *Journal of Research in Science Teaching, 37*(4), 318–339.

Zembal-Saul, C., McNeill, K. L., and Hershberger, K. (2013). *What's Your Evidence?: Engaging K-5 Children in Constructing Explanations in Science.* Boston, MA: Pearson Higher Education.

9 Scaffolding Beginning Teaching Practices

An Analysis of the Roles Played by Tools Provided to Preservice Elementary Science Teachers

Sarah J. Fick
UNIVERSITY OF VIRGINIA

Anna Maria Arias
KENNESAW STATE UNIVERSITY

Science teaching that supports student sensemaking is complex, and beginning teachers often miss the nuances and complexity of ambitious teaching (Lampert and Graziani, 2009; Ball and Forzani, 2009). Thus, beginning teachers need focused guidance to understand the how and why involved in teaching (Ball and Forzani, 2009; Thompson *et al.*, 2013). Research suggests that a practice-based approach to teacher education focused on development of the knowledge and doing of teaching can support learning to teach (Ball and Forzani, 2009; Grossman *et al.*, 2009). Within a practice-based approach, a variety of tools can support preservice teachers learning this complexity of pedagogical practices (Windschitl *et al.*, 2012; Ross and Cartier, 2015; see also Benedict-Chambers, this volume, Chapter 10; Kademian and Davis, this volume, Chapter 8). By tool, we mean a physical or digital object designed to support one in accomplishing a task. For example, primer tools supported secondary teachers in planning discussions for ambitious science teaching (Windschitl *et al.*, 2012). Often, a suite of these tools is used within elementary practice-based science methods courses (e.g., Benedict-Chambers and Aram, 2017; Davis, 2016). However, little is known about the characteristics of these tools and the support they might provide around learning to facilitate student sensemaking in science education. To begin to address this gap, we engaged in collaborative analysis of the tools used within our methods courses to examine, *What characterizes tools developed to support preservice elementary science teachers during practice-based science method courses?* We answer this question through asking the analytical questions: *(1) What is the purpose of the tools?; (2) What teaching practices do the tools provide support for?; (3) How might the tools support preservice teachers' practice?*

Our Collaboration

We, Anna and Sarah, share many similar characteristics that bring us to teacher education. We both are alumni of the same graduate program at the University of Michigan. Before graduate school, we both taught science at the middle school level. Anna taught sixth through eighth grades, and Sarah taught seventh through 12th grade. Although we had different advisors, we had the opportunity to apprentice and collaborate with Elizabeth Davis, Amanda Benedict-Chambers, Sylvie Kademian, and others in the design and implementation of elementary science method courses, as part of the long-standing University of Michigan Elementary Science Planning Group headed by Davis. In graduate school, Anna focused on K-8 science teaching and worked with the elementary science methods courses for five years. Focusing on secondary education, Sarah spent two years as a field instructor for Teach for America corp members in Detroit and co-teacher for their secondary science methods course. She also apprenticed for one iteration of the elementary science methods course. After graduate school, we started our careers at different universities as tenure-track assistant professors with a focus on elementary science methods.

When we began this retrospective analysis, Sarah had taught elementary science methods three times in three years at Wake Forest University, and Anna had taught the course seven times in two years at Illinois State University. The contexts of our teaching varied due to the size and location of the universities and the culture of the teacher education programs. Illinois State typically graduates 350 teachers annually in the elementary education program, and the state of Illinois has adopted the Next Generation Science Standards (NGSS). In contrast, Wake Forest graduates fewer than ten elementary education students annually and is in North Carolina, which has state science standards that are more science content focused, without a clear foundation in the science and engineering practices (SEPs) and crosscutting concepts (CCCs) as described by NGSS (NGSS Lead States, 2013), although the graduates might teach in NGSS states in the future.

Our Theoretical Approach for Science Methods Using Tools

In the design and teaching of science methods courses as well as our analysis, we share a social constructivist perspective to learning. From this perspective, learning involves the co-construction of meaning with others and with tools to make sense of and to act as part of the community of practice within a particular context (Vygotsky, 1978; Putnam and Borko, 2000). To support the co-construction of knowledge, we draw on a practice-based approach that emphasizes the work of teaching which has been shown to support preservice teacher learning (e.g., Arias and Davis, 2017; Ball and Forzani, 2009; Thompson et al., 2013; see also Davis, Palincsar, and Kademian, this volume, Chapter 13).

A practice-based approach uses three pedagogies of professional teaching practice: representing, decomposing, and approximating practice (Grossman *et al.*, 2009). When representing the practice, we support a structured discussion of video records or lesson plans of exemplary teaching in order to help preservice teachers (PSTs) notice and reflect on important elements of teaching practice. Decomposing the practice involves breaking down the practice into smaller pieces. For instance, in our courses, we break down the practice of planning for a single lesson into smaller chunks which we call the Engage, Explore, and Explain elements of a lesson, drawing on Bybee's (2013) 5E model. Example approximations of practice from our courses included interviews focused on an individual's science ideas and rehearsals. During rehearsals, the PSTs teach a part of a lesson to a set of peers acting as the appropriately aged students (see Benedict-Chambers, this volume, Chapter 10; Davis, this volume, Chapter 7). Our course concludes with the PSTs teaching a full science lesson to elementary students at the end of the semester. These designs draw from our experiences with the University of Michigan Elementary Science Planning Group, but we adapted the design of the rehearsals to meet the needs of preservice teachers in our local contexts. We also use similar assignments within the methods courses that the tools support. These include: interviewing someone about their science ideas, teaching a decomposed lesson to peers, planning and teaching a lesson within an elementary classroom, and planning a sequence of science lessons that build towards a broader science content goal. We also focus on the role of reflection to help PSTs in reasoning with evidence about how their actions support student learning.

In our practice-based approach, we focus on a collection of selected teaching practices, called high-leverage practices, along with important subject matter knowledge to support beginning teacher learning (Ball *et al.*, 2009; Davis and Boerst, 2014). As educators, we selected these high-leverage practices for their centrality, frequency, applicability, effectiveness, and the possibility that a novice could learn the practice (Ball *et al.*, 2009). Some of the focal high-leverage practices for our courses include eliciting and interpreting student thinking and leading a class discussion (Ball *et al.*, 2009; Boerst *et al.*, 2011).

To support this set of teaching practices, we as teacher educators, researchers, and former teachers have developed a set of tools (discussed below). The tools we use for our courses are based in Vygotsky's understanding of learning as a socially constructed process which occurs within the range of an individual's independent and assisted abilities, the *zone of proximal development* (Vygotsky, 1978). This process is facilitated by interactions with others, tools, and signs (Vygotsky, 1978). In this frame, we describe *material tools* as physical or digital objects that are provided to students to support them to accomplish a task that they would not be able to do independently through scaffolding learning (Vygotsky, 1978; Wood *et al.*, 1976). As scaffolds, material tools can support student learning through structuring the task

132 *Fick and Arias*

or problematizing the content (Reiser, 2004). In structuring a task, a scaffold might provide limited options. In problematizing the content, a scaffold might highlight inconsistencies between the work being done and the intended goal (Reiser and Tabak, 2014).

Our Analyses of the Tools

Similar to others (e.g., Davis, 2016; Peercy and Troyan, 2017), we are conducting a self-study (Buck and Akerson, 2016) of our work as teacher educators by analyzing 32 tools developed to support PSTs in their learning as a part of their practice-based elementary methods courses at our two universities. As a result of our similar academic backgrounds as well as our personal and professional friendship, some overlap existed in the tools we used. In addition, some of the tools build directly on work done with colleagues within the Elementary Science Methods Planning Group at the University of Michigan, led by Elizabeth Davis, or on tools provided to the Teach for America teachers to support their instructional practices. In other words, these tools evolved from our experiences at Michigan, and we adapted them to address challenges we identified in our individual contexts. We also created tools to support particular PST struggles. Thus, we used different sets of tools across our courses at different times depending on the needs of our students and changing emphases within our courses and the program. For any given iteration of our courses we intentionally used some of the tools; we never used all 32 of them at once.

In our analysis of the tools, we began by developing a set of codes around the purpose of the tool drawing on research about tools in science teacher education (e.g., Windschitl *et al.*, 2012; Ross and Cartier, 2015). Then, we segmented the tools into parts to allow for closer coding. For example, we separated a lesson planning tool (Figure 9.1) into the parts focused on writing the scientific understanding goal for students ("the desired results") from the part of the tool focused on describing the planned sequence of events ("learning plan") because we saw these segments as serving two distinct yet related purposes (writing a learning goal vs. planning an instructional sequence). Then, we developed additional coding schemes based on our reading of relevant literatures (e.g., Grossman *et al.*, 2009; Kloser, 2014; Reiser, 2004; TeachingWorks, 2016). Table 9.1 presents examples of the coding schemes that we applied to each segment of a tool and to the tool as a whole.

We created a matrix of the codes to analyze patterns across the tools (Miles *et al.*, 2014). To ensure trustworthiness, we both coded all of the tools and resolved disagreements within our coding.

Our Theory of Action

Our analyses of the tools enabled us to articulate a theory of action (Figure 9.2). In this theory of action, our tools were designed to support PSTs to engage in different tasks (i.e., engaging in authentic science; noticing; planning; reflecting),

DESIRED RESULTS

Learning Goal (should be specific and measurable)		
Learning Goal:		
Investigation Question:		
Scientific Explanation:	Claim:	
	Evidence:	
	Reasoning (If appropriate):	

LEARNING PLAN

For each of the following sections of the lesson, describe the activities that students will participate in. Make sure you provide enough detail so that 1) someone else could follow your lesson plan, 2) you provide descriptions of how you will facilitate the activity. What questions will you be asking students? What will you be listening for? What practices will you incorporate in the various stages of the lessons?

	Teaching Plan	Anticipated Student Responses
Engage:		
Experience:		

Figure 9.1 Lesson Planning Tool

Table 9.1 Coding Schemes, Example Codes, and Example Tools

Scheme	Example Codes	Example Tool with this Applied Code included in Figures
Purpose of Tool	Noticing teaching practice Reflecting on teaching practice	Explore Observation Tool (Figure 9.3) Approximation Reflection Tool (Figure 9.6)
High-leverage teaching practice (TeachingWorks, 2016)	Leading a group discussion Explaining and modeling content, practices, and strategies	Sensemaking Planning Tool (Figure 9.5) Scientific Modeling Tool (Figure 9.4)
Science Core Teaching Practices (Kloser, 2014)	Engaging students in investigations Facilitating classroom discourse	Explore Observation Tool (Figure 9.3) Lesson Planning Tool (Figure 9.1)
Pedagogies of Practice (Grossman et al., 2009)	Approximation Representations	Approximation Reflection Tool (Figure 9.6) Explore Observation Tool (Figure 9.3)
Roles for scaffolding (Reiser and Tabak, 2014)	Making Implicit Explicit Breaks down the task into smaller elements	Scientific Modeling Tool (Figure 9.4) Lesson Planning Tool (Figure 9.1)

which are described below. The tools provide this support by making implicit features of different aspects of high-leverage teaching practice explicit through limiting options, breaking down the practice into obvious steps, or requiring consideration of the how or why involved in the practice. We use these tools within the context of the pedagogies of practice—approximating, representing, and decomposing teaching—that we use in our course. In the next sections, we describe each of these process and provide examples of how the tools do this work in order to explicate our thinking about each element of our theory of action. The elements of the theory of action in Figure 9.2 are highlighted in the text using italics when we refer back to a specific construct.

Supporting Engagement in Different Tasks

Our analyses identified four different potential tasks that we designed the tools to support PSTs to be able to do: *engaging in authentic science, planning for instruction, noticing and analyzing teaching practice,* and *reflecting on teaching practice*, the boxes in Figure 9.2. Table 9.1 lists example tools that supported each type of task. These tasks matched expectations in our courses around

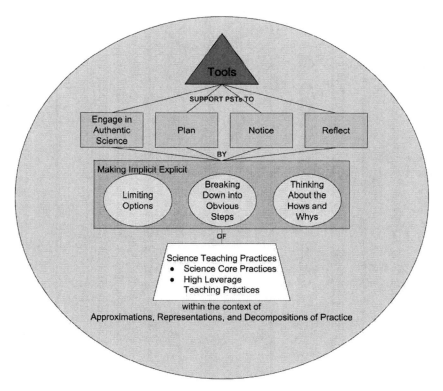

Figure 9.2 Theory of Action for the Support Provided by Tools

the work that we felt would help the PSTs to develop elements of teaching. The tasks also align with the research on the struggles of learning to teach (e.g., Davis *et al.*, 2006).

We used the *Tools for Engaging in Authentic Science* to support the PSTs to engage in aspects of science learning that include engaging in science and engineering practices and developing understanding of the disciplinary core ideas (DCIs) and crosscutting concepts (CCCs). These tools are similar to Ross and Cartier's (2015) discussion of tools that would support students in engaging in authentic science tasks. We used these tools to support the PSTs in developing their own content knowledge for teaching. We also saw tools, such as the Scientific Model Tool (Figure 9.3), as potential exemplars of the types of tools that the PSTs would use with elementary students to scaffold science learning. Anna used this tool, which is based on existing tools for engaging students in scientific modeling (e.g., Windschitl *et al.*, 2012; Tools for Ambitious Teaching, 2018), to support PSTs to engage in a process of modeling and revising their models based on new information and experiences. Other examples supported students in making sense of data, representing data, and writing evidence-based explanations depending on the lessons and activities we modeled in our methods courses.

We designed the *Tools for Planning and Priming* to support the PSTs to engage in all aspects of developing and writing plans for teaching elementary students, from anticipating student ideas to creating unit plans. Similar

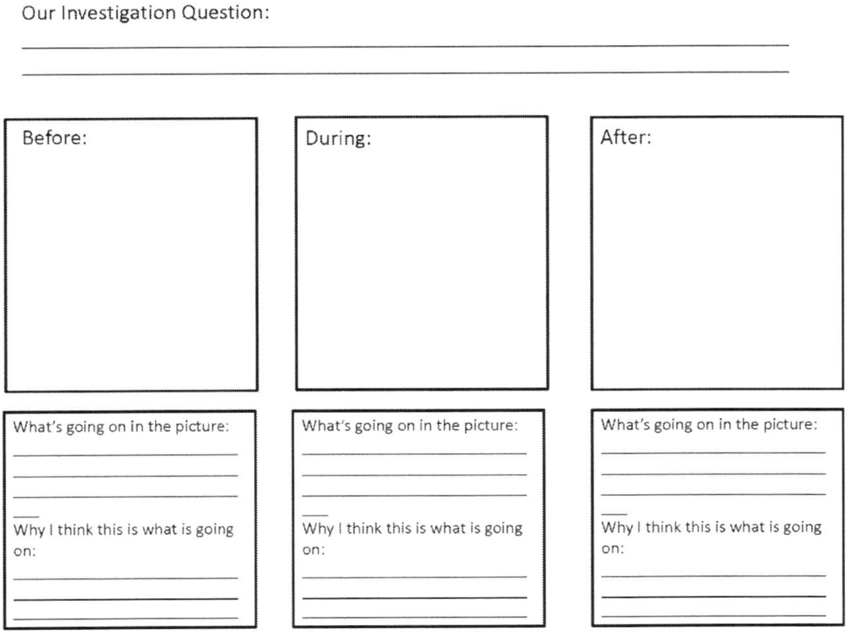
Our Investigation Question:
Before:
During:
After:
What's going on in the picture:
Why I think this is what is going on:
What's going on in the picture:
Why I think this is what is going on:
What's going on in the picture:
Why I think this is what is going on:

Figure 9.3 Scientific Modeling Tool

136 Fick and Arias

to the use of tools that Windschitl and colleagues (2012) described for secondary teachers, we used these tools to prepare our teachers for *approximating* practice through *decomposing* elements of lesson planning (Grossman *et al.*, 2009). With our intention to support the PSTs in preparing for instruction, our planning tools frequently broke down the parts of a lesson plan into smaller pieces in order to support the process of developing a lesson that has a single cohesive learning goal. Sarah used the Lesson Planning Tool (Figure 9.1) to facilitate the development of lesson plans in her methods course. This template purposefully highlights the importance of learning goals and investigation questions, and includes a scientific explanation as a desired result. Then, the teaching plan is broken down into parts using the 5E lesson framework (Bybee, 2013), and has a section where the PST is responsible for anticipating the responses of students during the lesson. Another example of a planning tool is the Sensemaking Planning Tool (Figure 9.4), which requires PSTs to make decisions about how the students will collect data, represent data, and show their understanding of the phenomenon. We used this tool to focus PSTs on how the evidence collected during investigation of a phenomenon might be best represented in order to support student learning. We found that a key aspect of these tools was their priming of the PSTs for diverse science ideas, such as possible student responses, [mis]conceptions, or evidence-based claims that they might propose. These tools supported the PSTs to see value in and use the diversity of students' initial and developing ideas as productive foundations for science learning, supporting rigorous and equitable teaching practice.

Lesson Goal:		
Investigation Question:		
How Ss collected the data	☐ Qualitative ☐ Quantitative ☐ Table ☐ Drawing ☐ Written Description ☐ Other:	This is what the data looked like:
Possible Representations of the Data that Would Answer the investigation question	☐ T-chart ☐ Graph: line, bar, pie, double line, double bar, box and whiskers, pictogram ☐ Venn-diagram ☐ Flow chart ☐ A new model/picture of mechanism ☐ Other:	This is an example of what the representations might look like:
This is how students will make the representation	☐ Individually ☐ As partners ☐ Whole class ☐ On their papers ☐ On a template ☐ On the board ☐ Other:	This is how I will help the students make the representation and understand why to make a representation:

Figure 9.4 Sensemaking Planning Tool

We designed the *Tools for Noticing and Analyzing* to support PSTs in identifying key aspects of teaching practice when observing representations of teaching, including both video records of experienced teachers as well as observations of peers. We used these in conjunction with the pedagogy of *representing* practice (Grossman *et al.*, 2009). These tools build on the tools and strategies that others have used to support PSTs to notice and reason about evidence of supporting student learning (e.g., Benedict-Chambers and Aram, 2017; Sherin and van Es, 2009; also see Benedict-Chambers, this volume, Chapter 10). Knowing that PSTs often notice issues of management, we designed these tools to focus the PSTs on other aspects of science teaching relevant to our courses. For example, the Explore Observation Tool (Figure 9.5) supports PSTs in noticing student and teacher actions and ideas during the investigation portion ("Explore") of a science lesson. Anna used this tool with PSTs when watching video records of an experienced teacher and when the PSTs watched their colleagues teach during the class rehearsals. Designing this tool based on those used at the University of Michigan, Anna included a section describing the relevant teaching practices that could be anticipated to exist within the type of lesson being taught. She used this tool to support the PSTs to be more cognizant observers by targeting their noticing towards specific teaching practices. The tool includes space for the PSTs to record both observations of what the teacher said or did and inferences about these observations connected to student learning. Through including space for observations and inferences, the tool helps the PSTs make the connections between their observation and reasoning about teaching. The other tools for noticing similarly included spaces for making observations and reasoning about these ideas.

Dimensions	**Relevant teaching practices**
Establish data collection (entails *planning and carrying out investigations*)	Support students in setting up one or more investigations that allow them to gather data that they can use as evidence to answer the question or problem. With varying degrees of guidance, have students... • Determine what data will be gathered and how and why it will be collected and recorded • Make justified predictions about the outcome of the investigation. • Discuss safety issues involved in the lesson
Carry out the investigation (entails *planning and carrying out investigations*)	Support students in systematically collecting and recording data (e.g., making scientific observations, making systematic measurements) to generate evidence to answer the investigation question or problem. This includes... • Observing and listening to students as they interact • Asking questions to help students begin to make sense of what their data mean, rather than "telling" students the answer. • Redirecting students' investigations to be more systematic, precise, and objective when necessary • Managing the distribution and collection of materials • Facilitating productive small group work

What the teacher said or did	Inferences about student learning (e.g., How would this support student learning)

Figure 9.5 Explore Observation Tool

138   *Fick and Arias*

Tools for Reflecting supported PSTs to consider how to continue to develop their own teaching practice through purposeful reflection on their teaching. In particular, we designed these tools to aid the PSTs in making evidence-based observations about areas of strength or revision after engaging in the pedagogy of *approximating*. In the Approximation Reflection Tool (Figure 9.6), PSTs are supported to find evidence of success and struggle in videos of their own instructional practice. PSTs are also supported to make connections between what they notice and the high-leverage practices of science teaching discussed in the course. Sarah used this tool after PSTs *approximated* teaching for their peers or at the end of the semester to reflect on teaching full science lessons to elementary students.

Considering the tasks of tools described above, when we looked across all of the tools from our courses we found that they fit into one, or sometimes multiple, of the four tasks of teaching shown in Figure 9.2. Of the tools, 17% supported the task of *engaging in authentic science*; 29% *planning*; 31% *noticing*; and 46% *reflecting*. We designed some of the tools to support more than one task, which is why the percentages add up to more than 100%. For example, a set of tools like the Explore Observation Tool (Figure 9.3) included a section for reflecting where the tools asked the PSTs to apply their noticing of others' teaching practice to consider their own teaching. This connection between noticing and application to one's own teaching seemed particularly important to helping PSTs realize the purpose of observing the teaching of others. In this analysis, we saw how making clear the role of the tools used to support teacher learning might help teacher educators and researchers build on each other's work and develop stronger tools.

For each of the 3 positives and 3 deltas (things you would like to improve), describe a moment when the situation took place using the following format:		
Positive #1		
Evidence	What I observed in the video:	
Analysis	What that segment indicates to me:	
Connections	How does this instance connect to the descriptions of best practices in Science Teaching we've read about? (Include citations to appropriate readings)	
Conclusions	How will your observation influence your future teaching?	

Figure 9.6 Approximation Reflection Tool

The Work of the Tools

In our analysis of the work that the tools, and our use of the tools, did to support PST learning, we saw they provided several different types of scaffolding to support the PSTs in the different teaching tasks. These tools scaffolded the teachers learning through both problematizing and structuring (Reiser, 2004) similar to how Davis (this volume, Chapter 7) describes the role of approximations of practice. First, all of the tools worked to make *implicit features of teaching practice explicit,* connecting to Reiser and Tabak's (2014) description of how scaffolding can highlight critical elements of a task to support learning. These tools scaffolded the teachers learning through both problematizing and structuring (Reiser, 2004). Thus, we used all of the tools in support of the pedagogy of *decomposing* teaching. Given the often implicit nature of teaching practices, these tools seem to facilitate teacher learning by pushing the PSTs to notice elements of science teaching that might be overlooked, a common struggle for PSTs (Davis *et al.*, 2006). The tools required the PSTs to attend to particular aspects of the work of teaching that beginners may not realize are important. For example, the Sensemaking Planning Tool (Figure 9.4) required teachers to consider how students collected the data before deciding which representations to use; we found this to be a part of planning for data representation that is often implicit and not considered by beginning teachers. Likewise, the Approximation Reflection Tool (Figure 9.6) highlights the need to include both evidence as well as analysis of the positive aspects of the lesson, which are often implicit or overlooked aspects of the task of reflecting on practice.

In addition to highlighting implicit elements of the practice, we saw that the tools focused PSTs on discrepancies between typically beginners' work and the desired outcome of the task, suggesting other ways in which a tool could scaffold the PSTs' learning (Reiser, 2004; Reiser and Tabak, 2014). For instance, because PSTs often struggle to think about the variety of ways that data can be represented to support students to identify patterns, the options presented in the Sensemaking Planning Tool (Figure 9.4) provides the PSTs with some ideas to consider. Three ways that the tools might change the way that the preservice teacher approached the task were: 1) *limiting options*; 2) *breaking down the work of the task into obvious steps*; and 3) *highlighting the need to think about how and why they might use a particular approach* as represented by the ovals in Figure 9.2. Not all of the tools used all three strategies; however, we found that each of the tools used at least one of these strategies to support PSTs in the task. *Highlighting the need to think about how and why* (62%) and *breaking down the work* (54%) were more common in the tools than *limiting options* (11%).

When *limiting options*, the tools provided the PSTs with a list of options to select from, focusing the PST to a smaller set of possible options. In the Sensemaking Planning Tool (Figure 9.4) the PST is supported to choose from provided options (column 2). While this tool gives the PST a more limited

140   *Fick and Arias*

sense of choice, it also may provide new ideas from which to select, prompting them to consider which choice might make the most sense for the context.

We often designed the tools to *break down the work of the task into obvious steps*. The Sensemaking Planning Tool (Figure 9.4) includes three boxes on the right side that PSTs complete sequentially, building on the decisions that they made in the previous box. Likewise, the Explore Observation Tool (Figure 9.3) breaks down noticing teaching practice into observing and making inferences; two important elements in the work of observing. Breaking down the work involved both making the pivotal elements apparent and providing the PST with support for how to approach these elements.

Many of the tools focused on *highlighting the need to think about the how and/or why* involved in making decisions about their teaching practice. The third column of the Sensemaking Planning Tool (Figure 9.4) supports PSTs to articulate how they plan to have students represent their data and how they will support students to be able to do that. The final box in the column also asks the PST to consider how they will support elementary students to understand why they are using the representation of data. This requires the teachers to consider deeply the *how* involved in teaching students to analyze data and *why* a particular data representation is appropriate. Similarly, the Approximation Reflection Tool (Figure 9.6) asks teachers to think about *why* a particular instance is a success or a struggle in need of revision.

Supporting Teaching Practices

Our analyses highlighted that the tools supported at least one high-leverage teaching practice or core science teaching practice as represented by the trapezoid in Figure 9.2 (Ball and Forzani, 2009; Kloser, 2014); this is not unexpected given the focus on teaching practices within the courses. The tools we analyzed supported some high-leverage teaching practices (TeachingWorks, 2016) more than others. Common high-leverage practices supported by the tools included "analyzing instruction for the purpose of improving it" (20 of 32 tools), "explaining and modeling content, practices, and strategies" (18 of 32 tools), "eliciting student thinking" (14 of 32 tools), "diagnosing student thinking" (9 of 32 tools), and "designing single lessons" (9 of 32 tools). The analysis of the core science teaching practices (Kloser, 2014) supported by the tools showed similar trends. The tools more commonly supported the core science teaching practices of "focusing on core science ideas, practices, and crosscutting concepts," "engaging students in investigations," and "eliciting, assessing and using student thinking about science."

Our analysis showed that often the tools linked several teaching practices together. Approximately three-quarters of the tools supported multiple high-leverage teaching practices. For instance, the Sensemaking Planning Tool (Figure 9.4) includes emphasis on "explaining and modeling content and practices," "setting long-term goals," and "designing a single lesson." Likewise, the Explore Observation Tool (Figure 9.5) connected "eliciting student thinking" to "analyzing instruction for the purpose of improving it." Some of this linking seemed to be connected to the purpose of the tools. All of the planning tools linked more than one teaching practice together. In contrast, almost all of the tools for engaging in authentic practices, such as the Science Modeling Tool (Figure 9.3), only focused on one high-leverage teaching practice, typically, "explaining and modeling content and practices."

The linking of teaching practices not only occurred across an entire tool but within each component of the tool. For example, each component of the Lesson Planning Tool (Figure 9.1) supported at least two high-leverage teaching practices. The "Desired Results" portion of the Lesson Planning Tool (Figure 9.1) required the PSTs to engage in elements of the high-leverage teaching practice of *explaining and modeling content, practices, and strategies* by asking the preservice teacher to consider how they will support students to explain a phenomena by "write an example scientific explanation that students should be able to construct as a result of your lesson." This section of the tool also engages the user in elements of "setting long- and short-term learning goals" in the section of "learning goal (should be specific and measurable)." Because Sarah designed the Lesson Plan Tool to support the construction of a lesson, this tool links these two high-leverage practices with a third teaching practice "designing a single lesson." We found similar linking of the core science teaching practices.

Our analysis revealed that these tools often decomposed elements of individual teaching practices while linking the teaching practices. For example, the high leverage practice, "designing a single lesson" is decomposed into the smaller components within the Lesson Planning Tool (Figure 9.1) by breaking down a science lesson into the "5Es" (Bybee, 2013). Likewise, Sarah designed the tool to decompose elements of "explaining and modeling content" by highlighting the need to consider the claim, evidence, and reasoning expected from the students and then considering how to support students to reach this goal through the components of the lesson. In addition to decomposing elements of individual teaching practices and linking the teaching practices, the tools also nest practices within each other (Boerst *et al.*, 2011). This nesting and linking highlights the potential of the tools to recompose teaching practices and support the enactment of teaching practices together which occurs within elementary classrooms. This ability to link practices together has implications for how to develop and use similar tools within teacher education programs.

Missed Opportunities for Supporting Learning

Our analysis of the tools also illuminated potential missed opportunities for supporting learning. When looking at each other's tools with the eyes of an outsider, we noticed that we did not often include in the tools explicit descriptions of the rationale for the tool, such as when to use the tool in the future or which teaching practice(s) it was decomposing. For example, the title of the Sensemaking Planning Tool (Figure 9.4) might give PSTs a potential reason for using this tool, however, the title of the tool and the tool itself do not make the rationale for using this tool clear, nor why a teacher might want to use this tool in the future. Likewise, this tool breaks down aspects of the teaching practice "explaining and modeling content, practices, and strategies," yet this is not made clear for the PSTs. Providing a reason for using this tool and how it is connected to teaching practice within the tool itself might support PSTs to gain deeper understanding of teaching practice and better motivate them in using this tool. We felt particular concern about this because we know that PSTs struggle to bring ideas about science teaching into their future teaching (e.g., Arias and Davis, 2017; Thompson, *et al.*, 2013).

Another area of missed opportunity was the lack of precise language to ensure the tool can support particular teaching practices. As we coded each other's tools, often we noticed instances where the tool was not worded precisely enough to highlight important elements of the task or underscore common discrepancies between the preservice teachers' thinking and the expectations for the task. For example, one tool asked for "evidence" to support why a particular aspect of a video was productive, but this tool was unclear about what might count as evidence. We also found varying level of explicitness in requiring consideration of the DCIs, SEPs, and CCCs (NGSS Lead States, 2013). We have been working together for a number of years, so we have a common language. This common language might mean that we understood each other's meanings and intentions more than another teacher educator or novice teacher might. Similarly, new to the practice of teaching, PSTs may not pick up on some of the nuanced intentions of the tools. Thus, the tool along with guidance from the teacher educator may not be supporting the PSTs within their zone of proximal development (Vygotsky, 1978). Additionally, a tool does not operate in isolation; all of these tools are used within the context of a learning environment that provides meaning and opportunities to interact with the tools and others (Putnam and Borko, 2000). A teacher educator might make this clear when using the tool in class with students, yet we wonder if more explicitness in the tool might provide a synergistic relationship between the teacher educator and the scaffolding of the tool (Reiser and Tabak, 2014).

Conclusion

In describing a theory of action for how our tools might facilitate PSTs' development of the teaching practices involved in supporting elementary students' sensemaking, we add to the conversation about how tools can support ambitious teaching within the varying contexts of practice-based teacher education programs (e.g., Arias and Davis, 2017; Boerst *et al.*, 2011;

Lampert and Grazani, 2011; Windschitl *et al.*, 2012; see also Davis, Palincsar, and Kademian, this volume, Chapter 13; Kademian and Davis, this volume, Chapter 8). Our analyses enabled us to articulate our vision for how these tools can support PSTs' learning. Through naming the tasks that tools support, the type of scaffolding they provide, and the teaching practices they inform, we are able to consider how and why we use these tools within our courses as well as how to improve the clarity and quality of their use. For example, the tools' abilities to link and nest teaching practices implies the great potential of these tools and the need for careful consideration of when and how to use the tools. An important consideration is how to support PSTs to fade use of these tools over time and how to internalize enactment of tasks supported by the tool (Reiser and Tabak, 2014; Vygotsky, 1978; Wood, Bruner, and Ross, 1976). The conception of scaffolding implied fading the support over time. Thus, some of these tools can serve as scaffolds, but we need intentional planning about which are supports and which are scaffolds. Some of the tools might be faded throughout a course or over the course of a teacher preparation program, whereas other tools might follow teachers into their beginning teaching careers. Still other tools may act as supports that teachers will use indefinitely.

Through our collaboration, we learned the importance of sharing, analyzing, adapting tools for our local context. These experiences highlight the potential for developing greater collaboration among teacher educators. We suggest that other teacher educators might apply this theory of action and process of analyzing tools within the design and teaching of their own courses. This more purposeful development, adaptation, and use of tools can lead to supporting beginning teachers to learn and enact the nuanced, complex, rigorous teaching that supports student sensemaking in science.

References

Arias, A. M., and Davis, E. A. (2017). Supporting children to construct evidence-based claims in science: Individual learning trajectories in a practice-based program. *Teaching and Teacher Education*, *66*, 204–218.

Ball, D. L., and Forzani, F. (2009). The work of teaching and the challenge for teacher education. *Journal of Teacher Education*, *60*(5), 497–511.

Ball, D. L., Sleep, L., Boerst, T. A., and Bass, H. (2009). Combining the development of practice and the practice of development in teacher education. *The Elementary School Journal*, *109*(5), 458–474.

Benedict-Chambers, A., and Aram, R. (2017). Tools for teacher noticing: Helping preservice teachers notice and analyze student thinking and scientific practice use. *Journal of Science Teacher Education*, *28*(3), 294–318.

Boerst, T. A., Sleep, L., Ball, D. L., and Bass, H. (2011). Preparing teachers to lead mathematics discussions. *Teachers College Record*, *113*(12), 2844–2877.

Buck, G., and Akerson, V. (Eds.). (2016). *Enhancing Professional Knowledge of Pre-Service Science Teacher Education by Self-Study Research*. Switzerland: Springer International Publishing.

Bybee, R. W. (2013). *Translating the NGSS for Classroom Instruction*. Arlington, VA: NSTA Press.

Davis, E. A. (2016). Evolving goals, pedagogies, and identities as an elementary science teacher educator: Prioritizing practice. In G. Buck and V. Akerson (Eds.), *Enhancing Professional Knowledge of Pre-Service Science Teacher Education by Self-Study Research* (pp. 151–176). Switzerland: Springer International Publishing.

Davis, E. A., and T. A. Boerst. (2014). Designing elementary teacher education to prepare well-started beginners. Retrieved from: http://www.teachingworks.org/images/files/TeachingWorks_Davis_Boerst_WorkingPapers_March_2014.pdf

Davis, E. A., Petish, D., and Smithey, J. (2006). Challenges new science teachers face. *Review of Educational Research*, 76(4), 607–651.

Grossman, P., Compton, C., Igra, D., Ronfeldt, M., Shahan, E., and Williamson, P. (2009). Teaching practice: A cross-professional perspective. *Teachers College Record*, 111(9), 2055–2100.

Kloser, M. (2014). Identifying a core set of science teaching practices: A delphi expert panel approach. *Journal of Research in Science Teaching*, 51(9), 1185–1217.

Lampert, M., and Graziani, F. (2009). Instructional activities as a tool for teachers' and teacher educators' learning. *The Elementary School Journal*, 109(5), 491–509.

Miles, M. B., Huberman, A. M., and Saldana, J. (2014). *Qualitative Data Analysis: A Methods Sources* (3rd edn.). Los Angeles: Sage Publications, Inc.

NGSS Lead States. (2013). *Next Generation Science Standards: For States, By States*. Washington, DC: National Academies Press.

Peercy, M. M., and Troyan, F. J. (2017). Making transparent the challenges of developing a practice-based pedagogy of teacher education. *Teaching and Teacher Education*, 61, 26–36.

Putnam, R., and Borko, H. (2000). What do new views of knowledge and thinking have to say about research on teacher learning? *Educational Researcher*, 29(1), 4–15.

Reiser, B. J. (2004). Scaffolding complex learning: The mechanisms of structuring and problematizing student work. *Journal of the Learning Sciences*, 13(3), 273–304.

Reiser, B. J., and Tabak, I. (2014). Scaffolding. In R. K. Sawyer (Ed.), *Cambridge Handbook of the Learning Sciences* (2nd edn.). New York.

Ross, D. K., and Cartier, J. L. (2015). Developing pre-service elementary teachers' pedagogical practices while planning using the learning cycle. *Journal of Science Teacher Education*, 26(6), 573–591.

Sherin, M. G., and van Es, E. (2009). Effects of video club participation on teachers' professional vision. *Journal of Teacher Education*, 60(1), 20–37.

TeachingWorks. (2016). High leverage teaching practices. Retrieved from http://www.teachingworks.org/work-of-teaching/high-leverage-practices

Thompson, J., Windschitl, M., and Braaten, M. (2013). Developing a theory of ambitious early-career teacher practice. *American Educational Research Journal*, 50(3), 574–615.

Tools for Ambitious Teaching. (2018). Scaffolding tools. Retrieved from https://ambitiousscienceteaching.org/tools-scaffolding/

Vygotsky, L. S. (1978). *Mind in Society: The Development of High Psychological Processes*. Cambridge, MA: Harvard University Press.

Windschitl, M., Thompson, J., Braaten, M., and Stroupe, D. (2012). Proposing a core set of instructional practices and tools for teachers of science. *Science Education*, 96(5), 878–903.

Wood, D., Bruner, J. S., and Ross, G. (1976). The role of tutoring in problem solving. *Journal of Child Psychology and Psychiatry*, 17(2), 89–100.

10 Using Tools to Notice Student Ideas and Support Student Sensemaking in Rehearsal and Classroom Lesson Reflections

Amanda Benedict-Chambers
MISSOURI STATE UNIVERSITY

Introduction

To teach effectively, preservice teachers need to learn to notice student ideas and support student sensemaking. However, classrooms are complex, busy settings and preservice teachers may struggle to know what is most important to focus on, interpret, and to use what they see (van Es *et al.*, 2017). Scholars refer to this important practice as *teacher noticing*, which consists of three main aspects: (a) attending to students' ideas and strategies; (b) using evidence of students' understandings to interpret instruction; and (c) deciding how to respond on the basis of students' understandings (Jacobs *et al.*, 2010; van Es *et al.*, 2017).

In science, sensemaking is the process through which students use science practices to develop an understanding of disciplinary core ideas (NGSS Lead States, 2013). Jacobs and colleagues (2010) found that preservice teachers (PSTs) struggle to respond on the basis of student sensemaking when reflecting on practice. Rather than referencing student thinking, the study showed that they made assumptions about student understanding and focused on the teachers' thinking. Noticing student sensemaking requires teachers to develop content knowledge and pedagogical content knowledge (Avraamidou and Zembal-Saul, 2010). Without a clear understanding of the phenomenon, teachers may not be prepared for students' ideas or know how to engage students in using scientific practices.

Rehearsals and tools have been shown to support PST learning (Davis, this volume; Grossman *et al.*, 2009; Stroupe and Gotwals, 2017; Windschitl *et al.*, 2012). The rehearsal is an example of a pedagogical approach that draws on representations, decompositions, and approximations of practice. These three pedagogical approaches, as described by Grossman and colleagues (2009), prepare preservice teachers for challenging aspects of teaching in a context, such as a methods course, that is less authentic and less complex than the busy classroom setting. Representations of practice, such as video recordings of instruction, demonstrate key teaching practices in action. Decompositions of practice, such as a set of frameworks, identify important features that may not

146 *Benedict-Chambers*

be visible to PSTs. Approximations of practice, like rehearsals, allow PSTs to enact and receive feedback on difficult teaching practices.

Tools play an important role in promoting the learning opportunities afforded in rehearsals (see, e.g., Kademian and Davis, this volume, Chapter 8). For instance, lists of possible student ideas about a phenomenon can represent what is important for teachers to notice during instruction. Tools such as reflection prompts can decompose specific aspects of instruction and guide teachers to interpret instructional interactions in evidence-based ways (e.g., van Es *et al.*, 2017). Finally, tools can support authentic teacher–student interactions in approximations by guiding the classmates to respond as "elementary students" with alternative conceptions (e.g., Benedict-Chambers, 2016; Benedict-Chambers and Aram, 2017). Although rehearsals can foster PST noticing (Benedict-Chambers and Aram, 2017), little is known about the role that tools play *with rehearsals* to help preservice teachers engage in the important work of noticing student ideas and supporting student sensemaking. In this chapter, I share two sets of data from a study of the role of tools during rehearsals: (a) PSTs' written rehearsal and classroom reflections that refer to student understandings; and (b) interviews with PSTs about their tool use. These data were collected in my elementary science methods course. In particular, I was interested in investigating: *How might tool-supported rehearsals help preservice teachers to notice student ideas and support student sensemaking?* I focused on two questions: (a) *In what ways did preservice teachers notice student ideas and support student sensemaking in rehearsal and classroom teaching reflections?*; and (b) *How do preservice teachers describe the role of the tools with the rehearsals in helping them to notice student ideas and support student sensemaking?*

Tool-Supported Rehearsals in the Elementary Science Methods Course

In the science methods course, the preservice teachers learned to enact and analyze the core practices of science teaching, focusing specifically on noticing students' ideas and supporting student sensemaking. I used three tools with rehearsals to support the PSTs in preparing for, enacting, and analyzing interactions with student sensemaking. The rehearsals and tools were informed by and adapted from my graduate work at the University of Michigan. While at U-M, I was part of the Elementary Science Methods Planning Group (ESMPG), a long-term instructional group headed by Davis. After leaving Michigan, I adapted the rehearsals for my own context and continued to develop them locally. Two of the tools I describe in this chapter were also originally developed in the ESMPG (see also Kademian and Davis, this volume, Chapter 8; Fick and Arias, this volume, Chapter 9).

At the beginning of the course, I arranged the preservice teachers in three-person teams for their rehearsals. Each team was responsible for teaching a specific disciplinary core idea in an elementary classroom at the end of the semester in a school that partnered with the science methods course. To prepare for the lesson, the teams enacted three 20-minute Engage-Explore-Explain (EEE) rehearsals during the course. The EEE framework, similar to the 5E model often used in science classrooms (Bybee *et al.*, 2006), provides an instructional framework for novice elementary teachers. I collaborated with the U-M ESMPG in developing the framework. The EEE rehearsals allowed PSTs to focus on the practices and principles that supported student learning within three phases of a science lesson:

- *Engage phase:* Elicit and engage students' ideas with an investigation question.
- *Explore phase:* Support students' observations and data collection explorations.
- *Explain phase:* Help students notice patterns and develop evidence-based explanations.

During the rehearsals, the teams taught a phase of the science lesson to the rest of the methods course, during which the other preservice teachers, and the teacher educator, simulated the actions and ideas of elementary students. The teacher educator also offered feedback during each rehearsal and afterwards as the class debriefed the instruction. Each rehearsal was video recorded, and the PSTs individually analyzed the instruction after the rehearsals for a course assignment.

The *student alternative ideas tool*, the first tool, was based on two tools that were originally developed by the U-M ESMPG (cf. Kademian and Davis, this volume, Chapter 8) and modified locally. Each semester, I compiled a list of student alternative ideas to represent the alternative ideas that elementary students might have about the concepts investigated in each lesson (e.g., Driver *et al.*, 1985). For instance, students investigating how light travels may believe that light travels from a person's eye to an object, rather than from the object to the eye. This tool provided a summary of student ideas and the accurate scientific explanation for each idea, and it was discussed in class prior to the rehearsals (Benedict-Chambers and Aram, 2017). Each PST in the methods course selected specific ideas to role-play for each team's rehearsal. As a part of their role-play, they responded to the instruction with alternative ideas and explanations. The teams studied the alternative ideas prior to the rehearsals and included questions in their lesson plans to elicit and respond to the students' ideas.

The *science practice challenges tool*, the second tool, highlighted the difficulties often experienced by elementary students as they learn to use science practices. Anna Arias led the development of an initial version of this tool, as a part of the U-M ESMPG. For instance, when recording their observations, students may make inferences rather than observations, or interpret their observations to match what they predicted, rather than what actually

148 *Benedict-Chambers*

happens in the investigation. Similar to the *student alternative ideas tool,* each preservice teacher in the course selected and role-played a science practice challenge to simulate interactions where students struggled to use the practices as they developed evidence-based explanations. Although the two tools treated the disciplinary core ideas and science practices separately, during the enactment of the lesson, the two worked in tandem as the PSTs role-played students using science practices to understand disciplinary core ideas. The teachers also reviewed the science practice challenges prior to the rehearsals and included teaching moves in their lesson plans to anticipate and respond to potential student difficulties.

The preservice teachers generated the third tool, *lesson artifacts of student thinking,* as they role-played the ideas and actions of elementary students in the rehearsal. This tool provided the teachers with an opportunity to analyze simulated elementary students' efforts to integrate science practices with the learning of disciplinary core ideas. For instance, in the Engage rehearsal, the simulated students may have written predictions that reflected their alternative ideas about the phenomenon or lacked justification. In the Explore rehearsals, students may have recorded observations in a data table that reflected alternative conceptions, or recorded observations in an inaccurate manner. In the Explain rehearsals, students may have struggled to make sense of patterns in their data or to write claims supported by evidence from the investigation. At the end of their rehearsals, the PSTs collected these lesson artifacts of student thinking and analyzed them as a part of their rehearsal reflections. The teaching teams taught the same lesson in an elementary classroom at the end of the semester, collected similar artifacts of student thinking, and individually analyzed their instruction in a final teaching reflection.

Research Design

This study took place in the elementary teacher education program at Missouri State University where preservice teachers were earning a bachelor's of science degree in elementary education. The science methods course occurred in the third semester of the five-semester teacher education program, and I was the instructor of the course.

Data Sources

The primary source of data for the first research question was written teaching reflections collected from 53 students (48 females, five males) from three sections of a science methods course. The PSTs were typical undergraduate seniors, at approximately 21 years of age, and all but one of the PSTs were white. To investigate the ways PSTs responded to their students' ideas, I focused on teaching reflections where they attended to students' ideas from their lessons, thus eliminating from my investigation the reflections that privileged their own teaching moves or student management. Of the 212 reflections collected (three rehearsal and one classroom lesson reflection per PST), I analyzed 93 reflections for this study. My investigation focused on one (four-part) question in the reflection.

> First, indicate one new area you or your team could revise from your lesson and what you could have done to improve the instruction. Second, provide evidence (different timestamp or student work evidence) from the lesson to prove that revision is needed to better support student learning. Third, provide a rationale to explain why your idea for revision could have more effectively supported student learning of the specific science concept of your lesson. Fourth, indicate specific moves that describe what you could have done to improve the instruction.

This question prompted PSTs to draw on evidence of student understandings from their lesson and to reflect on their interactions with student sensemaking. I also drew on four semi-structured interviews conducted with five randomly selected preservice teachers (Julianne, Tina, Jenny, Kacie, and Ben) in the science methods course (20 total interviews). Research assistants, familiar with the course, conducted the interviews after each of the three rehearsals and the classroom lesson to understand the PSTs' tool use. As the instructor, I did not review them until after course grades were posted. In the interviews, the research assistants asked PSTs to describe how they did or did not use the tools before, during, and after the rehearsal and classroom lessons. Ben was the only PST who discussed feeling comfortable teaching science from opportunities to substitute and teach summer school; the other four teachers mentioned having few experiences observing or teaching science in classroom settings.

Data Analysis

To code the written reflections, I first tagged the parts of the reflections where the PSTs wrote about revising their instruction. Next, drawing on previous research about teacher noticing (e.g., Benedict-Chambers and Aram, 2017; Jacobs *et al.*, 2010; van Es *et al.*, 2017) and student sensemaking in science (e.g., Benedict-Chambers *et al.*, 2017; Berland and Reiser, 2009). I developed a coding scheme to describe the ways the PSTs attended to students' ideas and strategies and supported student sensemaking as the process of helping students use science practices (SP) to develop an understanding of a disciplinary core idea (DCI). I examined the extent to which their responses emphasized the connections among specific student ideas, students' use of science practices, and students' understanding of the disciplinary core idea. Three major categories emerged; examples are provided in the text below.

150   *Benedict-Chambers*

1   PSTs attended to students' ideas about phenomena and responded by integrating students' use of science practices *and* learning of disciplinary core ideas;
2   PSTs attended to students' ideas about phenomena, but responded by focusing on students' use of science practices, *or* their understanding of the DCI, without a SP-DCI integration;
3   PSTs attended to student confusion about an aspect of the instruction (worksheet, materials, post-test), but omitted details of students' thinking about the phenomenon, and the responses did not build on students' understandings.

After checking for agreement on the codes, two researchers coded the written reflections, and we achieved over 90% interrater reliability. The second researcher was a graduate student who served as a teaching assistant in the course and was present for all of the rehearsals. Any coding discrepancies were resolved through discussion, and data were re-coded as needed.

After coding the rehearsal and classroom reflections, we coded the 20 transcribed interviews to understand the ways the PSTs used the tools to notice student ideas and support student sensemaking. We coded each interview question and response (Miles *et al.*, 2014) and looked for commonalities and discrepancies in how the PSTs discussed using the tools before, during, and after the instruction.

Findings

Findings indicate that in their rehearsal reflections almost two-thirds of preservice teachers attended to students' ideas in ways that supported sensemaking—that is, they responded by integrating students' use of science practices *and* learning of disciplinary core ideas. Similarly, in their classroom lesson reflections, almost half of the PSTs in the study attended to students' ideas and focused on promoting sensemaking. Next, I examine the ways the tool-supported rehearsals afforded opportunities for PSTs to support student sensemaking.

Supporting Student Sensemaking by Integrating Students' Use of Science Practices and Learning of DCI

Table 10.1 shows that in almost two-thirds (63%) of the rehearsal reflections PSTs attended to students' ideas, interpreted the scientific thinking reflected in those ideas, *and* responded by integrating students' use of science practices *and* learning of disciplinary core idea. A little less than half (43%) of the classroom lesson reflections also attended to students' ideas and focused on supporting sensemaking. To illustrate, in the following example from an Explore rehearsal reflection, the PST noticed the students' observations

Using Tools to Notice Student Ideas 151

Table 10.1 Supporting Student Sensemaking in Rehearsal and Classroom Lesson Reflections

Dimensions of supporting student sensemaking	Rehearsal reflections N=56	Classroom lesson reflections N=37
Attending to students' ideas about phenomena *and* responding by integrating students' use of science practices *and* learning of disciplinary core ideas	63% (35/56)	43% (16/37)
Attending to students' ideas about phenomena, but responding by focusing on students' use of science practices *or* their understanding of the disciplinary core idea, without a SP-DCI integration	13% (7/56)	19% (7/37)
Attending to student confusion about an aspect of the instruction (worksheet, materials, post-test), but omitting details of students' thinking about the phenomenon; the responses did not build on students' understandings	25% (14/56)	38% (14/37)

from the investigation would likely not support their understanding of how light energy travels when it reflects off different surfaces. In the reflections that focused on student sensemaking, the PST's reasons for adapting their instruction focused on the connections they noticed among three aspects from instruction: (a) specific student ideas; (b) student use of science practices; and (c) goals for the lesson's disciplinary core idea.

> I would revise the Explore handout … it would get students to think critically about where light comes from, how it travels, and how it helps us to see [disciplinary core idea] … For the mirror activity, I would ask students to draw pictures [science practice] of how the mirror and light was positioned and how the light traveled … To make the handout better, I will name each activity and include questions for each … For the foil activity, I would ask students to describe how the light traveled when reflected off the crumpled piece and off of the flat piece. This would discourage students from writing a general statement such as "it was brighter on the flat piece." [student idea]
>
> (PST 23, Explore Reflection)

In this example, the PST's response to noticing student ideas on the data table was to revise her instruction to better support student sensemaking. She noticed that students' observations of light energy were not very specific, and their observations would likely not deepen their understanding of how light energy travels. Her response to what she saw—students were not noticing important aspects of the phenomena—informed her decision to revise the handout guiding the investigation to enhance student understanding of how

152 *Benedict-Chambers*

light energy travels when it reflects off different surfaces. This response is typical in that the reflections that supported student sensemaking considered students' use of science practices and their developing ideas about the phenomenon in relation to the lesson's disciplinary core idea. In this reflection, the PST reasoned that providing opportunities for sensemaking would come from integrating the students' content and practice understanding.

Attending to Students' Ideas about Phenomena without Integrating Students' Use of Science Practices or Their Understanding of the DCI

Table 10.1 also indicates that in a small number of rehearsal and classroom reflections, 13% and 19% respectively, PSTs attended to students' ideas, but they responded by focusing on students' use of science practices *or* their understanding of the disciplinary core idea, without integrating the two. The next excerpt from an Explore Rehearsal reflection shows how a PST noticed a specific student idea, but he overlooked the connection between students recording accurate observations (an aspect of carrying out an investigation) and learning about how to change the pitch of a sound.

> One area that could be revised … as we go over each station students should point to the column they will be writing their observation in. This way students are sure to write their observations in the correct column. It would also help to make sure they all write the correct observations down. One of my students wrote, "The big rubber band is louder" [student idea] in the straw section. I believe this happened because it was their first station they went to and the straw section is the first column. We want students' observations to be written correctly [science practice] so that they can come to a correct conclusion.
>
> (PST 12, Explore Reflection)

Although this PST suggested revising his instruction of the pitch stations based on noticing that a student in the rehearsal recorded her observation of the rubber band station in the straw station column, he used the student's understandings in a very general way. That is, he did not make an explicit connection between where the student recorded her observations and her learning of pitch. He focused instead on guiding students to come to a correct conclusion, rather than on using their observations to understand how to create a high or low pitch. While helping a first-grade student learn where and how to record observations may seem like an obvious and insignificant thing to notice, it is an important step in scaffolding students' use of science practices to understand phenomena. This challenge was specifically noted on the *science practices tool*, so a classmate may have selected this to role-play as a student in the lesson.

Attending to Student Confusion

In one-fourth (25%) of the rehearsal reflections and 38% of the classroom lesson reflections, the PSTs attended to student confusion about an aspect of the instruction, but they did not include details of student thinking about the phenomenon, and they did not respond in a way that added to students' understandings of the practice–idea integration. In the following excerpt from an Explain rehearsal reflection, a PST noticed her student mixed up the definitions of insulators and conductors. Although she recognized her student's confusion, she omitted details of the student's thinking about the phenomenon and did not consider the student's use of science practices in understanding conductors and insulators.

> One thing we could improve on is making sure that we clearly say what the definitions of conductors and insulators are by either writing them on the board or in our PowerPoint ... because we had one student who got the definitions mixed up [student confusion]. This would have helped the students more clearly understand our main topics of conductors and insulators.
>
> (PST 25, Explain Reflection)

In reflecting on her lesson, the PST realized that some students did not fully grasp the meaning of insulators and conductors. Although her ideas to emphasize the definitions would have likely supported student understanding, she did not consider how the students used *science practices* to investigate insulators and conductors. In addition, she did not mention any specific student ideas about insulators or conductors that she could build on to foster their sensemaking. While the responses coded in this way show that the PSTs are not yet all attending consistently to students' ideas and supporting sensemaking, recognizing student confusion is an important step in learning to notice and respond to student thinking.

In summary, the analyses of the rehearsal and classroom lesson reflections suggest the tool-supported rehearsals afforded opportunities for preservice teachers to attend to students' ideas and promote student sensemaking. In particular, these opportunities enabled the novices to consider the connections among specific student ideas, their use of science practices, and their understanding of the disciplinary core idea. Many of the preservice teachers focused their reflections on these practice–idea integrations.

Preservice Teachers' Tool Use Before, During, and After Instruction

In this section, I discuss how the five focal preservice teachers described, in their interviews, the ways the tools with the rehearsals helped them to notice student ideas and support student sensemaking. The interviews suggest they used the tools to: (a) anticipate and manage the complexity of working with students' ideas and use of science practices before the instruction; (b) respond to student ideas during instruction; and (c) reflect on how they supported student sensemaking after instruction.

Using the Tools to Anticipate and Manage the Complexity of Working with Students' Ideas and Use of Science Practices

Four of five focal preservice teachers described using the *student alternative ideas tool* and the *science practice challenges tool* to prepare for the uncertain work of supporting student thinking and use of science practices. To illustrate, Ben explained that he and his teaching team used the tools to plan for the kinds of ideas they might face in their lesson,

> The [list of] misconceptions ... got us thinking about what students might [say], if we put ourselves in the first and second graders' shoes, some questions that they might have, that they can throw at us, that we can start to prepare for and then kind of build our lesson around.
>
> (Ben, Engage rehearsal interview)

Similarly, Kacie said,

> I really like the list of student misconceptions, it's nice to just know that because when we went and did our pre-test [in the classroom], there were a lot of those [ideas] on there, so it was good to be familiar with those so whenever they say something you're not just like, "Oh my goodness." Especially since we weren't really familiar with our topic.
>
> (Kacie, Explain rehearsal interview)

Kacie highlighted how the *student alternative ideas tool* enabled her to feel more equipped to reply when she encountered students' alternative ideas during instruction. Jenny also emphasized that she reviewed the *science practice challenges tool* prior to her classroom lesson to anticipate what difficulties her students might face as they learned to record data. She said, "The scientific practice challenges tool ... was helpful to look over and remember how students were supposed to record data and what things they might struggle with" (Jenny, Classroom lesson interview). These responses suggest the PSTs used the tools to prepare for and manage some of the complex aspects they might face in practice—such as supporting student thinking and use of science practices.

The PSTs also emphasized that the tools not only helped them anticipate students' ideas and use of science practices, but when their classmates did not use the tools to simulate student thinking, they missed an opportunity to practice. After her classroom lesson, Tina expressed frustration about the missed opportunity to respond to students' ideas because her classmates did not role-play the alternative ideas during her team's rehearsals. She said,

Using Tools to Notice Student Ideas 155

For the misconceptions, when we were doing the rehearsals, we were supposed to mark what we should act out, but no one really did, so it didn't really help; when we were actually teaching [in the classroom] if one of the kids had a misconception we didn't really know how to explain it without giving them the answer.

(Tina, Classroom lesson interview)

Here, she made connections between the opportunity to practice working with simulated students' ideas in the rehearsals and the chance to develop the skills to support student sensemaking in the classroom. These responses suggest the PSTs valued the learning opportunities afforded by the simulated teacher–student interactions.

Using the Tools to Respond to Student Ideas During Instruction

When asked to describe how they used the tools during the Engage rehearsal, three of the five PSTs noted they did not use the *student alternative ideas tool* because they did not expect to respond to students' ideas in the Engage rehearsal. Jenny said,

I did not use [*the student alternative ideas tool*] to create the lesson, did not think they would come up so soon … I think I just kind of figured, especially in the classroom when I go in, that they will not have the misconceptions.

(Jenny, Engage rehearsal interview)

Similarly, Julianne assumed that alternative ideas would not surface because the Engage rehearsal did not emphasize vocabulary terms, saying, "for the Engage phase, we didn't really think it was going to be that into [the students' alternative ideas] yet because we didn't have to use vocab" (Julianne, Engage rehearsal interview). As the instructor, I was surprised that they did not expect to work with their students' ideas in the Engage rehearsal, given that we had reviewed the *student alternative ideas tool* and discussed students' alternative ideas during the two class sessions prior to the Engage rehearsal. In later interviews, Jenny and Julianne emphasized that students might share ideas during the lesson, and they described reviewing the *student alternative ideas tool* to help them be ready to respond to those ideas during instruction. In reference to her Explore rehearsal, Julianne commented, "We studied [the *student alternative ideas tool*]. Just made sure if the students asked some of those questions we'd be able to answer their questions" (Julianne, Explore rehearsal interview). Similarly, after the Explain rehearsal, Jenny said, "I took the advice of myself when I didn't read the misconception sheet [before the Engage and Explore rehearsal]. I read it before just in case in the Explain, if a misconception did come up" (Jenny, Explain rehearsal interview).

156   *Benedict-Chambers*

Given the familiarity of instruction, preservice teachers may make assumptions about what is involved in supporting student sensemaking. Moreover, they may underestimate the complexity of this work, and as a result overlook important aspects of supporting student sensemaking. However, as the interviews suggest, the artificial nature of the rehearsals may help make familiar aspects of teaching more complex, which directs them to focus on important aspects of practice (Grossman *et al.*, 2009) such as working with students' ideas. In particular, the rehearsals may reveal how difficult it is to respond to and support students' scientific thinking, which could lead PSTs to embrace the scaffolds afforded by the tools.

Using the Tools to Reflect on How They Supported Student Sensemaking

All five of the focal preservice teachers mentioned using the *student alternative ideas tool, science practice challenges tool,* and *lesson artifacts of student thinking* to reflect on how they supported student sensemaking in their lessons. For instance, Kacie described using the *student alternative ideas tool* after her lesson to analyze a student's thinking about pitch and to identify an alternative idea on a *lesson artifact of student thinking* (student work sample in which a classmate used an assigned student idea to complete a handout). She said,

> One of the [alternative ideas] was "hitting an object harder changes the sound." We had to redirect them that we're not looking for the sound, we want pitch...I did have a student write that hitting an object harder made [the sound] change [on the student work], so I said [in my reflection] how I thought they were confused.
>
> (Kacie, Explain rehearsal interview)

Ben also discussed using the *student alternative ideas tool* to reflect on his video recorded instruction. He emphasized using the "scientifically accurate ideas" column on the *student alternative ideas tool* to analyze whether his team used accurate scientific language as they talked about the phenomenon and responded to student confusions during the rehearsal. He said,

> Whenever we wrote our memos, we went back and where the misconceptions were listed [on the student work], we saw what we said [in the video], but then we looked back and saw what the correct response to this misconception was [as indicated on the tool in the scientifically accurate ideas column]. We were like, "How did we do on the fly? Did it come out the same way that it was written?"
>
> (Ben, Explore rehearsal interview)

Julianne described using the *scientific practice challenges tool* to identify difficulties her fourth-grade students may have faced in making observations, "I did use this [tool] when writing my memo, [I] referred back to that, like [the student] didn't draw pictures with detail, [then] I wrote about what we could change or revise" (Julianne, Classroom lesson interview).

For PSTs to learn to support student sensemaking, they need opportunities to see this work decomposed and the chance to approximate it (Grossman *et al.*, 2009). The findings suggest the tools identify the components that make up this work, such as the range of ideas students may have during instruction or the challenges that students might face as they learn to make and record observations. The findings also indicate the rehearsals help PSTs practice using precise scientific language and responding to "elementary students" with alternative conceptions.

Conclusions

In this chapter, I investigated how tool-supported rehearsals might offer opportunities for preservice teachers to notice student ideas and support student sensemaking. One important finding of this work is the opportunity for PSTs to attend to student ideas about phenomena and to respond by integrating students' use of science practices and learning of disciplinary core ideas. This focus on supporting student sensemaking as the integration of content and practice is ambitious work, and typical elementary teaching does not exemplify this kind of science instruction. As such, this study offers an image of what it can look like for preservice teachers to work towards supporting students' sensemaking about phenomena in ways articulated by the vision of the *Next Generation Science Standards* when they are engaged in highly scaffolded rehearsals.

This study also suggests that when PSTs have opportunities to prepare for, work with, and reflect on how to engage student thinking and use of science practices, their sophisticated acts of teaching may surprise even their teacher educators. I know my assumptions about what the PSTs are capable of were challenged as a result of this study. In particular, I was surprised by the way they used the tools together to enhance the opportunities afforded through the rehearsals. For instance, although the *student alternative ideas tool* and the *science practice challenges tool* separately identified the difficult aspects of supporting students' content and practice learning, the PSTs were able to combine the two tools to advance an integrated approach to learning in science. Other science teacher educators have been impressed with how PSTs have used tools to reshape the work they do with science learners (e.g., Kademian and Davis, this volume, Chapter 8; Windschitl *et al.*, 2012).

The PSTs' ability in this study to begin to support their students' sensemaking in sophisticated ways offers insights about the affordances of tool-supported rehearsals. First, consistent with prior research that has underscored the difficulty of learning to see and use students' ideas in instruction (Jacobs *et al.*, 2010; van Es *et al.*, 2017), this study suggests that PSTs may benefit from tools that enable them to develop the necessary content knowledge and pedagogical content knowledge (Avraamidou and Zembal-Saul, 2010) to work with student ideas. In classroom settings, many factors compete for teachers' attention, and focusing on the nuances of children's thinking may not be prioritized (Jacobs *et al.*, 2010). In fact, as a result of this study, I have incorporated more scaffolds in my science methods course to prepare the PSTs to anticipate and work with students' ideas; I no longer assume that a few class discussions will prepare them for this important teaching practice. Before the rehearsals begin, I require the PSTs to research their phenomenon and to investigate possible alternative ideas students may have. I also ask them to find children's literature that discusses the phenomenon in accessible and kid-friendly language. These assignments serve to complement the tools used with the rehearsals and emphasize that preparing for and attending to students' ideas is an important aspect of science instruction.

Second, as others have reported (e.g., Lampert *et al.*, 2013), this study reveals that rehearsals allow PSTs to experience and learn from mistakes. It is much better that they realize that students have ideas that need to be elicited and supported after their first rehearsal, than realizing that in the classroom where students' learning could be impacted (Grossman *et al.*, 2009). As Jenny and Julianne emphasized after their Engage rehearsal, they had assumed that students would not share their initial ideas until later in the lesson. Recognizing their assumptions about teaching and student learning prior to teaching in classroom contexts is an important benefit of the rehearsals. As teacher educators, we want to design learning experiences that enable PSTs to face their assumptions and to learn from their mistakes, but to do so in the safety of the methods course classroom.

Third, this study builds on prior research by showing that even though the PSTs recognized the artificial nature of the rehearsal, they valued the learning opportunities afforded by the simulated interactions (Grossman *et al.*, 2009; Lampert *et al.*, 2013). Although rehearsals are designed to engage PSTs in instructional interactions that are less authentic than those they would encounter in a complex classroom setting, PSTs may become frustrated with the inauthenticity of rehearsals (Benedict-Chambers, 2016; Stroupe and Gotwals, 2017). They may not embrace the learning opportunities because they don't understand the goals of rehearsals. After the PSTs in my science methods course expressed these frustrations, I created a new tool that outlines the challenges they might face in preparing for, enacting, and reflecting on their rehearsals and the opportunities for growth. I introduce this tool at the beginning of the course and then revisit it at the end, and the PSTs have shared that this helps them to understand the rationale for the rehearsal as a vehicle for professional growth. Another explanation for the PSTs' buy-in may be that the tools enabled them to recognize the complexity of teaching and the challenges their students might face in instruction in the elementary classroom. As such, they appreciated their classmates' simulated responses to their instruction and the deliberate practice that afforded. Further research should examine the connections between peers' use of the tools to simulate elementary student thinking and PST buy-in and learning in approximations of practice.

In conclusion, by investigating how tool-supported rehearsals afford opportunities for PSTs to support student sensemaking as an integrated process of using science practices to develop an understanding of a disciplinary core idea, teacher educators can better leverage the opportunities they offer in promoting PST learning. While rehearsals will never replace the need for PSTs to engage with students in classroom contexts, the simulated interactions can highlight important features of science teaching and learning, prepare PSTs to manage some of the complex aspects they might face in practice, and help them reflect on specific elements of supporting student sensemaking.

References

Avraamidou, L., and Zembal-Saul, C. (2010). In search of well-started beginning science teachers: Insights from two first-year elementary teachers. *Journal of Research in Science Teaching*, 47(6), 661–686.

Benedict-Chambers, A. (2016). Using tools to promote novice teacher noticing of science teaching practices in post-rehearsal discussions. *Teaching and Teacher Education*, 59, 28–44.

Benedict-Chambers, A., and Aram, R. (2017). Tools for teacher noticing: Helping preservice teachers notice and analyze student thinking and scientific practice use. *Journal of Science Teacher Education*, 3, 1–25.

Benedict-Chambers, A., Kademian, S. M., Davis, E. A., and Palincsar, A. S. (2017). Guiding students towards sensemaking: Teacher questions focused on integrating scientific practices with science content. *International Journal of Science Education*, 39 (15), 1–25.

Berland, L. K., and Reiser, B. J. (2009). Making sense of argumentation and explanation. *Science Education*, 93(1), 26–55.

Bybee, R., Taylor, J., Gardner, A., Van Scotter, P., Powell, J. C., Westbrook, A., and Landes, N. (2006). *The BSCS 5E Instructional Model: Origins and Effectiveness*. Colorado Springs: BSCS.

Driver, R., Guesne, E., and Tiberghien, A. (1985). *Children's Ideas and the Learning of Science*. Milton Keynes, England: Open University Press.

Grossman, P. L., Compton, C., Igra, D., Ronfeldt, M., Shahan, E., and Williamson, P. W. (2009). Teaching practice: A cross-professional perspective. *Teachers College Record*, 111(9), 2055–2100.

Jacobs, V. R., Lamb, L. L., and Philipp, R. A. (2010). Professional noticing of children's mathematical thinking. *Journal for Research in Mathematics Education*, 41(2), 169–202.

Lampert, M., Franke, M. L., Kazemi, E., Ghousseini, H. N., Turrou, A. C., Beasley, H., and Crowe, K. (2013). Keeping it complex: Using rehearsals to support novice teacher learning of ambitious teaching. *Journal of Teacher Education*, 64(3), 226–243.

Miles, M. B., Huberman, A. M., and Saldaña, J. (2014). *Qualitative Data Analysis: A Methods Sourcebook*. Thousand Oaks, CA: Sage Publications, Inc.

NGSS Lead States. (2013). *Next Generation Science Standards: For States, By States.* Washington, DC: National Academies Press.

Stroupe, D., and Gotwals, A. W. (2017). "It's 1000 degrees in here when I teach": Providing preservice teachers with an extended opportunity to approximate ambitious instruction. *Journal of Teacher Education, 69*(3), 294–306.

van Es, E. A., Cashen, M., Barnhart, T., and Auger, A. (2017). Learning to notice mathematics instruction: Using Video to develop preservice teachers' vision of ambitious pedagogy. *Cognition and Instruction, 35*(3), 165–187.

Windschitl, M., Thompson, J., Braaten, M., and Stroupe, D. (2012). Proposing a core set of instructional practices and tools for teachers of science. *Science Education, 96*(5), 878–903.

11 A Framework for the Teaching Practice of Supporting Students to Construct Evidence-Based Claims Through Data Analysis

A Lens for Considering Teacher Learning Opportunities

Anna Maria Arias
KENNESAW STATE UNIVERSITY

Learning to support sensemaking in elementary science in equitable and rigorous ways is complex work. Given this complexity, description and decomposition of the teaching practices at the elementary level are needed for teacher educators to be able to develop coherent methods and strategies for supporting beginning teachers in learning these practices. In this chapter, I zoom in on one aspect of supporting sensemaking: the teaching practice of supporting children to engage in the science practice of constructing evidence-based claims of natural phenomena. The science practice of constructing evidence-based claims involves aspects of several science practices described in new reforms including constructing explanations, argumentation, and analyzing and interpreting data (National Research Council, 2007; NGSS Lead States, 2013). I describe a framework for the teaching practice of supporting children in constructing evidence-based claims of natural phenomena through data analysis called the Supporting Evidence-Based Claims Framework. I developed the Supporting Evidence-Based Claims Framework by looking at three areas of research and understanding: a) how scientists engage in the science practice; b) expectations and research about how elementary students might engage in this science practice; and c) exemplars and research on how teachers can support students in the science practice. Then, I use the framework as a lens for providing examples of promising practices used within a teacher education program to facilitate learning over time of the teaching practice of supporting constructing evidence-based claims through data analysis.

How Scientists Engage in Constructing Evidence-Based Claims Through Data Analysis

Considering how scientists engage in constructing evidence-based claims through data analysis within their work provides vision, direction, and

162   *Arias*

context for considering the expectations for how elementary student might meaningfully engage in these science practices. For scientists, the process of identifying claims involves starting with data collected from direct observation or models of the phenomenon of interest. Then, the scientist recursively distills and interprets the data using representations to analyze the data, making claims that summarize the expansive data collected (Latour, 1999; Popper, 1972). The data analysis entails studying and determining the nature and relationship of the patterns and interpretation requires explaining the meaning of this analysis (Rivet and Ingber, 2017). Because of the social nature of science, scientists do this work in conversation with others and drawing on the tools and knowledge of the community.

Constructing an evidence-based claim about a natural phenomenon also involves justifying one's claim in the complex interaction of theory, data, and evidence in science. As a scientist analyzes data and identifies a claim, the individual also needs to simultaneously consider and argue how the evidence sufficiently and appropriately fits the claim and belongs in the theories of the discipline (Duschl and Osborne, 2002; Latour, 1999; Popper, 1972). This work involves considering why other refuting claims do not fit the data collected (Popper, 1972) and providing a logical argument for why this particular claim best fits the data (see Toulmin's (2007) discussion of logical arguments). This construction of evidence-based claims enables the scientist to extend and refine the body of knowledge of the phenomenon in question.

Constructing Evidence-Based Claims in Elementary Science

New reforms for students to engage in science practices (see Figure 11.1) and science education research describe how elementary students might do work similar to scientists in the service of moving from data collection to construction of evidence-based claims. Students might analyze and interpret data by noting patterns, comparing groups, and comparing predicted results to actual results (NGSS Lead States, 2013; Rivet and Ingber, 2017; see Zembal-Saul and Hershberger, this volume, Chapter 1, for an example of what this can look like in the classroom). The data can be analyzed and interpreted through the use of representations (e.g., tables or graph) or through mathematical and statistical computation in the context of discussion with others (NGSS Lead States, 2013; Rivet and Ingber, 2017).

Constructing evidence-based claims in elementary classrooms requires justification of one's claims, an aspect of scientific argumentation, involving both understanding why one claim is stronger than other claims and persuading others of one's claim (Berland and McNeill, 2012; National Research Council, 2012; Osborne and Patterson, 2011). This justification of one's claim might occur through a consensus discussion where students select the most appropriate claim and persuade others of their choice (Herrenkohl and Cornelius, 2013). I draw on Toulmin's (2007) framework for

Analyzing and Interpreting Data	• "Use observations (first hand or from media) to describe patterns and/or relationships in the natural and designed world(s) in order to answer scientific questions and solve problems" • "Represent data in tables and/or various graphical displays ... to reveal patterns that indicate relationships" • "Analyze and interpret data to make sense of phenomena, using logical reasoning, mathematics, and/or computation" • "Compare and contrast data collected by different groups in order to discuss similarities and differences in their findings" (NGSS Lead States, 2013, Appendix F, p. 9)
Engage in Argument from Evidence	• "Compare and refine arguments based on an evaluation of the evidence presented" • "Identify arguments that are supported by evidence" • "Distinguish between explanations that accounts for all gathered evidence and those that do not" • "Analyze why some evidence is relevant to a scientific question and some is not" • "Construct and/or support an argument with evidence, data, and/or a model" • "Use data to evaluate claims about cause and effect" (NGSS Lead States, 2013, Appendix F, p. 13)
Constructing Explanations	• "Construct an explanation of observed relationships (e.g., the distribution of plants in the back yard)" • "Use evidence (e.g., measurements, observations, patterns) to construct or support an explanation or design a solution to a problem" • "Identify the evidence that supports particular points in an explanation" (NGSS Lead States, 2013, Appendix F, p. 11)

Figure 11.1 Goals for Elementary Students Described in NGSS

thinking about argumentation (e.g., Bell, 2000; Erduran *et al.*, 2004), focusing on role of linking claims to evidence and reasoning. Drawing on aspects of scientific explanations, reasoning involves beginning to consider and describe the "how" and "why" of a phenomenon (Berland and McNeill, 2012; Osborne and Patterson, 2011; Windschitl *et al.*, 2012).

The science practices, including analyzing data, constructing explanations, and scientific argumentation, co-occur as scientists work to make sense of data and construct meaning in an iterative process (Berland and McNeill, 2012; National Research Council, 2007, 2012). In elementary classrooms, mirroring the practice of science, constructing explanations, analyzing data, and argumentation overlap in constructing evidence-based claims where claims are identified from analysis of the data to make sense of a phenomenon and justification is used to support the claim made (Berland and McNeill, 2012; Osborne and Patterson, 2011). Thus, I consider this process as one larger science practice with intersectional components.

Figure 11.2 shows the Students Constructing Evidence-Based Claims Framework that I developed for describing my theoretical understanding of the construction evidence-based claims through data analysis in an elementary setting. The Students Constructing Evidence-Based Claims Framework splits the science practice two subpractices: analyzing the data to reveal patterns and relationships and making a claim justified by evidence and reasoning. To analyze the data to reveal patterns and relationships, a learner

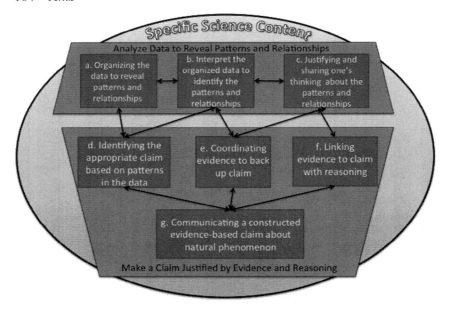

Figure 11.2 The Students Constructing Evidence-Based Claims Framework: Science Practice of Constructing Evidence-Based Claims in Elementary Classroom

within a community of learners needs to: (a) organize the data to reveal patterns and relationships; (b) interpret the organized data to identify the patterns and relationships; and (c) share and justify thinking about the patterns and relationships. Then, to make a claim justified by evidence and reasoning, the same learner would: (d) identify appropriate and accurate claims based on the patterns in the data; (e) coordinate evidence to back up the claim; (f) link evidence to the claim with reasoning or scientific principles; and (g) communicate a constructed evidence-based claim about the natural phenomenon in a logical structure. As learners engage in this process, they work with others in their community of learners to develop the knowledge socially through interaction and feedback. All of this work is integrated with the specific science content (i.e., the disciplinary core idea and/or crosscutting concept) that is the focus of the evidence-based claim. The lines in the model represent the web of iterative connections that are required to engage in this work.

Given the complexity of this work, students likely can learn this science practice by adding components over time. For example, a learner may first learn to align evidence with claims and then move to provide evidence and reasoning to justify their claims. Supporting the progressive movement toward more complex work in constructing evidence-based claims helps students to develop their understandings and practices over time. Given the progression that students take in learning the practices of science, using reasoning in evidence-based claims may not be expected in lower elementary grades, yet these students are capable of naming reasoning in particular cases (Berland and McNeill, 2010; Metz, 2000; Zembal-Saul *et al.*, 2013).

As suggested in the introduction to this volume, elementary students can learn to construct evidence-based claims through data analysis with increasing complexity over time by drawing on their nascent abilities as investigators and sensemakers (e.g., Herrenkohl *et al.*, 1999; Metz, 2000). However, students struggle with aspects of this science practice including coordinating evidence or reasoning with claims (Bell, 2000; Sandoval and Millwood, 2005) and making appropriate representations to analyze data (e.g., Lehrer and Schauble, 2004; Shah *et al.*, 1999). Thus, learners face many challenges in constructing evidence-based claims, pointing to the need to support students in this work. Moreover, variations in teachers' support for explanations connect to differences in students' ability to do this work (Erduran *et al.*, 2004; McNeill and Krajcik, 2009), pointing to the importance of considering and naming the type of support that can lead to equitable and rigorous student learning.

The Teaching Practice of *Supporting Students to Construct Evidence-Based Claims*

Drawing directly on the Students Constructing Evidence-Based Claims Framework, my Supporting Evidence-Based Claims Framework decomposes (Grossman *et al.*, 2009) the teaching practice of supporting students to construct evidence-based claims of natural phenomena into two subpractices: *supporting students to analyze the data to reveal patterns and relationships* and *supporting students to make claims justified by evidence and reasoning* (represented by dark hexagons in Figure 11.3). I break down the subpractice of *supporting students to analyze the data to reveal patterns and relationships* into two components (represented by the light rounded rectangles): (a) "supporting students to analyze the data;" and (b) "supporting students to share their thinking about the pattern." These components, then, align with the components of the Students Constructing Evidence-Based Claims Framework from Figure 11.2 (represented by the dark rectangles). For example, in order to support students in the subpractice of *supporting students to analyze the data to reveal patterns and relationships*, a teacher engages in the component "supporting students to analyze data to reveal patterns" by facilitating students in organizing data (e.g., create a graph) and interpreting the organized data to identify the patterns and relationships (e.g., discuss the graph with students). Enacting this subpractice also entails the other component "supporting students to share their thinking about the pattern" by facilitating students' engagement in justifying and sharing one's thinking about the pattern (e.g., asking students to share their ideas).

Similar to the subpractice of *supporting students to analyze the data to reveal patterns and relationships*, the subpractice of *supporting students to make a claim justified by evidence and reasoning* can be decomposed into two components:

166 *Arias*

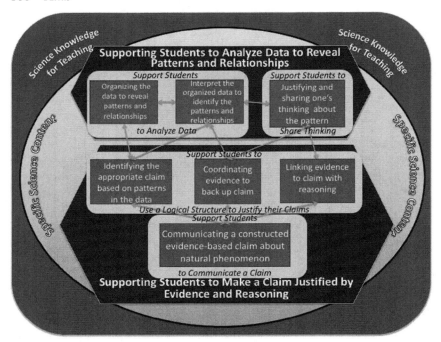

Figure 11.3 The Supporting Evidence-Based Claims Framework to Describe the Teaching Practice of Supporting Students to Construct Evidence-Based Claims Through Data Analysis

Note: The figure shows how this framework wraps around the Students Constructing Evidence-Based Claims from Figure 11.2 (with the light arrows and rectangles).

(a) "supporting students to use a logical structure to justify their claims;" and (b) "supporting students to make a claim." This subpractice for the teaching practice also aligns with the components of the science practice from Figure 11.2. This teaching practice is situated within specific science and requires coordination with one's science knowledge for teaching, signified by the large gray box in Figure 11.3. In a manner similar to the way Ball and colleagues (2009) describe components of the practice of leading a classroom discussion, I theorize these subpractices and their components as decomposed pieces of the practice of supporting students to construct evidence-based claims. In the following sections, I describe the decomposed elements of the Supporting Evidence-Based Claims Framework.

Supporting Students to Analyze the Data to Reveal Patterns and Relationships

In enacting the component of "supporting students to analyze the data" of the teaching subpractice *supporting students to analyze the data to reveal patterns and relationships*, a teacher can facilitate the selection of appropriate representations that organize data to answer the investigation question. Other teaching moves include explicitly discussing features in a representation, linking the investigation to the data, and highlighting inconsistencies in the data (Herrenkohl *et al.*, 1999; Rivet and Ingber, 2017; Wu and Krajcik, 2006). Tools such as graphs and charts can facilitate this work for learners in the same way they do for scientists (Rivet and Ingber, 2017; Shah *et al.*, 1999). Discussions of why and how analyzing the data leads to evidence-based claims and providing a clear rationale for using a representation may facilitate learners' development of knowledge for this science practice (Herrenkohl *et al.*, 1999; Wu and Krajcik, 2006). For example, a teacher may provide opportunities for student groups to make individual representations of the data they collected and lead a whole class discussion about how particular representations enable interpretation of the evidence to identify claims (Cartier, *et al.*, 2013). These teaching moves make the work of analyzing data accessible to all students, allowing for equitable and rigorous learning opportunities.

A second component of the subpractice of *supporting students to analyze the data to reveal patterns and relationships* is "supporting students to share their thinking," which facilitates students' ability to justify and share their thinking about the pattern. This component involve teaching moves such as probing student thinking to facilitate students to make their thinking about patterns visible, or having student consider alternative ideas about the patterns (Windschitl *et al.*, 2012; Zembal-Saul, 2009). To engage students in the process of justification, teachers may provide tools like verbal prompts such as, "Why do you think that?" or even facilitate students to use these prompts with one another (Chen *et al.*, 2017; Herrenkohl *et al.*, 1999; Zembal-Saul *et al.*, 2013). Several studies point to the small-group and whole-class opportunities to discuss ideas and consider one another's claims as key steps in students' development of evidence-based claims (Erduran *et al.*, 2004; Herrenkohl and Cornelius, 2013). These discussions facilitate sensemaking about the natural phenomenon as students try out their thinking and build on one another's thinking (Herrenkohl *et al.*, 1999). In these discussions, teachers acknowledge and build on the resources and ideas that all students bring to the classroom in making sense of phenomena and create equitable opportunities for students to contribute their thinking.

Supporting Students to Make a Claim Justified by Evidence and Reasoning

The second teaching subpractice is *supporting students to make a claim justified by evidence and reasoning*. As seen in Figure 11.3, the first component of this subpractice is supporting students to "use a logical structure to justify their claims," which involves facilitating elementary students in identifying the claim, evidence, and reasoning. One tool to support this work is an

168　*Arias*

application of Toulmin's (2007) framework for argumentation. The application of this framework involves students using a claim–evidence–reasoning (CER) framework such as, "I think ___ (claim). I think this because I have seen or done___ (evidence). I know this because ___ (reasoning)" (McNeill *et al.*, 2006; see also Kademian and Davis, this volume, Chapter 8; Zembal-Saul and Hershberger, this volume, Chapter 1). Students' use of written or verbal scaffolding around this framework helps learners develop evidence-based claims (Bell, 2000; McNeill and Krajcik, 2009; Songer and Gotwals, 2012).

Other teaching moves that can provide students with the support to understand a logical structure for evidence-based claims include: (1) modeling how to make an evidence-based claim; (2) discussing a framework for evidence-based claims; (3) connecting to everyday use of arguments; and (4) using appropriate and accurate scientific language (Avraamidou and Zembal-Saul, 2010; McNeill, 2011; Zembal-Saul *et al.*, 2013). Providing a rationale for having a claim, evidence, and reasoning can support students' knowledge development of why to engage in the science practices and improve students' engagement in the science practice (McNeill and Krajcik, 2009). To support students in developing epistemic understanding around this science practice, teachers can discuss how claims need evidence, asking students to consider alternative claims, and considering what evidence is used in making the claim (Herrenkohl and Cornelius, 2013).

The second component of the teaching practice subpractice of *supporting students to make a claim justified by evidence and reasoning* is "supporting students to communicate an evidence-based claim." To support this communication, a teacher may provide opportunities for students to share claims with the class and to receive feedback for their claims (Erduran *et al.*, 2004; McNeill, 2011). Support for this communication may involve facilitation of writing and speaking one's claim (see Hooper and Zembal-Saul, this volume, Chapter 4). This also allows for multiple claims to be considered and built on in constructing understanding of the phenomenon (Berland and McNeill, 2010; McNeill *et al.*, 2006; Songer and Gotwals, 2012; Zembal-Saul *et al.*, 2013). Tools such as shared representations of thinking, prompts or graphic organizers for writing, and scaffolded questions support students' engagement in communicating their claims (Herrenkohl and Cornelius, 2013; Songer and Gotwals, 2012). For example, supporting students to take on questioning roles focused on linking theory and evidence seemed to facilitate complex discussions of how to develop science theory (Herrenkohl *et al.*, 1999).

Another strategy for supporting the communication of claims is providing feedback. Students can receive feedback from the teacher or classmates on how they are able to support and defend their claims (Herrenkohl and Cornelius, 2013). Using rubrics can facilitate making these expectations of evidence-based claims clear and allow for directed feedback to promote continued improvement in their development of the practice and in their thinking about the practice (e.g., Zembal-Saul *et al.*, 2013).

Supporting Students to Do the Intellectual Work

Underlying each teaching subpractice of the Supporting Evidence-Based Claims Framework is the assumption that students will do the intellectual work so that the epistemic agency—the shaping of the knowledge and practice of the science community—is shifted to the students (see Zembal-Saul and Hershberger, this volume, Chapter 1). However, several examples exist of teachers and tasks taking on the epistemic agency and intellectual work involved constructing evidence-based claims, limiting all students' access to equitable and rigorous learning opportunities (e.g., Tekkumru-Kisa et al., 2015). These examples include naming claims or justification for students rather than pressing students to name the claim and justify their responses with reasoning and evidence, lowering expectations by minimizing the scientific ideas involved and focusing on memorization, and not allowing students to communicate and consider one another's ideas (Chen et al., 2017; Cartier, et al., 2013; McNeill and Krajcik, 2009; Tekkumru-Kisa et al., 2015). However, when all students are supported to do the work of constructing evidence-based claims themselves, they are capable of this work and develop more connected understandings of science practice and content (Herrenkohl et al., 1999; Songer and Gotwals, 2012).

The Connection between the Teaching Practice and Knowledge for Teaching

The knowledge that teachers have intertwines with the practices that teachers enact; teachers use their knowledge in action as they interact with students in a classroom (Hammerness et al., 2005; Lampert, 2010). This knowledge includes the specific content knowledge of the discipline in which the claim is being made represented by the light gray oval in Figure 11.3. Other aspects of science knowledge for teaching (cf. Ball et al., 2008) also intertwine with this practice as represented by the rectangular background in Figure 11.3. Some examples of aspects of this knowledge are: (a) subject matter knowledge of how to analyze data to reveal patterns and relationships; (b) pedagogical knowledge of making knowledge explicit to learners; (c) pedagogical content knowledge of instructional strategies involved in constructing explanations; (d) pedagogical content knowledge of students as science learners to know how students might struggle; and (e) pedagogical content knowledge of instructional aims (Abell, 2007). For instance, a teacher might draw on multiple types of knowledge to support students to construct evidence-based claims to answer the question "How does a batteries in parallel circuit compare to a batteries in series circuit?" including: knowledge of creating a chart to compare circuits (subject matter of how to analyze data), alternative ideas that students may have about electrical energy (knowledge of science learners), and representing the flow of electrons in electric circuits that allow productive understandings (pedagogical knowledge of making knowledge explicit to learners). Additional

170   *Arias*

forms of knowledge and abilities that enable the teacher to plan for and enact these practices are needed, but this limited list highlights the many intersections of knowledge and ability required for enacting the high-leverage practices that facilitate student learning.

Using the Framework for Teaching Practice to Consider How to Support Teacher Learning

Drawing on a longitudinal qualitative case study of the learning of 54 pre-service teachers (called interns) enrolled in a two-year practice-based teacher education program at the University of Michigan, I use the Supporting Evidence-Based Claims Framework to highlight examples of facilitating the development of the teaching practice of supporting children to engage in constructing evidence-based claims through data analysis (see Arias, 2015; Arias and Davis, 2017, for more information about the study). The teacher educators in the program used the pedagogies of practices including decomposition (i.e., breaking down the practice into components), representations (e.g., using video records of experienced teachers), and approximations of practice. In approximations, teacher educators provide opportunities for the interns to enact aspects of teaching practice in less complex, less authentic settings such as rehearsing with peers (Grossman *et al.*, 2009; see Davis, this volume, Chapter 7; Davis, Palincsar, and Kademian, this volume, Chapter 13, for more about these experiences and the teacher education program). I highlight two courses—the first of two Children as Sensemakers courses and a Science Methods Course—as well as other program experiences that provided learning opportunities for developing the focal teaching practice over time during the program. Davis, Palincsar, and Kademian (this volume, Chapter 13) provide more detail about both of these courses, so here, I provide an overview as it relates to constructing evidence-based claims.

Children as Sensemakers I Course

Occurring during the first month of the first year in the program, the first of two Children as Sensemakers courses aimed to highlight how elementary children make sense of the natural world through their everyday experiences. The interns engaged in three approximations of practice—two interviews with an early elementary student about their understanding of what causes day and night, and a read-aloud with the same student using a physical model to represent the phenomenon. Along with its broader focus on the high-leverage practice of eliciting students' thinking, this course emphasized three components of the teaching practice of constructing evidence-based claims: supporting students to: (1) communicate claims; (2) interpret representations to make claims and analyze data to reveal patterns; and (3) share and justify their thinking.

In terms of supporting students to communicate claims, the protocols for the interviews with a student required the interns to have children share their answer to the question, "Please tell me how you think we have day and night" (CaSM#1InterviewProtocol). Using the protocol, the interns first supported students to state their answers verbally; second, they supported students to draw representations of their thinking; and finally, they asked students to represent their thinking using models (including clay and a flashlight). The course discussions included conversation about how and why to support students to communicate their claims in this way. The tool used to assess the interns' work and provide feedback included an expectation that the intern "asked a clear question to introduce the task that appeared to be understood by the child" (Interview2_FeedbackTool).

The class assignments, class discussions, protocols, and feedback tools also had an emphasis on drawing representations to make claims and analyze data to reveal patterns. The read-aloud included an emphasis on supporting a student to make sense of a representation in the text as well as in a model. In class, interns discussed challenges of using and understanding representations to make claims such as how to match the model with the drawn representation in the book and highlighting implicit features of the representations. The class discussion also pointed out the importance of allowing students the opportunity to make sense of the representations in order to develop claims and evidence in service of an explanation. In class assignments, interns reflected on and received feedback about the use of representations to support students' thinking.

In terms of the teaching practice component of supporting students to share and justify their thinking, the course used representations of teaching including instructor modeling of eliciting student thinking and justification and video records of interviews prompting students to sharing their thinking about a natural phenomenon. The interview protocol also included example follow-up questions, such as "How does this happen?" (CaSMInterviewProtocol). The tools used for assessment and feedback included these two expectations:

1 Asked follow-up questions that targeted the scientific phenomenon, including questions that elicited the child's understanding of what causes day and night;
2 Asked follow-up questions that were tied to what the child said or did. (CaSMInterviewFeedbackTool)

Science Methods Course

During the first semester of year two of the program, the Science Methods Course included focus on all components of the teaching practice of supporting students to construct evidence-based claims as well as the associated science knowledge for teaching. To support the teaching practice, the course instructors utilized the EEE framework (Benedict-Chambers, 2014;

172 Arias

Kademian and Davis, this volume, Chapter 8), which decomposed a science lesson into smaller elements, as well as representations of teaching and approximations of practice (Grossman, *et al.*, 2009).

In focusing on the subpractice of supporting students to analyze the data to reveal patterns and relationship, the instructors first decomposed the elements of this work with the EEE framework (Figure 11.4). They also provided a video record of a teacher working with students in analyzing their data from an investigation. After watching the videos, the class discussed how the teacher highlighted patterns in the representation of data and followed-up with students to justify the patterns they named. The interns had opportunities to consider how they might support students at different grade levels to make representations of weather data. Then, the interns enacted this subpractice in their approximations of practice.

The instructors used a similar set of pedagogical moves as they focused on the subpractice of supporting students to make a claim justified by evidence and reasoning, including decomposing the subpractice (Figure 11.5), watching video records of teachers supporting students in the work across grade levels, and discussing how and why to focus on claims, evidence, and reason. For example, course discussions explored why having students

Identify patterns and trends in the data for answering the investigation question or problem *(entails analyzing and interpreting data, using mathematics thinking)*	Support students in making sense of the data so that they can generate claims with evidence. This includes … • Compiling class data, and if relevant, organize or represent the data in meaningful ways (e.g., in tables or graphs); • Directing students to particular aspects of the data to help them identify and make meaning of patterns or trends in the data; • Helping students select appropriate and sufficient data to use as evidence to support claims.

Figure 11.4 The Decomposed Practice of Supporting Students to Analyze the Data from the EEE Framework

Generate scientific claims with evidence and reasoning *(entails constructing explanations, engaging in argument from evidence)*	Facilitate a discussion that enables students to answer the investigation question by using the data to generate evidence-based claims. Provide students with scaffolds, such as "I think ____ *(claim)* because I observed ____ *(evidence)*" or "What I know: ____ *(claim)*. How I know it: ____ *(evidence)*." Provide opportunities for students to share their explanations with others, including peers, parents, etc. Help students to … • Revisit their initial ideas about the investigation question, expanding upon or developing new evidence-based claims; • Compare their own explanations with explanations reflecting scientific understanding, via direct instruction, textbooks, models, etc. (this includes introducing new terms to students, as appropriate); • Question one another about their explanations.

Figure 11.5 The Decomposed Practice of Supporting Students to Make Claims Justified by Evidence and Reasoning from the EEE Framework

include evidence is important for their learning. The discussions also highlighted specific teaching moves such as using a sentence stem to support learning or connecting students' ideas to each other.

The methods course also facilitated opportunities to develop science knowledge for teaching. Course instructors introduced the claim, evidence, and reasoning framework through class discussion and readings. The interns wrote several evidence-based claims in the class, discussed these claims, and practiced assessing samples of student work with evidenced-based claims. The course also included an emphasis on struggles elementary students might have in constructing evidence-based claims through focused readings and looking at patterns in student work.

The approximations of practice provided interns with opportunities to recompose the subpractices and knowledge for teaching into one teaching practice. One approximation, the Peer Teaching Assignment, where one intern teaches elements of a science lesson to a small group of peers, provided a focused opportunity to enact all of the components of the teaching practice of supporting students to construct evidence-based claims through data analysis (see Davis, this volume, Chapter 7, for a description of peer teaching and other approximations of practice in the course). In the final of three peer teaching approximations, each intern co-planned for, taught, discussed with colleagues, and reflected on a 20-minute section of a lesson focused on this teaching practice. After the enactment, colleagues and the teacher educator provided feedback using a form that asked how the interns enacted the decomposed elements seen in Figures 11.4 and 11.5 with questions such as, "How did the teacher facilitate a discussion that enables students to use data as evidence to answer the original question or problem? Give specific examples" (PeerTeachingFocusQuestions).

The methods course supported the interns to situate this focal teaching practice within an elementary science lesson through a Reflective Teaching Assignment. In this assignment, the preservice teachers planned for, taught, and reflected on teaching an investigation-based science lesson that involves constructing evidence-based claims to a classroom of elementary teachers. This assignment required interns to identify instances in the video records of their lesson when they enacted these decomposed elements of the focal teaching practice, and to reflect on how their enactments supported student learning. The instructors commented on these reflections as well as on their enactment of the teaching practice, with focused feedback on the decomposed subpractices emphasized throughout the course.

Other Opportunities to Learn throughout the Program

Beyond the Children as Sensemakers and Science Methods courses, other opportunities for learning elements of the Supporting Evidence-Based Claims Framework also existed in the program. One opportunity was teaching a science unit during the final semester, which involved student

174   *Arias*

teaching full-time in an elementary classroom. Some but not all of the interns taught a sequence of science lessons, providing them a chance to plan for, enact, and assess students' engagement in constructing evidence-based claims.

Other courses in the program also offered learning opportunities for focusing on particular components of the Framework. For example, the Mathematics Methods course, literacy courses, and other methods courses also focused on asking questions that would facilitate students to make a claim and use evidence within their particular discipline. They also focused on supporting students to share their claim and communicate with others. In their interviews, the interns identified these links across the course in the teacher education program. For instance, one participant described how her mathematics methods professor encouraged the use of discussion moves that helped her "make it more in depth" in supporting students to construct evidence-based claims (A_Intervivew4: 176–185). Similar to others' comments, this comment suggests that the interns made connections across courses in the program in learning the focal teaching practice, which suggests program coherence (Zembal-Saul, 2009).

Conclusions and Implications

This chapter describes the Supporting Evidence-Based Claims Framework, which decomposes the teaching practice of supporting students to construct evidence-based claims through data analysis based on research on science teaching and learning and new reform documents. The framework highlights the complexity of knowledge, ability, and actions involved in enacting one teaching practice involved in supporting student sensemaking. This complexity underscores the need to both name the components of the practice and facilitate teacher learning across these components. Using the framework as a lens, I discussed in this chapter examples of promising teacher education practices for the focal practice. These examples from a practice-based teacher education program show that courses and experiences provided opportunities to learn about different components of and approximate the practice in increasingly complex ways as seen in Figure 11.6. Figure 11.6 suggests that the interns had opportunities to develop elements of the teaching practice of supporting students to construct evidence-based claims through data analysis over time. The potential to support the development of the teaching practice implies the need for careful consideration of the scaffolding and connection across teacher learning opportunities, leading to more coherent teacher education programs and professional development. I also highlight the potential of engaging in a process of describing a research-based framework that decomposes a teaching practice in order to use it for designing, describing, and evaluating learning opportunities for teachers. Using a framework that decomposes a teaching practice might support teacher educators in building on these examples of promising practices to develop more coherent, connected experiences for learning to support student sensemaking in science.

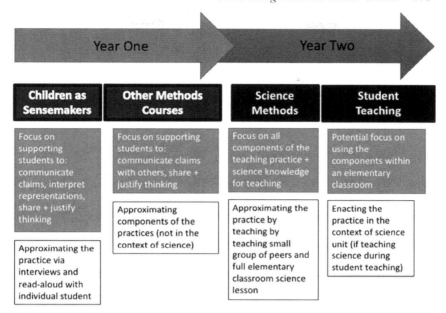

Figure 11.6 Learning Opportunities Across the Teacher Education Program

References

Abell, S. K. (2007). Research on science teacher knowledge. In S. K. Abell and N. Lederman (Eds.), *Handbook of Research on Science Education* (pp. 1105–1149). Mahwah, NJ: Lawrence Erlbaum Associates.

Arias, A. (2015). Learning to teach elementary students to construct evidence-based claims. Unpublished doctoral dissertation. University of Michigan, Ann Arbor.

Arias, A., and Davis, E. A. (2017). Supporting children to construct evidence-based claims in science: Individual learning trajectories in a practice-based program. *Teaching and Teacher Education, 66,* 204–218.

Avraamidou, L., and Zembal-Saul, C. (2010). In search of well-started beginning science teachers: Insights from two first-year elementary teachers. *Journal of Research in Science Teaching, 47*(6), 661–686.

Ball, D. L., Thames, M. H., and Phelps, G. (2008). Content knowledge for teaching: What makes it special? *Journal of Teacher Education, 59*(5), 389–407.

Ball, D. L., Sleep, L., Boerst, T. A., and Bass, H. (2009). Combining the development of practice and the practice of development in teacher education. *The Elementary School Journal, 109*(5), 458–474.

Bell, P. (2000). Scientific arguments as learning artifacts: Designing for learning from the web with KIE. *International Journal of Science Education, 22*(8), 797–817.

Benedict-Chambers, A. (2014). Developing professional vision for practice: Preservice teachers using students' scientific ideas in simulations of practice. Unpublished doctoral dissertation. University of Michigan, Ann Arbor.

176 *Arias*

Berland, L. K., and McNeill, K. L. (2010). A learning progression for scientific argumentation: Understanding student work and designing supportive instructional contexts. *Science Education, 94*(5), 765–793.

Berland, L. K., and McNeill, K. L. (2012). For whom is argument and explanation a necessary distinction? A response to Osborne and Patterson. *Science Education, 96*(5), 808–813.

Cartier, J., Smith, M. S., Stein, M. K., and Ross, D. (2013). *Practices for Orchestrating Task-Based Discussions in Science.* Arlington, VA: NSTA Press.

Chen, Y.-C., Hand, B., and Norton-Meier, L. (2017). Teacher roles of questioning in early elementary science classrooms: A framework promoting student cognitive complexities in argumentation. *Research in Science Education, 47*(2), 373–405.

Davis, E. A., and Boerst, T. A. (2014). Designing elementary teacher education to prepare well-started beginners. TeachingWorks Working Papers. University of Michigan, Ann Arbor. Retrieved from: http://www.teachingworks.org/images/files/TeachingWorks_Davis_Boerst_WorkingPapers_March_2014.pdf

Duschl, R. A., and Osborne, J. (2002). Supporting and promoting argumentation discourse in science education. *Studies in Science Education, 38*(1), 39–72.

Erduran, S., Simon, S., and Osborne, J. (2004). TAPping into argumentation: Developments in the application of Toulmin's Argument Pattern for studying science discourse. *Science Education, 88*(6), 915–933.

Grossman, P., Compton, C., Igra, D., Ronfeldt, M., Shahan, E., and Williamson, P. (2009). Teaching practice: A cross-professional perspective. *Teachers College Record, 111*(9), 2055–2100.

Hammerness, K., Darling-Hammond, L., Bransford, J., Berliner, D. C., Cochran-Smith, M., McDonald, M., and Zeichner, K. (2005). How teachers learn and develop. In L. Darling-Hammond and J. Bransford (Eds.), *Preparing Teachers for a Changing World: What Teachers Should Learn and be Able to Do.* San Francisco: John Wiley & Sons, Inc.

Herrenkohl, L. R., and Cornelius, L. (2013). Investigating elementary students' scientific and historical argumentation. *Journal of the Learning Sciences, 22,* 413–461.

Herrenkohl, L. R., Palincsar, A. S., DeWater, L. S., and Kawasaki, K. (1999). Developing scientific communities in classrooms: A sociocognitive approach. *Journal of the Learning Sciences, 8*(3–4), 451–493.

Lampert, M. (2010). Theory, practice and the education of professionals. *The Elementary School Journal, 98*(5), 511–526.

Latour, B. (1999). *Pandora's Hope: Essays on the Reality of Science Studies.* Cambridge, MA: Harvard University Press.

Lehrer, R., and Schauble, L. (2004). Modeling natural variation through distribution. *American Educational Research Journal, 41*(3), 635–679.

McNeill, K. L. (2011). Elementary students' views of explanation, argumentation, and evidence, and their abilities to construct arguments over the school year. *Journal of Research in Science Teaching, 48*(7), 793–823.

McNeill, K. L., and Krajcik, J. (2009). Synergy between teacher practices and curricular scaffolds to support students in using domain-specific and domain-general knowledge in writing arguments to explain phenomena. *Journal of the Learning Sciences, 18*(3), 416–460.

McNeill, K. L., Lizotte, D. J., Krajcik, J., and Marx, R. W. (2006). Supporting students' construction of scientific explanations by fading scaffolds in instructional materials. *Journal of the Learning Sciences, 15*(2), 153–191.

Metz, K. E. (2000). Young children's inquiry in biology: Building the knowledge bases to empower independent inquiry. In *Inquiry into Inquiring Learning and Teaching in Science* (pp. 371–404). Washington, DC: American Association for the Advancement of Science.

National Research Council (NRC). (2007). *Taking Science to School: Learning and Teaching Science in Grades K-8.* Washington, DC: National Academies Press.

National Research Council (NRC). (2012). *A Framework for K-12 Science Education: Practices, Crosscutting Concepts, and Core Ideas.* Committee on a Conceptual Framework for New K-12 Science Education Standards. Board on Science Education, Division of Behavioral and Social Sciences and Education. Washington, DC: National Academies Press.

NGSS Lead States. (2013). *Next Generation Science Standards: For States, By States.* Washington, DC: National Academies Press.

Osborne, J. F., and Patterson, A. (2011). Scientific argument and explanation: A necessary distinction? *Science Education, 95*(4), 627–638.

Popper, K. (1972). *Conjectures and Refutations: The Growth of Scientific Knowledge* (4th edn.). London: Routledge & Kegan Paul.

Rivet, A., and Ingber, J. (2017). Analyzing and interpreting data. In C. V. Schwarz, C. Passmore, and B. J. Reiser (Eds.), *Helping Students Make Sense of the World Using Next Generation Science and Engineering Practices* (pp. 159–180). Arlington, VA: NSTA Press.

Sandoval, W. A., and Millwood, K. A. (2005). The quality of students' use of evidence in written scientific explanations. *Cognition and Instruction, 23*(1), 23–55.

Shah, P., Mayer, R. E., and Hegarty, M. (1999). Graphs as aids to knowledge construction: Signaling techniques for guiding the process of graph comprehension. *Journal of Educational Psychology, 91*(4), 690–702.

Songer, N. B., and Gotwals, A. (2012). Guiding explanation construction by children at the entry points of learning progressions. *Journal of Research in Science Teaching, 49*(2), 141–165.

Tekkumru-Kisa, M., Stein, M. K., and Schunn, C. (2015). A framework for analyzing cognitive demand and content-practices integration: Task analysis guide in science. *Journal of Research in Science Teaching, 52*(5), 659–685.

Toulmin, S. E. (2007). *The Uses of Argument* (updated edn.) Cambridge: Cambridge University Press.

Windschitl, M., Thompson, J., Braaten, M., and Stroupe, D. (2012). Proposing a core set of instructional practices and tools for teachers of science. *Science Education, 96*(5), 878–903.

Wu, H.-K., and Krajcik, J. S. (2006). Inscriptional practices in two inquiry-based classrooms: A case study of seventh graders' use of data tables and graphs. *Journal of Research in Science Teaching, 43*(1), 63–95.

Zembal-Saul, C. (2009). Learning to teach elementary school science as argument. *Science Education, 93*(4), 687–719.

Zembal-Saul, C., McNeill, K. L., and Hershberger, K. (2013). *What's Your Evidence?: Engaging K-5 Children in Constructing Explanations in Science.* Columbus, OH: Pearson.

12 *Response:* Scaffolds, Tools, and Transitions Toward Disciplined Improvisation

Matthew Kloser
UNIVERSITY OF NOTRE DAME

Mark Windschitl
UNIVERSITY OF WASHINGTON

The authors' visions of exemplary teaching features young learners' use of disciplinary activity and discourse to foster meaningful learning about events and processes in the natural world. This commitment disrupts the status quo conception of hands-on work as valuable for its own sake in elementary classrooms (see Roth, 2014). To accomplish this more ambitious vision, preservice teachers are asked to take up forms of instructional practice that are so attentive to the meaning-making of learners and contingent upon the gritty particulars of the classroom, that they have to be parsed and studied "in pieces" (Davis, this volume, Chapter 7). In our review, we explore how perspectives in the preceding five chapters contribute to our understanding of the development of instructional practice holistically and in pieces, how the articulation of core principles may be necessary for providing structure yet allowing the flexibility to respond to students' needs, and how scaffolds and tools used to support this work can be productively problematized.

What Do These Chapters Mean by Practice?

The turn toward practice has taken root in elementary science teacher preparation and in recent reforms in elementary science education. Whether reflecting on engaging young people in disciplinary activity as a means for sensemaking about core science ideas (Kademian and Davis, this volume, Chapter 8) or on the development of teaching expertise, the preceding authors implicitly and explicitly frame a vision of what high-quality teaching "practice" is, is not, and why it is important.

Foremost, the authors' discussions of teaching practice move the enterprise well beyond prescribed skills. Teaching practices are *not* scripts, competencies, or behaviors, rather, they are thought of more expansively. As Davis (this volume, Chapter 7) notes, "teaching is interactive, contingent, and intricate with students contributing ideas in real time" and "support[s] the learning of students with different needs, backgrounds, interests, and experiences" (this volume, Chapter 7, p. 97). The nature of this professional practice extends beyond the procedural as it is imbued with professional judgment, knowledge of the content and students, and respectful of the emotional environment in which it is carried out.

Davis (this volume, Chapter 7) argues for the coordinated use of specialized scaffolds and tools as a means for novice teachers to monitor learners' movement toward learning goals. Within this view, instructional practices are undertaken jointly *with* children to negotiate and help make progress on reasoning and valued performances, some of which may emerge from the work as it unfolds. Thus, practice is viewed, again, not as discrete skills or teacher moves, but rather as goal-directed enactments, engaging students in coherent and broader learning objectives that extend beyond the boundaries of a single activity. A central goal of the practice-based approach and the tools identified in these chapters is that practice is designed to be sensitive to the classroom context and to students' backgrounds and needs.

Collectively, the authors suggest that responsive science teaching can "raise the bar" for learners' engagement in rigorous scientific thinking and disciplinary practices. Arias (this volume, Chapter 11) acknowledges the level of complex reasoning that is attainable, even by young children in science classrooms, through the teaching practice of "supporting students to construct evidence-based claims through data analysis." This enactment necessarily moves beyond a single skill or script-following on the teacher's part and engages students in the work of finding and interpreting patterns in data and making connections between theory, data, and evidence, in order to make sense of the world around them. As framed in these chapters, effective teaching practice can create and maintain equitable conditions for students from all backgrounds to engage in challenging intellectual work related to the subject matter (Windschitl *et al.*, 2018).

Disciplined Improvisation and Articulating Central Principles

In the classrooms described in this book, teachers "work on and with students' ideas." This is neither formulaic nor free-form pedagogy, rather the teacher is accountable to students' contributions, to the nature of science ideas, and the norms of the discipline. And while not free-form, we suggest that the vision of practice portrayed across these chapters could benefit from drawing on Sawyer's (2011) notion of *disciplined improvisation*. He interprets this kind of creative teaching as disciplined because it always occurs within broad frameworks that guide practitioner responses. So, while archetypical models of science teaching practices exist—like supporting students' analysis and interpretation of data as described by Arias (this volume, Chapter 11)—teachers may, at times, best address students' needs by creatively using, adapting, or discarding elements of a core instructional practice. This type of improvisation, however, can only be considered disciplined if it is bound by a set of principles that adhere to values

180　*Kloser and Windschitl*

about teaching, learning, and equity. These principles constrain "what counts" as an example of a particular practice. At the same time, they allow flexibility and innovation around talk routines, tasks, and tools that can foster student learning or participation (Leinhardt and Greeno, 1986).

What do we mean by "principles" that are central to disciplined improvisation and how might these chapter authors respond to this critique? To explore this idea, we provide a brief vignette of Karin, a secondary science educator who participated as a preservice teacher in a study with both authors of this chapter— Mark and Matt. Karin was working on moderating sensemaking discussions in small groups through the practice of "moving among the tables" (sometimes referred to as "circulating"). As with all practices, moving among the tables is goal-directed; the teacher uses questions and prompts to help all students in each group engage in collaborative science reasoning and help them think with one another to pose problems about phenomena or make sense of science ideas. Similar to Arias' (this volume, Chapter 11) decomposition of supporting students in analyzing and interpreting data, or Kademian and Davis's (this volume, Chapter 8) features embedded within their set of scaffolds, this practice is composed of multiple elements that can be used flexibly depending on students' needs:

- The teacher moves to group, listens first to students' current thinking;
- Teacher asks questions that probe students' ideas, provide an entry point for struggling students, or points to a specific part of some problem or representation that students have been talking about (not generically asking, "How are you thinking?");
- Teacher asks follow-ups to student responses: "Can you say more?" "What do you mean?" "Why do you think that?";
- Prompts group members to take positions on their peers' ideas, reasoning, or hypotheses, "Do you agree?" "Want to add on?";
- Teacher asks a "leaving question" that extends students' thinking further and keeps them talking after she/he moves to next group.

What one sees and hears during these visits will vary depending upon the unique conditions of each conversation. Yet there should also be a family resemblance across these exchanges, structured by three principles (P) that, ideally, underlie novices' decision-making:

P1. Create openings for *all* students to participate in equitable and meaningful ways.
P2. Be open to diverse ways of making sense by students; recognize and build on partial ideas, out-of-school experiences, hunches they think are relevant to the task. Acknowledge these and position their ideas as *science ideas* to be built upon.
P3. Hold students accountable for using science ideas and other resources introduced in class to reason about phenomena—individually and together. Give them opportunities to make visible what they know and how they are thinking.

Toward Disciplined Improvisation 181

In a previous lesson, Karin's students had ignited a dish of ethanol in a large transparent container. The next day, students in groups of four were given the task of drawing a model on small whiteboards that represented what they thought happened at the molecular level during the combustion. If Karin had viewed the circulating practice as a rigid set of steps, she would likely end up engaging in checklist-like behavior with each table visit. However, when observed addressing small groups, she set aside a tool designed to remind her of the practice's elements, so she could better attend to the needs of students while holding fast to the core principles of the practice. This occurred when she approached a small group: two Somali girls, Cadey and Nuuro, and a Somali boy, Abbas. She noticed that the students had copied down the formula for ethanol, but their hesitation when asked about it suggested that they were not sure what the symbolism meant—that molecules are made of atoms and those are being rearranged during the burning of ethanol to produce new compounds.

As Abbas drew on the whiteboard, Karin saw that Nuuro, standing opposite, had to read the model upside down. She worried that this English Language Learner was being disadvantaged by having to decode text from that angle and by Abbas's assertiveness in taking on the drawing responsibilities without much consultation with his peers.

Karin retrieved a marker from the front of the room and handed it to Nuuro. As Cadey and Abbas busied themselves showing atoms of different kinds on the model, Karin noticed that Nuuro was still at the other end of the table, looking on but not drawing. Karin gestured for the reluctant student to come stand next to her. As Nuuro repositioned herself, Karin turned the whiteboard so it faced her and asked the group: "What atoms do you think are in this container?" A long silence followed, but Karin resisted breaking her wait time with another question. After a minute, Nuuro offered: "Hydrogen?" Karin replied "Great, can you show me that? There is no wrong or right answer, I just want to see what you are all thinking." The conversation continued for another minute before the passing bell rang to end the class.

Any classroom observer expecting Karin to mechanically replicate the elements of this practice as she moved from table to table would likely be puzzled about which could be checked off as "done." But this would be missing the point of a practice-based preparation. After using a number of scaffolds and tools in her university coursework, her actions reflected judgment about how to interact with young learners in the context of an ELL classroom—informed by these previous supports but not dictated by them. She ensured that all students had an opening for participation (P1) while referencing visual representations (P3) in order to build on initial ideas (P2). Her visit to this group was shaped by her concern for the students' insecurity about the chemical symbolism they had copied down, but also by the lack of physical access one of the girls had to seeing what was being represented by her peers. As Karin retrieved the marker and placed it in Nuuro's

182 *Kloser and Windschitl*

hand, she sent a clear message about who should participate and whose ideas were going to be valued.

Our point here is that the novice has to be adaptable in using different elements of a practice. Karin's actions reflected the situated work of noticing student ideas and relating it to her practice (see also Benedict-Chambers, this volume, Chapter 10). As such, a supporting mentor or teacher educator would not follow a checklist of moves to determine effective practice, but rather monitor alignment of the novices' interactions with students with these underlying principles. The preceding chapters reflect this thinking in both implicit and explicit ways. For instance, Kademian and Davis (this volume, Chapter 8) highlight that instructional practices and the full complement of supports that go with them are effective only to the degree that, together, they reflect a coherent vision of teaching and learning. They are attending to the importance of core principles that underlie why particular moves or routines are successful for supporting student sensemaking. For the benefit of teacher educators and novice teachers, making fully explicit the underlying principles for all practices will make the moves, tools, and judgments more accessible and logically sound.

Optimizing Supports for Developing Professional Practice

Perhaps most salient across the set of chapters is the essential role of supports for the complex work of teaching. For preservice elementary science teachers, as for all novices, taking up ambitious instruction requires specialized tools, scaffolding, and opportunities to learn. Using these forms of assistance, novices gradually move from trying out parts of practices in the protected environment of university coursework, to facilitating whole science lessons for energetic children in crowded classrooms. These supports not only help guide early practice and may be used throughout even expert practice, but we argue that they set the stage for the kind of disciplined improvisation described above.

For example, Davis (this volume, Chapter 7) emphasizes that scaffolds and tools must be developed in ways that support, but do not constrain practices. In describing the suite of three different approximations that she uses as enactment scaffolds for novice teachers, she discusses a scenario in which an intern might make a move that broadens students' sense of who is scientifically proficient. Here, the teacher educator could pause and comment publicly about how the interns' move helps promote "more equitable and just science teaching" (this volume, Chapter 7, p. 103). In this case, the teacher educator would likely not have a decomposition that specifically points to the novice's preceding move as it is situated within a particular classroom interaction. But because core principles—particularly the commitment to promoting equity—underlie the teacher educator's own noticing (Benedict-Chambers, this volume, Chapter 10) and decision-making, attending to this interaction in the context of a rehearsal exemplifies practice as disciplined improvisation.

Kademian and Davis (this volume, Chapter 8) provide another example in which supports for teachers attend to broader principles rather than to just discrete moves or skills. In describing their monitoring tool, they emphasize that the tool is in place to do more than ensure that children are on task. Rather the tools help novices attend to what students say, allowing them to address the core principle that students' ideas are central to sensemaking. Furthermore, as articulated by Benedict-Chambers (this volume, Chapter 10), disciplined improvisation does not mean being unprepared for the uncertainties of the classroom. Two scaffolds that she introduces, namely the *student alternative ideas tool* and the *science practice challenge tool*, recognize that through experience and research, even novices can be aware of common scenarios to which they must respond. Similar to improv performers who grow more effective when they have a deep understanding of the context and the other performers with whom they are interacting, planfully thinking about common alternative ideas or ways in which students might run into difficulties engaging in scientific practices positions novices to make more effective decisions.

In addition, several chapters (Davis, Chapter 7; Kademian and Davis, Chapter 8; Fick and Arias, Chapter 9; Benedict-Chambers, Chapter 10) frame different supports as suites of scaffolds and tools rather than supports for novices that operate independently. The authors' discussions of suites of scaffolds and tools have important implications for teacher educators who foster a practice-based approach. Kademian and Davis's range of tools—from instructional planning templates and card sorts to talk move and monitoring tools—exist within the broader framework for knowledge needed for science teaching. These supports especially help novice elementary science teachers, who may be more hesitant to push for ambitious practice due to content knowledge constraints, see how the major tasks of integrating students' ideas with empirical evidence work in concert with each other to help learners develop useful explanations of the natural world. Benedict-Chambers' conclusions note that while the tools allow novices to notice individual parts of the practice, they must work together to be more broadly effective in helping student sensemaking.

Fick and Arias also explored a range of 32 tools that help support the development of novice elementary science teachers. Their chapter described the purposefulness of these as they innovated tools to support particular preservice science teacher struggle. This extensive use of tools acknowledges the level of support especially needed by elementary teachers, but it also raises the question of how teacher educators can avoid *over-structuring* experiences. The authors state that they only used some of the tools for any given course and never used them all at once, but the question remains: How might teacher educators make decisions about when too many frameworks, scaffolds, and tools are being used, such that novices become overwhelmed by the supports themselves rather than recognizing how the varied forms of assistance can work together toward a more holistic practice?

184 *Kloser and Windschitl*

Differentiating between Frameworks, Scaffolds, and Tools

Given the clearly important role of frameworks, scaffolding, and tools discussed in these chapters, is it important to more clearly conceptualize and problematize these terms? Frameworks are mentioned across each of the chapters in different ways, including those by Davis (e.g., frameworks that decompose a practice into salient features), Kademian and Davis (e.g., framework for knowledge needed for science teaching), Arias (e.g., framework for teaching practice to consider how to support teacher learning), and Fick and Arias and Benedict-Chambers (e.g., the EEE framework for science instruction). Our interpretation is that these structures intend to provide guidance about practice while also organizing a variety of interrelated ideas.

Taken literally, scaffolds are temporary supports used in construction that help builders accomplish tasks that would normally be difficult or impossible without them. When the task is completed, the scaffolds are taken down while other work continues on the project. In education, scaffolds serve an analogous function. As Davis (this volume, Chapter 7) describes, scaffolds provide "appropriate assistance [so that] a learner can attain a goal or engage in a practice otherwise out of reach" (this volume, Chapter 7, p. 98). For example, she describes how scaffolds like peer-teaching rehearsal experiences allow novices to engage in the interactional work of teaching in a low-stakes setting. Like construction scaffolds, the rehearsals and other approximations are eventually faded and give way to more authentic teaching practice.

Indeed, in teacher education, scaffolds for practice should be considered temporary supports that allow novice teachers to construct an understanding of the variety of ways in which the essential principles of practice can play out. For example, Davis's use of peer rehearsals are scaffolds that will disappear once independent teaching begins, whereas the set of talk moves or monitoring tools that are used within the rehearsal may carry over permanently into practice. It may be important, then, to more clearly differentiate between scaffolds, which are temporary supports, and frameworks and tools which become parts of the teacher's repertoire. We propose that frameworks help implicitly or explicitly acknowledge the central principles of a practice and therefore are permanent supports for teaching. Similarly, tools like talk moves or ways of ensuring equity of voice are used in an ongoing manner in professional practice as a means to meet instructional goals.

These chapters invite us to clarify distinctions between frameworks, scaffolds, and tools. Each provide a form of support for novice teachers, but the terms seem to be occasionally used interchangeably by the authors. Making explicit what frameworks are necessary will push teacher educators and novices toward a set of core principles that can allow for disciplined improvisation. Clearly naming which supports are scaffolds will push teacher educators to think more consciously about their *temporary* nature and the trajectory for when they can be faded or removed entirely, thus better preparing novices for more independent practice. And finally, it is important for teacher educators to recognize, within our conceptualization, the *permanence* of tools. Thus, when certain scaffolds are pulled away, allowing for more disciplined improvisation that addresses the principles of a core practice outlined by a framework, some tools still remain that can be used or tabled based on the professional judgment of the teacher. As discussed in several chapters (e.g., Fick and Arias, this volume, Chapter 9), the tools can evolve in the context of professional work. Furthermore, recognizing the permanence of tools may help teacher educators avoid the introduction of superfluous assistance that can overwhelm novices, veritably "overloading their toolbelt", which in turn could lead to ad hoc or perfunctory uses of supports that end up being counterproductive to the aims of ambitious science teaching.

We close with this quote by Dutro and Cartun (2016): "[T]he long-circulating question of which practices of teaching hold the most promise for children's learning must be pursued in ways that foster movement toward useful clarity while sustaining attention on complexities of practice" (p. 120). These chapters contribute in concrete ways to this sentiment. Davis (this volume, Chapter 7) provides a lens for teacher educators to shape approximations—by providing enough structure to narrow the focus of learning, but also recognizing the complexity and problematizing the learning opportunities. Kademian and Davis (this volume, Chapter 8) reflect on a set of tools that exist not as individual supports, but take a systems approach to the integrated practice of facilitating investigation-based discussions. Arias, Benedict-Chambers, and Fick and Arias (this volume, Chapter 9) all present frameworks and tools that move elementary science teachers beyond scripts and toward instruction that responds to students' ideas and ongoing sensemaking. In sum, these chapters themselves represent a disciplined improvisation on the nature of elementary science teacher education. They draw on overarching principles that value and respect each child, they recognize the complexities and situated nature of teaching, and they provide a variety of supports to help novices—and teacher educators— advance their practice.

References

Dutro, E., and Cartun, A. (2016). Cut to the core Practices: Toward visceral disruptions of binaries in practice-based teacher education. *Teaching and Teacher Education, 58*, 119–128.

Leinhardt, G., and Greeno, J. G. (1986). The cognitive skill of teaching. *Journal of Educational Psychology, 78*(2), 75–95.

Roth, K. (2014). Elementary science teaching. In N. Lederman and S. Abell (Eds.) *Handbook of Research on Science Teaching* (Vol. II). New York: Routledge.

Sawyer, R. K. (2011). What makes good teachers great? The artful balance of structure and improvisation. In R. K. Sawyer (Ed.), *Structure and Improvisation in Creative Teaching* (pp. 1–26). New York: Cambridge University Press.

Windschitl, M., Thompson, J., and Braaten, M. (2018). *Ambitious Science Teaching*. Boston, MA: Harvard Education Press.

Section III

Supportive Contexts for Professional Learning

13 Designing a Practice-Based Elementary Teacher Education Program and Supporting Professional Learning in Science Teaching

Elizabeth A. Davis, Annemarie S. Palincsar and Sylvie M. Kademian
UNIVERSITY OF MICHIGAN

Acknowledgments

Parts of this research were funded by Lyle Spencer Award from the Spencer Foundation. Any opinions, findings, conclusions, or recommendations expressed in this material are those of the authors. The authors thank the Elementary Science Methods Planning Group, the Elementary Curriculum Design Group, and the elementary interns at the University of Michigan for supporting the authors' growth as teacher educators.

Introduction

Elementary science teaching, as has been established throughout this volume, presents many challenges to teachers, yet effective teaching is crucial for supporting children's sensemaking in science. How can teacher educators support beginning teachers in learning to teach science? We describe our approach at the University of Michigan. Our program reflects a "practice-based" approach to teacher education. We discuss how practice-based teacher education is reflected in our instructional designs and how preservice teachers learn to engage in authentic, equitable, and rigorous elementary science teaching.

Elementary Science and Meanings of "Practice"

Since the 1990s, science education has increasingly assumed an orientation toward teaching scientific practice in the context of investigations of phenomena (e.g., Arias, 2015; McNeill and Krajcik, 2008). The United States' standards emphasize "three-dimensional learning" that integrates disciplinary core ideas, scientific and engineering practices, and crosscutting concepts (National Research Council, 2012; NGSS Lead States, 2013). Other countries, too, emphasize similar integration (e.g., UK Department for Education, 2014).

190 Davis, Palincsar, and Kademian

Science and engineering practices represent the work scientists and engineers do. A set of scientific and engineering practices is developed in the *Framework for K-12 Science Education* (National Research Council, 2012) including practices such as planning and carrying out investigations and arguing from evidence.

During roughly the same time period, the field of teacher education has moved away from emphasizing only teachers' knowledge development and analytic skills and toward what is referred to as practice-based teacher education (Ball and Forzani, 2009; Grossman *et al.*, 2009b), the goal of which is to support novices to use a rich knowledge base as they engage in a set of key teaching practices.

Arias (2015) analyzed how Lampert (2010) uses "practice" and explicated the term in reference to both science education and teacher education. First, as Lampert states, practice can refer to *a collection of practices*. In learning to teach, we refer to a set of (content-neutral) high-leverage or core teaching practices, which can include planning practices as well as interactional practices (e.g., meeting with a parent, or planning and leading a discussion). In learning science, we refer to the scientific practices used to learn about natural phenomena. Second, practice can be used as a verb as in *to rehearse*. In learning to teach, a beginning teacher may rehearse a lesson with colleagues before teaching it to children. In learning science, a child might develop scientific arguments as a part of every unit across the year, practicing them across time. Finally, practice can be used in reference to *a profession*. In learning to teach, the profession is teaching. In learning science, it would be a discipline of science. We draw on all three meanings in our work with preservice teachers (called "interns" in our program).

Pillars of the Teacher Education Program

We organize our elementary program around a taxonomy of 19 *high-leverage teaching practices* that were developed collaboratively (Davis and Boerst, 2014). We wanted to identify teaching practices that were likely to be powerful in advancing students' learning, effective in acknowledging differences among students and confronting inequities, and useful across many different contexts and content areas. We also wanted to identify teaching practices that could serve as building blocks for learning to teach, could be learned by a beginner, could be assessed, had face validity, and were unlikely to be learned well only through teaching experience.

We developed the program's high-leverage practices to work across content areas. Yet much of teaching is content-specific. Thus, in our coursework specific to science teaching, we focus on a handful of high-leverage science teaching practices, including:

1 Supporting students to construct scientific explanations;
2 Choosing and using representations, examples, and models of science content and practices;
3 Leading discussions that integrate science disciplinary core ideas and practices;

Practice-Based Teacher Education   191

4 Eliciting, probing, and developing students' thinking about science;
5 Setting up and managing small-group investigations;
6 Developing norms for discourse and work that reflect the discipline of science; and
7 Appraising and modifying science lesson plans.

Our decision-making about foci in science was informed by our program design as a whole, as well as the scholarship of others who have worked to identify high-leverage science teaching practices (Cartier *et al.*, 2013; Kloser, 2014; Windschitl *et al.*, 2012).

A second pillar of our program is *content knowledge for teaching*, by which we mean the subject matter knowledge and pedagogical content knowledge (Shulman, 1986) needed for teaching academic content—including knowledge of content and students, knowledge of content and teaching, and common and specialized content knowledge (Ball *et al.*, 2008). This knowledge is not separate from teaching practice, but an inherent part of the work of teaching.

The third pillar grounding our program is a set of *ethical obligations* (TEI Ethics Project Working Group, 2009). Teachers have an obligation to, for example, treat all learners with respect and take responsibility for obstacles to student success. These ethical obligations are worked on throughout the program toward the goal of more equitable and just teaching.[1] The intent is for interns to be able to enact teaching that reflects the obligations—not for them to be able to espouse the "right" beliefs.

How are these three pillars reflected in elementary science teaching? Imagine a fifth-grade teacher teaching a lesson on condensation and scientific modeling. The teacher needs to elicit students' ideas about the change of state from gas to liquid, adapt a lesson plan to meet the needs of her students, and develop classroom norms for critiquing others' scientific models. These are some of the high-leverage science teaching practices she would need. The teacher also needs to understand the explanatory mechanism for condensation, students' typical alternative ideas about condensation (e.g., that cold water *leaks through* a glass to the outside surface), struggles they may have with scientific modeling, and experiences with the phenomenon that could help to address specific ideas. These are some of the dimensions of content knowledge for teaching needed. Furthermore, the teacher needs to consider that *each* student enters the classroom with ideas that can be used as resources for learning and engage *each* child in sensemaking. These are some of her ethical obligations.

Teacher Education Pedagogies for Well-Started Beginners

Our program is designed with the intention of supporting the development of well-started beginners, effective from their initial days in the classroom. Teacher education pedagogies include pedagogies of investigation,

192 *Davis, Palincsar, and Kademian*

reflection, and practice (Grossman *et al.*, 2009b). *Pedagogies of investigation* involve analytic work. *Pedagogies of reflection* involve reflection on one's own or others' teaching. *Pedagogies of practice* include *decomposition, representation,* and *approximation* (Grossman *et al.*, 2009a). Table 13.1 summarizes these pedagogies of teacher education, and the pedagogies of practice are unpacked below.

Decomposition of practice involves "breaking down practice into its constituent parts for the purposes of teaching and learning" (Grossman *et al.*, 2009a, p. 2056). Representation of practice refers to "the different ways that practice is represented in professional education and what these various representations make visible to novices" (Grossman *et al.*, 2009a, p. 2055–56). Representations can include videos of classroom teaching, samples of student work, or lesson plans. Approximations of practice "refer to opportunities to engage in practices that are more or less proximal to the practices of a profession" (Grossman *et al.*, 2009a, p. 2056). A key approximation of practice, rehearsal, involves "publicly and deliberately practicing" (Lampert *et al.*, 2013, p. 227) how to teach specific content using specific teaching practices.

These pedagogies help teacher educators support preservice teachers in developing knowledge and ability. Next, we describe the design of and rationale for two practice-based courses from our undergraduate program.

Early in the Program: Seeing Children as Sensemakers

Our undergraduate elementary teacher education program is four semesters long, culminating in student teaching. Figure 13.1 presents an overview of the timeline of the program. The program is small, with approximately 40–50

Table 13.1 Teacher Education Pedagogies

Pedagogies of Teacher Education	Description and Example: The preservice teacher …
Pedagogies of investigation	analyzes something (e.g., a case depicting a teacher's decision-making)
Pedagogies of reflection	reflects on their own or another's teaching (e.g., responding to focused questions about one's enactment)
Pedagogies of practice (or of enactment)	
Decomposition of practice	uses a breakdown a practice (e.g., using a framework)
Representation of practice	reads about or watches an example of teaching (e.g., watching a video of an expert teaching a lesson)
Approximation of practice	enacts a smaller or less authentic version of a practice or lesson (e.g., rehearsing a practice with colleagues)

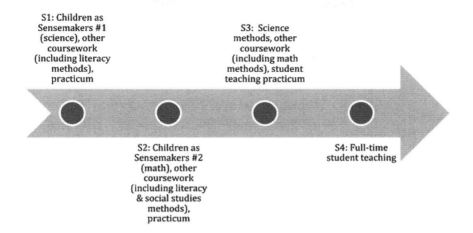

Figure 13.1 Timeline of the Four-Semester Elementary Teacher Education Program

interns in each year (so 80–100 interns total at any given time), typically taught in two cohorts or sections.

When interns first enter our program, they experience a course entitled Children as Sensemakers. This course meets for four weeks, three hours a week, and makes pivotal use of experiences in the interns' field placements in grades K-2. The intent is for interns to recognize that students are constantly engaged in making sense of the world, and that teachers influence this sensemaking by mediating students' interactions with others and with physical objects. The main high-leverage science teaching practice of focus is eliciting students' thinking about phenomena. By focusing on eliciting students' thinking, the course supports interns to acknowledge and prioritize students' ideas in their teaching. Interns begin to take on the role of teacher as facilitator, guiding students toward more accurate understanding of phenomena, rather than conveyor of scientific knowledge (Kucan and Palincsar, 2013). Shifting their stance in this way is crucial for the interns' movement through the rest of the teacher education program—they need to begin to see children as making sense of the world in reasonable ways, recognize the value of children's ideas, and see teachers as those who support that sensemaking.

Interns interact with a single student in their field placement classroom on three occasions. First, using a fully developed interview protocol, they ask the child to share what they think about how we have day and night; the child is encouraged to *tell, draw,* and *show* what they know (using objects to represent the sun, the earth, and a person on the earth). On the second occasion, interns do an interactive reading of a book entitled *What Makes Day and Night* (Branley, 1986) with their student. Again, we provide the protocol for the discussion about the reading. Interns follow the reading by repeating the initial interview to assess student sensemaking for change. Third, the interns interview their child about how objects make sounds and what causes the pitch of a sound to change. The protocol for this interview is co-constructed as a class, and the interns select the materials that they will use for this interview to meet the needs and interests of their student, as well as their own interests and experiences.

Several literatures inform the content, spirit, and design of this course. These literatures are specific to how people learn, how educators' decision-making should be influenced by an understanding of learning, and how novice educators should be supported to learn to elicit, probe, and extend student thinking.

With respect to how people learn, this course reflects cognitive tenets of learning, which point to how humans construct understanding in the process of interpreting experiences in particular contexts (e.g., Bransford *et al.*, 1999). As the interns interview their students and ask questions designed to probe their thinking about a phenomenon that everyone experiences (i.e., the day/night cycle), they see the ways that children build explanations that fit with their observations and experiences of the world (e.g., the sun travels across the sky during the day). As interns introduce their students to new, more scientific explanations for day/night (through the reading and through modeling), they experience the variation in children's responses. These responses range from making the new information conform to their preconceptions, to making slight modifications to their explanations, to embracing the scientific explanation (Vosniadou and Brewer, 1994).

The role of the conversations, experiences with text, and experiences with modeling materials demonstrate how thought, learning, and knowledge building occur in socially and culturally shaped contexts. Rather than viewing cognition as an individual process, the interns are encouraged to consider how cognition is a collaborative process (Rogoff, 1997), and that thought and learning are, in fact, internalized discourse (John-Steiner and Mahn, 1996). Emphasis is placed on the role of the teacher in understanding student understanding (Duckworth, 2009) and mediating student sensemaking (Palincsar, 1998).

We use representations, decompositions, and approximations of teaching practice (Grossman *et al.*, 2009a) in teaching interns how to mediate sensemaking. We show a video of an expert eliciting and probing two fifth-graders' thinking about how humans are able to see objects—a *representation of practice*. Interns are guided to notice the moves the expert makes to engage the students in elaborating on their thinking and to test the limits of the explanations they generate for how we see. Their own videos are another important resource for supporting the learning of the group as interns engage in guided study of one another's representations of practice.

Practice-Based Teacher Education 195

The metascripts (Tharp and Gallimore, 1991) that we provide interns serve to *decompose the practice* of eliciting and supporting student thinking. For example, the metascript models having a small conversation with a student; engaging in an initial elicitation of the child's thinking; probing the student's thinking; supporting the productive use of the text and modeling materials; and closing the interview.

With each iteration of the interview, interns are engaged in *approximations of practice*, or the opportunity to engage in practices that are proximal to the practices they will engage in as teachers of record.

Later in the Program: Putting the Pieces Together

The elementary science methods course meets in the third semester for nine weeks, three hours a week. Like Children as Sensemakers, this course draws on experiences in the interns' field placements. Interns are in the field part-time in K-7th-grade classrooms. These placements become their full-time student teaching placements in the fourth semester.

We focus on the development of the high-leverage science teaching practices listed above, but also focus on the recomposition (Janssen *et al.*, 2015) of the practices into sets, because of this course's timing during the semester immediately preceding student teaching. We count on interns having knowledge and skills related to the high-leverage practice of eliciting students' ideas, among others, due to their experiences in the Children as Sensemakers classes taken earlier.

We also use an instructional framework to help preservice teachers decompose the work of science teaching. Similar to other models (e.g., the 5E model; Bybee *et al.*, 2006), it organizes and names the typical components of an investigation-based science lesson. The EEE+A framework (see Benedict-Chambers, 2016; Kademian and Davis, this volume, Chapter 8) decomposes science teaching into an *Engage* element (establishing an investigation question and eliciting students' initial ideas); an *Experience* element (investigating a natural phenomenon); and an *Explain+Argue with Evidence* element (making sense of data, making claims based on evidence, and applying knowledge to a new situation).

The EEE+A framework links to the high-leverage teaching practices and to the scientific practices named in the *Next Generation Science Standards*. The framework also supports interns to build on experiences with eliciting, prioritizing, and using students' ideas from Children as Sensemakers, with the goal of moving toward more equitable and just teaching that values children's ideas and supports their sensemaking.

We also draw on representations of practice, primarily through video, for three related reasons. First, novice elementary teachers often do not have much enthusiasm for teaching science and sometimes are nervous about doing so; they often lack the rich subject matter knowledge of their secondary colleagues (Abell, 2007). Second, science is rarely taught at the elementary level, at least in the US (e.g., Banilower *et al.*, 2018). This means that there are relatively few opportunities for interns to observe science teaching in their field placements, and interns' experiences with young children learning science probably are limited to those they had in Children as Sensemakers. Third, it is even more rare to see the kind of integration of science content and scientific practices recommended by current reforms (cf. NASEM, 2015). Representations of high-quality science teaching practice help us to overcome these three limitations.

Typically, we look for videos that demonstrate science teaching that integrates content and practice as we are urging our interns to engage in with their students. For example, we use videos from our class text (Zembal-Saul *et al.*, 2013) showing skillful elementary teachers engaging their students in such teaching. Centering some representations on children's sensemaking is important because we know that elementary teachers may avoid supporting sensemaking. We sample across the grade levels our interns will be teaching, including the lowest elementary grades. This is important because we know that, while young children are capable of engaging in sophisticated scientific thought and work (Metz, 1995), some teachers do not recognize their capabilities, and we want to reinforce the messages from the Children as Sensemakers course sequence. Providing video examples from early grades can support novice teachers in changing their expectations of young children (cf. Arias, 2015). Finally, we look for videos that reflect the demographics of American classrooms. Too often, novice teachers make assumptions about who can and cannot do science; we try to challenge those assumptions. We use a guide to support novices' engagement with video (cf. Kademian and Davis, this volume, Chapter 8).

We also engage in a series of approximations of practice (Davis, this volume, Chapter 7). For example, interns rehearse segments of a carefully selected lesson intended to highlight common problems of practice in teaching science, such as working with data gathered by children. The teacher educator provides specific, focused feedback. The rehearsals "quiet the background noise" (Grossman *et al.*, 2009a, p. 2083) and lower the stakes.

Interns also teach science in their field placement classroom twice during the course, culminating in teaching a full investigation-based science lesson. They plan these lessons using our instructional planning template (see Kademian and Davis, this volume, Chapter 8), enact the lessons with the children in their field placement, and reflect on the enactments using video.

How These Experiences Support Interns' Development

Drawing upon multiple methods, we explored how these experiences in Children as Sensemakers and elementary science methods support interns' development in terms of their knowledge and practice.

Practice-Based Teacher Education 197

Interns' Experiences with Children as Sensemakers

We interviewed nine interns following the course, in the late fall or early winter of their first year in the program, when they were juniors. We selected these interns to be representative of their cohort in terms of their subject matter major, achievement in science courses, racial/ethnic identity, and gender. We designed the interview questions to inquire into the interns' reflections on the development of teaching practices specific to supporting students' sensemaking and knowledge building.

In response to asking *why the course focused on eliciting and probing children's thinking*, the most frequent response was to identify insights achieved regarding children's thinking. For example, interns said, "It's valuable and important to understand that children make sense of the world in their own way" (Maddison) and "How are you supposed to even consider being a teacher and go through this program without really thinking about [how children learn] first?" (Jess).

Interns also identified skills they associated with the course. For example, Na'imah said, "Probing and having the children think and express their thoughts to you is very important. That's one of the first things that we should know how to do." Sabrina noted, "This is the first class where I was posed with the idea that the way I phrase my questions or the way that I ask students, they respond accordingly." She continued, "You want to be open-minded, but you need a goal so you know how to phrase questions."

Other responses revealed that a subset of the interns engaged in identity work (Luehman, 2007; Avraamidou, this volume, Chapter 5). For example, Maddison commented that the course was useful to her in confronting preconceived ideas, saying, "eliciting without correcting is not something I had really thought about much … At first, I did not even know what to do with myself."

Maddison's response was a frequent refrain in the class discussions. The interns were initially distressed that their goal was to elicit children's thinking and refrain from what they conceived of as "teaching," which, they represented as synonymous with "telling." Similarly, Jess commented in the interview, "We had no clue what we were doing or what teaching was." The crucial shift toward seeing students as sensemakers and teachers as facilitators was beginning.

Cumulatively, interns' responses to this initial question suggest that they "got" the primary purpose of the course; they reflected ways in which the course both influenced their orientation to teaching and provided a context for acquiring useful teaching skills.

The second interview question asked: "*What do you think you got better at with regard to eliciting and probing students' ideas?*" The nine responses were variations on the theme of acquiring and/or extending their repertoires for eliciting and probing student thinking and prioritizing student thinking. Jacey said, for example, "I got better at asking questions in different ways."

Maddison said that she became "more adept at asking questions that would give actual student-thought answers ... using prompts like 'tell me more about that'." Harper noted, "I find myself more confident and comfortable ... with pauses and to have students talk more."

The third question was designed to elicit the experiences that helped them to get better with the skills they identified in response to question 2. Four respondents referenced the opportunity to view their own videos and the videos of one another. Additional responses noted the importance of the interview protocols and feedback from the instructor.

Given the prominent role that recording and viewing videos[2] of themselves, as well as one another, played in this course, we were curious how the interns experienced this process. Their responses to the question that asked them to *reflect on their experiences learning from their own and others' videos* were encouraging, but also pointed to the conditions necessary for this approach to work well. All nine interns referenced how their learning was enhanced by video viewing. For example, "watching others was helpful because I spotted some things I should have done and took some of their ideas." When probed to elaborate, Na'imah answered, "I am very wordy; one of our colleagues was very explicit and clear. I need to work on that and I am still working on that." Three interns commented on the value of seeing how other children responded to the same interview. Typically, the interns found that their colleagues helped them to identify a strength in their own teaching that they had not observed about themselves.

In summary, the interview data were useful to characterizing the kinds—and value—of experiences the interns had in Children as Sensemakers, how these experiences influenced their thinking about teaching and about themselves as teachers, and their awareness of skills and knowledge they believed they needed to acquire. Interns acknowledged that student ideas are important and should be a priority when teaching. They recognized shifts in their own practice—such as developing improved questioning—that helped support that new stance. They also recognized that the experiences they had in Children as Sensemakers supported them in making these improvements; however, they also identified the need to expand their repertoire of moves to probe (rather than simply elicit) students' thinking and they expressed uncertainty about how students come to new and/or deeper understandings.

Interns' Development around Multiple High-Leverage Practices

A year later, after this shift in identity had begun and the development of some teaching skills had started, interns took their science methods course. By this point, interns experienced a year in the field, in both lower- and upper-elementary classroom placements. They also, by this point, had worked on several different high-leverage teaching practices as well as content knowledge for teaching across multiple content areas. Here, we explore how these individuals developed a few high-leverage science teaching practices in the science methods course, investigating their classroom practice through video of their science lessons.

Using a longitudinal design, we analyzed videos of science teaching from four individuals while they were (a) interns in our program and then (b) first-year teachers. We looked at how they engaged in a set of high-leverage science teaching practices, using specialized coding keys that reflected a progression of performance along relevant sub-practices (Davis and Palincsar, 2017). Our analyses highlighted the variability of practice within and across teachers, as well as within and across high-leverage practices.

Here, we focus on interns' performances related to *eliciting students' ideas in science, leading a sensemaking discussion in science,* and *supporting students in constructing scientific explanations.* The practice of eliciting is of interest to us because it is initially supported in Children as Sensemakers, and is supported consistently throughout the program. The practice of leading a discussion is of interest because it is *not* particularly supported in the elementary science methods course—it is a focal teaching practice in other subject areas' methods courses, instead. Third, the practice of supporting explanation construction is of interest because it is a strong focus in the undergraduate elementary science methods course.

The practice of *eliciting students' ideas in science* seemed straightforward for interns and first-year teachers. They experienced the most success with this practice during their time in the program (compared with other high-leverage practices) and maintained about the same level of success as first-year teachers (approximately 80% of the scored lessons at both time points met or exceeded expectations). Characteristics of this practice included using effective questions and tasks or models to elicit ideas (skills interns worked on in Children as Sensemakers). They also made reasonable interpretations of what students said or did, and followed up on their language as appropriate. We attribute some of the interns' success to the work they did early on in the Children as Sensemakers course and continued throughout the subsequent course- and field-work in the program.

Interns and first-year teachers were similar with regard to experiencing success with *leading a sensemaking discussion in science* (around two-thirds of lessons at both time-points were scored as "meeting" or "exceeding" expectations for this practice), but neither group demonstrated as much success here as we had hoped based on the extent of work in the program on this practice. (Of course, leading sensemaking discussions is challenging for veteran teachers, as well!) Teachers consistently used multiple children's ideas to work toward a key idea. We saw less evidence of teachers supporting children in building on one another's ideas, and we saw almost no evidence of the teachers purposely sequencing students' ideas in the discussion. We hypothesize that, despite extensive work on leading a discussion in other academic subject areas, leading a discussion in science is uniquely challenging due in part to the challenge of knowing a lesson's intellectual point (Sleep, 2012; see also Windschitl *et al.*, 2012). Without deep, rich subject matter knowledge in science, it may be hard to transfer knowledge and skill related to this practice to another subject area. Furthermore, while this practice builds on the work of eliciting student thinking, it requires navigating many students' thinking at once.

First-year teachers were more likely to experience success with *supporting students in constructing scientific explanations*, compared with interns (79% of first-year teachers' lessons "met" or "exceeded" expectations, compared to 56% of the in-program lessons). We provided numerous intentional supports for interns in learning how to support students in constructing scientific explanations (see, e.g., Arias, this volume, Chapter 11). Characteristics of this practice that we saw included the use of a claim-evidence-reasoning framework (e.g., McNeill and Krajcik, 2008) and the use of appropriate and sufficient evidence. We saw less evidence of discursive engagement in student–student argumentation. That some success continued and even increased into the first year of teaching was exciting. We suspect that some of this success was due to a fundamental recognition that children *are* sensemakers and thus teachers must engage in sensemaking of some sort with their students—ideas developed initially in the Children as Sensemakers course and reinforced throughout the program.

Conclusions and Implications

These practice-based teacher education experiences work cumulatively and synergistically to help us prepare well-started beginning elementary teachers who can effectively teach science as well as the other subject areas for which they are responsible. We see evidence of the importance of these practice-based experiences, in promoting identity shifts and knowledge growth, as well as the development of high-leverage science teaching practices. Thus a practice-based teacher education program can serve as a supportive context for professional learning.

We take from these findings a set of implications for our own program design and, by extension, science teacher education more generally. For example, the interviews after Children as Sensemakers suggested that we should do more to prepare interns for the role that video viewing will play in their preparation. The interviews also suggested the importance of being more explicit about the role of the teacher in responding to sensemaking that culminates in erroneous ideas and providing additional information regarding how learning occurs. Finally, these interviews suggested the importance of supporting interns to work on verbal skills particular to any specific teaching practice.

Similarly, with regard to the analysis of interns' development of high-leverage science teaching practices, interns' struggles with the high-leverage science teaching practice of leading a sensemaking discussion in science has implications for our program design, which currently hinges on an assumption of transfer of knowledge and skill around discussion from other subject areas to science. Indeed, the version of the course in the master's-and-certification program included more focus on (and success with) the high-leverage science teaching practice of leading a discussion (Kademian and Davis, this volume, Chapter 8). In the undergraduate program, in contrast, the complexity of the task may increase too quickly and without sufficient scaffolding. We need to do more to support the transfer of knowledge and skill related to discussion across subject areas. We are developing tools that should support this kind of development and transfer (Kademian and Davis, this volume, Chapter 8), because of the centrality of this practice in promoting sensemaking for all children.

As they move into full-time teaching positions, teachers prepared in these ways are positioned to take advantage of ongoing opportunities for professional learning. Such opportunities to learn should be coherent and responsive to teachers' needs, can include both pull-out and school-embedded opportunities, and must be informed by the best available research (NASEM, 2015; cf. Roth, this volume, Chapter 17). Practice-based teacher education experiences can support beginning teachers in important development that can set the stage for their later growth. These initial practice-based experiences require careful sequencing and scaffolding. Experiences like these help to form supportive contexts for teachers' professional learning and growth over time.

Notes

1 In contrast with a recent critique of practice-based teacher education (Philip *et al.*, 2018), the program at the University of Michigan takes issues related to diversity, equity, justice, and inclusion seriously and works to prepare well-started beginners who are able to engage in skillful, equitable, and just teaching in all subject areas (as do other practice-based programs with which we are familiar).
2 Each intern had a subscription to a video-management application called Edthena. They uploaded their video, and tagged events in the video that were significant. Class time was dedicated to viewing and discussing one another's videos.

References

Abell, S. (2007). Research on science teacher knowledge. In S. Abell and N. Lederman (Eds.), *Handbook of Research on Science Education* (pp. 1105–1149). Mahwah, NJ: Lawrence Erlbaum Associates.

Arias, A. (2015). Learning to teach elementary students to construct evidence-based claims. (Unpublished doctoral dissertation), University of Michigan, Ann Arbor.

Ball, D., and Forzani, F. (2009). The work of teaching and the challenge for teacher education. *Journal of Teacher Education, 60*(5), 497–511.

Ball, D., Thames, M., and Phelps, G. (2008). Content knowledge for teaching: What makes it special? *Journal of Teacher Education, 29*(5), 389–407.

Banilower, E., Smith, P. S., Malzahn, K., Plumley, C., Gordon, E., and Hayes, M. (2018). *Report of the 2018 NSSME+*. Chapel Hill, NC: Horizon Research, Inc.

Benedict-Chambers, A. (2016). Using tools to promote novice teacher noticing of science teaching practices in post-rehearsal discussions. *Teaching and Teacher Education*, *49*, 28–44.

Branley, F. (1986). *What Makes Day and Night*. New York: HarperCollins.

Bransford, J. D., Brown, A. L., and Cocking, R. R. (Eds.). (1999). *How People Learn: Brain, Mind, Experience, and School*. Washington, DC: National Academies Press.

Bybee, R., Taylor, J., Gardner, A., Van Scotter, P., Powell, J. C., Westbrook, A., and Landes, N. (2006). *The BSCS 5E Instructional Model: Origins and Effectiveness*. Colorado Springs: BSCS.

Cartier, J., Smith, M., Stein, M. K., and Ross, D. (2013). *5 Practices for Orchestrating Productive Task-Based Discussions in Science*. Reston, VA: National Council of Teachers of Mathematics.

Davis, E. A., and Boerst, T. (2014). Designing elementary teacher education to prepare well-started beginners. Retrieved from http://www.teachingworks.org/images/files/TeachingWorks_Davis_Boerst_WorkingPapers_March_2014.pdf

Davis, E. A., and Palincsar, A. S. (2017). Investigating high-leverage science teaching practices. Paper presented at the annual meeting of NARST, San Antonio, TX.

Duckworth, E. R. (2009). *Tell Me More: Listening to Learners Explain*. Cambridge, MA: Harvard University Press.

Grossman, P., Compton, C., Igra, D., Ronfeldt, M., Shahan, E., and Williamson, P. (2009a). Teaching practice: A cross-professional perspective. *Teachers College Record*, *111*(9), 2055–2100.

Grossman, P., Hammerness, K., and McDonald, M. (2009b). Redefining teaching, re-imagining teacher education. *Teachers and Teaching: Theory and Practice*, *15*(2), 273–289.

Janssen, F., Grossman, P., and Westbroek, H. (2015). Facilitating decomposition and recomposition in practice-based teacher education: The power of modularity. *Teaching and Teacher Education*, *51*, 137–146.

John-Steiner, V. and Mahn, H. (1996). Sociocultural approaches to learning and development. *Educational Psychology*, *31*, 191–206.

Kloser, M. (2014). Identifying a core set of science teaching practices: A Delphi expert approach. *Journal of Research in Science Teaching*, *51*(9), 1184–1217.

Kucan, L., and Palincsar, A. S. (2013). *Comprehension Instruction through Text-Based Discussion*. Newark, DE: International Reading Association.

Lampert, M. (2010). Learning teaching in, from, and for practice: What do we mean? *Journal of Teacher Education*, *61*(1–2), 21–34.

Lampert, M., Franke, M., Kazemi, E., Ghousseini, H., Turrou, A., Beasley, H., and Crowe, K. (2013). Keeping it complex: Using rehearsals to support novice teacher learning of ambitious teaching. *Journal of Teacher Education*, *64*(3), 226–243.

Luehmann, A. L. (2007). Identity development as a lens to science teacher preparation. *Science Education*, *91*(5), 822–839.

McNeill, K., and Krajcik, J. (2008). Scientific explanations: Characterizing and evaluating the effects of teachers' instructional practices on student learning. *Journal of Research in Science Teaching*, *45*(1), 53–78.

Metz, K. (1995). Reassessment of developmental constraints on children's science instruction. *Review of Educational Research*, *65*(2), 93–127.

NASEM (National Academies of Sciences Engineering and Medicine). (2015). Science Teachers' Learning: Enhancing Opportunities, Creating Supportive Contexts. Committee on Strengthening Science Education through a Teacher Learning Continuum

Board on Science Education and Teacher Advisory Council Division of Behavioral and Social Science and Education. Washington, DC: National Academies Press.

National Research Council. (2012). *A Framework for K-12 Science Education: Practices, Crosscutting Concepts, and Core Ideas*. Committee on a Conceptual Framework for New K-12 Science Education Standards. Board on Science Education, Division of Behavioral and Social Sciences and Education. Washington, DC: National Academies Press.

NGSS Lead States. (2013). *Next Generation Science Standards: For States, By States*. Washington, DC: National Academies Press.

Palincsar, A. S. (1998). Keeping the metaphor of scaffolding fresh—A response to C. Addison Stone's "The metaphor of scaffolding: Its utility for the field of learning disabilities". *Journal of Learning Disabilities*, *31*(4), 370–373.

Philip, T., Souto-Manning, M., Anderson, L., Horn, I., Carter Andrews, D., Stillman, J., and Varghese, M. (2019). Making justice peripheral by constructing practice as "core": How the increasing prominence of core practices challenges teacher education. *Journal of Teacher Education*, *70*(3), 251–264.

Rogoff, B. (1997). Cognition as a collaborative process. In R. S. Siegler and D. Kuhn (Eds.), *Handbook of Child Psychology, Volume 2: Cognitive, Language, and Perceptual Development*. New York: Wiley.

Shulman, L. S. (1986). Those who understand: Knowledge growth in teaching. *Educational Researcher*, *15*(2), 4–14.

Sleep, L. (2012). The work of steering instruction toward the mathematical point: A decomposition of teaching practice. *American Educational Research Journal*, *49*(5), 935–970.

TEI (Teacher Education Initiative) Ethics Project Working Group. (2009). Ethical obligations of teachers. Retrieved from: http://www.soe.umich.edu/academics/bachelors/elementary-teacher-education/ethical-obligations

Tharp, R. G., and Gallimore, R. (1991). *Rousing Minds to Life: Teaching, Learning, and Schooling in Social Context*. New York: Cambridge University Press.

UK Department for Education. (2014). *National Curriculum in England: Science Programmes of Study (No. DFE-00182–2013)*. London: Crown Publishing.

Vosniadou, S., and Brewer, W. F. (1994). Mental models of the day/night cycle. *Cognitive Science*, *18*(1), 123–183.

Windschitl, M., Thompson, J., Braaten, M., and Stroupe, D. (2012). Proposing a core set of instructional practices and tools for teachers of science. *Science Education*, *96*(5), 878–903.

Zembal-Saul, C., McNeill, K., and Hershberger, K. (2013). *What's Your Evidence?: Engaging K-5 Students in Constructing Explanations in Science*. Boston, MA: Pearson Education.

14 Learning to Teach Science in an Elementary Professional Development School Partnership

Carla Zembal-Saul, Bernard Badiali, and Alicia M. McDyre
THE PENNSYLVANIA STATE UNIVERSITY

Brittany Mueller
BABYLON MEMORIAL GRADE SCHOOL, NEW YORK

Introduction

At a time when there is increasing progress toward coherence among what we know about learners and learning, robust standards, the importance of formative assessment, and features of effective professional development, it is more necessary than ever to address the role of context in professional learning. Barriers to change in teachers' practices are well documented (NASEM, 2015). These include local, state, and federal policies; staffing practices; lack of coherence among curriculum, instruction, assessment and professional learning opportunities; high stakes assessment practices; school leadership; and more.

Our aim in this chapter is to share our knowledge and experiences with a long standing professional development school (PDS) partnership between the Penn State College of Education and the State College Area School District as one example of a supportive context for teacher learning and development across the professional continuum—from preservice teachers to experienced practicing teachers to teacher educators. Before describing the partnership, we summarize the literature on the important role of context in teacher learning, and school–university partnerships specifically. We then describe a 20+-year partnership, highlighting our work with elementary school science. Co-author Brittany Mueller, who graduated from the program in 2016, shares her experiences and the role of teacher inquiry as part of her learning to teach science, as well as how her continuing development as a teacher is influenced by her preparation and current school context. To illustrate that interns are not the sole beneficiaries of the PDS partnership, we share the results of a mixed methods study that examined changes in mentor teachers' instructional practices across content areas resulting from PDS involvement (Nolan *et al.*, 2011). At the end of the chapter, we return to the important need to intentionally address supportive contexts as a key feature of professional learning opportunities for preservice and practicing teachers.

Educational Contexts and Teacher Learning

In the NASEM (2015) report on science teachers' learning, the committee critically addressed the ever-changing landscape of the educational systems in which teachers work, including the influence of federal and state policies and changing student and teacher demographics. We recognize the powerful influence of education policy, high stakes assessment, and other factors on teachers' practices and decision-making related to professional learning. While we acknowledge the numerous factors that influence teacher development, here we foreground features of local partnership work as it relates to supporting elementary teacher learning in science.

Davis and her colleagues (2006) reviewed the literature on beginning science teachers and reported that they have limited opportunities to learn science content in depth or engage in scientific practices as part of their own teacher preparation in science learning, which negatively influences their self-efficacy. Most beginning teachers have limited understanding of their students' ideas and interests, as well as other aspects of pedagogical content knowledge for science teaching (Luft *et al.*, 2011). In the current context of reform in science education (NRC, 2012), most K-12 teachers, beginning and experienced, have not learned science in ways that they are now expected to teach it. Further, they have not had opportunities to engage children in scientific discourse and practices for understanding and explaining phenomena. This is especially true of elementary teachers (Banilower *et al.*, 2018; Davis *et al.*, 2006). To be clear, we are not disparaging teachers for these deficits, but rather highlighting them as learning needs that must be carefully and intentionally considered when designing professional learning opportunities and supportive contexts for learning to teach science.

Schools and districts are complex organizations that can "feed or starve teachers' efforts to grow" (NASEM, 2015, p. 175). Studies of comprehensive school reform have revealed a number of overlapping conditions necessary for productive change (Cohen et al., 2013; Rowan *et al.*, 2009). These include coherent curricula and supports (Davis *et al.*, 2017), aligned and meaningful teacher professional learning, and a well-articulated vision of effective teaching. Of particular interest to our work is the development of collaborative and interdisciplinary learning communities in which experienced and beginning teachers critically examine their instructional practices and student learning, as well as make their thinking and growth public. This kind of critical and collaborative inquiry is a fundamental component of professional capacity (Bryk *et al.*, 2010)—one which transcends a single teacher, coach, or teacher educator. Unfortunately, the literature is clear that opportunities for teachers to collaborate for the purpose

206 Zembal-Saul, Badiali, Mueller, and McDyre

of strengthening instruction is uncommon (Banilower *et al.*, 2018; Hopkins, Zembal-Saul, Lee, and Cody, this volume, Chapter 15).

In the section that follows, we address the historical roots of school–university partnerships. We encourage readers to consider the aforementioned teacher learning needs and the importance of contexts that support norms of collaboration, critique, and inquiry focused on student learning.

Professional Development Schools: Past and Present

The term Professional Development School (PDS) first appeared in *Tomorrow's Teachers: A report of the Holmes Group* (Holmes Group, 1986). The Holmes Group was a consortium of deans and a number of chief academic officers from research institutions in each of the 50 states, organized around the twin goals of reforming teacher education and the teaching profession. The stated goals of The Holmes Group were to: (1) make the education of teachers intellectually more solid; (2) recognize differences in teachers' knowledge, skill, and commitment, as well as in their education, certification, and work; (3) create standards of entry to the profession (e.g., examinations and educational requirements that are professionally relevant and intellectually defensible); (4) connect the group's institutions with K-12 schools; and (5) make schools better places for teachers to work and learn.

Professional Development School (PDS) Origins

For the purpose of this chapter, we focus on goals four and five, since these recommendations resulted in the concept of school–university partnerships—and ultimately Professional Development Schools (PDSs). The Holmes Group report asserted that university faculties were to become more expert educators of teachers and that professors should make better use of expert teachers in the education of other teachers through collaboration. Specifically, they recommended that the collaboration should include joint research on teaching. In short, schools were called to become places where both teachers and university faculty interested in teaching could systematically inquire into teaching practices and improve them (NCATE, 1990).

The report also recommended making schools better places for teachers to work and to learn, which resonates with contemporary thinking about supportive contexts for teacher professional learning (NASEM, 2015). An emphasis on school improvement assumes that less bureaucracy will result in more professional autonomy and more leadership for teachers. The Holmes Group envisioned schools where teachers could learn from one another, and from other education professionals. Central to this vision was reorganizing schools as places where effective teachers would want to work. The Holmes Group argued that connecting colleges of education with schools would provide teachers with opportunities to contribute to the development of knowledge in their profession. The group viewed working partnerships as a way to continue developing knowledge and reflective practice among professional educators, much the way that teaching hospitals do (Shulman, 2005). The initial conceptualization of PDSs grew out of partnership models and was based on four key ideas: (1) reciprocity and mutual exchange within the partnership; (2) reasonable experimentation; (3) systematic inquiry into teaching; and (4) an emphasis on working with students with different academic backgrounds and experiences.

While not all of the recommendations and proposals offered by The Holmes Group (1990) were realized, the idea of the professional development school persisted. In 1996, the National Council for Accreditation of Teacher Education (NCATE) launched its work on instituting standards for PDSs (Wise, 2005). According to Marsha Levine who spearheaded the development and implementation of these standards, professional development schools are institutions created through partnerships among universities, schools, and other organizations, including school districts and teacher organizations. "They are intended to improve teacher preparation and professional development, and to promote inquiry through collaboration of the partnering institutions in the context of the school" (Levine, 1998, p. 1).

Although there are essential elements that characterize PDS partnerships from other kinds of school–university relationships, each PDS is unique. Structural features within PDS partnerships can, and do, vary widely. Institutional histories, cultures, and expectations give shape to the roles and responsibilities found in professional development schools (Clark, 1999). Today we are fortunate to have detailed descriptive accounts of PDS structures and practices given a burgeoning literature in the field (Buchanan and Cosenza, 2018; Bullough and Rosenberg, 2018; Ferrara *et al.*, 2014; Neapolitan, 2010).

The following section describes one PDS partnership, which was strongly influenced by the original recommendations of The Holmes Group. During its existence, this PDS has grown into, and in many ways beyond, those original recommendations.

Our PDS Context

The Penn State University College of Education and State College Area School District have been engaged in collaborative teacher preparation and professional development work for twenty years. During this time, the PDS has grown from 14 interns and mentors in two elementary schools, to roughly 40 interns per year with the participation of more than 50 mentor teachers in the district.

The mission of this professional development school partnership, which both encompasses and extends the mission of each partner, is expressed by four goals:

1   *Enhance* the educational experiences of all learners;
2   *Ensure* high-quality induction into the profession for new teachers;
3   *Engage* in furthering our own professional growth as teachers and teacher educators; and
4   *Educate* the next generation of teacher educators.

We attribute much of our success over many years of transition, expansion, and educational change to grounding our relationship in these goals.

PDS Roles and Commitments

Unlike most PDSs across the nation that define each separate school as a PDS, our partnership made a conscious decision to conceive of the PDS as one community—a community of ideals that is geographically distributed across all eight elementary schools in the school district. Our belief is that collaboration across buildings is a powerful vehicle for innovation, inquiry, and reflection. Because we have defined ourselves as one community, a variety of structural features and working relationships that encourage collaboration across buildings have been created, and they are essential in sustaining the idea of a single community (Badiali *et al.*, 2012). Potentially the most powerful of these is the practice of engaging all members of the PDS community in decision-making by consensus. We argue that teachers, administrators, university faculty, and curriculum and assessment specialists thrive together when they have an active voice in the community. Only in that way do all members of the community feel ownership of the PDS. Moreover, mentor teachers, administrators, curriculum support personnel, doctoral students, and university faculty are considered teacher educators in the PDS context. Our work together takes place in large part in professional learning teams that co-plan, collaboratively implement, and evaluate methods courses and other professional learning experiences. This model serves as powerful professional development for the diverse members of our context, and affords a welcoming intellectual community for newcomers to the PDS.

PDS interns demonstrate a high level of commitment to the program by following the district calendar throughout the entire school year. The internship year begins before the start of the academic year with an orientation program, and interns begin working with their mentor teachers on the first district inservice day. Interns graduate in May, and return to continue through the last school day for children in June. Throughout the school year, interns participate fully in all school activities including Back to School Night, student goal setting conferences with parents, school-wide faculty meetings, weekly grade-level meetings, unit planning meetings with mentors, other teachers, and curriculum support personnel, response to intervention (RTI) work, professional development and inservice activities, individualized education program (IEP) meetings, and instructional support team meetings. Interns also

Learning to Teach Science in a PDS 209

participate in parent-teacher organization meetings and other school–community activities and gatherings. Put another way, PDS interns are fully integrated into the school districts' activities and systems of supports, just as they would be as first-year teachers.

Professional learning in the PDS is intentionally designed to transition interns from observing and analyzing mentor teacher instruction to incrementally talking over more responsibility for instructional decision-making and co-teaching. In the fall semester, interns are enrolled in four intensive teaching methods courses, including science methods. These courses are embedded in interns' weekly schedules and co-taught by mentor teachers and university faculty onsite in PDS classrooms. The PDS science methods course, which is described in more detail elsewhere (see Zembal-Saul, 2009), engages interns in scientific discourse and practices to understand and explain phenomena, and to analyze their learning experiences from the perspective of students. Interns' experiences as science learners are paired with video-based cases of mentors teaching similar content to children in their classrooms. These videos are analyzed by interns from both the perspective of the teacher and the student. In particular, we emphasize sensemaking discourse and the role of the teacher in orchestrating such discussions. Interns have an opportunity to co-plan and teach a series of lessons that engage students with phenomena, involve investigating phenomena and collecting data, and require analyzing a subset of data to construct a Claims–Evidence–Reasoning sequence (Zembal-Saul and Hershberger, this volume, Chapter 1; Zembal-Saul, _et al._, 2013) that contributes to developing a deeper understanding of the phenomena. Interns video record their teaching and individually and collaboratively analyze it using a coherent conceptual framework that unfolds across the semester in the science methods course.

As mentioned previously, interns take over increasing responsibility for instruction and assessment as the year progresses, as well as engage in teacher inquiry (see next section). PDS partners advocate a co-teaching model as opposed to solo teaching, which is common during traditional student teaching. Mentors and professors endorse co-teaching given that it increases attention to individual students, reflective dialogue between mentor and intern, and opportunities for professional growth for interns and mentors alike (Badiali and Titus, 2010). Co-teaching positions mentor-intern pairs to achieve the primary goal of enhancing learning experiences for all students.

Teacher Inquiry as Signature Pedagogy

From the inception of this PDS partnership, teacher inquiry (Dana and Yendol-Silva, 2009) as a form of professional learning and knowledge building has been the centerpiece of our work together. It is the signature

210   Zembal-Saul, Badiali, Mueller, and McDyre

pedagogy for our program. Signature pedagogies (Shulman, 2005) are characterized as commitments to teaching and learning that organize the ways in which future practitioners are educated for their professions. In our case, teacher inquiry as signature pedagogy conveys an explicit embrace of teachers and teacher educators as knowledge producers who collaboratively address problems of practice and are continuously engaged in professional growth—all in the service of school improvement.

Ultimately our aim is for educators across the professional continuum to adopt an inquiry stance toward their practice (Cochran-Smith and Lytle, 2009). Put another way, we treat the continuous study of teaching and learning as something that effective professionals do. As part of this effort, each PDS intern conducts a practitioner inquiry project and makes their learning public to the larger community of educators and guests at an annual Teacher Inquiry Conference. Mentor teachers agree, as a condition of becoming a mentor, to engage in inquiry on an annual basis in one of three ways: (1) by conducting an independent inquiry project; (2) by conducting a collaborative inquiry project with their intern; or (3) by supporting their intern's inquiry. Inquiry in the PDS is not limited to mentors and interns. Principals, curriculum personnel, doctoral students, and university faculty also engage in practitioner inquiry each year and share their findings at the conference. A number of these projects have gone on to be published in practitioner journals and books (e.g., Kur and Heitzman, 2008; Hershberger *et al.*, 2013; Zembal-Saul and Hershberger, this volume, Chapter 1).

Teacher Inquiry in Action

Our goal in the remainder of the chapter is to highlight examples of how teacher inquiry as signature pedagogy has contributed to the intellectual work of the PDS community. We provide an example of a PDS intern's investigation of integrating science and literacy in kindergarten, which was conducted as part of her teacher inquiry project. Brittany Mueller (third author) makes her work public so that others may learn, and she shares the continued impact of teacher inquiry on her science teaching practices as a beginning teacher. Because of the tendency to associate the affordances of PDS partnership work for preservice teachers, we provide a second example intended to foreground benefits to mentors and simultaneous renewal of university faculty and graduate students. In reading these examples, keep in mind the role that inquiry into practice plays in maintaining a focus on the four goals of our PDS work: *Enhance* the educational experiences of all learners; *Ensure* high-quality induction into the profession for new teachers; *Engage* in furthering our own professional growth as teachers and teacher educators; and *Educate* the next generation of teacher educators.

Example 1: Integrating Science and Literacy in Kindergarten

Ms. Brittany Mueller (third author) was a PDS intern in 2015–2016. She now teaches third grade at Babylon Memorial Grade School in New York. In the narrative that follows, she shares her teacher inquiry journey. Brittany's science methods instructor (Alicia McDyre, fourth author) and mentor teacher supported her throughout the process.

Ms. Mueller (in her own words):

As part of my inquiry project, I explain my professional experiences as a kindergarten intern at Bluebird Elementary School. My goal is to provide evidence to support the assertion that science and literacy can be connected (Hooper and Zembal-Saul, this volume, Chapter 4), and these connections can be enhanced in a variety of ways. I provide examples from my practice that illustrate how science and engineering investigations were integrated into the curriculum, as well as the process I used.

The PDS program requires interns to have a partner classroom that is at least two grade levels away from their main placement to ensure that each intern gains sufficient experience observing and teaching students in other grades. After spending a great deal of time in my 3rd grade partner classroom, I was left wondering why I saw science instruction in the daily schedule there, but not in my kindergarten placement. I had learned through previous instruction and experiences that young children are capable of learning science concepts and participating in science practices. This wondering inspired me to make a change in my teaching. The focus of my inquiry was to design a series of science and engineering lessons that were integrated into our existing literacy program and based on standards and research, reflect on my implementation experiences through reflective journaling, and examine samples of student writing from each lesson.

After discussing my desire to integrate science and engineering into our classroom with my mentor teacher, we agreed that I would start by implementing one extended science investigation per week. I was extremely fortunate to have a mentor teacher who gave me the time and support I needed to do this work with the 25 children in our class. The investigations that I developed ranged from 50 minutes to 2 hours long depending on the schedule for that week. These investigations were aligned to both Pennsylvania State Standards, the school district's kindergarten science curriculum objectives, and the three dimensions of the NGSS framework. In addition, I was intentional about maintaining and strengthening the connection of science and literacy. When planning I used the following instructional strategies to achieve science and literacy integration: three dimensional investigations, read alouds (nonfiction and fiction), science talks, science journals, and visual representations.

Based on extensive research, which included the Next Generation Science Standards (NGSS Lead States, 2013), the supporting Framework

(NRC, 2012) and associated studies, I planned, implemented, and analyzed a series of ten science and/or engineering investigations that were integrated with literacy instruction (Mueller, 2016). Initially, I organized learning opportunities around a focus on science, adding on journal writing and read-alouds. After several lessons, it became clear that given the importance of engaging with phenomena and participating in science talks as a form of sensemaking, we would never have enough time for writing and reading.

I worked with my mentor teacher to adjust our plans to include a science station as one of our literacy centers. By doing this, we were able to focus on the science and engineering without rushing, devoting the necessary time to investigation and science talks. The science writing center provided time for students to receive support with drawing and writing about their observations, ideas and explanations in their journals. In other words, science became the context for kid writing, a child-centered program for emergent writers in early grades.

In the implementation process, I was fortunate to have a variety of colleagues to help support my students in learning and engaging in science investigations. I found it extremely helpful to work with my science methods instructor, Dr. McDyre, to co-plan and co-teach lessons. When students worked in small groups, it was ideal to have an adult to monitor and facilitate discussion among the children at each table. This gave me time to review children's journals to better understand and be responsive to what they were thinking.

The process of planning and implementing the series of ten weekly science investigations involved continuous data collection and analysis, which included samples of student writing and systematic reflection on small group discussions. Each iteration of lesson planning and implementation was informed by my observations and analysis, especially the major structural shift to small group work as part of Writer's Workshop. Some of what I learned is captured in the list that follows.

- In order for students to produce quality science journal entries, they need to be given a sufficient amount of time and support to document their thinking and experiences. The 15-minute time slot that I was often able to give my students after an investigation was not enough.
- The science journals my students completed during literacy centers had more writing than the ones completed during science instruction.
- Structuring science journals in a way that gives students freedom in what they want to draw and/or write about after an investigation serves as a formative assessment and helped me gauge what to do next in terms of instruction.

- Read-alouds with students can help deepen their understanding of a topic, as well as introduce or reinforce new science vocabulary terms after an investigation. The read-alouds that I selected purposefully contained science vocabulary aligned with particular investigations.
- Allowing students to contribute to building visual representations of science ideas (e.g., charts, models, examples) and posting them around the classroom helped foster student discussion and meaning-making.

Through the inquiry process, I was able to improve on my own practice for integrating science and language arts. Today, in my new elementary school context, I not only have the knowledge of how to research, plan, and implement integrated curriculum, but I also understand the importance of utilizing student work to inform my teaching. I am fortunate to work with a network of colleagues with whom I can collaborate on instruction and share both past and present teaching experiences.

Example 2: Changes in Mentor Teachers' Science Instruction

It should not be assumed that PDS interns are the sole beneficiaries of our focus on teacher inquiry as signature pedagogy. As an example of the broader impacts of PDS interactions, we share the results of a mixed methods study that examined changes in mentor teachers' instructional practices across content areas resulting from PDS involvement (Nolan *et al.*, 2011). We developed, administered, and analyzed a survey to purposefully select participants for the qualitative portion of the study. Then we utilized semi-structured interviews with participating mentors to better understand their science teaching practices and how their development was perceived over time.

There was greater than 80% return rate on the survey, with 76% of mentors reporting that their science teaching practices had changed through participation in the PDS. This aligned with the extensive professional development opportunities for elementary teachers in science as compared with other subject areas. From this group, we selected 11 mentors to be interviewed about their stories of change. All of the mentors addressed interactions with their interns as part of the change process. For instance, mentors reported that when their interns taught science, children were more engaged and excited about it than when they themselves taught science. This focused their attention in ways that allowed mentors to notice that interns were not intent on eliciting or providing "right answers," but rather creating opportunities for students to observe, question, investigate, discuss, and construct explanations based on evidence. Most interns were intentionally using approaches and scaffolds that they were learning about in the science methods course, such as Claims–Evidence–Reasoning and argument mapping tools (Zembal-Saul *et al.*, 2013).

Given that interns were attempting to implement these practices for the first time, they frequently encountered issues commonly associated with noviceness. Additionally, because the interns' teaching practices were new for many mentors, they were motivated to learn more in order to support their interns (Nolan *et al.*, 2011). Mentors' attempts to understand contemporary science instruction led them to consult with university faculty, seek out resources, and conduct their own teacher inquiry projects of science teaching. Notably, interns were typically the ones who facilitated connections to more experienced others and relevant resources. Not surprisingly, the mentors who reported the most productive changes in their science teaching also engaged in teacher inquiry. We argue that it is the supportive context of the PDS, and in particular the norms of inquiry and collaboration, that created the conditions for productive change.

Concluding Remarks

There is no single most effective approach when it comes to creating supportive contexts for teacher professional learning; however, there are many documented obstacles associated with educational contexts (Banilower *et al.*, 2018; NASEM, 2015). There has been a persistent call for school reform to be paired with teacher preparation and professional development (Goodlad, 1994). A healthy educational ecology for change has coherent curricula and supports, aligned with meaningful teacher professional learning and a well-articulated vision of effective teaching. The aim is to rise above the individual work of one teacher or one school and to build professional capacity through critical and collaborative inquiry (Bryk *et al.*, 2010).

In our PDS partnership, we embrace teacher inquiry as signature pedagogy and coalesce around shared goals: *Enhance* the educational experiences of all learners; *Ensure* high-quality induction into the profession for new teachers; *Engage* in furthering our own professional growth as teachers and teacher educators; and *Educate* the next generation of teacher educators. Ms. Mueller's example of an intern's inquiry in the PDS context highlights the pairing of induction into the profession with designing rigorous, equitable and consequential science and literacy experiences for children. Similarly, the study of mentor teachers' stories of change features engaging educators in professional learning that benefits children, as well as interns. Additionally, investigation of changes in mentor teachers' science instruction was conducted by a team of researchers that included a graduate student in science education. In this way, the fourth goal of the PDS is addressed—educating the next generation of teacher educators. Both examples of life in the PDS are intended to illustrate the powerful nature of developing an inquiry stance toward teaching and learning, participating in a supportive professional community, and making our work public.

The PDS serves as a "living laboratory" for innovation and knowledge generation for all members of the eight participating schools. In a supportive context where norms are built around examining one's practice, university faculty and graduate students are welcomed to work alongside mentors and interns (and administrators and curriculum specialists) to investigate teaching, learning, curriculum, assessment, teacher development, curricular changes, parent interactions/involvement, and more. This is not to say that there are not tensions in our collaborative work and professional learning; however, we embrace these as tools for uncovering rich problems of practice that require diverse perspectives to investigate and understand.

References

Badiali, B. and Titus, N. (2010) Co-teaching: Enhancing student learning through mentor-intern partnerships. *School-University Partnerships*, *4*(2), 74–80.

Badiali, B., Zembal-Saul, C., DeWitt, K. and Stoicovy, D. (2012). *SHARED INQUIRY: Placing Practitioner Knowledge at the Center of Teacher Education: Rethinking the Policy and Practice of the Education Doctorate*, ed. Margaret Macintyre Latta and Susan Wunder. Education Policy in Practice: Critical Cultural Studies Series. Greenwich, CT: Information Age Publishing.

Banilower, E., Smith, P. S., Malzahn, K., Plumley, C., Gordon, E., and Hayes, M. (2018). *Report of the 2018 NSSME+*. Chapel Hill, NC: Horizon Research, Inc.

Bryk, A., Sebring, P., Allensworth, E., Easton, J. and Luppescu, S. (2010). *Organizing Schools for Improvement: Lessons from Chicago*. Chicago: University of Chicago Press.

Buchanan, M., Cosenza, M. (2018). *Visions from Professional Development School Partnerships: Connecting Professional Development and Clinical Practice*. Charlotte, NC: Information Age Publishing.

Bullough, R. and Rosenberg, J. (2018). *Schooling, Democracy, and the Quest for Wisdom: Partnerships and the Moral Dimensions of Teaching*. New Brunswick, NJ: Rutgers University Press.

Clark, R. W. (1999). *Effective Professional Development Schools*. San Francisco, CA: Jossey-Bass.

Cochran-Smith, M. and Lytle, S. (2009). *Inquiry as Stance: Practitioner Research for the Next Generation*. New York: Teachers College Press.

Cohen, D., Peurach, D., Glazer, J., Gates, K., and Goldin, S. (2013). *Improvement by Design: The Promise of Better Schools*. Chicago: University of Chicago Press.

Dana, N. F., and Yendol-Hoppey, D. (2014). *The Reflective Educator's Guide to Classroom Research: Learning to Teach and Teaching to Learn Through Practitioner Inquiry*. Thousand Oaks, CA: Corwin Press.

216 *Zembal-Saul, Badiali, Mueller, and McDyre*

Davis, E. A., Palincsar, A. S., Smith, P. S., Arias, A., and Kademian, S. (2017). Educative curriculum materials: Uptake, impact, and implications for research and design. *Educational Researcher, 46*(6), 293–304. Retrieved from: https://doi-org.proxy.lib.umich.edu/10.3102/0013189X17727502

Davis, E. A., Petish, D., and Smithey, J. (2006). Challenges new science teachers face. *Review of Educational Research, 76*(4), 607–651.

Ferrara, J., Nath, J., and Guadarrama, I. (2014). *Creating Visions for University School Partnerships.* Charlotte, NC: Information Age Publishing.

Goodlad, J. I. (1994). *Educational Renewal: Better Teachers, Better Schools.* San Francisco, CA: Jossey-Bass.

Guadarrama, I. N., Ramsey, J. L. (Eds.) *University and School Connections: Research Studies in Professional Development Schools.* Charlotte, NC: Information Age Publishing.

Hershberger, K., Kur, J., and Haefner, L. (2013) ... and action! *Science and Children, 51*(3), 56–63.

Holmes Group (1986). *Tomorrow's Teachers.* East Lansing, MI: Holmes Group.

Holmes Group (1990). *Tomorrow's Schools: Principles for the Design of Professional Development Schools.* East Lansing, MI: Holmes Group (ERIC Document reproduction Service No. 328 533).

Kur, J. and Heitzman, M. (2008). Attracting student wonderings. *Science and Children, 45*(5), 28–32.

Levine, M. (Ed.) (1998). *Designing Standards that Work for Professional Development Schools.* Commissioned Papers of the NCATE PDS Standards Project. Washington, DC: National Council for Accreditation of Teacher Education.

Levine, M. and Trachtman, R. (Eds.) (2005) *Implementing PDS Standards: Stories from the Field.* Washington, DC: National Council for Accreditation of Teacher Education.

Luft, J., Firestone, J., Wong, S., Ortega, I., Adams, K., and Bang, E. (2011). Beginning secondary science teacher induction: A two-year mixed methods study. *Journal for Research in Science Teaching, 48*(10), 1199–1224.

Mueller, B. (2016). Strengthening the connections between science and literacy through inquiry- based investigations in kindergarten. Thesis. The Pennsylvania State University, University Park, PA.

NASEM (National Academies of Sciences Engineering and Medicine). (2015). *Science Teachers' Learning: Enhancing Opportunities, Creating Supportive Contexts* (Committee on Strengthening Science Education through a Teacher Learning Continuum Board on Science Education and Teacher Advisory Council Division of Behavioral and Social Science and Education Ed.). Washington, DC: National Academies Press.

NCATE (National Council for the Accreditation of Teacher Education). (1990). *NCATE Standards, Procedures and Policies for the Accreditation of Professional Education Units.* Washington, DC: NCATE.

Neapolitan, J. (Ed.) (2010). *Taking Stock of Professional Development Schools: What's Needed Now.* Yearbook of the National Society for the Study of Education, Vol. 110, Part 2. New York: Teachers College, Columbia University.

NRC (National Research Council). (2012). *A Framework for K-12 Science Education: Practices, Crosscutting Concepts, and Core Ideas.* Washington, DC: National Academies Press.

NGSS Lead States. (2013). *Next Generation Science Standards: For States, By States.* Washington, DC: National Academies Press.

Nolan, J., Badiali, B., Zembal-Saul, C. and Manno, J. (2011). Affirmation and change: Assessing the impact of the professional development school on mentors' classroom practice. In J. Nath, I. Guadarrama and J. Ramsey (Eds.), *Investigating University School Partnerships*. Charlotte, NC: Information Age Publishing.

Rowan, B., Correnti, R., Miller, R., and Camburn, E. (2009, August). *School Improvement by Design: Lessons from a Study of Comprehensive School Reform Programs*. Philadelphia, PA: Consortium for Policy Research in Education.

Shulman, L. S. (2005). Signature pedagogies in the professions. *Daedalus*, *134*(3), 52–59.

Wise, A. E. (2005). Foreword. In M. Levine, and R. Trachtman (Eds.), *Implementing PDS Standards: Stories from the Field*. Washington, DC: National Council for Accreditation of Teacher Education.

Zembal-Saul, C. (2009). Learning to teach elementary school science as argument. *Science Education*, *93*(4), 687–719.

Zembal-Saul, C., McNeil, K., and Hershberger, K. (2013). *What's Your Evidence? Engaging K-5 Students in Constructing Explanations in Science*. Boston, MA: Pearson.

15 Starting Small

Creating a Supportive Context for Professional Learning that Fosters Emergent Bilingual Children's Sensemaking in Elementary Science

Megan Hopkins
UNIVERSITY OF CALIFORNIA, SAN DIEGO

Carla Zembal-Saul, May H. Lee, and Jennifer L. Cody
THE PENNSYLVANIA STATE UNIVERSITY

Acknowledgments

The authors thank Mr. Hill, Ms. Garrison, and their students for welcoming us into their classrooms and sharing their learning with us. We are grateful to school district administrators, and in particular Mr. Berger, for their support of Science 20/20 and the teachers engaged in the work.

Introduction

Immigration to the United States has changed over the last two decades such that communities with little recent history of ethnic or racial diversity are experiencing rapid shifts in their cultural and linguistic compositions (Wortham *et al.*, 2002). In this context of demographic change, emergent bilingual (EB)[1] students are expected to comprise one-quarter of the overall US school population by 2025 (Suárez-Orozco *et al.*, 2008). Nonetheless, research indicates that most general education teachers feel underprepared to work with EBs (Gándara *et al.*, 2005). Teachers' under-preparation to serve EBs is concerning given that teacher quality and preparation is the strongest school-related predictor of achievement for all students, including EBs (Darling-Hammond, 2000; López *et al.*, 2013). Thus, it is critical to identify approaches that support teachers' professional learning related to EB instruction, especially in new immigrant destinations where EB instructional capacity tends to be most limited (Lowenhaupt and Reeves, 2015).

In this chapter, we describe lessons learned from the pilot year of the professional development project, *Science 20/20: Bringing Language Learners into Focus through School–University–Community Partnership* [2]. Drawing on the term 20/20, which denotes visual acuity (sharpness and clarity), our goal is to bring EBs into focus through language learning opportunities afforded by an emphasis on sensemaking in elementary science. Science offers authentic opportunities for classroom discourse associated with investigating phenomena, constructing and critiquing evidence-based explanations, and negotiating and using scientific ideas and vocabulary (see Hooper and Zembal-Saul, this volume, Chapter 4, and Zembal-Saul and Hershberger, this volume, Chapter 1). Such opportunities support sensemaking and language development for all children, especially EBs (Lee *et al.*, 2013; NASEM, 2018). Unfortunately, as Banilower and colleagues explain (2018), discourse-rich science teaching is not common in most US classrooms, particularly in the early grades.

The school district in which Science 20/20 is situated is a microcosm for the demographic change that is taking place in communities across the country. It is located in a mid-size city in the Northeastern United States, where the city's Latinx population increased from 0% to 40% over the last ten years, and the district's EB population increased from 1% to 15%. Most new families to the area are from the Dominican Republic, and Spanish is their home language. Like many districts in new immigrant destinations, where capacity and resources to meet EBs' needs are often sparse, especially in STEM (NASEM, 2018), district and school leaders have struggled to respond. With respect to science, the district has no formal curriculum in the early grades, meaning that science is not taught systematically in K-2. In grades 3–6, the science curriculum is highly prescribed and textbook-driven, leaving little room for science teaching and learning focused on sensemaking. We viewed this as an opportunity to capitalize on the potential of science as the content around which to engage teachers, administrators, and other education professionals in creating rigorous, equitable and consequential language learning opportunities for EBs.

Our initial work was full of stops and starts as we navigated this new terrain—developing relationships with teachers, administrators and community members, coming to understand more about the organizational context, and continuously refining our professional learning model. Throughout the planning process and pilot year, we sought opportunities to connect project goals with complementary school and district initiatives. Whereas many district-university PD efforts take place in contexts "ready for change," we sought to initiate change were capacity was more limited and to tailor the PD design to that context (Penuel *et al.*, 2011, p. 334). This work came to be guided by a philosophy of "starting small." We started small in many ways: around the young age of learners, the intimate size of the professional learning community, and our emphasis on a single content storyline. Starting small allowed us to facilitate PD focused on fostering language learning opportunities afforded by investigating the natural world, while remaining true to our PD model (described next). We share

220 *Hopkins, Zembal-Saul, Lee, and Cody*

these early lessons with the hope that they are useful to others engaged in the difficult yet important work of creating contexts that support teacher professional learning focused on transforming instruction for EBs in science.

Professional Development Model

Science 20/20 is informed by sociocultural learning theories and contemporary scholarship on teacher professional development (NASEM, 2015). While there is still much research to be done, a consensus view has emerged that suggests professional learning opportunities should: engage teachers as active participants, be contextualized in teachers' work, involve the analysis of artifacts (e.g., student work samples), be subject-matter rich, align with school and district practices and policies, and be of adequate duration to provide opportunities for cycles of learning, practice, and reflection (Garet *et al.*, 2001; van Driel and Berry, 2012). Furthermore, research highlights the importance of supportive contexts that allow for teachers to try new approaches and inquire into their own teaching practices (NASEM, 2015). With these findings in mind, we describe two components of our PD model: foundational principles of teaching and learning and PD design features.

Project Principles of Teaching and Learning

Three research-based principles about teaching and learning serve as the foundation for Science 20/20 and inform the integration of science and language instruction.

Engaging Students as Partners in Knowledge Building

Scientific knowledge and understandings come in many forms and often draw upon our everyday lived experiences. Classroom instruction that is informed by the knowledge and resources embedded in students' homes and community, or *funds of knowledge* (Moll *et al.*, 1992), has the potential to support the conceptual development of students' scientific thinking and sensemaking (Gutiérrez *et al.*, 1999; Moje *et al.*, 2004). When science teachers engage students as partners in developing scientific understandings by making connections to students' prior experiences and linguistic and cultural resources, this instructional congruence can have positive effects on performance (Lee *et al.*, 2002; Lee and Fradd, 1998).

One way that teachers facilitate this congruence is through the use of relevant and interesting phenomena, around which students engage in scientific practices to investigate and explain. This approach, in which EBs are engaged in science and engineering practices to make sense of a phenomenon, can facilitate their inclusion in the science classroom as well as their

Starting Small 221

access to science knowledge (Lyon *et al.*, 2016; NASEM, 2018). Further, by inviting questions from students related to their interests, teachers cultivate natural curiosity, which is critical for students' engagement in and motivation to learn science.

Creating Opportunities for Productive Participation

For students to engage with phenomena, it is important for teachers to create learning environments that promote active construction of students' understanding through authentic experiences (Krajcik *et al.*, 2008). However, research has demonstrated that if science is taught at all in the elementary grades, the emphasis tends to be on fun activities, or, at the other extreme, reading informational texts, memorizing vocabulary, and completing worksheets. These approaches do not reflect the work of scientists, nor do they capture children's natural curiosity about how the world works. There is thus a need for teachers to engage in inquiry-oriented instruction that fosters productive participation among students. This is especially true for EBs, as a recent meta-analysis revealed that inquiry-based instruction has a positive and significant effect on EBs' science achievement (Estrella *et al.*, 2018).

Of the scientific practices described in the *Framework for K-12 Science Education* (NRC, 2012), we emphasize constructing evidence-based explanations because of its role in contributing to iterative sensemaking in science and to language development (see Zembal-Saul and Hershberger, this volume, Chapter 1). The use of phenomena that captivate students' interests and create a "need to know" can lead to investigation and analyses of relevant data. The claims-evidence-reasoning (CER) framework (McNeill, 2009; McNeill and Krajcik, 2008) is particularly helpful for engaging EBs in scientific practices because it scaffolds the process of co-constructing arguments and explanations orally and generating written explanations. Creating a classroom environment rich with oral and written discourse is necessary for EBs to make their thinking visible as they grapple with sensemaking in science (Lee *et al.*, 2018).

Using Formative Assessment to Drive Instruction

Given limitations to validity, large-scale assessments rarely provide teachers with accurate data of EBs' capabilities, nor do they provide information teachers can use to inform their instruction of EBs (Cheuk *et al.*, 2018; Durán, 2008). Recent research indicates that many EBs who successfully engage in interactive classroom activities are deemed struggling on standardized tests (Rodriguez-Mojica, 2018). Rather than viewing assessment as a means to evaluate students' knowledge and abilities, Science 20/20 draws on formative assessment to ensure that instruction is contingent upon and responsive to students' needs. Formative assessment is an ongoing process of gathering evidence of learning as it occurs so that teachers can use the information and feedback during real-time instruction or to inform future instruction (Heritage and Chang, 2012).

We use formative assessment to foster science and language learning across domains of language. With respect to oral language (i.e., listening and speaking), teachers can assess EBs' scientific thinking and language learning during sustained classroom conversations and close questioning that occur amidst investigating phenomena (Alvarez *et al.*, 2014). By interacting with students in real time, teachers can modify their language to foster EBs' language comprehension and production (Bailey, 2017). In terms of written language, teachers may ask EBs to express their ideas with drawings and to explain ideas in their own words. Drawings and writing provide a teacher with useful information related to EB learning, and they help to contextualize sensemaking for EBs (Kang *et al.*, 2014). Overall, the use of formative assessment can help teachers create a rich language environment as EBs make sense of scientific phenomena (Solano-Flores, 2016).

Design Features of the Professional Development Model

We designed and continue to refine Science 20/20 as an intensive PD program that integrates formal and classroom-embedded components around the three principles of teaching and learning described above. We host three PD institutes throughout the year[3] (i.e., summer, winter, spring) in which teachers are introduced to these principles and associated practices. A sustained focus on our principles is intentional and allows us to foreground attention to equity in all aspects of our work. In between institutes, project personnel meet weekly with groups of teachers in their classrooms. School-based professional learning involves multiple cycles of implementation and co-design throughout the year. Drawing on the work of Penuel and colleagues (2007), the co-design process involves teachers as collaborators in shaping how Science 20/20 will play out in their classroom contexts. Co-design of instruction and resources is highly facilitated, focused on problems of practice, and involves multiple cycles of collaborative work between teachers and researchers that include:

- Planning instruction and assessment based on project principles;
- Teaching and documenting student learning;
- Analyzing samples of student work to inform subsequent instruction; and
- Creating, implementing, and refining instructional tools and resources.

Additionally, weekly interactions are intended to be responsive to teachers' in-the-moment needs and questions, and to keep Science 20/20 work at the forefront of their thinking and practices as their day-to-day demands unfold. In the next section, we describe the opportunities and challenges we experienced as we worked to cultivate a supportive context for teacher learning in this district, and how we came to embrace "starting small" as our mantra for this work.

Cultivating a Supportive Context for Teacher Learning

In our pilot year (2017–2018), one English-as-a-second-language (ESL) teacher and seven third-grade teachers were recruited from a grade 3–6 school serving 28% EBs, which we call Tartarville Elementary-Middle School. The principal at Tartarville was enthusiastic about Science 20/20 and encouraged participation among teachers. After the summer PD institute, one of the third-grade teachers, Mr. Hill, was transferred to his previous assignment teaching kindergarten at Tartarville's feeder K-2 school, Fulbright Elementary. Although PD with Tartarville teachers continued throughout the pilot year, it is our work at Fulbright Elementary, and with Mr. Hill, around which our philosophy of starting small emerged.

Engaging Teachers with Project Principles

Our three-day summer institute introduced participating teachers to research-based strategies known to support student engagement in language learning, with an emphasis on investigating phenomena and attending to students' funds of knowledge. A unique feature of the institute was a concurrent science camp for EBs that was taught by an experienced elementary educator. Participating teachers engaged in scientific discourse and practices, and then were able to observe children participating in similar learning experiences. For each lesson that was observed, teachers interacted with children to consider their science thinking and use of linguistic and cultural resources, and debriefed with the science camp teacher about her instructional decision making and insights about student learning.

For example, after being introduced to scientific practices and engaging in a CER sequence as "students," participating teachers observed a lesson in which children were investigating structure and function by interacting with insects. They observed how the teacher engaged students in closely observing insects and asking questions about their appearance and behaviors, questions that were then sorted into those that were testable and those that required information from a scientific source. Children kept science notebooks to record their observations and drawings of physical adaptations. In small groups and as a whole class, students discussed the functions of various adaptations, and investigated behaviors and habitat preferences. Children ultimately used evidence to co-construct an explanation for how insects survive in their environment. Throughout the process of engaging children in scientific practices and sensemaking, the teacher modeled research-based language development and translanguaging practices (García and Kleyn, 2016). Once teachers experienced multiple rounds of science and language learning based on project principles, and had opportunities to analyze

224 Hopkins, Zembal-Saul, Lee, and Cody

student learning and consider students' interests, capabilities, and linguistic resources, they were guided to develop an implementation plan for the beginning of the academic year.

Finding Openings in the Organizational Context

During the summer institute and first months of the academic year, we began to more fully appreciate how district policies and practices might hinder long-term implementation. For example, beginning in third grade, classes are no longer self-contained; teachers specialize in particular subject areas, and students rotate among classes. Our work at Tartarville Elementary-Middle thus quickly shifted to curriculum integration across subjects, with science and language instruction as the centerpiece. However, teachers were anxious about deviating from the prescribed curriculum, which relied heavily on textbooks and direct instruction, offering few opportunities for the kinds of sensemaking practices supported by Science 20/20.

As we wrestled with the challenges of implementation at Tartarville, Mr. Hill contacted us and asked to continue participating in the project even though he transferred back to Fulbright as a kindergarten teacher. Leveraging his prior experiences at Fulbright, we were able to identify opportunities to integrate Science 20/20 initiatives into kindergarten classrooms. First, the district shifted from half-day to full-day kindergarten, providing additional instructional time that was not designated to a particular subject area. Second, there was no formal science curriculum for kindergarten, and science had rarely been taught in the half-day model. Thus, there was space and flexibility to integrate science into the curriculum. Third, given the ESL teacher's large caseload and limited capacity to serve all EBs, our focus on EBs was viewed as an asset.

Mr. Hill worked with two Science 20/20 researchers, Ms. Lee and Ms. Cody (third and fourth authors), to articulate alignment between project principles and the district's two early literacy initiatives: 1) "hybrid," a model for literacy instruction that combines direct instruction, small group collaborative work, and self-directed learning via computer-based language programs; and 2) "kid writing" (Feldgus and Cardonick, 1999), a program that integrates writing workshop, journals, and phonics across the curriculum. First, Mr. Hill and project team members developed a plan in which Science 20/20 could be woven into hybrid instruction. Mr. Hill proposed working with small groups of students during hybrid to engage them with scientific phenomena and elicit their observations, questions, and interests. Then, kid writing was highlighted as a natural extension of these activities, both as a process for students to construct written explanations as they engaged in sensemaking and conducted investigations, and as a means for Mr. Hill to use formative assessment to guide instruction for students at all English language proficiency levels. The team shared these ideas with the principal at Fulbright, Mr. Berger, and he approved Mr. Hill's continued participation.

While these openings in the organizational context paved the way for Science 20/20 at Fulbright Elementary, an important factor that facilitated our collaboration with Mr. Hill is that he is an ESL certified teacher who is fluent in Spanish. In addition, he previously taught in Florida where resources for EBs tend to be more established. Although Mr. Hill had few experiences teaching science, his background with EBs provided under-standings that deepened his appreciation for Science 20/20. He shared these insights with a kindergarten colleague, Ms. Garrison, and invited her to informally join project meetings. Ms. Garrison was in her fifth year of teaching, yet had participated in limited PD related to EBs and none in science. The addition of Ms. Garrison to our Fulbright team allowed us to develop a small professional learning community (PLC) of teachers and researchers where our work could unfold.

Creating Authentic Purposes for Continued Professional Learning

In the absence of a formal science curriculum, a central focus for our PLC at Fulbright was developing and implementing a coherent science content storyline (Roth *et al.*, 2011) that featured sensemaking opportunities for science learning and language development. Given Mr. Hill's interest in using his experiences from the summer institute, similarities and differences among plants and animals and what they need to survive in their environ-ments (NGSS Performance Expectation K-LS1) emerged as the centerpiece for sustained cycles of co-design. Across the year, students hosted a number of living organisms in their classrooms, observed them daily, and recorded observations and questions. Students' questions became fodder for investi-gations and provided opportunities to speak, listen, write and read about plants and animals (see Hooper and Zembal-Saul, this volume, Chapter 4). Repetition with productive ideas (e.g., similarities and differences, sequen-cing) allowed students to anticipate the characteristics and needs of new organisms as they were introduced. The development of this storyline occurred across three phases that created authentic purposes for professional learning, which we describe below.

Building from Teachers' Formal PD Experiences

The vision for the content storyline stemmed from the lessons teachers observed at science camp in the summer institute, during which the teacher used live organisms—Madagascar hissing cockroaches—to invite student participation and capture their observations, interests, and questions. This approach created a rich context for both science and language learning, and revealed the richness of students' cultural and linguistic resources. While preparing for the beginning of the year, Mr.

226 *Hopkins, Zembal-Saul, Lee, and Cody*

Hill shared his excitement about having live organisms in his classroom with two members of the research team, Ms. Lee and Ms. Cody. They took this opportunity to highlight how, in addition to the organisms, the institute classroom had spaces where the teacher recorded students' thinking over time. Mr. Hill was receptive to this idea and collaborated with the researchers to rearrange his classroom to facilitate science investigations.

Although Mr. Hill's classroom was thoughtfully designed to support implementation, he was apprehensive about teaching science. Ms. Lee and Ms. Cody took the lead in co-planning the first lessons of the year in which students explored communities—both their new school and that of the Madagascar hissing cockroaches. Mr. Hill, Ms. Lee, and Ms. Cody each facilitated a small group of students using the hybrid model for literacy instruction. Mr. Hill led students on a school tour where they took photographs and discussed various settings and their purposes. Ms. Lee facilitated kid writing with students by providing the sentence frame, "I see … " and guiding students to write about a photograph in their science journals. Ms. Cody introduced the cockroaches as classroom pets, and students shared their observations and questions, which she recorded and posted in the classroom. These initial experiences helped establish classroom norms around making and sharing observations, welcoming questions, honoring students' funds of knowledge, and identifying linguistic resources through talking, drawing, and writing.

Co-Investigating Learning and Teaching

After laying the groundwork with these initial learning experiences, the team developed two variations of a content storyline that was based on characteristics and behaviors of plants and animals, their environments, and their life cycles—one for Madagascar hissing cockroaches and another for chickens. Mr. Hill was willing to teach these unfamiliar ideas, but he was not yet comfortable with planning sequences of instruction. The PLC, which included Mr. Hill and his colleague Ms. Garrison, as well as researchers Ms. Lee and Ms. Cody, met weekly to co-plan a series of integrated science and language lessons that were modeled by or co-taught with researchers. Weekly meetings allowed the storyline work to unfold collaboratively and in context, and the consistent presence of the research team meant that they knew Mr. Hill's students and could highlight often overlooked evidence of progress, especially for EBs at beginning levels of English language proficiency.

Researchers were careful to approach their work with teachers collaboratively and felt the PLC was developing positive and productive norms as well as a sense of trust. By the end of the first semester, however, Ms. Lee and Ms. Cody expressed unease that they were still leading most of the team's activities. Concerned that they were viewed as outside experts rather than co-designers, Ms. Lee and Ms. Cody utilized the winter institute to enlist Mr. Hill and Ms. Garrison as co-investigators of student learning and instructional practices. Given that Mr. Hill and Ms. Garrison often related anecdotes about how the use of live organisms facilitated connections between scientific concepts and students' background knowledge and experiences, and how their EBs demonstrated more sophisticated language as they had more entry points into the content, we focused the winter institute on the principle of formative assessment to support teachers in seeing students' progress and responding in real time. We engaged in joint analysis of student work guided by the ATLAS—Looking at Data Protocol (National School Reform Faculty, 2014), which is designed to describe formative assessment information and other data, make inferences, and share implications for future work. This approach shifts attention away from what students did "right or wrong" toward how teachers could support students' intellectual work and progress. Mr. Hill and Ms. Garrison each selected a writing sample from a student's science journal, and had opportunities to hear outside perspectives on their student's capabilities and how they might build upon them in future instruction. Ms. Lee and Ms. Cody also challenged Mr. Hill and Ms. Garrison to consider each student's proficiency in English and Spanish, and how individual variation in language development might factor into their analyses. The PLC then created a plan for monitoring changes in students' writing and their corresponding understandings of science content and scientific practices.

Utilizing Evidence to Build Capacity

After the winter institute, Ms. Lee and Ms. Cody urged Mr. Hill and Ms. Garrison to assume more responsibility for their joint work and co-designed a unit on how seeds grow into plants, which evolved from a "failed plant experiment," as Mr. Hill described it. To the teachers' surprise, even though several attempts to grow seeds were unsuccessful, students were still eager to explore why the seeds did not grow. Students' questions served as the foundation for an extended unit on seeds around which the PLC co-planned a series of investigations. Students' work samples served as tools for formative assessment that helped to inform planning decisions. Continuing to examine students' writing helped the PLC center on students' knowledge, experiences, and interests, and consider different ways to create spaces for productive participation for EBs at all proficiency levels.

By the end of the academic year, students in Mr. Hill and Ms. Garrison's classes showed significant growth on district measures of reading performance compared to students in the four other kindergarten classrooms at Fulbright Elementary. Further, the PLC collected evidence of students' understanding of scientific practices and core ideas, as well as their oral language and literacy development, over time. For example, by the end of the year, the kindergarteners collaboratively constructed and explained a Venn diagram for characteristics of plants and animals, needs for survival in their environment, and life cycles. Given that these successes were visible in the district data and on the classroom walls, the principal at Fulbright Elementary became eager to scale up Science 20/20 at his site.

Lessons Learned from Starting Small

Our experience reveals several considerations for those engaged in teacher professional development in science and language learning in a new immigrant community. Creating a supportive context for professional learning in a community undergoing rapid demographic change is necessarily an ongoing process that begins with investing substantial human and financial resources in a small number of teachers. Starting small in this way allowed us to better understand the district and school environment, capitalize on affordances of the existing setting, engage in a sustained collaborative process that helped develop trusting relationships between teachers and researchers, and demonstrate positive impact using multiple sources of evidence.

The goal in these final paragraphs is not to repeat all of the ways in which starting small played out in our work, but rather to underscore the lessons we learned that inform our ongoing work. First is attention to the projects' three foundational principles, which we keep at the forefront during all of our interactions with teachers. These include: 1) embracing all children as knowers and partners in knowledge building; 2) inviting productive participation in sensemaking in science and language development; and 3) utilizing formative assessment across domains of language to inform instruction. By attending to these principles in all aspects of project life, from PD institutes to co-planning to lunchtime conversations, we kept issues of equity for EBs at the forefront. We cannot overstate the importance of everyone involved in the project, researchers and teachers alike, understanding and using the principles to inform cycles of co-teaching and co-design.

Like much of the scholarship on teacher professional learning suggests (e. g., Garet et al., 2001; NASEM, 2015; van Driel and Berry, 2012), our work at Fulbright Elementary revealed the importance of engaging teachers as active participants. Co-planning and co-teaching are central to our PD model; however, the full benefit of the collaborative process was not realized until it was reframed to include co-investigating students' sensemaking in science and language development. Not only did the shift to teachers as co-investigators foreground the importance of formative assessment and using evidence to inform instruction, but it afforded an authentic purpose for the collaborative work that took place between teachers and researchers. This work enabled the development of more trusting relationships and a transition of roles and responsibilities for co-teaching and co-design to teachers as part of their professional learning.

Although they occurred on a small scale, these early wins during our pilot PD year were essential to the continuation of Science 20/20. We were not surprised to find that many high-priority district initiatives at the elementary level were focused on language and literacy, and we were nimble enough to make the most of connections among sensemaking in science and literacy (see Hooper and Zembal-Saul, this volume, Chapter 4) and language development. Given that our work with teachers yielded positive results for EBs that were meaningful to school leaders and teachers, we were invited back to continue—and to expand—with strengthened administrative support. In this way, starting small created opportunities for the larger-scale capacity building that is so often necessary in schools in new immigrant destinations, where EBs are often not afforded access to equitable science and language learning opportunities (NASEM, 2018).

The lessons we have learned are woven into the fabric of the project as we move forward. Overall, develop supportive contexts for professional learning based on co-teaching and co-design in the midst of rapid demographic change is demanding and time-intensive work. In fact, some might say our investment in two teachers at Fulbright Elementary was too great. Our experiences, however, tell a different story, and highlight the need to start small so that capacity can be built from the ground up in response to the local context.

Notes

1 We use the term emergent bilingual to refer to students whose primary language is not English and whose level of English language proficiency may be sufficient to deny them access to content where the language of instruction is English. Although federal policy uses the term "English learner" to refer to this group of students, we use emergent bilingual to acknowledge the bilingual assets these students bring to our schools and communities.
2 Science 20/20 is a National Professional Development grant funded by the US Department of Education, Office of English Language Acquisition (2016–2021). Any opinions, findings, conclusions, or recommendations expressed here are those of the authors.
3 The school district contributes inservice days for teachers participating in Science 20/20 winter and spring professional development institutes.

References

Alvarez, L., Ananda, S., Walqui, A., Sato, E., and Rabinowitz, S. (2014). *Focusing Formative Assessment on the Needs of English Language Learners*. San Francisco, CA: WestEd.

Bailey, A.L. (2017). Progressions of a new language: Characterizing explanation development for assessment with young language learners. *Annual Review of Applied Linguistics*, 37, 241–263.

Banilower, E., Smith, P. S., Malzahn, K., Plumley, C., Gordon, E., and Hayes, M. (2018). *Report of the 2018 NSSME+*. Chapel Hill, NC: Horizon Research, Inc.

Brooks, K., Adams, S. R., and Morita-Mullaney, T. (2010). Creating inclusive learning communities for ELL students: Transforming school principals' perspectives. *Theory into Practice*, *49*(2), 145–151.

Cheuk, T., Daro, P., and Daro, V. (2018). The language of mathematics and summative assessment: Interactions that matter for English learners. In A. L. Bailey, C. A. Maher, and L. C. Wilkinson (Eds.). *Language, Literacy and Learning in the STEM Disciplines: How Language Counts for English Learners*. New York: Routledge.

Ciechanowski, K. M. (2014). Weaving together science and English: An interconnected model of language development for emergent bilinguals. *Bilingual Research Journal*, *37*(3), 237–262.

Darling-Hammond, L. (2000). Teacher quality and student achievement: A review of state policy evidence. *Education Policy Analysis Archives*, *8*(1).

Durán, R. P. (2008). Assessing English-language learners' achievement. *Review of Research in Education*, *32*(1), 292–327.

Estrella, G., Au, J., Jaeggi, S. M., and Collins, P. (2018). Is inquiry science instruction effective for English language learners? A meta-analytic review. *AERA Open*, *4*(2), 1–23.

Feldgus, E. and Cardonick, I. (1999). *Kid Writing: A Systematic Approach to Phonics, Journals, and Writing Workshop*. New York: McGraw Hill.

Gándara, P. C., Maxwell-Jolly, J., and Driscoll, A. (2005). *Listening to Teachers of English Language Learners*. Santa Cruz, CA: Center for the Future of Teaching and Learning.

García, O., and Kleyn, T. (2016). Translanguaging theory in education. In O. García and T. Kleyn (Eds.), *Translanguaging with Multilingual Students: Learning from Classroom Moments* (pp. 9–33). New York: Routledge.

Garet, M. S., Porter, A. C., Desimone, L., Birman, B. F., and Yoon, K. S. (2001). What makes professional development effective? Results from a national sample of teachers. *American Educational Research Journal*, *38*(4), 915–945.

Gutiérrez, K., Baquedano-Lopez, P., and Tejada, C. (1999). Rethinking diversity: Hybridity and hybrid language practices in the third space. *Mind, Culture, and Activity*, *6*(4), 286–303.

Heritage, M., and Chang, S. (2012). *Teacher Use of Formative Assessment Data for English Language Learners*. Los Angeles, CA: CRESST/UCLA.

Kang, H., Thompson, J., and Windschitl, M. (2014). Creating opportunities for students to show what they know: The role of scaffolding in assessment tasks. *Science Education*, *98*(4), 674–704.

Krajcik, J., McNeill, K. L., and Reiser, B. J. (2008). Learning-goals-driven design model: Developing curriculum materials that align with national standards and incorporate project-based pedagogy. *Science Education*, *92*(1), 1–32.

Lee, O., and Fradd, S. H. (1998). Science for all, including students from non-English-language backgrounds. *Educational Researcher*, *27*(4), 12–21.

Lee, O., Deaktor, R.A., Hart, J.E., Cuevas, P., and Enders, C. (2005). An instructional intervention's impact on the science and literacy achievement of culturally and linguistically diverse elementary students. *Journal of Research in Science Teaching*, *42*(8), 857–887.

Lee, O., Quinn, H., and Valdés, G. (2013). Science and language for English language learners in relation to Next Generation Science Standards and with implications for Common Core State Standards for English Language Arts and mathematics. *Educational Researcher, 42*(4), 223–233.

Lee, O., Grapin, S., and Haas, A. (2018). How science instructional shifts and language instructional shifts support each other for English learners: Talk in the science classroom. In A. Bailey, C. Maher, and L. Wilkinson (Eds.), *Language, Literacy and Learning in the STEM Disciplines: How Language Counts for English Learners* (pp. 35–52). New York: Routledge.

López, F., Scanlan, M., and Grundrum, B. (2013). Preparing teachers of English language learners: Empirical evidence and policy implications. *Education Policy Analysis Archives, 21*, 1–35.

Lowenhaupt, R., and Reeves, T. (2015). Toward a theory of school capacity in new immigrant destinations: Instructional and organizational considerations. *Leadership and Policy in Schools, 14*(3), 308–340.

Lyon, E. G., Tolbert, S., Solís, J., Stoddart, P., and Bunch, G. C. (2016). *Secondary Science Teaching for English Learners.* Lanham, MD: Rowman & Littlefield.

McNeill, K. L. (2009). Teachers' use of curriculum to support students in writing scientific arguments to explain phenomena. *Science Education, 93*(2), 233–268.

McNeill, K. L., and Krajcik, J. (2008). Scientific explanations: Characterizing and evaluating the effects of teachers' instructional practices on student learning. *Journal of Research in Science Teaching, 45*(1), 53–78.

Moje, E. B., Ciechanowski, K. M., Kramer, K., Ellis, L., Carrillo, R., and Collazo, T. (2004). Working toward third space in content area literacy: An examination of everyday funds of knowledge and discourse. *Reading Research Quarterly, 39*(1), 38–70.

Moll, L. C., Amanti, C., Neff, D., and González, N. (1992). Funds of knowledge for teaching: Using a qualitative approach to connect homes and classrooms. *Theory into Practice, 31*(1), 132–141.

NASEM (National Academies of Sciences, Engineering, and Medicine). (2015). *Science Teachers' Learning: Enhancing Opportunities, Creating Supportive Contexts.* Washington, DC: National Academies Press.

NASEM (National Academies of Sciences, Engineering, and Medicine). (2018). *English Learners in STEM Subjects: Transforming Classrooms, Schools and Lives.* Washington, DC: National Academies Press.

NRC (National Research Council). (2012). *A Framework for K-12 Science Education: Practices, Crosscutting Concepts, and Core Ideas.* Washington, DC: National Academies Press.

Penuel, W. R., Roschelle, J., and Shechtman, N. (2007). Designing formative assessment software with teachers: An analysis of the co-design process. *Research and Practice in Technology Enhanced Learning, 2*(1), 51–74.

Penuel, W. R., Fishman, B. J., Cheng, B. H., Sabelli, N. (2011). Organizing research and development at the intersection of learning, implementation, and design. *Educational Researcher, 40*(7), 331–337.

Rodriguez-Mojica, C. (2018). From test scores to language use: Emergent bilinguals using English to accomplish academic tasks. *International Multilingual Research Journal, 12*(1), 31–61.

Roth, K. J., Garnier, H. E., Chen, C., Lemmens, M., Schwille, K., and Wickler, N. I. (2011). Videobased lesson analysis: Effective science PD for teacher and student learning. *Journal of Research in Science Teaching, 48*(2), 117–148.

Solano-Flores, G. (2016). *Assessing English Language Learners: Theory and Practice.* New York: Routledge.

Suárez-Orozco, C., Suárez-Orozco, M. M., and Todorova, I. (2008). *Learning a New Land: Immigrant Students an American Society*. Cambridge, MA: Harvard University Press.

van Driel, J. H. and Berry, A. (2012). Teacher professional development focusing on pedagogical content knowledge. *Educational Researcher, 41*(1), 26–28.

Wortham, S., Murillo, E. G., and Hamann, E. T. (Eds.). (2002). *Education in the New Latino Diaspora: Policy and the Politics of Identity*. Westport, CT: Ablex.

16 *Response:* Supporting Elementary Teacher Learning to Teach Science

Jan H. van Driel
MELBOURNE GRADUATE SCHOOL OF EDUCATION,
THE UNIVERSITY OF MELBOURNE

Introduction

The three chapters in this section describe an interesting collection of projects that, taken together, paint a rich picture of what is needed in terms of supportive contexts to scaffold elementary teachers' journeys to become experts in science teaching. Since policy papers and research literature, around the world, continue to point at the lack of competence and confidence of elementary teachers in the domain of science, the work described in these chapters is very important and timely. In this response, I will discuss these chapters in the light of the broader international research literature on science teacher learning.

Many publications lament elementary science education. It tends to be marginalized in elementary curricula across the world, and whenever it is taught, it is often of low quality. Reviewing the research literature, Roth (2014) identified several factors that contribute to this. These include instructional approaches that are not adapted to students' level of understanding, do not support understanding or scientific thinking, and that portray science as a static collection of facts rather than a dynamic body of knowledge. At best, elementary science teaching contributes to students becoming interested in science. Given the central role of teachers in the education process, it is vital that elementary teachers become empowered to teach science in ways that engage all students in the development of scientific understanding and skills. This implies that elementary teachers have rich science subject matter themselves, and know how their students learn this subject matter, and what students find difficult, or interesting. To promote student learning of specific subject matter, teachers need to have a repertoire of instructional strategies, and, most importantly, to know when and how to apply which strategy. This professional expertise of teachers is often referred to as pedagogical content knowledge (PCK; Gess-Newsome, 2015) or content knowledge for teaching (Ball *et al.*, 2008). The development of this expertise needs to start during initial teacher education and sustained through ongoing professional learning.

Teacher professional learning

Professional learning of teachers, both preservice and inservice, has been studied for quite some time, but it is still not well understood what and how teachers learn from teacher education and professional development programs, and how this impacts on the development of their knowledge and practice (Desimone *et al.*, 2002; Fishman *et al.*, 2003). Studies on teachers' professional learning have shown that high-quality teacher education programs emphasize forms of inquiry (Little, 2001; Lotter *et al.*, 2006) that enable preservice and inservice teachers to actively construct knowledge through practice and reflection (Guskey, 1986; 2002). Moreover, research in this domain has demonstrated that effective programs typically include the following elements: (a) an explicit focus on teachers' initial knowledge, beliefs and concerns; (b) opportunities for teachers to experiment in their own practice; (c) collegial cooperation, including teachers, teacher educators, or others; and, (d) sufficient time for changes to occur (e.g., Bell and Gilbert, 1996; Garet *et al.*, 2001; Van Driel *et al.*, 2012).

There is general agreement in the broader educational community about the importance of teachers' professional learning as one of the ways to improve education. However, a major question in the teacher learning literature concerns how changes in knowledge, beliefs, and attitudes, relate to changes in actual teaching practice (Richardson and Placier, 2002), and how this relationship can be fostered. For a long time, it has been widely assumed that when teachers change their knowledge, beliefs, and attitudes on, for example, new instructional methods, their teaching practice will improve, leading to better student learning outcomes (Guskey, 1986). More recently, ideas about teacher learning have focused on reflection on one's own practice as a lever to changes in both teachers' knowledge and practice (Korthagen *et al.*, 2001). Teacher learning is now commonly seen as a complex system of processes in which teachers are engaged in active and meaningful learning (Borko, 2004).

Within this perspective, one of the models proposed for teachers' professional learning is the Interconnected Model of Teacher Professional Growth (IMTPG; Clarke and Hollingsworth, 2002). This model is constituted of four different domains: (1) the Personal Domain, which is concerned with teachers' knowledge, beliefs, and attitudes; (2) the External Domain, which is associated with external sources of information or stimuli; (3) the Domain of Practice which involves professional experimentation; and (4) the Domain of Consequence, which is comprised of salient outcomes related to classroom practice (see Figure 16.1). According to this model, teachers' professional learning is represented by changes in these four domains, through the mediating processes of reflection and enactment (represented as arrows linking the domains). Although the model was primarily developed in the context of the ongoing professional learning of inservice teachers, it can also be applied to programs of initial teacher education, in particular, on the learning that takes place during internships or placements.

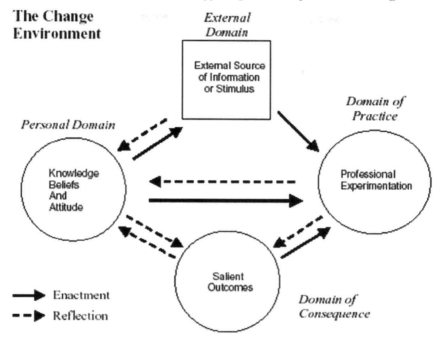

Figure 16.1 The Interconnected Model of Teacher Professional Growth
Source: Clarke and Hollingsworth, 2002

The processes of professional growth represented in this model occur within an enveloping change environment: "Change in every domain and the effect of every mediating process are facilitated or retarded by the affordances and constraints of the workplace of each teacher" (Clarke and Hollingsworth, 2002, p. 965). I have found the IMTPG a useful framework to design and study teacher learning processes in different contexts (Justi and Van Driel, 2006; Wongsopawiro et al., 2016), and I will therefore refer to it in the next sections as to discuss the three chapters in this section.

Practice-Based Teacher Education

The chapter by Davis, Palincsar, and Kademian (this volume, Chapter 13) outlines the principles underlying the design of a practice-based elementary teacher education program and describes some of its outcomes as evidenced in interviews with participants, and video registrations of their classroom teaching. The authors provide a strong case for a practice-based approach to elementary teacher education, which is based on three pillars: high-leverage practices, content knowledge for teaching, and ethical obligations of teaching. The practices are the focus of this chapter. Drawing on the work of Grossman et al. (2009), the design of the four-semester program, is outlined

236   *van Driel*

as a coherent sequence of coursework and practicum. An important focus of the program is the idea of "children as sensemakers." This idea underpins a very fundamental notion, that is, that children are trying to make sense of the world they live in, and that as a teacher, your responsibility is not so much to tell or explain this world to them, but to elicit and value their thinking and engage in conversations to further that thinking. If understood well, this notion challenges some of the persistent problems in science teaching, in particular, at the elementary level, as described above.

The authors describe how this notion is central in a course early in the program, which takes place concurrently with a placement, where interns work closely with individual students, through conversations, texts and modeling materials. This experience aims to assist the interns to see that knowledge building, rather than an individual process, is shaped by the social and cultural contexts in which it takes place. Interviews with interns about halfway through the program reveal that they recognize the value of understanding children's ways to make sense of the natural world. Later in the program, videos, both of the interns' own teaching, as from exemplary elementary teachers, are used as representations of practice.

Interestingly, the authors briefly report on a longitudinal study of four participants in the program into their first year as teachers. The findings show that interns and first-year teachers are similarly capable to apply the practice of eliciting students' ideas in science, however, both groups experienced limited success with leading a sensemaking discussion in science. Finally, the first-year teachers were more successful than interns with the practice of supporting students in constructing scientific explanations. In summary, this chapter demonstrates that a practice-based approach can successfully prepare elementary teachers to teach science, competently and confidently. In my view, the strengths of the program are its focus on practices, and the design that combines various high-leverage practices in a coherent and consistent way, over a substantial amount of time. My main comment would be that the focus on practices in the chapter somewhat obscures the two other pillars of the program, that is, content knowledge for teaching, and ethical obligations of teaching. I appreciate that this knowledge is not separate from teaching practice, but it would have been interesting, for instance, to read more about the PCK that interns develop through eliciting students' ideas in science and analyzing videos of science lessons, and how PCK is further developed by reflection on the practice of supporting students to construct scientific understandings.

It's not difficult to recognize the four domains of the IMTPG in this program: the external domain (i.e., the coursework) provides interns with ideas, language and frameworks that inspire and scaffold their experimentation in practice (Domain of Practice), focusing on specific practices rather than confronting the interns with the full complexity of classroom teaching. It seems that the representations of practice (i.e., the videos) played a vital role to promote reflection on the salient outcomes of practice (i.e., student

Supporting Elementary Teacher Learning   237

responses during interactions and lessons), leading to changes in interns' knowledge and understanding. The small-scale longitudinal study indicates that, if scaffolded this way, beginning teachers will engage in new cycles of experimentation in practice, reflection on outcomes, and developing their professional understanding.

School–University Partnerships

In the chapter by Zembal-Saul, Badiali, Mueller and McDyre (this volume, Chapter 14) the supportive context provided by the Professional Development School (PDS) is central. It is good that the authors refresh the history of the PDS. The five goals in the Holmes Group report are as relevant today as they were in 1986, especially in the light of the barriers to teacher learning identified in the NASEM (2015) report. Many of these barriers concern the organizational and broader policy context in which teachers operate, that constitute the Change Environment in the IMTPG. The collaborative multidisciplinary communities that a PDS can offer, in which experienced and beginning teachers learn together, may not exist at a large scale, however, similar ideas underpin the notion of Professional Learning Communities (PLCs) which is central in the chapter by Hopkins *et al.* (Chapter 15). The chapter demonstrates how powerful such communities can be to promote teacher learning.

The four goals defined by the PDS that was established by Penn State University College of Education and State College Area School District are aligned with those of the Holmes Group, and extend these by including professional growth among teacher educators. Decision-making by consensus among all PDS participants is an important feature of this PDS. It ensures that beginning and experienced teachers, school leaders, teacher educators and researchers have equal voices in the community. Another important feature is the use of video. Similar to the Davis *et al.* chapter (Chapter 13), videos of beginning and experienced teachers *teaching the same content* are used as a learning resource. Other strengths of the approach include the way that beginning teachers are allowed increasing levels of responsibility, and the role of teacher inquiry as a signature pedagogy.

Inquiry is a key element of the learning journey of one of the authors, Ms. Mueller, a graduate from the program. Her account focuses on the combination of teaching literacy and science, integrating science lessons inspired by the NGSS in literacy instruction. The eminent role of her mentor teacher and teacher educator in the processes of co-planning and co-teaching emerge clearly from this case study. The inquiry process led her to collect and analyze the writing, reading and visualizations of her students, which allowed her a deeper understanding of her students' thinking. In terms of the IMTPG, this chapter illustrates how reflection on professional experimentation (Domain of Practice), followed by a reflection on salient outcomes (Domain of Consequence), enables the development of knowledge in the Personal Domain, feeding back into the Domain of Practice.

238   *van Driel*

Ms. Mueller describes the benefits of the process in generic terms: *"Through the inquiry process, I was able to improve on my own practice for integrating science and language arts"* (this volume, Chapter 14, p. 213). It would have been interesting to read a few examples of how she made sense of the domain-specific learning of her students, to which specific insights this led (e.g., in terms of PCK), and how she enacted these in a next cycle. The chapter concludes by providing some evidence that teacher mentors also benefited from engaging in collaborative teacher inquiry. In summary, this chapter provides a convincing account of how powerful a PDS as a change or learning environment can be.

A Supportive PD Context

The final chapter in this section, by Hopkins, Zembal-Saul, Lee, and Cody (Chapter 15), focuses on the design of, and experiences with, a professional development approach that focuses on teaching science to English learners (ELs). This requires teaching science with a strong focus on language and literacy, somewhat similar to the previous chapter. Specifically, the teaching approach is inquiry-oriented and discourse-rich, implying that ELs use language extensively (talking, writing) to build knowledge and construct scientific understanding. Formative assessment is an integral part of this approach, enabling responsive teaching and fostering inclusive learning.

Creating these kinds of learning opportunities can be challenging for elementary teachers. The authors propose a sociocultural PD model ("Science 20/20"), that combines institutes with weekly meetings of a Professional Learning Community including teachers and teacher educators, co-planning and co-designing science lessons. Being aware of the challenges facing teachers to implement and test their ideas in their professional practice, the authors decided to choose a nimble and responsive approach, reflected in the phrase "Starting small."

The remainder of the chapter focuses on one of the teachers, Mr. Hill, who worked with a colleague and two teacher educators, co-designing and co-teaching lessons with "living things" in K-2, making use of the fact that there was no formal science curriculum for K-2 in the district. The authors stress the importance of ongoing collaboration within the team, and of making co-investigation (i.e., of students' sense-making in science and language) an integral element of the cycles of jointly planning, designing and teaching. They conclude that this approach fosters the kind of capacity building that is needed to successfully implement the teaching of science in elementary settings. That may be so, but the chapter is not very explicit about the specific capacity that the team members built, for instance, in terms of knowledge or PCK, attitudes, or self-efficacy.

In terms of the IMTPG, the four domains, again, are clearly present: The institutes providing external input (External Domain), which inspires professional experimentation (Domain of Practice) and co-investigation leading to analyzing the salient outcomes (Domain of Consequence) and fostering changes in professional knowledge and understanding (Personal Domain). However, this chapter highlights the role of the change environment even more than the two other chapters in this section. The chapter details how the constraints (organizational, curricular) that could hinder the implementation of the teaching approach and the PD process, inspired the "starting small" mantra. Through working with a small team, ensuring the support from school administrators and staff, and focusing on K-2 (i.e., no formal science curriculum), the authors created a supportive change environment, which facilitated teacher professional learning.

Conclusion

The chapters in this section demonstrate the complexity of educational processes, and how these depend on relationships between various groups of people. Teachers need to recognize their students as knowledge builders and be willing to support and join them in their journeys of constructing meaning and making sense of the natural world. In turn, teachers need to be supported by educators, parents and administrators, to develop their professional expertise and become confident to improve their science teaching practice. The approaches to teacher learning in the domain of elementary science, described in these chapters, show that supportive communities, sustained over time, can be empowering. The teachers who participated in these communities learned with and from others, including their students.

Taken together, these chapters add insight in what it takes to develop, implement and sustain exemplary science teaching at the elementary level. Specifically, by focusing on the contexts or environments that are needed to support teacher learning, these chapters extend the research-based knowledge on teacher professional learning. The chapters provide some evidence of the efficacy of the respective approaches, however, more research is needed to better understand how these, and other, supportive contexts foster elementary teachers' learning, and to what kind of learning outcomes they contribute, in terms of enhanced knowledge, practices, or confidence. Such research will help to inform the design of programs for preservice and inservice teacher learning that can boost the science learning experiences of all elementary students.

References

Ball, D., Thames, M., and Phelps, G. (2008). Content knowledge for teaching: What makes it special? *Journal of Teacher Education, 29*, 389–407.

Bell, B. and Gilbert, J. K. (1996). *Teacher Development: A Model from Science Education.* London: Falmer Press.

Borko, H. (2004) Professional development and teacher learning: Mapping the terrain. *Educational Researcher, 33*, 3–15.

240   van Driel

Clarke, D. and Hollingsworth, H. (2002) Elaborating a model of teacher professional growth. *Teaching and Teacher Education, 18,* 947–967.

Desimone, L., Porter, A. C., Garet, M., Yoon, K. S., and Birman, B. (2002) Does professional development change teachers' instruction? Results from a three-year study. *Educational Evaluation and Policy Analysis, 24,* 81–112.

Fishman, B. J., Marx, R. W., Best, S., and Tal, R. T. (2003) Linking teacher and student learning to improve professional development in systematic reform. *Teaching and Teacher Education, 19,* 643–658.

Garet, M., Porter, A., Desimone, L., Birman, B. and Yoon, K. S. (2001) What makes professional development effective? Results from a national sample of teachers. *American Education Research Journal, 38,* 915–945.

Gess-Newsome, J. (2015). A model of teacher professional knowledge and skill including PCK. In A. Berry, P. Friedrichsen and J. Loughran (Eds.), *Re-examining Pedagogical Content Knowledge in Science Education* (pp. 28–42). New York and London: Routledge.

Grossman, P., Compton, C., Igra, D., Ronfeldt, M., Shahan, E., and Williamson, P. (2009). Teaching practice: A cross-professional perspective. *Teachers College Record, 111,* 2055–2100.

Guskey, T. R. (1986) Staff development and the process of teacher change. *Educational Researcher, 15,* 5–12.

Guskey, T. R. (2002) Professional development and teacher change. *Teachers and Teaching: Theory and Practice, 8,* 381–391.

Justi, R., and Van Driel, J. H. (2006). The use of the IMTPG as a framework for understanding the development of science teachers' knowledge on models and modelling. *Teaching & Teacher Education, 22,* 437–450.

Korthagen, F. A. J., Kessels, J., Koster, B., Lagerwerf, B., and Wubbels, T. (2001) *Linking Practice and Theory: The Pedagogy of Realistic Teacher Education.* Mahwah, NJ: Lawrence Erlbaum Associates.

Little, J. W. (2001) Professional development in pursuit of school reform. In A. Lieberman and L. Miller (Eds.), *Teachers Caught in the Action: Professional Development that Matters* (pp. 28–44). New York: Teachers College Press.

Lotter, C., Harwood, W. S., and Bonner, J. J. (2006) Overcoming a learning bottleneck: Inquiry professional development for secondary science teachers. *Journal of Science Teacher Education, 17,* 185–216.

NASEM (National Academies of Sciences, Engineering, and Medicine). (2015). *Science Teachers' Learning: Enhancing Opportunities, Creating Supportive Contexts.* Washington, DC: National Academies Press.

Richardson, V. and Placier, P. (2002) Teacher change. In V. Richardson (Ed.), *Handbook of Research on Teaching* (4th edn, pp. 905–947) Washington, DC: American Educational Research Association.

Roth, K. J. (2014). Elementary science teaching. In N. Lederman and S. Abell (Eds.), *Handbook of Research on Science Education,* Vol. II (pp. 361–394). New York and London: Routledge.

Van Driel, J. H., Meirink, J.A ., Van Veen, K., and Zwart, R. C. (2012) Current trends and missing links in studies on teacher professional development in science education: A review of design features and quality of research. *Studies in Science Education, 48,* 129–160.

Wongsopawiro, D., Zwart, R. C., and Van Driel, J. H. (2016). Identifying pathways of teachers' PCK development. *Teachers and Teaching: Theory and Practice, 23*(2), 191–210.

17 *Response:* Two Lenses for Looking at Supportive Contexts for Science Teacher Learning

Kathleen Roth

CENTER FOR EXCELLENCE IN SCIENCE AND MATHEMATICS TEACHING,
CALIFORNIA STATE POLYTECHNIC UNIVERSITY

The three chapters in Section III each describe a coherent set of science teacher learning experiences along with some evidence of the success of these experiences in helping teachers understand, value, and use teaching practices that engage student sensemaking in science. In Chapter 13 Betsy Davis and colleagues report on a practice-based teacher education program. Chapter 14 focuses on 20 years of partnership work between Pennsylvania State University and a local school district to develop a professional development school (PDS) that supports both preservice and inservice teachers. In Chapter 15 Hopkins and colleagues report on a small one-year pilot effort to reshape a professional development (PD) program for inservice teachers so that it better fits the policies and practices of a partner school district in a nascent immigrant community to support the needs of emergent bilingual children. I was interested in examining both the commonalities and the unique features of these efforts that might contribute to deepening our thinking and questioning about supportive contexts for science teacher learning.

To help in this task, I turned to two resources: dictionaries and a National Academies report on the status of research knowledge about supporting science teacher learning (NASEM, 2015). Each of these resources provided me with a new lens with which to analyze and reflect on the efforts described in these three chapters: a Multiple Meanings Lens and a Multiple Fronts Lens. I describe these two lenses next and then use these lenses to highlight ways in which the efforts described in the Section III chapters contribute to and raise questions about our understanding of supportive contexts for science teaching learning.

The Multiple Meanings Lens

In the Section III chapters, there are frequent mentions of *supports* and *supportive contexts* for teacher learning. Wondering about how we are defining the words, "support" and "supportive," I investigated dictionary definitions and found examples of these words being used in a variety of ways. Looking across different dictionaries, I found that a frequently used definition for the word "support" is as a verb: providing assistance that enables a function or act. This strikes me as the meaning that we might most often have in mind when we talk about supporting teachers' professional growth. A second definition of *support* (this time as a noun) also seems appropriate for thinking about teacher learning programs: a base, foundation, or underpinning. The most commonly cited definition of the word *supportive* takes a different slant that might also be relevant to thinking about teacher learning contexts: providing encouragement, approval, comfort, reassurance. This definition focuses more on emotional supports.

Because my own experiences working with teachers challenged me to consider all three of these definitions, I examined the chapters through a Multiple Meanings Lens: To what extent are these three meanings of *support/supportive* important in creating supportive contexts for science teacher learning?

The Multiple Fronts Lens

My revisiting of the NASEM report led me to consider a second analytical lens. An idea emphasized repeatedly in the report is that teachers work in *multiple* contexts and that they need to be supported in improving their knowledge and practice across these multiple contexts, not just one or two of them. The NASEM report notes that "a sustained weakness in any one support undermines attempts to improve students' learning" (2015, p. 176). The report goes on to emphasize that to effect change for individual teachers and improve collective capacity, "it is important to consider how a variety of factors work together to support teachers" (2015, p. 176).

The NASEM report lists the multiple fronts that research suggests are important to address in constructing supportive learning contexts for science teachers. Their list of multiple fronts provided a productive taking off spot for my examination of the three professional learning experiences described in Section III: What are the "multiple fronts" they are tackling in their work? What can we learn about supportive teacher learning contexts by looking across the multiple fronts addressed in these three efforts?

The Multiple Meanings Lens

How are the three contexts described in this section similar and different in addressing three different meanings of support: support as a foundation, support as assistance, and support as encouragement? In discussing the three contexts in these chapters, I will refer to them by the following shorthand abbreviations: TE for the University of Michigan teacher education program, PDS for the Penn State work in professional development schools, and PD-ELL for the university-school collaborative PD program focused on the needs of English Language Learners in science.

Supports as foundational. Two aspects of professional development experiences for teachers that have not been well researched are:

- The use of a conceptual framework that provides coherence to the ideas and practices that define the substance of teachers' learning (Roth *et al.*, 2017; Roth *et al.*, 2018), and
- The use of a theory of teacher learning that informs the nature, structure, and sequence of teacher learning experiences (Ball and Cohen, 1999; Roth *et al.*, 2017).

Both of these can provide a foundation for a teacher learning program. A conceptual framework can bring focus to the substance of what teachers are learning. A theory of teacher learning can guide decisions about the types of activities that are used to engage teacher learning and how those activities are sequenced over time. Given that the research is not strong enough to identify these foundational features in the conclusions made in the NASEM report about effective PD programs, it is striking that each of the three teacher learning contexts reviewed here is built on these types of foundations.

In terms of defining what teachers will learn, the three contexts—TE, PDS, and PD-ELL—share a foundational vision of science teaching that focuses on student sensemaking through the investigation of phenomena and the construction of evidence-based scientific explanations and arguments. To make this vision accessible to preservice teachers, the TE program specifies a framework that structures this vision in three phases: *Engage, Experience*, and *Explain+Argue with Evidence (EEE+A)*. The PD-ELL program characterizes this vision of science teaching in terms of three principles: students are partners in knowledge construction; students construct understanding through authentic activities; formative assessment drives instruction. All three programs foreground equity issues in their vision of science teaching. The first of four defined goals of the PDS work, for example, is to enhance learning for *all* students. This shared vision of science teaching and learning serves as a conceptual framework that defines one aspect of teacher learning and is at the core of the work in all three contexts.

The TE program goes beyond presenting a framework for thinking about science teaching and also provides a conceptual framework that defines what teachers will learn in their program. Their framework describes the substance of the program as three "pillars": seven high-leverage science teaching practices, science content knowledge for teaching, and ethical obligations of teachers. The PDS and PD-ELL contexts do not specify an equivalent framework for defining *what* teachers will learn, although these chapters focus more strongly on *how* teachers will learn.

In describing *how* teachers learn, only the PD-ELL description explicitly mentions a theory of teacher learning that guides the design, structure, and

244 *Roth*

sequencing of teachers' learning experiences. However, it is clear that all three efforts share a sociocultural perspective on teacher learning, consistent with a situated cognition theory of teacher learning and a cognitive apprenticeship pedagogy to support teacher learning. Situated cognition posits that learning is naturally tied to authentic activity, context, and culture (Lave and Wenger, 1991). A cognitive apprenticeship instructional model focuses on initial modeling by experts, followed by scaffolded opportunities for learners to practice with gradual fading of supports as learners develop more skill and expertise (Collins, 2006). In line with this theoretical stance, the TE, PDS, and PD-ELL experiences are all founded in classroom-based ("situated") learning over time. In all three contexts, teachers examine and analyze more expert teachers first and then are supported in various ways as they begin to use new science teaching practices themselves. For example, preservice teachers in the TE program first practice teaching parts of lessons to their peers. Interns' learning in the PDS context starts with a focus on observing and analyzing mentor teacher instruction and moves gradually to taking over more responsibility for instructional decision-making and co-teaching with their mentors. In the PD-ELL context, teachers are first introduced to the guiding principles of science teaching and learning as they observe and analyze an experienced teacher's work with ELLs in a summer science camp. Later, they work with university partners in cycles of co-planning, co-teaching, and collaborative analysis.

Supports as providing assistance. In all three contexts, there is a focus on three main types of activities and related tools and resources to assist teachers in changing their science teaching practice: models of practice, supports for analysis of practice, and supports for implementing new practices. Table 17.1 highlights how each program assists teacher growth through these activities.

A fourth type of assistance was the people who teachers were able to work with and learn from as they engaged in these activities, including course instructors, colleagues, mentor teachers, and other teacher educators. Intern teachers in the PDS context had the opportunity to learn from the widest variety of people: their peers, a mentor teacher who co-taught the methods course, the intern's host mentor teacher, other mentor teachers, the methods course instructor, and other university-based teacher educators.

Supports as encouragement. Although providing encouragement, approval, comfort, and reassurance likely occurred frequently in all three contexts, this type of support was only hinted at in these chapters. Certainly giving feedback to preservice teachers in the TE program, and co-teaching with science-shy teachers in the PD-ELL context and with teacher interns in the PDS context included multiple messages of this kind of support. I am curious how tending to this emotional side of supporting teachers played out in consensus decision making in the PDS setting and in challenging teachers' deficit language about learners in the PD-ELL work. In my own

Supportive Contexts for Teacher Learning 245

Table 17.1 Three Types of Assistance for Supporting Teachers

Type of assistance	TE Context (Chapter 13)	PDS Context (Chapter 14)	PD-ELL Context (Chapter 15)
Models of practice	Videos of expert teaching in two courses	Videos of mentor teachers teaching similar content	Observations of experienced summer science teacher
Supports for analysis of practice	Preservice teachers analyze their own and their peers' teaching of lessons Analytical Tool: Framework observation guide	Interns analyze video of experts and own teaching Interns, Mentor Teachers, Teacher Educators engage in inquiry projects Analytical Tool: Coherent conceptual framework	Inservice teachers and university partners analyze student work Analytical Tools: <ul><li>Science 20/20 guiding principles</li><li>ATLAS protocol for analyzing student work</li></ul>
Supports for implementing new practices	Preservice teachers start with peer teaching to rehearse with a carefully selected lesson Tool: Instructional planning template	Interns co-plan with peers and mentor teachers Interns co-teach with mentor teachers Tool: Claim-evidence-reasoning framework	Inservice teachers and university partners: Co-plan instruction and assessment <ul><li>Co-plan instruction and assessment</li><li>Co-teach and document student learning</li><li>Collaboratively analyze student work</li></ul> Tool: Project 20/20 guiding principles

work, I have been struck by the need to strike a careful balance between supporting teachers in an encouraging way and challenging teachers to reconsider, to examine things more deeply and with new lenses, and to change long-held beliefs and teaching practices. My experience has taught me that providing encouragement is not enough. Transforming science teaching practice is hard work that almost always requires some uncomfortable moments. How can teacher educators find productive ways to challenge as well as support teachers?

The Multiple Fronts Lens

The NASEM report describes the many contexts in which teachers work. Each of these contexts has the potential to nurture or constrain teacher learning. We can think of these contexts as different organizational levels: classrooms, departments, schools, districts, professional organizations and networks, state and national reform efforts, and each

246 Roth

teacher's individual characteristics and efforts. In addition to these organizational levels of support, the NASEM report identifies five overlapping categories of work that research has shown to be linked to student learning in math and literacy (see Table 17.2) (NASEM, 2015). Each of these five categories can be addressed at multiple organizational levels. While each of the organizational levels and the categories defined in Table 17.2 is complex in its own right, the complexities are compounded by the ways they overlap and influence each other. This is why school reform research emphasizes the importance of addressing these contexts simultaneously (Bryk *et al.*, 2010).

Table 17.2 Multiple Fronts for Supporting Teacher Learning

Categories of Fronts (NASEM, 2015)	Examples
1. Professional learning experiences that include research-supported features	Consensus model features: • Engage teachers in analysis of practice • Subject matter content focus • Align with district/state policies and practices • Sufficient duration to allow repeated practice and reflection Nominated features with emerging evidence of impact (NASEM, 2015): • Science content learning intertwined with analysis of practice • Focus on a few targeted teaching strategies • Learning scaffolded by knowledgeable leaders • Analytical tools support deep analysis
2. Development of professional capacity	• Professional networks • Coaching • Partnerships • Professional learning communities • Staffing policies • Science specialists • Teacher evaluation
3. Coherent instruction	• Arrangement and pacing of subject matter content within and across grades • Expected depth of student learning • Pedagogical strategies, tools, curriculum materials • State and district curriculum standards • Assessment and accountability policies
4. Leadership advocacy and support	• Instructional leadership by principals • Development of teacher leaders
5. Time and funding	

Supportive Contexts for Teacher Learning   247

To what extent are the TE, PDS, and PD-ELL efforts addressing multiple fronts simultaneously? All three provide teacher learning experiences that meet the research-supported criteria for effective teacher learning experiences that are referred to in the literature as the "consensus model" (Desimone, 2009; NASEM, 2015). The PDS and PD-ELL efforts explicitly develop professional capacity through the creation of professional learning communities and partnerships between university- and school-based educators. All three programs contribute in a limited way to the coherence of the school science curriculum, largely by focusing on helping teachers develop a new vision of science learning goals and skill in using target teaching strategies to enact that vision. They have less control over the content and organization of the science curriculum within and across grade levels or the assessments used for accountability. The PDS most explicitly includes school administrators and involves the development of teachers as leaders in preparing new teachers and in conducting and sharing inquiry projects. While none of the chapters discuss issues of funding and access to resources, these issues were no doubt addressed in establishing the programs, and it would be helpful to know ways in which funding at state, district, school, and university levels has been leveraged to support these programs.

The PDS context stands out as addressing multiple (but not all) fronts simultaneously. In this school-district-university partnership, the PDS has a simultaneous focus on the learning of elementary students, preservice teachers, inservice teachers, university-based teacher educators, and administrators. The PDS also works at multiple organizational levels—elementary classrooms, university courses, schools, the district, and the university. There is more limited connection to state level policies and the national NGSS initiative, where the PDS is more on the receiving ends of state and national reforms. It is interesting to note that the PDS context has a long, 20-year history that may be an important factor to consider in aiming to work across multiple fronts simultaneously. The PD-ELL description represents a much newer effort, and the authors make a strong case for the power of starting small because it enabled university-based educators to be flexible in shaping a PD program to fit with priorities and ongoing commitments in the schools. This led to small successes that served as entry points for larger scale work and partnership in the future.

While these three efforts each involve work at the intersection of multiple fronts, it is clear from looking at the list of examples in Table 17.2 that there are many levels or fronts that they do not address. Rather than look at this as a criticism or a deficit, I think we need to do more to acknowledge and fully understand what it takes to develop the kinds of teacher learning contexts described in this section. I particularly am struck by how helpful it is to include a description of the relatively young PD-ELL effort. In that report we get to see more of the struggles and problem solving and compromises that tend to be glossed over in reporting about more mature projects.

248   *Roth*

Reflections and Implications for Future Work

What do we learn from looking at these three teacher learning contexts through the Multiple Meanings and Multiple Fronts lenses, and what are the implications for future work? What are important questions that are identified by this analysis?

Commonalities and Implications for Future Work

Looking at these chapters through the Multiple Meanings Lens, I was struck by the similarities across contexts in terms of how they addressed three meanings of "support": support as a foundational framework, support as providing assistance to help teachers enact more effective teaching practices, and support as providing encouragement and reassurance. The Multiple Fronts Lens reveals a common effort to create coherent teacher learning experiences by aligning work across organizational levels (national, state, school, university) and addressing multiple contexts of teachers' learning (Table 17.2).

I was particularly interested in the ways in which these three efforts all include but go beyond the long-held consensus model of effective teacher professional development (Desimone, 2009; NASEM, 2015). Consistent with the consensus model, all three programs engage teachers in analysis of practice, have a science content focus, are aligned with district, state, national efforts, and are of sufficient duration and intensity. Moving beyond this model, however, they also: integrate science content learning and pedagogical learning in analysis of practice activities, focus on a few targeted teaching practices, provide scaffolding by knowledgeable others, and provide analytical tools for analysis of practice. These four features are of special interest because they are also identified in a handful of rigorously studied PD programs cited in the NASEM report (2015). The TE, PDS, and PD-ELL efforts also share a conceptual framework that defines the core substance of teacher learning, and they all use an implied socio-cultural, situated cognition theory of teacher learning to guide the design and sequence of teacher learning activities over time. Future research might examine the extent to which these are critical features for supportive teacher learning contexts that can advance our thinking beyond the current consensus model.

Differences and Implications for Future Work

An important difference across the three efforts is the nature of the evidence to support their claims for effectiveness in creating supportive learning contexts. While all three chapters present qualitative descriptions of the teacher learning programs and include examples of successful teacher learning, only the TE chapter examined teachers' practice directly. Their analysis of teaching videos of four teachers at two points in time provided a richer sense of the successes and limitations of the program's impact than the surveys and interviews used in the PDS study and the qualitative description in the PD-ELL chapter. To better support my suggestion in the previous section that these programs can advance our knowledge about supportive teacher learning contexts, it is important to have stronger evidence for impact that includes analysis of both successes and failures as well as data about impact on teaching and impact on student learning, which none of these studies present.

A second important difference is the degree to which multiple fronts are addressed simultaneously. The longstanding PDS program demonstrates how a strong partnership can simultaneously support the learning of students, preservice teachers, inservice teachers, university science educators, and administrators while working across multiple organizational levels (school, district, university). While this is impressive, there is still much work to do to address the many contexts and organizational levels in which teachers work. For example, what role can the PDS effort play in shaping district- and state-defined policies and assessments so that they better support science teacher learning? At the opposite end of the spectrum is the PD-ELL work which is a fledgling school-university partnership. The contrast between the PDS and PD-ELL efforts highlights the need for research to fill the gap between the two: What does it take to develop partnerships that work effectively at multiple organizational levels simultaneously? How can we get better at working at multiple fronts, while acknowledging the dangers of starting too big?

Additional Questions to be Explored

In closing, I share several additional questions that these chapters raised for me that I think need further attention within these projects and in the larger science education community. I encourage readers to think about additional questions that this work raises for you.

- What makes for a useful conceptual framework that defines and focuses what teachers are learning? How might a conceptual framework define learning goals for inservice teachers differently from those of preservice teachers? What about learning goals for university-based educators?
- What do we know and what do we need to know about support as encouragement in science teacher learning contexts? What kinds of personal interactions and moves can be identified that provide encouragement and reassurance while also challenging teachers to experience some discomfort that comes with growth?
- In professional learning communities and school-district-university partnerships, how do we best define the roles of people with science expertise? In particular, science education researchers typically have

more expertise about science teaching and learning than elementary teachers. How do we use that expertise while respecting teachers as professionals?

- What do we know about teaching science content and science practices within the context of analysis of practice? What can each of these projects tell us about deepening teachers' understanding of science within practice-based work?

References

Ball, D. L., and Cohen, D. K. (1999). Developing practice, developing practitioners: toward a practice-based theory of professional education. In L. Darling- Hammond and G. Sykes (Eds.), *Teaching as the Learning Profession* (pp. 3–32). San Francisco: Jossey-Bass.

Bryk, A. S.Sebring, P.B., Allensworth, E.Luppescu, S., and Easton, J.Q. (2010). *Organizing Schools for Improvement.* Chicago: University of Chicago Press.

Collins, A. (2006). Cognitive apprenticeship. In R. K. Sawyer (Ed.), *The Cambridge Handbook of the Learning Sciences* (pp. 47–60). New York: Cambridge University Press.

Desimone, L. M. (2009). Improving impact studies of teachers' professional development: Toward better conceptualizations and measures. *Educational Researcher, 38,* 181–199.

Lave, J., and Wenger, E. (1991). *Situated Learning: Legitimate Peripheral Participation.* New York: Cambridge University Press.

NASEM (National Academies of Sciences, Engineering, and Medicine). (2015). *Science Teachers' Learning: Enhancing Opportunities, Creating Supportive Contexts.* Committee on Strengthening Science Education Through a Teacher Learning Continuum, Board on Science Education and Teacher Advisory Council, Division of Behavioral and Social Science and Education. Washington, DC: National Academies Press.

NGSS Lead States. (2013). *Next Generation Science Standards: For States, By States.* Washington, DC: National Academies Press.

Roth, K. J., Bintz, J., Wickler, N. I. Z., Hvidsten, C., Taylor, J., Beardsley, P.M., Caine, A., and Wilson, C. D. (2017). Design principles for effective video-based professional development. *International Journal of STEM Education, 4,* 31.

Roth, K. J., Wilson, C. D., Taylor, J. A., Stuhlsatz, M.A., and Hvidsten, C. (2018). Comparing the effects of analysis-of-practice and content-based professional development on teacher and student outcomes in science. *American Educational Research Journal.* Retrieved from: https://doi.org/10.3102/0002831218814759

Conclusion

Reflections on Science Teacher Education and Professional Development for Reform-Based Elementary Science

Cory T. Forbes

UNIVERSITY OF NEBRASKA

Introduction

Sensemaking in Elementary Science: Supporting Teacher Learning draws from expertise and cutting-edge work spanning the fields of science education and teacher education to collectively articulate a vision for elementary science teacher education and professional development that supports contemporary science education reform efforts. The *Framework for K-12 Science Education* (NRC, 2012) and *Next Generation Science Standards* (NGSS Lead States, 2013) have ushered in a new era of science education that, while building upon the past (e.g., NRC, 1996; 2000), presents novel opportunities and foundations for science teaching and learning in K-12 classrooms. This is no less the case for elementary (K-5) settings, where the emphasis on three-dimensional learning (disciplinary core ideas, science and engineering practices, and crosscutting concepts) demand a reconceptualization of elementary science that foregrounds student sensemaking. And, as noted in the volume's introduction, illustrated in contributed chapters, and supported by an ever-growing body of research, early learners are capable of productively engaging with the natural world and science in this way (e.g., Baumfalk *et al.*, 2019; Beyer and Davis, 2008; Manz, 2012; McNeill, 2011). Opportunities for them to do so help ensure that "all students are provided with equitable opportunities to learn science and become engaged in science and engineering practices" (NRC, 2012, p. 28), building a solid foundation for lifelong science learning not influenced by gender, socioeconomic status, and other similar factors. While achieving this vision requires comprehensive reform of all aspects of elementary science (e.g., instruction, curriculum, and assessment), teachers will remain the critical linchpin in science learning environments. And while NGSS presents new opportunities for both teachers and students, they will undoubtedly also present teachers with new questions and challenges related to elementary science. As such, ongoing efforts to support elementary teachers—both preservice and inservice—to cultivate elementary science learning environments that reflect contemporary science education reform priorities are more important than ever.

252   *Forbes*

But how do we actively promote this refined vision of elementary science education? This book is grounded in the assumption that we can affect change in the teaching and learning of science in elementary classrooms through teacher education, professional development, and other intentional and designed learning experiences for teachers at all stages of their careers. As professional practitioners, teachers naturally have unique learning needs defined by their own individual characteristics (knowledge, beliefs, self-efficacy, prior experience, etc.), the goals and objectives driving their instructional practice, and the characteristics of the context(s) in which they work (e.g., Appleton, 2006). Supporting teachers' professional growth is the crucial charge of teacher educators, whether they are university faculty, staff developers, or others engaged in this work with preservice and/or inservice teachers. We must acknowledge that many of the same principles we apply to instruction with early learners—building upon students' ideas and experience, embedding learning in meaningful contexts, promoting equity, and cultivating communities of learners—apply to current and future teachers as well. As such, professional learning experiences for elementary teachers of science should honor and leverage what individuals bring to the table to help them refine and expand their capacities for effective elementary science teaching. In doing so, teacher educators can significantly influence both the nature and outcomes of elementary science teaching and learning. This is an important and highly motivating mission upon which elementary science teacher education and professional development rest.

However, this assumption is high-level and general, providing little in the way of specific guidance for how such learning experiences for teachers can and should be designed. The articulation and use of what Roth (this volume, Chapter 17) describes as "consensus models" for elementary teacher education and professional development is critical to translating these and similar broad assumptions into realized and observable impact. Such models are comprised of key theoretical and empirically grounded orientations, principles, and components that can provide a skeleton around which to build specific learning experiences for teachers. Discussed throughout the contributions to this book, both explicitly and implicitly, are concrete principles, strategies, and heuristics that drive the design and activity of elementary science teacher education and professional development. These tenets of effective program design not only help define such programs, but also help make important linkages between contexts of teacher learning and connected contexts (elementary classrooms, policy, etc.), thus establishing and enhancing coherence between all relevant domains and stakeholders. In this way, such consensus models help teacher educators communicate, explain, and justify their approaches to fostering teacher learning. However, questions about how to best support elementary teachers' learning for science teaching are as long-standing as the endeavor itself (e.g., Nichols and Koballa, 2006; Russell and Martin, 2014). The contents of this edited volume make great strides in illustrating innovative approaches to

Conclusion: Reflections 253

elementary science teacher education and professional development, raise important theoretical and empirical questions for the future, and help codify a shared perspective and knowledge base that strengthens and enhances the field and community of practice around elementary science teacher education and professional development. I am grateful for the authors' willingness to put their work forward and the opportunity to synthesize the work in this concluding chapter.

Core Themes for Elementary Science Teacher Education and Professional Development

The objective of this concluding chapter is to highlight key themes of the book and to make visible the most important take-aways in terms of supporting elementary science teachers' learning to support, in turn, their students' sense-making. To do this, I organize the discussion around three key arenas, each of which I believe is essential to a well-developed consensus model for elementary science teacher education and professional development. First, I discuss key elements of a perspective on the nature of teaching practice and teacher learning. Second, I revisit key elements of effective science teaching and learning in elementary classrooms. Finally, third, I articulate and, in many ways, reiterate important features of the design of teacher learning experiences for elementary teachers of science. I am sincerely hopeful that these observations serve to help advance the conversation around elementary science teaching and learning.

A Coherent Perspective on the Nature of Teaching and Teacher Learning

In order to design experiences for teachers that optimize their learning, we must first articulate a perspective on the nature of teaching and teacher learning. One consistent and clear theme that emerges from this edited volume is a shared vision for the work of teachers and its direct connection to their learning and development. As the editors note in the introduction (citing Putnam and Borko, 2000), they share a view of teacher learning as social, distributed, and situated in teachers' practice. This perspective resonates throughout the contributed chapters. While there are, of course, variations in the unique conceptual frameworks outlined by the various contributors, each broadly aligns with the overarching framing provided by the editors, with a shared emphasis on: a) teachers' personal characteristics (knowledge, beliefs, orientations, and self-efficacy); b) mutually constitutive nature of contexts of practice; c) translation of past experience into changes in practice through tools and scaffolds; and d) the goal-directedness of authentic practice. These key elements have critical implications for considerations about the second two themes, including the design of learning experiences for elementary teachers of science and what we might identify as "high-leverage" instructional practices (Ball and Forzani, 2009) we seek to promote.

254   *Forbes*

To synthesize these conceptual perspectives, I propose a framework for teachers' learning and practice across the continuum of professional teaching (Figure 18.1; see also Forbes and Biggers, 2015) that captures these core elements, building upon work presented in this book, as well as broader educational theory and research. These include Shulman's (1987) original ideas underlying the idea of pedagogical content knowledge (PCK), Remillard's (2005) work on teachers' use of curriculum materials, and cultural-historical activity theory (Engeström and Sannino, 2010), a domain-general conceptual perspective that is highly applicable to the work of teachers and teaching. These theoretical perspectives possess shared features, which we might characterize as the epistemic dimensions of instructional practice. I identify four shared epistemic dimensions of teaching based on these theoretical perspectives. First, teachers must *problematize* some aspect of teaching and learning related to their goals and objectives for instruction. Fundamentally, this involves questioning, analysis, and sensemaking, perhaps of their own direct experiences, but also underlying principles, their own personal characteristics, and the tools and resources with which they engage in practice. Second, teachers formulate a *plan* to address the issue they have identified which, again, is a process supported by available tools and scaffolds. Third, they *perform* or, more simply, engage in classroom teaching with their students. Finally, fourth, they *process* these experiences through reflection and distillation of essential elements of their experiences. Processing and problematization are key metacognitive processes for teachers through which they consider the what, how, and why of teaching and learning and internalize key observations and lessons learned for instructional practice. In contrast, planning and performance are externally oriented processes focused on impact, where teachers design and implement plans for teaching and learning intended to influence their environment. Figure 18.1 provides a visual form of this conceptual model for these epistemic dimensions of teachers' instructional practice.

This model, I argue, is a reflection of what Kloser and Windschitl (this volume, Chapter 12) describe as *disciplined improvisation*, where expertise is derived from the interplay of instructional practice, which by its nature demands flexibility and responsiveness, and principles of practice over time. This process is non-linear and iterative, meaning teachers experience this general cycle of activity repeatedly, may spend more time with some epistemic activities than others, and may engage in these activities in a non-sequential manner, ideally (and most importantly) in response to the needs of learners. There is an array of resources, both conceptual (content knowledge, beliefs about teaching and learning, instructional models, etc.) and physical (curriculum materials, equipment, etc.), that can serve as tools and scaffolds for teachers engaged in practice. However, the ideas and repertoires that they internalize as part of their normative core (NC in Figure 18.1) constitute principles of practice and provide a solid, disciplined

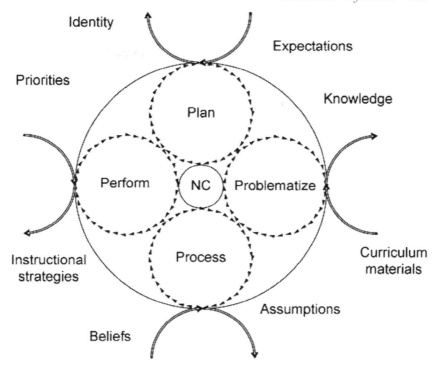

Figure 18.1 Conceptual Model of Instructional Practice
Source: Forbes and Biggers, 2015; NC: normative core

foundation upon which improvisation can occur. Consistent with this model, new ideas, strategies, and approaches to elementary science teaching introduced from without (i.e., through designed learning experiences for teachers) can be internalized by a teacher and become part of their normative core. The resources that become part of their normative core and serve as foundational principles of practice are those that have been best enable them to improvise pedagogically, with students, in learning environments, over time through engagement in these epistemic dimensions of authentic instructional practice

Critical Aspects of Elementary Science

With an overarching perspective on the nature of teaching and teacher learning in mind, a key question is, "What should an effective science teacher know and be able to do?" A sizable and ever-growing body of research helps define characteristics of "good" science teaching, including at the elementary level, that foster students' sensemaking. My objective here is not to provide a comprehensive summary of this research. However, teachers

256   Forbes

will continue to have a significant amount of latitude to select and use instructional strategies and approaches that help realize NGSS's vision and promote students' sensemaking about science. As such, my objective is to highlight elements of innovative pedagogy evident in this volume's contributed chapters, which help paint a clearer picture of innovative and effective elementary science teaching and learning.

First, as Kloser and Windschitl (this volume, Chapter 12) observe, and consistent with the perspective laid out in the previous section (Figure 18.1), teaching is goal-oriented, focused on "coherent and broader learning objectives." This is a somewhat obvious but perhaps underemphasized point. Effectively designed science curriculum, instruction, and assessment should be focused on pre-defined outcomes for students' science learning. Formal science classrooms should not be defined by totally student-directed "discovery learning," where the scope and sequence of students' science experiences is entirely emergent, which research has increasingly shown to be ineffective (e.g., Furtak *et al.*, 2012). However, the goal-oriented nature of formal education presents both affordances and constraints to teachers and students. On the one hand, it may constrain classroom teaching and learning to some degree. The notions of "off topic," "getting sidetracked," and "tangents" exist because there is a pre-defined purpose to classroom activity. On the other hand, these learning outcomes provide teachers and students parameters and resulting guidance in the focus and purpose of their classroom activity, which affords a structure within which meaningful science teaching and learning practices can exist.

As evident throughout the contributions to this volume, as well as its overall framing, the *Next Generation Science Standards* (NGSS Lead States, 2013) are highly influential in providing guidance and structure to science teaching and learning. NGSS is being adopted across the United States and even in states where they are not officially adopted, they are significantly influencing state and district-level science standards. The three dimensions of NGSS's performance expectations emphasize not only disciplinary and crosscutting concepts, but the sensemaking practices through which students should engage with these ideas. The shifts for elementary science are arguably most profound. For example, compared to the earlier *National Science Education Standards* (NSES; NRC, 1996), NGSS articulates specific performance expectations by grade level for elementary science. As compared to NSES, this affords teachers much more specificity for the kinds of activities in which students should engage in the elementary classroom and what learning would be expected to occur from these experiences.

Second, students' learning experiences are most meaningful and relevant when designed around concrete, localized phenomena that are relevant to their everyday lived experience. As McNeill (this volume, Chapter 6) describes, these phenomena should be most observable and focused on natural or designed systems related to target performance expectations. This perspective benefits from a long history of thinking in science education, whether it be from perspectives focused on Science-Technology-Society (STS; Bennett *et al.*, 2007), socio-scientific issues (SSIs; Sadler and Dawson, 2012), or the use of anchoring questions as driving frameworks for science teaching and learning (Krajcik and Mamlok-Naaman, 2006). Approaching classroom science through the entry point of such phenomena leverages a basic assumption of science education—that our own experiences drive our motivation to better understand the natural world. These phenomena help clarify linkages between classroom science and the world around us, cultivating a desire in students to develop understanding that can help them reason and ultimately address problems and challenges they may experience in day-to-day life. There are many examples of phenomena throughout the chapters in Section I (summarized by McNeill, this volume, Chapter 6), focused on topics that relate to an array of DCIs spanning scientific domains. For example, Cody and Biggers (this volume, Chapter 3) describe a unit situated within an authentic local controversy about water quality; at a smaller scale, Hooper and Zembal-Saul (this volume, Chapter 4) launch their chapter with a teacher's question about using simple machines to lift a load into the classroom treehouse. Phenomena such as these help, as Avraamidou (this volume, Chapter 5) notes, place Doing so not only serves as a motivator for learning, but also legitimizes the geographical, cultural, economic, and social dimensions of students' lived experience and sense of self (i.e., identity). This is essential to opening the doors of science learning to all students in ways that not only benefit and enrich students as individuals, but also the communities and societies in which they live. As such, localized phenomena contribute to the cultivation of equitable elementary science learning environments by helping students see science not only as part of *the* world, but, most importantly, *their* world.

Third, once these localized phenomena have set the stage for inquiry, teachers and students have a wide array of opportunities available to them to investigate the phenomena. While I use the term "inquiry" here, I do so utilizing its more general connotation as a scientific search for understanding. This may be contrasted with the notion of inquiry as "scientific processes" focused primarily on hands-on activities and investigations (e.g., experiments) that have driven discourse around elementary science for decades (NRC, 1996; 2000). While these kinds of experiences can certainly be a part of sensemaking in elementary science, there are other practices that are equally as important in science, such as modeling, which may not appear to align directly with more common and/or traditional perspectives on "hands-on science." Each of these practices is equally important for students to generate evidence about phenomena that serve as the basis for explanations and claims about how and why the natural world works. Several chapters in Section I describe how teachers can engage their students in such science practices; for example, Bismack and Haefner (this volume, Chapter 2) explore how practices work together to support sensemaking and Zembal-Saul and Hershberger (this volume, Chapter 1) zoom in on the role of grappling with data to foster sensemaking. Sensemaking about science is defined by the claims that students make, their evidence, and their reasoning about how evidence supports their claims (Zembal-Saul, McNeill, and Hershberger, 2013; see also Zembal-Saul and Hershberger, this volume, Chapter 1).

A critical point of discussion evident in these chapter is the varied and multifaceted ways in which students are afforded opportunities to articulate their claims, evidence, and reasoning. As Avraamidou (this volume, Chapter 5) observes about the case presented by Hooper and Zembal-Saul (this volume, Chapter 4), students benefit greatly from opportunities to represent phenomena (data and evidence), their ideas (claims), and their reasoning in many different forms. A defining characteristic of elementary science classrooms should be as "representation-rich" environments. By representation I refer not only to physical artifacts students might produce (diagrams, written products, 3D models or designs, etc.), but also verbal talk and discourse. Claims, evidence, and reasoning, the essential elements of sensemaking, are each constructions that can be represented in a wide variety of ways. There is no magic formula for specifying precisely what kinds of representations are most productive and when. That said, in the NGSS performance expectations, the nature of the phenomena and disciplinary concepts under study, and the teacher's and students' familiarity and/or abilities with different representational processes and forms can all help narrow the focus. Cultivating a "representation-rich" elementary science learning environment also enhances equity by affording students opportunities to represent and communicate their sensemaking in culturally meaningful ways.

Fourth, I specifically highlight one representational form—classroom discourse—as a critical component of effective elementary science learning environments. Classroom discourse should not be unidirectional, solely defined by teachers communicating *to* students. Rather, the teachers' role is to shape classroom discourse to immerse students in an "economy of ideas," fundamentally acting as a facilitator. This is not only conventional wisdom, but an underlying assumption of many programs designed to support science teacher learning, including those described in this book. In fact, an attunement to students' ideas and sensemaking repertoires as a critical component of classroom science, including instruction, is critical to broadening participation in science by leveraging resources students bring with them to the classroom and a key component of theoretical perspectives underlying the field of science education more generally (Driver *et al.*, 1985). The contributions to this book present many helpful examples of effective classroom talk. For example, Bişmack and Haefner (this volume, Chapter 2) provide a detailed account of how a highly experienced first-grade teacher used talk to engage students in various components of sensemaking, including articulating their ideas, describing patterns in data, and proposing explanations for magnetism, changes of state, and life cycles. However, learning to facilitate effective classroom discourse can be extremely challenging for science teachers, particularly new teachers. It is made so by a variety of factors, including the uncertainty associated with the ideas students bring to the classroom, specific strategies for facilitating classroom discourse, and identifying a balance between the free flow of ideas and guidance toward scientifically accurate ideas, as well as the temporal and cognitive demands this form of instruction places on both teachers and students. The growing array of resources focused on "talk moves" can help teachers develop confidence and expertise with facilitation of classroom discourse (Harris *et al.*, 2012), such as the *Talk Moves Tool* described by Kademian and Davis (this volume, Chapter 8). They outline specific types of prompts, questions, and redirects that give teachers an arsenal of concrete tools to use to facilitate discussions in their classrooms. These are critical tools that can support teachers to internalize discourse repertoires as a core component of their normative core for science instruction, particularly for preservice teachers when foregrounded through well-designed approximations of practice as described by Davis (this volume, Chapter 7).

Design Features for Programs that Support Teacher Learning

Having distilled these core themes from the contributions to this book, we must next consider how we optimally support elementary teachers to engage in these practices and support students' sensemaking about science. Elementary science teacher education and professional development is a sizable and important undertaking. However, as Avraamidou (this volume, Chapter 5) observes, For us as elementary science teacher educators, there are always opportunities to continue to refine our approaches and strategies, no matter how confidently we may believe they help teachers. However, like van Driel (this volume, Chapter 16), I do not believe that the chapters in this volume demand or even allude to redesigning elementary science teacher education from the ground up. Rather, the shifts for elementary science brought about by NGSS present opportunities to build off of the strengths of existing programmatic features to reconceptualize some aspects of the work we do to further help prepare and support teachers to cultivate reform-based elementary science learning environments.

There are many core features of effective science teacher education and professional development evident in contributions to this book. These constitute a consensus model comprised of "research-supported criteria for effective teacher learning experiences" that reflects our understanding of the nature of teaching, what we want teachers to learn, and how we support their learning. The last of these elements is the focus of this subsection— design features for effective programs that support elementary teachers to engage in ambitious, reform-based science teaching. The report by the National Academies of Sciences, Engineering, and Medicine (NASEM, 2015), also discussed by Roth (this volume, Chapter 17), foregrounds many of these features, including a focus on disciplinary concepts and opportunities for teachers to experience expert science teaching, as well as scaffolded practice engaging in these kinds of novel practices over a significant amount of time. The chapters in this volume present multiple and varied concrete examples of what these strategies and approaches can look like as part of programs designed for both preservice and inservice teachers, including student interviews (Arias, Chapter 11; Davis, Palincsar, and Kademian, Chapter 13), lesson planning and enactment (Arias, Chapter 11; Davis, Chapter 7; Hopkins, Zembal-Saul, Lee, and Cody, Chapter 15; Kademian and Davis, Chapter 8; Zembal-Saul, Badiali, Mueller, and McDyre, Chapter 14), and reflection and analysis (Benedict-Chambers, Chapter 10; Zembal-Saul, Badiali, Mueller, and McDyre, Chapter 14). They also illustrate a wide array of tools with which to support elementary teachers' learning, including talk moves and discourse (Arias, Chapter 11; Kademian and Davis, Chapter 8), noticing and accounting for students' ideas (Benedict-Chambers, Chapter 10; Kademian and Davis, Chapter 8), and various scientific practices (Fick and Arias, Chapter 9; Kademian and Davis, Chapter 8).

First, these perspectives share an emphasis on authentic practice as a core element. Teachers, including elementary teachers, are professional practitioners, which means having a defined domain of professional practice. The preparation and ongoing support of teachers is focused not on generically defined competencies and skills, but a targeted set of knowledge and skills necessary for a specific role—classroom science teaching. (Of course, an elementary teacher must develop this targeted knowledge and skill around each of the academic subjects they teach!) As such, expert practice must be the core feature of learning experiences for teachers. But what does this mean? A simple contrast could be articulated as engaging teachers in "learning about" as compared to "learning to do." "Learning about" focuses on teachers' developing understanding of ideas and strategies related to effective science teaching and learning. While this is an important component of "learning to do," it can also be undertaken in a practice-independent manner in more traditional settings (teaching methods courses, professional development workshops, etc.). Teachers may be introduced to new ideas and strategies but without parallel opportunities to actually implement and use these ideas in teaching practice (or approximations of practice; Davis, this volume, Chapter 7), they may not translate into the science that K-12 students experience in classrooms. "Learning to do' not only involves "learning about," but also opportunities for teachers to iteratively try out new ideas and approaches through authentic aspects of teaching practice, such as the analysis of lesson plans and curriculum materials, student artifacts, and video recordings of science instruction, as well as course-based microteaching and practicum-based experiences with students in K-12 classrooms. These activities reflect the key domains of teaching reflected in Figure 18.1 and, over time, help teachers develop robust routines that serve as a foundation for innovative instruction, or the *discipline* that grounds *improvisation*.

Conclusion: Reflections 261

This argument is not new, and certainly is not mine alone (e.g., Davis, Palincsar, and Kademian, this volume, Chapter 13; Forzani, 2014; McDonald *et al.*, 2013). It is well documented in theory, research, and policy underlying teacher education, as well as evidenced in the chapters that comprise this book. The contributors to this book are leaders in translating the idea of practice-based teacher education and professional development into effective learning experiences for current and future elementary teachers of science. I have been fortunate to work with and be mentored by some of them, including in the University of Michigan program (Davis, this volume, Chapter 7), and count them all as colleagues. However, in my professional work spanning multiple institutions of higher education, I have also experienced the challenges associated with programmatically pursuing elementary science teacher education and professional development experiences that foreground practice. And there are many. One of the most significant and glaring involves affording preservice elementary teachers meaningful, long-term experiences in elementary classrooms. Building programs across contexts of teacher education and professional development (postsecondary and K-12) continues to be one of the greatest challenges teacher educators face. Also, while inservice teachers have their own classrooms as contexts for implementing new ideas (e.g., Hopkins, Zembal-Saul, Lee, and Cody., this volume, Chapter 15), the often short timeframe of grant-funded, one-off professional development programs limits teachers' abilities to reflect collaboratively with colleagues, seek out and receive additional support, and engage in multiple cycles of instructional innovation so critical to systemic reform. These issues are not easily addressed by teacher educators because they are not usually under our direct control (e.g., limited institutional resources and/or capacity, grant funding, etc.). The chapters by Hopkins, Zembal-Saul, Lee, and Cody (this volume, Chapter 15) and Zembal-Saul, Badiali, Mueller, and McDyre (this volume, Chapter 14) illustrate critical examples of the design and impact of programs that are successfully navigating these challenges. For similar programs to become the norm rather than the exception, I argue that we, as teacher educators, must be consistent advocates and champions for the institutional support and structures necessary to afford teachers the most robust, theory-informed, empirically supported professional learning environments possible. We must be voices of reform not only with the teachers with whom we work, but also with university administrators, policymakers, and school district leaders who help shape these experiences for teachers.

Second, we know that the sheer volume of ideas and strategies related to elementary science teaching and learning can be overwhelming for teachers. As Kloser and Windschitl (this volume, Chapter 12) accurately note, this can result in an "overflowing toolbelt' and rote use of a wide array of teaching strategies. Focusing on key features of elementary science teaching, or packaging an array of tools and strategies within a coherent framework, it critical for effective teacher education and professional development. But

262 Forbes

what are these key elements and how might they be packaged in such a manner? Again, there are many examples throughout this volume, for example, Davis, Palincsar, and Kademian's emphasis (Chapter 13) on high-leverage practices, disciplinary content knowledge, and ethical obligations as three pillars of their program. All of these attend to core components of effective science teaching described in the first section of this concluding chapter, including classroom discourse and talk, students' evidence-based explanations, meaningful contexts, and varied representational forms of ideas and experiences. In particular I believe each of these attend to, in different ways, a focus on students' ideas as the primary driver of instruction which, as described previously, is a core underlying theoretical assumption of science teaching and learning (Driver *et al.*, 1985) and critical feature of equitable elementary science learning environments. However, one of the core challenges science teachers face, if not *the* fundamental tension of teaching, is learning to design and engage instruction that is simultaneously a) responsive to students' thinking and b) reflective of broader learning goals, a theme echoed throughout the chapters of this book. Vygotsky's zone of proximal development is still very much with us as a central feature of science teaching and learning, as well as science teacher education and professional development.

How do we support elementary teachers to use students' thinking to inform science instruction in this way? As Benedict-Chambers (this volume, Chapter 10) states, it is perhaps unproductive to so this emphasis on responsive instruction must be the defining feature of a foundational, overarching programmatic framework, or perhaps mission and core commitment, within which more concrete and specific instructional practices can be situated. One productive approach we and others have employed with both preservice (Otero and Nathan, 2008; Sabel *et al.*, 2015) and inservice (Falk, 2011; Forbes *et al.*, 2015; Sabel *et al.*, 2016) elementary teachers is formative assessment, an established, evidence-based instructional framework in which teachers use evidence of students' thinking to shape instruction and, thus, can better support students' scientific sensemaking, a core focus of this book. In its most simplified form, it involves an iterative and ongoing process of *eliciting* students' thinking, *interpreting* their ideas, *diagnosing* learning needs, and *designing instruction* to address those needs. Each of these steps affords multiple entry points for specific "high-leverage' instructional strategies highlighted throughout contributed chapters. For example, students' ideas can be elicited through discourse and student artifacts reflecting their claims, evidence, and/or reasoning about target phenomena. Interpretation of students' ideas requires teachers to employ their pedagogical content knowledge and reasoning to navigate disciplinary concepts, targeted learning outcomes, and evidence of student understanding. Designing instruction involves the use of available resources, including curriculum materials, to visualize and design opportunities for student sensemaking that are grounded in practice-based evidence. These phases overlap with common instructional models for science, such as the 5Es (Bybee *et al.*, 2006), which can be used to both illuminate and afford students opportunities to engage further with their ideas and phenomena. While the use of the word "assessment" may have loaded meaning for some, our experience suggests elementary teachers recognize the utility of this generalized approach, are able to readily connect it to more familiar language and terminology they experience in schools, and find it a valuable and workable conceptual space within which to engage in all aspects of instruction. Formative assessment can afford an overarching framework through which elementary teachers of science can engage in instructional *improvisation*, reflective of *disciplined* principles of practice, that is responsive to students' trajectories of learning.

Conclusion

Sensemaking in Elementary Science: Supporting Teacher Learning is an important and timely collection of work focused on elementary science teaching and learning. The contributions to this volume illustrate and reflect cutting-edge work and the field's current thinking about supporting elementary teachers to realize the vision for elementary science reflected in NGSS. I began this chapter with one assumption and will end it on another—as critical agents in shaping the science that students experience in elementary classrooms, teachers both require and deserve effective professional preparation and ongoing support. This, in turn, highlights the importance of elementary science teacher educators, professional developers, and all involved in these efforts. As a community of practice with shared assumptions and goals, we must continue working to enhance our collective capacity and overall impact on effective, meaningful, cognitively rich, and culturally relevant science sensemaking opportunities that promote science learning and equity for all students. This edited volume will serve as a tremendous resource in enabling us to do so.

References

Appleton, K. (2006). Science pedagogical content knowledge and elementary school teachers. In K. Appleton (Ed.), *Elementary Science Teacher Education: International Perspectives on Contemporary Issues and Practice* (pp. 31–54). Mahwah, NJ: Lawrence Erlbaum Associates.

Ball, D. L. and Forzani, F. M. (2009). The work of teaching and challenge of teacher education. *Journal of Teacher Education, 60*(5), 497–511.

Baumfalk, B., Bhattacharya, D., Vo, T., Forbes, C.T., Zangori, L., and Schwarz, C. (2019). Impact of model-based curriculum and instruction on elementary students' explanations for the hydrosphere. *Journal of Research in Science Teaching, 56*(5), 570–597.

Bennett, J., Lubben, F., and Hogarth, S. (2007). Bringing science to life: A synthesis of the research evidence on the effects of context-based and STS approaches to science teaching. *Science Education, 91*(3), 347–370.

264 *Forbes*

Beyer, C. J., and Davis, E. A. (2008). Fostering second graders' scientific explanations: A beginning elementary teacher's knowledge, beliefs, and practice. *The Journal of the Learning Sciences, 17*(3), 381–414.

Bybee, R., Taylor, J., Gardner, A., Van Scotter, P., Carlson, J., Westbrook, A., and Landes, N. (2006). *The BSCS 5E Instructional Model: Origins, Effectiveness, and Applications.* Colorado Springs: BSCS.

Driver, R., Guesne, E., and Tiberghien, A. (1985). *Children's Ideas in Science.* Philadelphia, PA: Open University Press.

Engeström, Y. and Sannino, A. (2010). Studies of expansive learning: Foundations, findings and future challenges. *Educational Research Review, 5,* 1–24.

Falk, A. (2011). Teachers learning from professional development in elementary science: Reciprocal relations between formative assessment and pedagogical content knowledge. *Science Education, 96,* 265–290.

Forbes, C.T. and Biggers, M. (2015). What kind of science teacher will I be? Teachers' curricular role identity for elementary science. In L. Avraamidou (Ed.), *Studying Teacher Identity: Theoretical Perspectives and Methodological Approaches* (pp. 129–152). Rotterdam: Sense Publishers.

Forbes, C.T., Sabel, J., and Biggers, M. (2015). Elementary teachers' use of formative assessment to support students' learning about interactions between the hydrosphere and geosphere. *Journal of Geoscience Education, 63*(3), 210–221.

Forzani, F. M. (2014). Understanding "core practices" and "practice-based" teacher education: Learning from the past. *Journal of Teacher Education, 65*(4), 357–368.

Furtak, E. M., Seidel, T., Iverson, H., and Briggs, D. C. (2012). Experimental and quasi-experimental studies of inquiry-based science teaching: A meta-analysis. *Review of Educational Research, 82*(3), 300–329.

Harris, C. J., Phillips, R. S., and Penuel, W. R. (2012). Examining teachers' instructional moves aimed at developing students' ideas and questions in learner-centered science classrooms. *Journal of Science Teacher Education, 23*(7), 769–788.

Krajcik, J. and Mamlok-Naaman, R. (2006). Using driving questions to motivate and sustain student interest in learning science. In K. Tobin (Ed.). *Teaching and Learning Science: An Encyclopedia* (pp. 317–327). Westport, CT: Greenwood Publishing Group.

Manz, E. (2012). Understanding the codevelopment of modeling practice and ecological knowledge. *Science Education, 96*(6), 1071–1105.

McDonald, M., Kazemi, E., and Kavanagh, S. S. (2013). Core practices and pedagogies of teacher education: A call for a common language and collective activity. *Journal of Teacher Education, 64*(5), 378–386.

McNeill, K. L. (2011). Elementary students' views of explanation, argumentation and evidence, and their abilities to construct arguments over the school year. *Journal of Research in Science Teaching, 48,* 793–823.

NASEM (National Academies of Sciences, Engineering, and Medicine). (2015). *Science Teachers' Learning: Enhancing Opportunities, Creating Supportive Contexts.* Washington, DC: National Academies Press.

Nichols, S. E., and Koballa, T. (2006). Framing issues of elementary science teacher education: Critical conversations. In K. Appleton (Ed.), *Elementary Science Teacher Education: International Perspectives on Contemporary Issues and Practice* (pp. 1–12). Mahwah, NJ: Lawrence Erlbaum Associates.

NRC (National Research Council). (1996). *National Science Education Standards.* Washington, DC: National Academies Press.

NRC (National Research Council). (2000). *Inquiry and the National Science Education Standards: A Guide for Teaching and Learning.* Washington, DC: National Academies Press.

NRC (National Research Council). (2012). *A Framework for K-12 Science Education: Practices, Crosscutting Concepts, and Core Ideas.* Washington, DC: National Academies Press.

Otero, V. K., and Nathan, M. J. (2008). Preservice elementary teachers' views of their students' prior knowledge of science. *Journal of Research in Science Teaching, 45*(4), 497–523.

Putnam, R. T., and Borko, H. (2000). What do new views of knowledge and thinking have to say about research on teacher learning? *Educational Researcher, 29*(1), 4–15.

Remillard, J. T. (2005). Examining key concepts in research on teachers' use of mathematics curricula. *Review of Educational Research, 75*(2), 211.

Russell, T., and Martin, A. K. (2014). Learning to teach science. In N. G. Lederman and S. K. Abell (Eds.), *Handbook of Research on Science Education*, Vol. II (pp. 885–902). New York: Routledge.

Sabel, J., Forbes, C. T., and Flynn, M.L. (2016). Elementary teachers' use of content knowledge to evaluate students' thinking in the life sciences. *International Journal of Science Education, 38*(7), 1077–1099.

Sabel, J., Forbes, C. T., and Zangori, L. (2015). Promoting prospective elementary teachers' learning to use formative assessment for life science instruction. *Journal of Science Teacher Education, 26*(4), 419–445.

Sadler, T. D., and Dawson, V. (2012). Socio-scientific issues in science education: Contexts for the promotion of key learning outcomes. In B. Fraser, K. Tobin, and C.J. McRobbie (Eds.), *Second International Handbook of Science Education* (pp. 799–809). Dordrecht, The Netherlands: Springer.

Shulman, L. (1987). Knowledge and teaching: Foundations of the new reform. *Harvard Educational Review, 57*(1), 1–22.

Zembal-Saul, C. L., McNeill, K. L., and Hershberger, K. (2012). *What's Your Evidence?: Engaging K-5 Children in Constructing Explanations in Science.* Boston, MA: Pearson.

Index

academic language 88, 92
access to resources 247
achievement 56, 61, 197, 218, 221
activities 18–19; authentic 243; contentless 93; and data generation 27; engineering 51; fun 221; hands-on 2, 16, 79; step-by-step 16
activity-centric approaches 25
administrators 208, 215, 218, 219, 239, 247, 249, 261
affective scaffolding 99, 106, 107, 108, 109, 110
affinity-identity 81
alternative ideas 121, 122; tool 116, 121, 122, 125
analysis: of artifacts 220; of ideas 70; to improve instruction 140; of learning opportunities 17; of practice 244–246, 248, 250; of student learning 223–224; of student work 222; of teaching practice 134; of tools 132; tools for 137, 143; of video recordings 209
anchoring questions 257
anchor phenomenon 23, 88
approximation 6, 97–110, 114, 131, 133, 134, 136, 145, 146, 157, 170, 173, 182, 185, 192, 194–196, 259
approximation reflection tool 133, 138, 139
assessment: 72, 117, 124, 174, 204, 215, 263; CER framework as support 17; formative 16, 19, 204, 221–222, 224, 227, 228, 238, 243, 262, 263; high-stakes 17, 205; large-scale 221; practices 16; of reading 56; of students 53
ATLAS – Looking at Data Protocol 227, 245

authentic activities 243, 244
authentic practice 141, 253, 260
authentic science 1, 3, 106, 132, 134, 135, 138
authoritative discourse 120
autonomy 100, 206

barriers: to learning 92, 237; to teaching science 75; to understanding scientific facts 72
big ideas 2; big ideas tool 126n2
bilingual children 85; see also emergent bilingual children

capabilities 34, 43, 196, 221, 224, 227
capacity 205, 214, 218, 219, 224, 227, 229, 238, 263
card sorting activity 116, 118–119, 183
CER framework see Claims–Evidence–Reasoning framework
CER Scaffolding Tool 116, 125
change environment 237, 239
children: bilingual 8, 85, 218–229, 241; as capable 9; ideas 3, 6, 16, 122, 123, 125, 193; and instructional practices 179; as partners 228; perspectives 121, 123; as sensemakers 2, 8, 9, 192–195, 236; thinking 158; understandings 122
Children as Sensemakers (course) 170–171, 193, 195, 196, 198, 200
claim-evidence-reasoning 80, 209; see also claim-evidence-reasoning (CER) framework
claim-evidence-reasoning (CER) framework 17, 18, 19, 22, 23, 25, 51, 69, 116, 124, 168, 200, 221, 223, 245
claim–evidence–reasoning instructional scaffold 33, 123–124

classroom culture 93
coaching 246
co-construction 74; of arguments 221; of claims 70
co-design 18, 26, 222, 229, 238
cognition as collaborative process 194
cognitive apprenticeship 65
cognitive scaffolding 106
co-investigation 226–227
collaboration 5, 8, 18, 23, 33, 60, 85, 115, 130, 143, 205, 206, 222, 225, 238, 245; and cognition 194; with researchers 226
collaborative inquiry 205, 210, 214
collaborative science reasoning 180
communities 61, 82, 89, 210, 239; collaborative 237; exploration of 226; of ideals 208; of learners 78, 164, 252; learning 65–66, 71, 73, 205, 219, 225, 237, 238, 247, 249; of practice 4–5, 66, 98, 130, 263; as sources of knowledge 220
community-based teacher educators 4
conceptual frameworks 115, 243, 249
conceptual model of instructional practice 255
conceptual scaffolding 99
conceptual tools 6, 125
consensus building 32, 41, 244
consensus model of professional development 247, 248, 252, 259
consequential learning 103, 105
content storylines 22–23, 26, 47, 48, 67, 226
context 85, 179, 190, 220, 229, 244; of learning 7, 194, 205–206, 214, 218–229, 239, 247, 248, 252; local 83; organizational 8, 219, 224–225; of practice 253; for skill acquisition 197; of tool use 113–114, 142
continued professional learning 204, 225–228
co-planning 228, 238, 244
core ideas 3, 31, 70, 148, 189, 227; disciplinary 1, 3, 65, 123, 135, 145, 149–152, 157, 159, 190, 251, *see also* disciplinary core ideas; in science 1, 16, 19, 22, 23, 67, 74, 140
core practices 65, 140, 141, 146, 179, 190
core principles 178, 181–184
co-reflection 102
co-teaching 209, 228, 229, 237, 244
critical inquiry 214

critical thinking 49, 54
crosscutting concepts (CCCs) 1, 3, 17, 31, 130, 135, 140, 164, 189, 251
cultural repertoires 83, 85
cultural-historical activity theory 254
cultural resources 223, 225

decision making 182, 183, 192, 205, 237, 244; and learning 194; in professional development schools 208; tools 18
demographic change 6, 228, 229
demographics 196, 205
design 26, 60, 89, 174, 258; guidelines 6; of instruction 262; of lessons 140, 141; of tools 115–126
diagnosing learning needs 262
dialogic interactions 85, 120
dialogue 116; reflective 209
disciplinary concepts 258, 259, 262
disciplinary content knowledge 262
disciplinary core ideas (DCIs) 1, 3, 65, 123, 135, 145, 149, 150–152, 157, 159, 190, 251
disciplined improvisation 179–182, 254
discursive engagement 200
diversity 85, 118, 201n1, 218
domains of literacy 70

early literacy initiatives 224
Edthena 201n2
EEE+A Framework *see* Engage-Experience-Explain + Argue Framework
Elementary Science Methods Planning Group (ESMPG) 6, 97, 110n2, 115, 130, 131, 132, 146, 147
eliciting 191–200; 71–72, 191, 236; thinking 193, 236, 262
emergent bilingual (EB) children 8, 218–229, 241; *see also* English language learners
Engage-Experience-Explain + Argue Framework (EEE+A Framework) 110n3, 116–120, 171, 172, 195, 243
Engage-Explore-Explain rehearsals 147
engagement 46, 49, 51, 60, 69, 73, 79, 89, 90, 102, 119, 120, 124, 131, 134–138, 145, 147, 148, 165, 174, 191, 195, 221; active 21, 65; with data 16; with multiple texts 70–71; with principles 223–224; in science practices 65, 66, 205; in sensemaking 9, 32
Engineering is Elementary (EiE) 47, 48, 51, 52, 56

268 *Index*

engineering practice 1, 5, 23, 47–51, 80, 83, 130, 135, 189, 220, 251

English language arts 6, 49

English Language Learners 42, 229n1, 242; *see also* emergent bilingual (EB) children

epistemic practices and agency 19, 22, 26, 65, 70, 72, 74, 169, 254

epistemic alignment 64–76

equity 2–4, 6, 19, 22–24, 48, 78–86, 108, 110, 117, 167, 169, 180, 182, 195, 219, 222, 252

ethics 4, 7, 191, 262, 235

evaluation 41, 66, 78; of EB students 221–222

excitement 54, 59, 80, 213

experimentation 18, 81, 85, 92, 207, 234, 237, 239

expert guidance 104, 107

expertise 249, 250, 254

explore observation tool 133, 137, 138, 140, 141

fading scaffolds 32, 100, 143, 184, 244

feedback 102, 104, 109, 147, 164, 168, 173, 196, 198, 244

field-based teaching 106, 114

field placements 118, 193, 195, 196

field trips 5, 46, 52, 80, 83

five-paragraph essay organizer scaffold 53

formative assessment 16, 19, 204, 221–222, 224, 227, 228, 238, 243, 262, 263

foundational principles of practice 255

Framework for K-12 Science Education 1, 5, 6, 9, 17, 25, 78, 221, 251

framework observation guide 245

frameworks 6, 104, 145, 161–174, 183–185, 195, 243; for argumentation 168; empirically grounded 6; function of 184; importance 7; for teaching practice 170

funds of knowledge 226

goal-directed enactments 179

goals 84, 132; learning 18; of professional development schools 207–208, 214; setting 208; of teacher education program 125

growth: of knowledge 200; opportunities for 158; professional 8, 201, 208–210, 214, 235; student 54, 205; *see also* Interconnected Model of Teacher Professional Growth

high-leverage practices 24, 114, 116, 131, 133, 138, 141, 170, 198–200, 235, 243, 253, 262; teaching practices 101, 105, 119, 134, 140, 190, 191

high-stakes assessments 17, 72, 204, 205

Holmes Group 206, 207, 237

identity 2, 6, 58, 78–86; shifts 200

immigrant communities 8, 241

improvisation 24, 178–185, 255, 260, 263

inclusive learning 238

independent inquiry projects 210

inequities 190; *see also* equity

inferences 137, 140, 147, 227

inquiry 19, 33, 206–208, 221, 257; collaborative 205, 210, 214; critical 214; practitioner 4, 19; and sensemaking 78–79; skills 78; teacher 209–214, 237

instruction 132, 233, 234

instructional planning templates 116–118, 124, 125, 183, 196, 245

integration: of curricula 47; of engineering practices 48; framework 50–52; practice for 46–61, 153; of science and language lessons 226; in science learning 1–2, 157; of science and literacy 210–213; of science practices 87–93

intellectual work 19, 169

Interconnected Model of Teacher Professional Growth (IMTPG) 234, 235, 236, 237, 238

interdisciplinary units 49

interests 27, 31, 43, 97, 61, 205; related to questions 221

interviews 131, 146, 150, 170, 171, 193–200, 213, 236, 260

investigation-based discussion 113–126

investigation-based science lessons 117, 173

investigations: planning 32; and questions 49; small group 34

journals 58, 211, 212, 227

justice 1, 3, 4, 108, 195, 201n1

justification 66, 165, 116, 124, 163, 170–172; by teachers 169

"kid talk" 19, 24, 25, 80, 84

"kid writing" 212, 224

knowledge 24, 81, 84, 206, 260; access to 221; awareness of 198; building 18, 19,

220–221, 228; community 162; conceptual framework for 115; construction 98, 130, 234, 243; content 7, 55, 115, 119, 120, 123, 124, 135, 145, 158, 169, 179, 183, 191, 198, 235, 243, 262; context of 194; control over 19; cultural funds of 120; development 9, 167, 196, 207; domains 115; evaluation in EB students 221–222; funds of 220, 226; growth of 200; and learners 170; local 27; pedagogical 169, 170; professional 98, 239; representation of 25; scientific 169, 193; shaping 169; social construction 6; of students 191; of subject matter 114–118, 131, 191; of teachers 7, 113–126; for teaching 1, 123, 124, 169–174; transfer 200–201

leadership 204, 206, 246
learning communities 65–66, 71, 73, 205, 219, 225, 237, 238, 247, 249
lesson artifacts of student thinking tool 148, 156
lesson planning tool 132, 133, 136, 141
lesson plans 101, 131, 192, 260
lessons in the field assignment (LiFE) 118, 121
lifelong learning 60, 251
linguistic resources 223, 225, 226
literacy 64–76, 80; centers 212; courses 174; definition 65; development 84, 227; domains 70; instruction 49; and place-based education 46–61; practices 5, 47, 50–52, 64–76; and science 49, 61, 64–65, 75, 80, 237; strategies 5, 52, 60; and teaching practices 64
Literacy Practices for Sensemaking in Science 65, 68, 70
local context 53, 59, 60, 61, 83, 256, 257
local knowledge 27
localized phenomena 256, 257

marginalization 1, 86, 233
mathematics 1; methods 174; teaching 114; thinking 172
Measurement of Academic Progress (MAP) 56
memorization 72, 74, 87, 93, 169
mentors 4, 98, 106, 107, 114, 182, 208–215, 244
metacognition 98, 106

metacognitive scaffolding 99, 104, 107, 108, 109, 110
methods course 33, 125, 130–131, 145, 174, 209
misconceptions 154, 155, 156
missed opportunities 141–142, 154
modeling 2, 135, 140, 141, 162, 171, 181, 191, 194, 195, 244, 245, 257; language 69
monitoring 99, 122
monitoring tools 115, 116, 121–123, 183
motivation 54, 75, 89, 221, 257
moves 183, 198, 249; pedagogical 172; talk 18, 91, 116, 120, 125, 183, 259, 260; teaching 119, 149, 167, 173
multiple fronts lens 8, 242, 245–248
multiple meaning lens 8, 241–244, 248

National Academies of Sciences, Engineering, and Medicine (NASEM) report 205, 237, 242, 243, 245, 246, 248, 259
National Council for Accreditation of Teacher Education (NCATE) 207
National Science Education Standards (NSES) 256
negotiation 3, 17, 24, 26, 179
Next Generation Science Standards (NGSS) 1, 5, 9, 17, 42, 47, 51, 67, 68, 78, 87, 116, 119, 130, 157, 195, 211, 237, 247, 251, 256, 259, 263; performance expectations 23, 225
norms 18, 22, 70, 71, 74, 191, 206, 215, 226
notebooks 69, 223
noticing 137, 138, 145–159; ideas 182

open-ended questions 33, 125
opportunities: for collaboration 205–206; for communication 83; for contribution 167; for data analysis 22; to discuss ideas 37–38; for investigation 67; for learning 17, 84, 121, 161–175, 182, 201, 204, 212, 219, 220; ; missed 141–142, 154; prioritizing 43; for professional development 43, 213; for questioning 64; for reasoning 67; scaffolded 244; for science practices 42, 64; for sensemaking 24, 57, 60, 67, 81, 87; for talk 67

participation 18, 22, 25, 92, 181; productive 19, 221, 228
participatory model of learning 49

270 *Index*

partner reading 52
partnerships 204–215, 237–238, 243, 246, 247, 249; productive 8; school-university 4, 66
pedagogical content knowledge (PCK) 233, 236, 254
pedagogical knowledge 169, 170
pedagogical learning 248
pedagogical moves and practices 17, 172, 246
pedagogies 110, 131; consistent 108; of enactment 97; of investigation 191, 192; of practice 4, 97, 133, 134, 170, 191, 192; of reflection 191, 192; signature 209–210, 213, 214, 237
peer teaching 103–105, 114, 118, 121, 184; assignment 173; rehearsal 100–101
Pennsylvania State University 4, 5, 8, 204, 207, 237, 241, 242
performance: expectations 256; reading 56; writing 56
persuasive writing 5
place-based education 5, 46–61, 80
policies 204, 205, 220, 224, 246, 249
practitioner inquiries 8, 210
preparation 1, 9, 49; as predictor of achievement 218
primer tools 129
principles 164, 179, 180, 182, 183, 252; articulation of 179–182; of practice 254, 263; of Science 20/20 project 220–224; scientific 33; and teacher engagement 223–224
prioritization 33, 43, 193, 195, 197
probing 191, 194, 195, 197
problematization 99, 100–110, 139, 178, 254; and scaffolding 132
problem-solving 50, 84, 99, 247
productive learning 105
productive participation 18, 19, 22, 25, 26, 70, 221, 228
productive partnerships 8
professional capacity 205, 214, 246, 247
professional development 4, 66, 67, 204–215, 220, 228, 238–239, 243, 248, 252, 261; model 222–223; opportunities 43, 213; programs 234, 241, 243, 261; school (PDS) 5, 204–215, 237, 241, 242
professional growth 8, 208, 210, 214, 235
professional identity 81
professional knowledge 239

professional learning 2, 7, 8, 189–201, 209, 214, 222, 228, 233–235; communities 237; contexts 214, 218–219, 229; continued 225–228; experiences 246;
professional networks 5, 246
professional practice 179, 182–184, 238, 260
programs supporting teacher learning 259–263
project-based inquiry science (PBIS) 50, 51, 52, 53, 56

read alouds 211, 212, 213
recommendations, evidence-based 53, 54
reflection 97, 102, 106, 131, 133, 134, 138, 145–159, 153, 156, 192, 197, 208, 212, 220, 234, 236, 246, 254, 260; prompts 146; on outcomes of experimentation 237
reflection 207, 209, 211
Reflective Teaching Assignment 173
reform research 246
reform-based discourse 81, 82
reforms 1, 2, 48–49, 81–82, 84, 87, 93, 124, 174, 196, 205, 214, 251, 259; recommendations 79; and science practice 64
relationships 19, 163–165, 169, 228; causal 25, and the educational processes 239
response to intervention (RTI) 208
responsiveness 16, 25, 238
rewinds 102–104, 109
role play 147, 148, 152, 154
rubrics 6, 104, 168

scaffolding 41, 51–53, 135, 168, 172, 174, 178–185, 253, 254, 260; affective 99, 106, 107, 110; for beginning teaching practice 129–143; CER framework as 17, 33; and co-construction of arguments 221; cognitive 106; and complexity 201; conceptual 99; definition 184; fading 32, 100, 143, 184, 244; intentions 98; material tools as 131, 313; metacognitive 99, 104, 107, 110; for preservice teachers 97–110; and problematizing 132; procedural 99; and rehearsals 157; roles 133; science practices 152; sociocognitive 99, 105, 106, 107, 110; and structuring 132;

and tools 139, 143; use in professional development schools 214; verbal 168; written 168
school-based professional learning 222
school-university partnership 4, 66, 204–215, 237–238, 249
Science 20/20 project 218–220, 224, 225, 228, 229; guiding principles 245
science and engineering practices (SEPs) 130; science practices 193, 195, 199
science methods course 6, 113, 114, 118, 120, 149, 170–173, 195, 198, 199, 209
science modeling tool 141
sentence stems 103, 116, 173
shifts: in pedagogy 17, 74; in science practices 64
signature pedagogy 8, 209–210, 213, 214, 237
situated cognition theory 244, 248
situated learning 244
skills 81, 108, 179, 183, 206, 260; allocation 54, 58; awareness of 198; cognitive 65; context for acquisition 197; critical thinking 54; development 198, 233; language 65; prescribed 178; process 87; social 65; transfer of 80; verbal 200
small-group work 84, 123, 191, 212
social construction of knowledge 6
social constructivist perspective 130
social discursive practices 2
social interactions 82
social positioning 86
sociocognitive activity 98–99
sociocultural theories 3, 220
socio-scientific issues 257
stakeholders 57–59, 91
standards 3, 48, 49, 67, 78, 204, 207
state-defined policies 249
STEM (science, technology, engineering, and mathematics) 219
stop-actions 102–104, 109
storylines 22–27, 47, 48, 67, 90
strategies 9, 67, 75, 84, 87, 120, 141, 223, 233, 252, 255
structuring 99, 100–107, 139, 166–168; affective 108, 109; metacognitive 108, 109; and scaffolding 132; science journals 212
student alternative ideas tool 154–157, 183
student artifacts 260
student-driven discourse 91–92

Students Constructing Evidence-Based Claims Framework 163, 164, 165
summer institute 224, 225
Supporting Evidence-Based Claims Framework 161–174
syntactic knowledge 115
systems approach 185

Taking Science to School 49
talk 34–36, 67, 68, 91, 258, 262; children's 80; classroom 73; opportunities for 67; *see also* talk moves
talk moves 18, 91, 116, 120, 125, 183, 259, 260; tool 116, 120–122, 124, 125, 259
teacher education pedagogies 191–192
teacher education programs 4, 5, 7, 8, 43, 118, 174, 189–201, 234, 235; goals 125
teacher inquiry 209–214, 237
teaching moves 119, 149, 167, 173
teaching practice 70, 131, 133, 161–174, 178, 193, 197, 206; analysis 134; authentic 184; decisions 140; decomposing 141, 142, 161; enactment 141, 173; frameworks for 170; and knowledge of teaching 169–170; linking 141; noticing 134; scaffolding 129–143; support for 140–141
templates 6, 48, 116–118, 121, 123, 125, 136, 183
terminology 36, 42, 43, 92, 263
theory of action 132–134
theory of teacher learning 243
three-dimensional learning 1, 7, 189, 211, 252
time: allocation 49; constraints 41, 42; lack of 61; prioritizing 43
TIMSS Video Study 18
tools: adapting 143; analysis 132, 143; analytical 137, 248; capabilities 43; conceptual 6, 125; and context 113–114, 142; creating 125; for decision making 18; definition 129; design 115–126; educator-provided 113; empirically grounded 6; explanation mapping 18; to guide teacher thinking 3; importance 7; and language 142; and learning 139; for lesson planning 132, 133, 136, 141; material 131; modification 115–126; monitoring 183; opportunities for

272 Index

development 9; planning 133, 135, 136; rationales for 142; for reflection 138; and rehearsal 150, 157; scaffolding 139, 143; and science practice 42–44; and sensemaking 154; sharing 143; and student ideas 145–159; suite of 115–126; tasks of 138–140; and teacher knowledge 113–126; use 124–126, 153–154

Tools for Engaging in Authentic Science 135

Tools for Noticing and Analyzing 137

Tools for Planning and Priming 135

Tools for Reflecting 138

trajectories of learning 263

transitions 178–185

translanguaging 223

University of Michigan 4, 6, 7, 97, 100, 110n2, 114, 115, 131, 132, 137, 146, 170, 189–201, 201n1, 242, 261

values 179–180

visualizations 59, 237

visual representations 181, 211, 213

vocabulary 18–19, 68, 71–73, 88, 93, 155, 221; academic 25; and experience 92–93; frontloading 74; and ideas 219; preteaching 92; scientific 36, 74; teaching 65

Vygotsky, Lev 98, 131, 262

well-started beginners 191–192

What's Your Evidence? (WYE) 17, 25

whole class discussion 35, 67, 69, 70, 73, 84, 119, 123, 133, 167, 212

wonderings 41, 90

words 6; and learning 73; and meaning 72–73, 80, 84

writing 50, 68, 69, 73–75, 87, 123, 124, 212, 226, 237, 258; as core science practice 65; eliciting ideas through 71–72, 80; facilitation 168; heuristics 18; performance 56; persuasive 5; and sensemaking 54

WYE *see What's Your Evidence?*

zone of proximal development 98, 131, 142, 262